Entrepreneur® MAGAZINE'S

ULTIMATE

GUIDE TO

BUYING OR SELLING A BUSINESS

IRA NOTTONSON

Entrepreneur® Press

Editorial Director: Jere Calmes
Cover Design: Beth Hanson-Winter
Composition: CWL Publishing Enterprises, Inc., Madison, Wisconsin, www.cwlpub.com

This publication is designed to provide accurate and authoritative information in regard to the subject matter covered. It is sold with the understanding that the publisher is not engaged in rendering legal, accounting, or other professional services. If legal advice or other expert assistance is required, the services of a competent professional person should be sought.

> —From a Declaration of Principles jointly adopted by a
> Committee of the American Bar Association and
> a Committee of Publishers and Associations

ISBN 1-932531-20-3

Library of Congress Cataloging-in-Publication Data

Nottonson, Ira N., 1933-
    Entrepreneur magazine's ultimate guide to buying or selling your business /
    by Ira N. Nottonson.—4th ed.
      p. cm.
    ISBN 1-932531-20-3
      1. Sale of small businesses. 2. Small business—Purchasing. I. Nottonson, Ira N., 1933-

HD1393.25.N68 2004
658.1'62—dc22

                                        2004043234

09 08 07 06 05   10 9 8 7 6 5 4 3 2 1

Contents

Preface

THE ONLY MAGIC CONTAINED IN THIS BOOK IS in understanding the reality that exists between a buyer and a seller. You cannot plug in a magic formula that will make your purchase or sale of a business successful. You need to establish a working relationship with the person opposite you at the negotiating table. Your ability to work together toward a mutually acceptable result, coupled with your ability to adjust your expectations about what that result will be, will determine your success or failure. Adjusting expectations is the key to successful negotiation.

If a sale requires the seller to receive a substantial portion of the purchase price over an extended period—in the form of a purchase money promissory note—the relationship between buyer and seller will likely last five to 10 years. In this case, the seller depends on the buyer to succeed in the business and make regular payments on the note. In turn, the buyer depends on the seller to have been truthful as to the business elements. Signing a note rather than paying cash for a business creates a greater sense of codependency. It requires buyer and seller to perform careful research before the sale and establish a common psychological and emotional understanding as sale negotiations proceed. How to establish this mutual understanding is the secret to buying or selling a business.

This book, therefore, presents both the buyer's and the seller's perspectives. I urge you to take advantage of this fact and read the entire book, regardless of the category to which you belong.

Making a judgment about the value of the business is just the beginning. The presentation, negotiation, and documentation of the sale are really the critical elements. You will find the basic strategies to valuing a business in the first four chapters. The remainder of the book works you through the preparation, decision making, and negotiating process. You will find worksheets and sample profit and loss statements throughout the book to help you pinpoint key issues involved in your particular situation and determine how to deal with them.

I have woven into the context wherever appropriate the methods by which a seller can reduce costs and maximize equity potential. Most of these methods focus on how to prepare the business for sale. Consequently, if you are considering selling, you will benefit from working through the exercises in this book, whether you ultimately sell the business or not. More importantly, the book will help you determine when a potential sale does not look good, saving you more time and money in the long run.

The book will teach you enough of the buzzwords and basic concepts to understand what your professionals are talking about. It will position you to frame a decent presentation as a seller and give you the tools necessary to understand the fundamentals as a buyer.

Finally, if complicated legal issues arise in your particular situation, this book should not take the place of using competent legal counsel. On the contrary, it is one of my strongest recommendations that you employ the services of professionals, such as an attorney and an accountant, early in the process. You will save money by avoiding costly mistakes!

Remember: your success as a buyer or a seller will depend on the frame of mind you take to the process. By the time you finish this book and the worksheet exercises it contains, you will know how much work you have yet to do to make your purchase or sale successful and where to find the help you need if you cannot do it all yourself.

This book has appeared in earlier editions under the title *Secrets to Buying and Selling a Business*. If you're familiar with that book, what I have tried to do in this new version is to bring the content up to date for the 21st-century businessperson. The need to generate dollars for growth has become much more the rule than the exception in the past decade. In addition, the need for the entrepreneur to completely understand the financial barometers of his or her business has made some additional information mandatory.

In revisiting the question of business basics, it is understandable that readers absorb the concepts of "basics" in different ways. Although the book was originally written with this in mind, it is clear that another approach can be helpful to those who learn more easily from a different style of presentation. It is for this reasons that a new part has been added.

Chapter 25 of Part VI, Revisiting the Financial Issues, is devoted to financial matters from a unique perspective. It offers a short series of definitions. It also includes narratives and charts that point out the differences among a profit and loss statement, a balance sheet, and a cash flow forecast. Some of the sample charts explain the real differences between accrual and cash methods of accounting. In addition, there are examples of what to look for in a profit and loss statement to better understand the business, a comparative analysis to show how to recognize the trends in a business before they become critical, a guide to establishing a solid balance sheet, and the all-important borrowing base, upon which a lending institution will predicate its thinking about lending to any company, based on the payback potential and stability of the business.

Chapter 26 of this new Part VI, Revisiting the Core Elements of This Book, is a reminder of the different goals of a buyer and a seller as well as the basic purpose of a business valuation, which should have a significant place in the hierarchy of the book's core materials.

And, in a somewhat unusual approach, each chapter has been reexamined by the author, who has prepared an 'opinion' to enhance the material, express the appropriate cautions when deemed necessary, and add a touch of the personal to the nature of the information contained.

—Ira N. Nottonson

ACKNOWLEDGMENTS

Considering the intricacies of the new content added to this book, it is with extreme gratitude that I thank Marilynn Force of The Force Group for her work in helping to create the complex charts and narratives having to do with the financial aspects of understanding business. An additional thank-you goes to Kelly Burton for converting to the appropriate format so much of the information that would otherwise have been quite disparate and difficult to follow.

How to Use This Book

THIS BOOK WAS DEVELOPED BY TYING together the things that are appropriate to buyers, sellers, entrepreneurs, and professionals and putting them into one book. Certain chapters have more information specific to one type of individual than to others. However, if you are a seller and only read Part III—The Seller's Perspective, you will completely lose the perspective of the buyer, an absolutely essential and necessary part of your thinking. The reverse is also true: if you are a buyer and only read Part II—The Buyer's Perspective, you will never have the necessary understanding of the seller's thinking that is so essential to the negotiating process. The only way to fully benefit from what this book has to offer is to read both the buyer's and the seller's perspectives.

ORGANIZATION

For the sake of clarity, the book is divided into six parts. The first is an introductory section that focuses on financial issues and the preliminary considerations any buyer or seller should make before entering negotiations. Parts II and III focus on a buyer's concerns and a seller's concerns, respectively, and Part V is about the con-

tract that brings them together. Part IV is for both you and the professionals—to become more familiar with the different roles they play in the buy-sell process. Part VI revisits the financial basics, together with an understanding of the principal elements involved in the core factors of the book.

Part I—Introduction to Buying and Selling a Business

Part I sets out some very specific language and concepts you need to know to properly negotiate a purchase price. If you are not close enough to that stage of the process, you may want to read Parts II and III first and then return to Part I after you understand all the elements involved in preparing for and negotiating the purchase and sale of a business.

Part II—The Buyer's Perspective

The buyer's section discusses strategies for initial market research, the emotions that sometimes interfere with a buyer's good business sense, and different ways to get into a business, such as buying a franchise start-up, buying an existing franchise, or buying an existing independent business.

The buyer's section also offers sellers important information. It enables a seller to prepare a selling portfolio that appeals to the right buyers and to recognize when a buyer is not right for the sale. Distinguishing between the right buyer and wrong buyer is a subtle, but vital part of a business sale. If a buyer fails after taking over the business and defaults on promissory note payments, the business is not sold, and the seller may return to a business so poorly managed in the interim that it is not salvageable. With this in mind, it is important for sellers to read Part II as well as buyers.

Part III—The Seller's Perspective

The seller's section walks you through the finer points of preparing a business for sale. You will run cost analyses, compare profit and loss statements, reconstitute your own financial data, and calculate an asking price. Chapters 16 and 17 also take you through the possibility of selling a business that is losing money or even operating under bankruptcy protection.

Because a buyer's success depends on taking over a sustainable business, buyers must recognize when a seller's financial information does not coincide with industry standards. Buyers will find in Part III all of the processes sellers must perform to prepare their business for sale. Buyers can then look for discrepancies in the disclosure documents they receive during sale negotiations and perform their own research into competition, customer base, location, lease, advertising methods, and product and labor costs. All of this research will not only help buyers secure the best deal during the sale, but also get them started in the right direction when they take over business operations.

If a buyer finances the purchase with a promissory note to the seller, the buyer-seller relationship will likely last several years. When a buyer knows how a seller prepares a business for sale, reconstitutes the profit and loss statement, and presents all the information, the relationship will be based on mutual understanding and trust rather than suspicion or misunderstanding.

Part IV—Legal and Financial Considerations

Part IV takes a unique twist in its point of view. Throughout the first three parts, the text is addressed directly to you, the reader, whether you are a buyer or seller. In Part IV, however, the "you" is addressed directly to accountants, lawyers, and brokers. Nevertheless, buyers and sellers should read these very important chapters—the chapters are intentionally written this way so buyers and sellers can read them and then have their accountants, lawyers, and brokers read the chapter that applies specifically to them.

Professionals will find three significant elements in this book:

- The technical methodology for valuing a business,
- The individual perspective of the buyer and seller, and
- The client's emotional involvement that professionals need to recognize throughout the negotiating process.

Part IV will help professional advisors prepare for their role in negotiating a business transfer, learn to work as a united team on behalf of the buyer or seller they represent, and make sure buyer and seller are protected from potential post-sale problems.

Buyers and sellers can benefit from Part IV by learning what professional advisors and consultants can and should do in a business sale.

This section is also designed to better prepare you for engagements with your lender. Business growth today, in great part, is based on the ability of a business to generate the dollars necessary to reach the next level of success. Often times this brings many business people to the banker or other lender without a real understanding of what is expected of them. Knowing the lender's job and perspective gives the borrower a clear understanding of how to succeed in getting the necessary dollars. Buyers preparing a loan will especially benefit from its content and the worksheet titled "Know the Lender's Job." Also, see the section in Chapter 26, "What Is a Borrowing Base?"

Part V—Contract Elements

The problem in today's small business marketplace seems to be centered, in the general business community, around competition. Fair competition is one thing; losing customers because of competition is quite another. In the franchise community, problems seem to be appearing due to the expiration of franchise contracts. The language of the contracts does not leave much room for survival after the contract expires. Look to this chapter for some solid advice.

Part VI–Revisiting the Essentials

It is clear in today's competitive business environment that the businessperson must have a complete understanding of his or her business barometers. Part VI includes material that will, for many readers, clear the air of the misunderstandings relative to basic financial paperwork. It includes an explanation of the following:

- What each item on a profit and loss statement (an income statement) is designed to show and how to handle "assumptions,"
- What the balance sheet is designed to show, including an understanding of the need for and the use of various ratios,
- The purpose of the cash flow forecast and how it relates to the difference between accounting on a cash basis and accounting on an accrual basis,
- The cumulative aspects of a break-even analysis,
- How you can read the financial information and understand what the indicators suggest in terms of trends in the business' history and how they can be recognized, analyzed, and prepared for.

This, Part VI also has some additional information that should revitalize the reader in terms of what the real goals should be relative to buyer and seller and the use of the valuation concept.

OTHER HELPFUL RESOURCES
Illustrations, Tables, and Samples

Buying or selling a business requires you to consider many different variables. Not all variables will apply to your particular situation. You will find throughout the book illustrations, tables, and samples that will help clarify the various concepts and apply them to real-life examples—particularly the purchase or sale you are considering. The illustrations, tables, and samples will expose you to many negotiating points, problem issues, and potential pitfalls. Read them carefully and apply the experiences of these former buyers and sellers to your experience.

Worksheets

Every chapter ends with a supplementary advice section in which the author offers some recommendations, opinions, and cautions and with a worksheet that reviews the most important points of the chapter and asks you to apply the chapter's advice or strategies to your own situation.

For example, if you are selling a business with a small operating profit, Worksheet 16 will help you target problem areas and improve your cost factors. If you are buying a business that includes many different assets as part of the package, Worksheet 7 will help you isolate and analyze those assets and their value to the business.

You may find that not all the worksheet questions require answers. Some are designed simply to make you think about the many elements involved in buying and selling a business. Sometimes, just looking over the questions and identifying the answers you don't know will prepare you to meet with your professional advisors.

Key Points to Remember

Finally, each chapter features a summary of the most important topics covered in the chapter. If you don't understand one or more of the points listed here after reading the chapter, go back and reread the area where the subject was covered. Understanding and feeling comfortable with the main points of each chapter may make the difference between your ultimate success and failure.

ABOUT THE AUTHOR

Ira N. Nottonson is a Law Review Graduate of Boston College Law School and licensed to practice in the Commonwealth of Massachusetts and the State of California. He has practiced general litigation and business/franchise law with partnerships in Boston, Massachusetts and Westwood, California. At present, he confines his consulting practice to the business of buying, selling, evaluation, and reconstruction of small businesses.

Mr. Nottonson has acted in different capacities for many companies, both private and public: chief executive officer, chief operating officer, chief legal counsel. He has also, at various times, been head of marketing, franchise sales and has acted as consultant for hundreds of companies throughout the United States and the United Kingdom. These companies include International House of Pancakes, Orange Julius of America, House of Pies, PIP Printing, PIP/UK (the British subsidiary of PIP Printing), Quickprint of America (the Big Red Q Quickprint Centers), Copper Penny Family Restaurants, The Bryman-Sawyer Schools, United Rent-All, and Icelandic Design.

In his legal capacity, Mr. Nottonson has been responsible as a member of the management committee for all of the above companies. He has been an integral part of the planning and implementation of basic business concepts.

Mr. Nottonson's qualifications are particularly unique, as he has also been an entrepreneur in his own right. He has been the owner of an advertising agency, a television production company, a publishing company, a law practice, and a nightclub. This diverse background has given him a better understanding of the day-to-day problems of business from a very personal perspective.

Mr. Nottonson currently works with both start-ups and problematic situations needing negotiation and reconstruction. He has been appointed as arbiter by the court and has testified on the subjects of small business and business valuations. He has written extensively on the subject of business generally for various newspapers and periodicals and writes a weekly business column for the *Boulder Daily Camera* in his hometown of Boulder, Colorado. In addition, he has been guest lecturer at various colleges and universities as well as a teacher at the Chamber of Commerce in Boulder under the auspices of the Small Business Development Center. As an articulate exponent of business concepts, he has appeared on radio and television over the years.

He is also the author of the book, *Before You Go into Business, Read This!*

Introduction to Buying and Selling a Business

CHAPTER 1

The Buyer-Seller Relationship

BUYING AND SELLING A BUSINESS CAN BE VERY complex, but it doesn't have to be. As you prepare for and negotiate a purchase or sale, you will encounter some specialized terminology that you will need to understand before you can find a sense of the buyer's and seller's financial realities. Both buyer and seller will need to consider a number of new ideas—and consider them from each other's point of view. A third possibility is the transfer of a family-owned business to the next generation. While many issues remain the same, some special issues must also be considered. You will find in this chapter some of the ideas upon which this book's valuation method is based. This chapter is only an introduction. Each concept is explained in more detail in succeeding chapters. You will develop a fuller understanding as each concept becomes integrated with other aspects of the buy-sell process.

THE BUYER WANTS AN INCOME

Buyers consider investing in an existing business because they want a new lifestyle and a respectable income—immediately. Some are willing to delay gratification of those desires; most are not. If a buyer says at the negotiating table, "It doesn't work for me," it usually means that the business would not produce enough profit to provide the buyer with an income.

Many sellers, believe it or not, don't consider this a valid criticism of their proposed deal. That is why many sellers are still waiting to find a buyer for their businesses.

Most buyers intend to buy a business and take an income from it the very next day. They don't want to be told that they will receive an income after they increase sales, decrease costs, or put into effect some other great plan that, for some reason or other, the seller didn't or couldn't do while he or she owned the business.

The Relationship Between Operating Profit and Asking Price

Unless a buyer purchases a business with cash—and in today's marketplace that is certainly the exception rather than the rule—the buyer will make a down payment and begin a long-term monthly payment schedule with someone.

The buyer might make payments to a lending institution, but in most cases, the buyer will pay off a purchase money promissory note to the seller. Once the buyer takes over the business, the business itself should be able to service the purchase money debt.

In terms of where these payments come from, picture a simple four-piece pie chart. Allocate a piece of the pie to fixed expenses, another piece to cost of product, and a third piece to labor. The remaining piece of pie is called operating profit. Although each business has its own particular percentages, this concept will help you prepare a mental skeleton of the percentage parameters within which any business should properly function.

For example, look at the numbers for a fictional quick-print shop. The Spry Print Shop has an annual gross revenue of $363,797. After paying for all the costs of producing the product (known as cost of product or cost of sales), the fixed expenses (including rent and utilities), and all salaries (including insurance, payroll taxes, and the like), there is an annual operating profit of 7.5%, or $27,285.

That doesn't look too bad right after a takeover, does it? Well, that depends. If the buyer paid $200,000 for the business, put down 20% ($40,000), and had a balance of $160,000 financed by the seller over a 10-year period with 10% interest, the annual payments are $25,372.

If the buyer uses the $27,285 per year to pay the promissory note to the seller of $25,372 per year, the operating profit of $27,285 is reduced to an income of $1,913. This is clearly not the respectable income the buyer is looking for, which suggests that the price is probably too high.

IT IS THE SELLER'S PROBLEM

Some sellers respond to the above situation with "That's not my problem!" But an income that is too small for the buyer certainly is the seller's problem if it stops the buyer from taking over the business. It is an even bigger problem if the buyer takes over the business without knowing that this is going to happen.

If the buyer takes over the business and is then unable to receive a decent income and make payments on the note to the seller, both the buyer and the seller have a big problem. Some sellers will say, "Well, that's OK. I'll just take back the business." There are two things the seller needs to consider before accepting that alternative.

- The purpose of the exercise is to make a sale—a permanent sale—so the seller can collect the money and start a new life.
- The seller might take back the business only to

find that it has been totally devastated while the buyer operated it.

If a seller has to return to a seriously mismanaged business now worth much less than the buyer paid, the sale was not successful.

METHODS OF VALUATION

How many methods are there to value a business? Some brokers and sellers develop selling price analyses one page long and others are dozens of pages long. Specifically, every method should involve costs of product, labor, rent, operating profit, and equipment capability and age. Generally, every method should also involve competition, geography, parking, new business, market value fluctuations for buildings, lease, location, and a variety of other considerations depending on the particular business and its relative position in the marketplace.

Some people actually use formulas like 100% of gross volume for 12 months. Others speak of a multiple of net profit, which depends on who created the profit and loss statement. Still others include economic values, such as the depreciated value of the equipment.

Most formulas are developed by taking the average selling price in a given trade or industry and working out a formula that fits the majority of the sales. The problem is that this method will normally give a business a bigger value if it is below average and a smaller value if it is above average. It does not necessarily represent a true value of any kind, and it certainly doesn't allow for the buyer's income as an important element.

Realistically, no formula will stand alone without a consideration of the buyer's income.

The Business Must Pay for Itself

When you buy a house, your loan officer will ask you many detailed questions about your personal income and whether it can support the monthly mortgage payments. If you buy a business, the business will be your personal income. If the business cannot support the monthly payments on a purchase money promissory note, you will default on the note and the sale will fail. The seller has a responsibility to set an asking price and establish a note payment structure that the business's operating profit can support.

As you will learn in the succeeding chapters, no single formula for valuing a business works without considering all the variables involved:

- Operating profit,
- Buyer's income,
- Asset variables—such as lease, location, equipment, competition, and customer base—and their value to the business,
- Return of investment, and
- The three primary price adjustors—size of down payment, interest rate, and the length of the note in a sale that involves a purchase money promissory note.

However, as a seller, if your business shows no operating profit or shows a loss, you will not be able to use this book's method for developing an asking price. You will have to show what your business could and should do if properly operated—when the buyer brings cost of product and cost of labor within industry standards. Some buyers and sellers will face the problem of a business with no profit. Many reasons why a business has not performed well are entirely fixable under new ownership. Chapters 16 and 17 discuss this situation at some length.

Seller's Equity Versus Buyer's Bonus

Some business brokers contend that a seller has the right to base the business' asking price on future profits. The more defensible position is that future profits belong to the buyer as a kind of bonus. The seller is entitled only to a purchase price based on the equity he or she has earned. Thus, the seller's equity is what he or she earns from building the business as the owner. The buyer's bonus is the additional profit the buyer will earn from what he or she puts into the business after taking it over.

Look at another example. Spry Print Shop's chief competitor, Bob's Printing, has a more effective management team and is paying less rent for its premises. Like Spry, Bob's Printing has a somewhat larger annual gross revenue of $379,289. However, after Bob pays for all the costs of product, fixed expenses, and salaries, he has an operating profit of 25%, or $94,822, more than three times that of Spry Print Shop. The price Bob can ask for his shop, based on the larger operating profit, is his earned equity.

The financial picture for Bob's Printing, therefore, looks much different. Bob has built so much equity into his business that he can justify a much higher asking price than Spry's owner, possibly as much as $500,000. Bob's Printing will pay for itself—meet promissory note payments from operating profit—and provide the new owner with an annual income of $15,532. If the buyer puts 20% down, or $100,000, and has a balance of $400,000 financed by the seller over a 10-year period at 10% interest, the annual payments are $63,432. Deduct this from the $94,822 operating profit and the buyer gets $31,390.

Furthermore, if you follow the manager's salary concept discussed in Chapter 2, the new owner of Bob's will eventually be able to take over management of the shop and enjoy the manager's salary in addition to this income from profit.

The format for selling is not as simple as the two examples just shown. You will need to factor in other variables, such as lease, equipment, marketplace, customer fluctuation, competition, and industry outlook. However, if, as a seller, you develop a selling price without considering the buyer's perspective, you will not negotiate a successful sale.

FAMILY BUSINESS TRANSITIONS

One other scenario that must be considered is when children take over the family business. While all of the information in this book will be valuable to parents and children making this transition, other factors also enter into the decision-making process.

It shouldn't surprise anyone who is contemplating such a takeover that preparation is the key word to the success of the transition and the survival of the business.

In some cases, two or more generations have been working together in the business before the concept of takeover enters the picture. This is not always the case, however. In the current marketplace, a business that a parent started offers a unique job opportunity to a son or daughter as well as a potential for the future. With the limitations of job availability and the competitive element being as strong a market force as it is, many young people are looking at the family business with a new perspective. However, the responsibilities of preparation to ensure a smooth transition rest on the shoulders of the parents. This section discusses the issues that parents must consider.

The Relationship Before the Takeover

Many variables can exist in terms of relationships just before a family takeover. In some cases, the son or daughter may have been working in the business for such a long time that he or she has actually become an integral part of the business operation. In other cases, although this is sometimes difficult to admit, the son or daughter may never have become an integral or necessary part of the operation, regardless of how long he or she may have been associated with the business.

With respect to a working relationship that already exists, some parents never think their children are capable, no matter how hard they may try and how effective they might appear to their peers. Other parents give their children credit for total competence without ever having done a really objective analysis of their value to the company if management were left exclusively in their hands. Other variations include having a good general manager who is not a member of the family and who is perfectly competent to maintain the continuity of the business. That person may seem to get along with the son or daughter when the parents are around, but is he or she capable of working well with the son or daughter in the absence of the parents? On the other hand, if there is a general manager and the parents give the operating responsibility to their son or daughter, will they lose the general manager and, in turn, jeopardize the continuity of the business, particularly as the parents will no longer be available for day-to-day consultation?

Day-to-Day Consultation After Takeover

The extent to which you will want to maintain a relationship with the business after takeover depends on your answers to a variety of questions.

- To what extent is the continuity of the business essential to your retirement?
- To what extent are you still responsible for certain contractual obligations, like the lease, even though you will no longer be connected with the operation of the business?

▼ **Illustration 1.1 Identify Suitable Successors**

In one situation, the owner of a business had both his son and daughter working in the business with him when he succumbed to a heart attack. Neither of his children had any intention of making the business a permanent part of his or her future. The business, however, represented so large a portion of the father's estate that both children agreed to maintain the continuity of the business for the sake of their mother. The problem of holding the pieces together during the takeover period, for which no preparation had been made, caused tremendous pressures between the children.

The daughter finally left. The son was not capable of handling much of the paperwork by himself. He was not trained for this responsibility and he did not have the inclination to handle the myriad details that had normally fallen on the shoulders of his sister. The business eventually got into trouble. It survives today, but its tempo will never be as dynamic as it was during the father's tenure. Adequate preparation could have avoided many, if not most, of the problems that the business and the children faced after the father's death.

- Are you ready to give up the business and its equity by telling your son and daughter that it is a sink-or-swim situation?
- To what extent are you obliged to make working capital available in the event the business enters a slow period or the industry takes a downturn?
- In other words, just how quickly are you prepared to cut the cord?

You will want to keep a number of factors in mind. Primarily, there is the question of the business concept. You have undoubtedly formed the business and maintained it with a certain philosophy and with the idea that it holds a certain position or niche in its particular trade or industry. It is very easy for someone to quickly and dynamically superimpose a whole new set of principles on the business in your absence. Some of these may be only subtle changes with little long-term effect; others may well impact the very nature of the business.

But here is a place to take care. On the one hand, staying the course and maintaining continuity are important. On the other hand, you must never lose sight of the creative juices of new blood and new energy and recognize that the business marketplace is constantly changing. It feeds on creativity and change. The competitive element can be quickly lost by not taking advantage of change when change is necessary or appropriate. It is for this reason that you should stay in touch. This does not mean "stay in charge." It means "stay in touch."

Make sure that you can monitor the changes and recognize the impact that each change will likely have on your position in the marketplace, before it is too late to cure. After all, larger companies do this by having a board of directors. Consider the next example.

Illustration 1.2 Stay in Touch

In one situation, the son took over the business after spending many years as an apprentice under the supervision of his father. Immediately after taking over, in an attempt to ensure a good competitive position, he leased some new state-of-the-art equipment. The increase in his productivity was minimal. The increase in his client base was also small. But the increase in monthly obligations was substantial. He had not generated the advertising necessary to "fill the time of the new equipment" and make the lease and the monthly payment workable.

The father would have taken a much more conservative position by saying, "Let's examine the market potential before we make the investment." The father was devastated, but the paperwork was already signed. The business, instead of generating a modest retirement income as the father had hoped, turned into a Chapter 7 bankruptcy. The father, instead of retirement, got a new job. Staying "in touch" after the takeover would, undoubtedly, have netted a different result.

Vulnerability of Assets After Takeover

Unfortunately, when you start a business, you sign a long-term lease for the premises, you sign a franchise agreement for 10 or 20 years, you sign leases or contracts for the use or purchase of equipment, and, indeed, you might very well sign a promissory note for money you borrow from a bank, other lending institution, or the seller if you purchase the business. These people might be very encouraging, from a personal standpoint, when you tell them that you are turning the business over to your son or daughter. However, they will normally not be inclined to release you from your obligation, since you are probably more stable in the community and likely have more assets than your son or daughter. In other words, your assets and your dollars will remain at risk even though you may no longer be personally involved in the business.

Remember: even though you may have a corporation that is responsible for most of those obligations, you have probably signed all the paperwork as an individual as well. Most banks, landlords, and purveyors of expensive equipment will not allow the corporate signature without either a co-signer or a guarantor. In either case, you will remain responsible until the entire debt is paid, as illustrated below.

Illustration 1.3 Getting off the Hook

A son, who was extremely knowledgeable in a particular business, took over from his mother and father. He operated the business very well for a number of years. In fact, he grew the business quite dramatically. Then, he hit a downturn and the business verged on the edge of disaster. The franchise company, the landlord, and the equipment companies all came after the mother and father, neither of whom was capable any longer of operating the business. They weren't even aware of the business's day-to-day activity, but their assets were still vulnerable.

This business has made all kinds of arrangements for readjusting its debts and will probably survive. In this case of a permanent takeover, arrangements should have been made to close out certain obliga-

> tions after a given time period and let the parents off the hook, providing the business showed proper stability in the early stages, which it did.

Moving their business into the hands of the next generation is a dream held by many parents. The children recognize the great opportunity that such a transition provides. It is unfortunate that, in the face of this joy, there are pitfalls to which little or no serious consideration is given—until it is too late. If you are involved in such a situation, make sure that all the parties involved completely understand the very nature of the business, its position in the marketplace, and its future in the competitive field. Make sure that you have a plan for the future and a pattern for its potential growth that all parties study and understand. Make sure that all of you discuss, analyze, and agree upon certain investments, particularly in the early days, rather than allowing individual, inexperienced judgments to prevail. It is in the nature of youth to reach out creatively toward the future. It is in the nature of parents to reflect on the past to ensure a conservative approach for the future. Neither is wrong. It is, in fact, in the combination of these things that you will find the most successful transitions. It is worthwhile to take the time for this exercise.

Uncle Sam: Your New Partner After the Sale

Because of the tax implications of every sale transaction, you would be careless not to consider the methods by which you can eliminate or, at least, minimize the taxes that might be payable upon the inheritance of your business by family members. The nature of the tax structure in this country allows for a variety of ways to approach this problem. Here are some alternatives:

- Form a legal entity that will allow incremental increase of ownership over a period of time.
- Give the family member participation on a gift basis, being sure not to incur a gift tax in the process.
- Set up a trust to hold the stock.
- Establish a family limited partnership.

Along with most of these alternatives, it will be crit-

ical to create an insurance program that will handle the tax problem by making dollars available for acquiring stock without diluting its value or the participation of ownership. Failure to do so will often defeat the intention of the original owner.

A brief analysis of some of these alternatives suggests that gifts, like irrevocable trusts, can be inappropriate, because they may cause the owner to lose active control of the enterprise during his or her lifetime. This is not usually the goal that the owner seeks to achieve. The limited partnership concept, on the contrary, allows the owner, as the general partner, to maintain control while having portions of the ownership in the hands of limited partners.

This brief examination should make it clear that any approach to the tax question and the owner's ability to maintain control during his or her lifetime will require the advice of an expert. Consult the team of your attorney, your accountant, and your insurance planner before any definitive move is contemplated. (See Part IV.) These are the key points for a smooth transition of a family business:

- Be sure that your children are properly trained to take charge of the daily responsibilities of the business.
- Be aware of potential conflict with your current key employees.
- Take the time to set the stage with the appropriate personnel, vendors, and customers.
- Make sure that your transition period is long enough to ensure success of the turnover.
- Understand the difference between "staying in charge" and "staying in touch."
- Structure the transition to minimize tax implications.

ADJUSTING EXPECTATIONS

The remainder of this book will closely examine several concepts vital to your buy-sell process, including the following:

- Operating profit,
- Return of investment,
- Reconstitution of the profit and loss statement,
- Owner's compensation versus manager's salary, and

- The need to adjust expectations to successfully negotiate a sale.

Many of these concepts require at the very least a calculator and at the most a skilled accountant. The last concept—adjusting your expectations—may be the most important and most difficult of all. If either buyer or seller remains inflexible about the terms of the deal, negotiations will fall apart. If you are a seller, you must adjust your expectations about the value of your business to meet your buyer's income needs. If you are a buyer, you must adjust your expectations about the immediate income you may receive to meet the reality of the business's operating profit and working capital requirements.

A buyer normally enters negotiations with only a casual understanding of the business and with several misconceptions. The seller's job is to put the buyer at ease and develop a comfort zone within which the buyer can contemplate his or her future. The seller should anticipate buyer questions and give answers that make sense.

Apart from all the calculations regarding operating profit and note payments, the buyer is going to have a number of other projects in mind. He or she may want to replace equipment, upgrade the cosmetics of the business, or add new personnel. The buyer will also be interested in how to increase his or her income. Again, when it comes to buyer's income, the objective valuation of a business must remain flexible.

Some buyers enter the world of business ownership after being behind a salaried desk at $40,000 per year. Others come from executive suites with compensation packages of $400,000 per year. The seller has no control over this disparity in the buyer's former income, yet it will play a very significant part in the conversation at the negotiating table. And not all the buyer's thinking takes place there; much of it takes place at his or her kitchen table. The seller must therefore give the buyer and the buyer's family as many positive elements to think about as possible.

If a buyer wants an income of $100,000 per year and your business, even at its maximum potential, can offer only half that, it is not the right investment. If, on the other hand, the buyer is looking for an annual income of $80,000 and your asking price, based on current operating profit, will afford the buyer only $60,000 per year, you may have the beginning of a negotiation. You must be willing to adjust your levels of expectation to make the potential sale a reality.

Examine the practical considerations apart from the technical or mathematical. The buyer needs sufficient funds to pay the purchase money promissory note and all other expenses, both in boom and in bust economic times. Although the seller's goal is to maximize his or her earned equity, the sale is never complete until the note is paid. The margin between note payments and operating profit cannot be too narrow. If the margin is too narrow, it is not a sale; it is a gamble. If there is a bad month, or the buyer doesn't maintain the business in the best tradition, or an employee leaves who is difficult to replace, or a particularly large client moves away, it could cause a glitch in the payment schedule. A seller should not let greed get in the way of his or her logic as a person.

In the succeeding pages, you will find many of these concepts repeated and explained in greater detail. However, the reigning mottos of this book will remain the same: if it doesn't work for the buyer, it doesn't work for the seller, and the sale isn't final until the last note payment is made.

KEY POINTS TO REMEMBER

- The buyer is interested in an immediate and dependable income based on the business and its profit as it exists the day it is purchased.
- Every business is based on four fundamental elements—cost of product, cost of labor, general administrative expenses, and profit.
- No pricing formula can be valid without considering the buyer's income.
- The seller is entitled to convert the earned equity of the business to a selling price. Any growth of the business and its profit after the sale is the buyer's bonus.
- Negotiation is the art of adjusting expectations.

Worksheet 1.1. Know the Other Party's Point of View

The following questions emphasize some of the most important points you need to consider while you prepare for, negotiate, and finalize the purchase or sale of a business.

What is the most important thing the buyer expects to enjoy after buying a business?

What is the second most important thing the buyer expects to enjoy after buying a business?

Why is it equally important to the buyer and seller that the business can afford to meet the payments on the purchase money promissory note?

What is the difference between "seller's earned equity" and "buyer's bonus"?

Why can it be a bad idea for the seller to take back the business if the buyer defaults on note payments?

Why is operating profit so important in structuring the value of a business?

Is there a magic formula that you can use to find the value of a business?

Why is adjusting expectations so important to the negotiation process?

Worksheet 1.2. Transitioning a Business to Your Family

These questions highlight those issues you must consider before you transfer your business to your children or other family members.

Are there contractual or financial obligations to which you, as the seller, will remain tied even after the business is taken over and operated by someone else? ❑ Yes ❑ No

Leases ❑ Yes ❑ No   How long will they last?

Contracts ❑ Yes ❑ No   How long will they last?

Promissory notes ❑ Yes ❑ No   How long will they last?

Have you trained your son or daughter to handle the myriad technical responsibilities involved in the operation of the business, such as:
Bookkeeping? ❑ Yes ❑ No   Quantity purchasing contracts and leases? ❑ Yes ❑ No
Employee review? ❑ Yes ❑ No   Working with professionals? ❑ Yes ❑ No

Have you imbued your son or daughter with the less technical aspects of the business, such as:
Customer relations? ❑ Yes ❑ No   Adjusting inventory? ❑ Yes ❑ No
Changing customs and styles? ❑ Yes ❑ No   Settling disputes? ❑ Yes ❑ No

Have you considered what impact, if any, the changes of control will have:
On your employees? ❑ Yes ❑ No   On your vendors? ❑ Yes ❑ No
On your customers? ❑ Yes ❑ No

Have you arranged for a slow transition period in order to handle the problems of changeover and minimize the impact of new directions? ❑ Yes ❑ No

Are there dramatic changes in the particular trade or industry that could devastate the business without your experienced input? ❑ Yes ❑ No

What kind of ongoing relationship do you intend to have after the takeover?

Will you have a right to approve or reject the purchase or lease of expensive equipment? ❑ Yes ❑ No

Do you understand the difference between "staying in charge" and "staying in touch"? ❑ Yes ❑ No

Are you prepared to make the transition? ❑ Yes ❑ No

Do you understand the potential conflict, after giving over the prerogatives of ownership, between a son or daughter and a key employee, especially a manager? ❑ Yes ❑ No

Are you prepared to handle this conflict? ❑ Yes ❑ No

VALUING A BUSINESS AS A BUYER: BE CAREFUL!

You will find a variety of organizations that sponsor valuation experts of all stripes. Some experts will have many capital letters after their names but may not yet have acquired substantial experience in the marketplace on a practical level. Some will be able to deal with the numbers but will fail to explain what they're doing or how they're doing it. If you can't understand the method they've used, the valuation will have little significance for you. And, don't forget: you're the person who counts.

It's a Lot More than the Dollars

Many people think that the dollar value of the business is the keynote. The fact of the matter is that many people want a valuation not because they want to sell the business but because they would like to know how the valuation works. In this way, they can figure out how to improve the business before they decide to sell, which, in the long term, will inevitably increase the price for which it will ultimately sell.

It's the Risk That Counts the Most

The basic concept of value consideration is an examination of the numbers. If you take the sales of a business and deduct essentially all the costs needed to achieve those sales, you will have, hopefully, a profit. Although it is clear that the profit represents the basic foundation of the business's value, the real key is the risk that the purchase of the business represents to the buyer.

If, for example, the business depends on a relationship with the seller's brother-in-law, the buyer is certainly vulnerable to the possibility or probability that the relationship will not continue after the sale. The diversity and number of customers on which the business depends are a key to spreading the risk.

The ability of the business to continue buying its raw materials or component parts is another key risk factor. If the source of the materials is likely to dry up or not be as readily available or be priced higher than previously, the risk to the buyer is great.

And what about key personnel who may decide to leave the business immediately after the sale? Do you think the buyer would end up with a risk not anticipated? And what about the obsolescence of equipment or innovations in equipment not disclosed to the buyer? Is this yet another risk that might not be obvious to the buyer but should be?

These are the kinds of risks that need to be examined, aside from the valuation of the business based on profit alone.

Examination Is the Key

It is certainly true that it may be less expensive to buy a business than to start one from scratch. Keep in mind, however, that, whatever your experience in a given trade or industry, there are those who understand the risk factors in business generally much better than you. Don't think that your industry experience will suffice as you examine a business you intend to buy. Buying a business is a business of its own. It requires an understanding of business basics and the subtleties involved in the transfer of a business from one person to another. It is not necessarily complex, but it is mired in details of all kinds, many of which the average businessperson has never dealt with.

The Competitive Factor

It is not necessary or even appropriate to be "concerned" about your competitors. The better word is to be "aware" of your competitors. You need to know the product they sell or the service they offer if it is similar to your own. You need to know the price they charge and the values they add to their product or service.

This is the only way to know where you stand with your potential customers relative to the prices at which you offer your goods or services. If you are offering less in terms of value, you might sell more by making your price more competitive. If you are offering more in terms of value, you might sell fewer but have a margin that allows you to prosper on that basis. If you're offering the same value at the same price, you might depend on your location as the key to maintaining success in your marketplace. Be careful that you understand these differences and that you are fully prepared to participate on a competitive level.

CHAPTER 2

The Financial Picture

AS MENTIONED IN CHAPTER 1, THIS BOOK discusses several concepts that may be difficult to understand at first. This chapter leads you through the financial ideas, almost as a glossary introduces and defines new terms you need to have in your vocabulary. This chapter includes:

- Where buyers get their money and how much it costs,
- How the risk of failure relates to the investment for success,
- What the purchase money promissory note represents,
- How to replace owner's compensation with an appropriate manager's salary,
- How to reconstitute the profit and loss statement, and
- What the receivables turnover period and working capital reservoir mean to buyer and seller.

One of this book's most important goals is to teach you the language of professionals and experts who work in small business investment every day. While you cannot commit to memory all the ideas and terms used by lawyers and accountants, you can become more familiar with them so you can better understand and interpret what your professionals tell you. Once you finish

reading this chapter, complete Worksheet 2 to help reinforce some of the financial concepts and terminology you will need when working with your professionals.

FINANCIAL CONSIDERATIONS FOR THE BUYER

The first decision you face as you consider buying a business is how to finance it. Below are the three essential factors involved in that decision: your cash return, your level of risk, and your financing method.

Buyer's Cash Return

Whenever you use your own cash in an investment, you lose the money you would have earned if you had left it where it was. Therefore, you need to compare the return your cash investment would yield in the business you buy and the return it would get in the stocks, mutual funds, or savings account where you have it now.

First, compare your percentage return from your current investment and the interest rate you would pay by leaving the cash there and borrowing the money for the business. In this example, use a percentage return of 8%, which is not an unreasonable expectation for a relatively secure investment in today's financial marketplace. As a buyer, if you pay $200,000 in cash for a business, you lose $16,000 per year ($200,000 x .08) by not investing that money elsewhere. On the other hand, if you do not use your own cash, you have to borrow money from the seller or elsewhere at 10% or greater. Taking the cash out of your invested capital is actually less expensive for you. (You can benefit from other advantages when you use cash for the purchase, as discussed in Chapter 3.)

Next, compare what your return will be from the business with your current market investment, again using 8% to represent the return on your current investment. If you invest $200,000 in a business with $200,000 gross revenues and 10% operating revenues, the $20,000 operating profit is the cash return on your investment. If you invest your own money, actually borrow money from yourself, you lose $16,000 per year ($200,000 x .08), but you gain $20,000 per year in operating profit. You get a better return on investment by paying cash for the business than you would have received had you invested the same $200,000 in another investment at 8%.

If, on the other hand, the operating profit is only $15,000, you will make more money by leaving your invested capital where it is earning 8%, $16,000 per year on $200,000, or negotiating a lower purchase price for the business.

No matter where the money comes from, it will cost you something. The trick is to compare all the percentages and come to the negotiating table knowing exactly what you can risk and how much it will cost.

High Risk

The interest, or return, you receive from an investment is often based on the level of risk involved in the investment. You can get a heck of a return by investing in the third race at Churchill Downs, but there is also a high risk of losing. High potential return represents high risk.

When you buy a business, there are other risks involved besides the financial percentages. For some businesses, a change in ownership can mean a dramatic change in stability—for example, if the business depends on the ability of the owner to go out and sell. On the other hand, if the business is a retail shop that depends primarily on location and longevity for its growth, a change in ownership could be an incidental factor. If the business's success depends more on location, you face less uncertainty in your investment as long as the location stays the same. If the business relies on the previous owner's contacts or personality, your risk is higher if you cannot produce similar resources. If the business you are considering buying has these types of risk, you want to negotiate a lower asking price to enjoy higher returns after you overcome the initial risks. The seller will counter your arguments by assuring you that your investment is secure. The seller will explain the history of the industry, the growth of the marketplace, and the need for the product or service. Learn what each of these things represents in terms of risk or stability of the business.

Financing Methods

Businesses rarely sell for cash. You are more likely to make a cash down payment and have your seller carry a note for the remainder of the purchase price, a purchase money promissory note. When this happens, it is certainly in the seller's best interest that you, the buyer, succeed after the purchase. Otherwise, the seller may be left with much litigation and aggravation. Ultimately, the sale has to work for the buyer in order to work for the seller as well. Remember: the sale is not final until the last check clears in final payment on the purchase money promissory note.

Even if you obtain the necessary money from a lending institution, that third-party lender will still have an investment in your success. The lender will hold the purchase money promissory note instead of the seller. Because payment of the promissory note depends so much on the buyer's success, banks and other lenders are normally not so inclined to put their money at risk in a business venture. The third-party lender can normally find a more secure investment in the real estate community involving hard assets that do not depend on the energies and abilities of an individual. The seller, on the other hand, has fewer alternatives if he or she wants to sell the business.

Many methods exist to adjust the purchase price or payment schedule on a note. The list is endless. If you consider any of the following methods, you may want to have an accountant by your side.

- Increase or decrease in the down payment
- Special arrangements for the buyer to pay the down payment in increments
- Services or products made available at a discount to the seller after the sale, so long as the seller does not remain in a competitive position
- Responsibility retained by the seller to pay certain payables, some of which may not be accrued
- An agreement that the buyer will pay the seller for a percentage of receivables in cash (rather than, as is usually the case, the seller being responsible for all accrued payables and entitled to all accrued receivables)
- Length of time to pay the purchase money promissory note
- Interest rate on the purchase money promissory note
- Particular assets to be retained by the seller or purchased separately by the buyer—often including personal computers, software, and office furniture
- Security given by the buyer in addition to the business itself, such as a second trust deed on personal real estate holdings
- Secondary elements, such as professional fees, to be absorbed by one party or the other
- An agreement by the buyer to pay completely or partly the seller's broker's fees
- A transition period in which the seller remains with the business after the sale as a paid consultant

Chapter 3 discusses some of these price adjustments in more detail, particularly the length of the note and the size of the down payment.

Both buyer and seller will have to be engaged in mathematical calculations and percentages. As a result, both need to know the many factors that can become a part of financing the purchase.

FINANCIAL CONSIDERATIONS FOR THE SELLER

Because your asking price is based on operating profit, you want to do everything in your power to make that operating profit look good. For most of your career, however, you have reported to the Internal Revenue Service (IRS) an operating profit that you wanted to look as small as possible because you paid taxes on it.

Changing your profit and loss statement (P&L) from one used for tax purposes to one used for selling purposes is called *reconstituting* your P&L. It is your first step to selling your business.

Reconstituting the Profit and Loss Statement

As a seller, you must reconstitute your P&L to present all the financial pieces in the right light and with the right continuity. Some things in your P&L are irrelevant to the buyer. As you know, a good P&L for the IRS is one that contains all the possible deductions the tax code allows. Your business shows a minimum of profit and the taxes you pay are lower. On the other hand, by taking out expense items allowed by the tax code that were appropriate but not mandatory to the operation of the business, you will show a bigger profit. In turn, your business will be valued at a higher price—even though some of the profit is currently being used for more personal, nonessential but allowable expense deductions.

Keep in mind that both presentations are legal and legitimate. You are not committing any deception here. In fact, you will probably show the buyer or the buyer's accountant both sets of numbers at some point, so that they understand how you prepared them and how the buyer can prepare a P&L for the IRS in the future.

Under no circumstances, however, do you have any flexibility relative to gross revenues or the cost of sales. These cannot be changed! While better marketing may increase revenues and attention to detail may save on cost of sales, these are not items personal to the owner. The profit and loss statement at the end of this chapter—presented before and after reconstitution—illustrates this point.

The time to present your financial information in the form most effective and most favorable for a positive selling atmosphere is during the initial negotiations. You want to look at the financials from your potential buyer's perspective. How will the bottom line work for him or her? Will there be enough left to feed the family after the purchase money payments? Is there enough potential in the business to satisfy the buyer's expectations now and in the future?

Some buyers are more sophisticated than others. If your buyer wants to discuss profit and loss only, you should be prepared with concrete figures. Be careful not to confuse the buyer with information you think is pertinent, but about which the buyer has not inquired or shown an inclination to examine.

Depreciating Equipment

Can you ask your buyer to pay for equipment that has depreciated to zero? Again, the Internal Revenue Code may allow a piece of equipment to be completely depreciated in five to seven years, but that does not mean the equipment is really worth zero at the end of that time. The notion that equipment the IRS allows you to depreciate is really worth nothing is one of the biggest fictions in negotiating a business sale. You may depreciate your car over a relatively short period as allowed by the IRS, but the depreciation period is an arbitrary life span given to the equipment and periodically changed by the legislature for tax purposes. It doesn't mean that your Ford, Cadillac, or Mercedes is then worth zero.

Some equipment simply does not change much over the years. You must examine and evaluate the life of equipment, including replacement parts, depending on the particular industry involved. The real question is whether the equipment ranks among the latest technology.

If buyers understand the business, a discussion about the equipment's value will be easy and productive. If they don't, the negotiations will be more difficult because buyers will be looking at depreciation as an essential element to include in the calculations. After all, they always see it in the P&L prepared for tax purposes. Remember: depreciation is designed to anticipate replacement cost of equipment as it becomes necessary. Since nobody knows when this will take place, the legislature has given it an arbitrary time period. In any case, you should be prepared to explain the role your equipment plays in the total picture of your business, its adequacy to perform the job for which it was designed, and the requirements for repair and replacement over a given period.

Owner's Compensation Package

In addition to equipment depreciation, another figure that affects your operating profit is the figure you use to represent owner's salary. Each owner is likely to take a different compensation package; you are not responsible for what your buyer decides to include as owner's compensation after buying the business. An owner can enhance his or her personal income in many ways, such as having the business pay for cars, insurance, travel, or other benefits. If you have included similar items in your compensation package, you will have a badly distorted set of costs and an operating profit produced by bad mathematics, unless you remove them from the P&L.

When you remove the P&L enhancements and equipment depreciation from your P&L, your business will show a higher operating profit. You will be able to show the buyer more easily that the business can stand on its own and pay its new obligations, like the note to the seller, out of current revenues.

The Absentee Owner Concept and Manager's Salary

One of the most important steps toward that goal is to establish an appropriate manager's salary in place of any inflated owner's salary you may currently enjoy. Although absentee ownership is not appropriate for most businesses, it is the basic concept used to develop an appropriate manager's salary. You need a manager's salary for one simple reason—because you deduct cost of labor to calculate your operating profit, you must create a standard for measuring the cost of labor that is consistent with the other financial elements of the business.

Just about every industry has developed a comparison of manager's salary and gross sales at some point in its history, and you can obtain industry information on which to base your ratio of manager's salary to gross sales. For example, in one industry, a manager might make $20,000 per year on sales of $2 million, or 1% of sales. In another industry, a manager might make $20,000 per year on sales of only $200,000, 10% of sales. You need to establish a standard appropriate for your industry and marketplace that is separate from the items you, as owner, included in your compensation package. Make this a priority item—it is that important!

Once you develop a formula, you won't have to arbitrarily allocate a manager's salary to show your true operating profit. If, for example, you are paying your son three times what you would pay another manager, there is no reason to lock that salary into your selling formula. You should use a manager's salary in all the P&Ls and refrain from talking about owner's compensation at all.

During the initial transition period, the buyer may retain the manager and act as an absentee owner. The new owner can spend time learning, stabilizing, and building the business. When the buyer has completed this initiation or training period, he or she may then choose to take on the manager's role and the manager's money. By adding this salary to the net profit and the P&L enhancements, the buyer will have an idea what the business can mean to his or her family in terms of total income.

The concept of manager's salary is vital to the valuation process. Many variables go into determining manager's salary, including industry standards, levels of responsibility, dollar volume, and cost of living in different geographical areas. For example, the salary for manager in San Francisco who handles a gross volume of $300,000 may not be the same for a manager in Kansas City handling the same gross volume of $300,000. In San Francisco, $27,000 represents much less purchasing power than $27,000 in Kansas City. Also, the manager's salary you choose must be appropriate to the talent necessary to handle the responsibilities of the business.

Receivable Turnover Period and Working Capital Reservoir

Finally, one last set of terms you need to be familiar with relates to the cash requirement you want your buyer to bring to the negotiating table. Years ago, people used to talk about certain businesses as *cash businesses*. The customers paid for the product or service at the counter in cash when they picked it up. Times have changed! Very few service businesses and only some product businesses can claim to be cash businesses today. Now, if IBM wants you to do its printing, but it pays bills 90 days after receipt of invoice, you will probably still take the job because you feel secure that IBM will pay. You are carrying its receivable for 90 days. IBM will not immediately reimburse you for the paper you used for that job, or the ink, or the labor, or, in some cases, outside work such as typesetting that you had to pay for right away. Some businesspeople call this the *receivable turnover period*.

Credit cards can decrease the gamble of collection and eliminate the turnover period. However, credit cards represent another percentage loss on the bottom line, because of the amount credit card companies charge for their service.

The buyer must always have a *working capital reservoir*. The amount you designate for this purpose can vary depending on the particular client mix in a given business. However, a reasonable request in the printing industry, just as an example, is an amount equal to a month and a half of gross revenues. In the case of a shop doing approximately $25,000 per month, this amounts to $37,500. Before your buyer can begin to think about a down payment, he or she must have a minimum of $37,500 in an operating account. So, if the buyer is going to put a $50,000 down payment on the purchase of the business, the buyer needs $87,500 in cash.

A cash requirement that size may be too big for many potential buyers. Chapter 3 will discuss some of the variables involved in getting past the cash requirement and making the sale a reality. It shows you some of the more creative and complex methods for financing or price structuring a business sale.

Before you move on, however, look at the reconstituted P&L on the following pages and the effect it has on operating profit and asking price.

KEY POINTS TO REMEMBER

- The buyer must consider risk as one of the elements involved in business investment and recognize the effect it may have on the buyer's return of investment.
- Many elements can be adjusted in the buy-sell negotiation, apart from the price.
- Reconstituting the P&L will maximize the profit picture in the seller's favor.
- The owner's compensation package must be converted to a manager's salary for the profit equation to make any sense in valuing the business.
- Both buyer and seller must be sure that the buyer has a strong working capital reservoir to ensure continuity and success of the business takeover.

Sample of a Reconstituted P&L—Alice's Print 'n' Copy

The two columns on the profit and loss statement for Alice's Print 'n' Copy—on this and the following page—represent the figures before and after reconstituting the P&L to sell the business.

The following items are personal to the owner and not to the business and are removed from the reconstituted P&L:

- Owner's draw in excess of appropriate manager's salary
- Owner's auto insurance payments and bank payments on car
- Health insurance for owner's spouse
- Airline tickets for a working holiday in London

Here are some other items a seller might consider for elimination:

- Legal and accounting costs attributable exclusively to sale preparation
- One-time equipment purchases that were expensed rather than depreciated

Be careful not to exclude things like dues and subscriptions or donations, repair and maintenance, or outside labor, all of which are integral parts of the going business regardless of who the owner is. If the new owner can find a way to eliminate the use of outside labor or decides to drop a membership in a trade organization, that savings is part of the buyer's bonus, not the seller's equity.

If you reconstitute your P&L carefully and reasonably, it is a very effective selling tool. Of course, the best way to achieve a better operating profit and asking price is to actually increase sales or decrease costs—tangibly and not just on paper.

The maximum asking price payable from an annual operating profit of $16,690 is $105,000 payable over 10 years at 10% interest. (You will learn how to calculate a maximum asking price in Chapter 3.) However, an asking price as high as $105,000 will leave nothing from the operating profit to serve as the buyer's income. Alice's Print 'n' Copy will more likely sell for much less, possibly as little as $80,000, depending on other negotiated items, such as a transition period, the value of equipment, location, and lease, or the size of the down payment, the interest rate, or the length of the promissory note.

With a selling price of $80,000, financed with a 10-year note at 10% interest and a 10% down payment, the buyer will have to meet annual note payments of $11,418 from the operating profit of $16,690 per year. This gives the buyer an annual income of $5,272.

The manager at Alice's is receiving $16,640 per year in salary. When the buyer feels comfortable enough running the business on his or her own, the buyer can release the manager and supplement his or her income with the manager's salary, creating a buyer income of $21,912 per year.

FIGURE 2.1   Alice's Print 'n' Copy Reconstituted P&L (continued on next page)

	BEFORE		AFTER	
	Year to Date	**%**	**Year to Date**	**%**
SALES				
Printing	$101,499	74.57%	$101,499	74.57%
Outside Services	$31,451	23.11%	$31,451	23.11%
Copier	$3,431	2.52%	$3,431	2.52%
Returns and Allowances	($275)	0.20%	($275)	0.20%
Total Sales	**$136,106**	**100%**	**$136,106**	**100%**

FIGURE 2.1 Alice's Print 'n' Copy Reconstituted P&L (continued)

	BEFORE		AFTER	
	Year to Date	%	Year to Date	%
COST OF SALES				
Beginning Inventory	$2,182	1.60%	$2,182	1.60%
Purchases	$18,637	13.69%	$18,637	13.69%
Outside Vendors	$15,208	11.17%	$15,208	11.17%
Ending Inventory	($1,514)	1.11%	($1,514)	1.11%
Equipment Supplies	$4,361	3.20%	$4,361	3.20%
Total Cost of Sales	**$38,874**	**28.55%**	**$38,874**	**28.55%**
GROSS PROFIT	**$97,232**	**71.45%**	**$97,232**	**71.45%**
OPERATING EXPENSES				
Salaries and Wages*	$14,645	10.76%	$14,560	10.70%
Partners' Salaries*	$20,800	15.28%	$16,640	12.23%
Taxes on Payroll*	$2,718	2.00%	$2,392	1.76%
Advertising	$6,197	4.55%	$6,197	4.55%
Auto Expenses†	$2,152	1.58%	$900	0.66%
Bad Debt Expense	$320	0.24%	$320	0.24%
Copier Service	$906	0.67%	$906	0.67%
Depreciation‡	$9,297	6.83%	$0	0.00%
Dues/Subscriptions	$417	0.31%	$417	0.31%
Franchise Royalty	$11,284	8.29%	$11,284	8.29%
Insurance	$2,434	1.79%	$2,434	1.79%
Health Insurance[1]	$1,474	1.08%	$874	0.06%
Legal and Accounting	$2,828	2.08%	$2,828	2.08%
Office Expense	$1,813	1.33%	$1,813	1.33%
Over and Short	($6)	0.00%	($6)	0.00%
Promotion	$229	0.17%	$229	0.17%
Rent	$11,760	8.64%	$11,760	8.64%
Repairs & Maintenance	$2,007	1.47%	$2,007	1.47%
Supplies	$356	0.26%	$356	0.26%
Taxes and License	$920	0.68%	$920	0.68%
Telephone	$1,612	1.18%	$1,612	1.18%
Travel & Entertainment[2]	$1,738	1.28%	$238	0.02%
Utilties	$1,861	1.37%	$1,861	1.37%
Total Operating Expenses	**$97,762**	**71.84%**	**$80,542**	**58.46%**
TOTAL OPERATING PROFIT	**($530)**	**−0.39%**	**$16,690**	**12.99%**

*Save $4,571 from the differential in salaries and payroll taxes.

†Save $1,252 after deducting payments on owner's car.

‡Save $9,297 on equipment depreciation.

[1]Save $600 after deducting spouse's insurance.

[2]Save $1,500 on owner's business/personal trip to Europe.

Worksheet 2. Expand Your Financial Vocabulary

The following questions will help you determine if you know the financial elements of a business sale and can understand what your professional advisors and the buyer or seller on the other side of the negotiating table are talking about.

Would you describe the business's operating profit as dependable and stable? ❏ Yes ❏ No

If you answered no, are you prepared to request (if you are a buyer) or concede (if you are a seller) a reduction in the purchase price to accommodate the level of risk involved in purchasing the business? ❏ Yes ❏ No

As a buyer, do you understand why you cannot demand that equipment be valued at zero just because the government allows the seller to depreciate equipment to zero after a certain period of time? ❏ Yes ❏ No

As a buyer, do you understand why a seller should not include items like the cost of a spouse's health insurance in a reconstituted profit and loss statement? ❏ Yes ❏ No

Do you understand the purpose of making a distinction between owner's compensation and manager's salary?
❏ Yes ❏ No

What are the most important factors in determining an appropriate manager's salary for your business?
- ❏ Standard of living in your geographical location
- ❏ Sales volume
- ❏ Other: _____

- ❏ Manager's level of responsibility
- ❏ Industry standards
- ❏ _____

How will you calculate an appropriate manager's salary for your business? _____
_____
_____

Do you understand the concept of receivable turnover period? ❏ Yes ❏ No

What type of receivable turnover period does the business you are buying or selling contend with? _____
_____
_____

Do you understand the need to have a working capital reservoir? ❏ Yes ❏ No

What size working capital reservoir does the business you are buying or selling require? _____
_____
_____

USING SOMEONE ELSE'S MONEY

Some money sources are more obvious than others. The first source of capital is likely to be reaching into your own pocket. After all, who has more faith in the concept you hope to build than yourself? In the event your pocket is empty, the next source is normally friends and family. Here again, the people most likely to be willing to invest in your creativity and your energies are the people who know you best.

Looking to Strangers

When the dollars for survival or for the next plateau of success are not available from your own pocket or from those who already know and trust you, your next approach will likely be the lender or the investor. For short-term financial problems, it makes more sense to borrow, if possible, rather than to get an investor who will be in your business for the long term.

Lender Concerns

The lender is usually interested in getting the money returned within a specific period of time and interest for the time you've had it. For this reason, the lender is usually not interested in the long-term goals of the company; it is interested in your ability to meet the repayment schedule established at the time of the borrowing. The lender will, of course, be interested in security to ensure payment of the loan in the event you fail to meet your periodic payment schedule, as this represents a certain vulnerability. Be sure you are comfortable with the schedule of payments.

The Investor Profile

Investors, on the other hand, will not usually take security for their investment; they are taking stock in your company with the intention of staying for the long term, hoping that the success of your company will mean a return of a multiple of their investment. The problem with investors is that they are going to want to watch your progress and are likely to exercise as much control as they can during the growth period of the company. One problem with this "looking over your shoulder" is that they may subvert your long-term interests to protect their investment in the short term. In other words, their goals and your goals may not be the same. Giving up control of your company's direction, even to a minor degree, can be adverse to the long-term interests of the company.

Money from Strange Sources

Often, a company can buy raw materials, component parts, and even inventory with a "postponed" payment schedule. If, for example, you can have material, parts, or inventory delivered and don't have to pay for them for 90 days, you have essentially enjoyed an investment in your company. It's possible to sell the goods and col-

lect on the sales before the dollars for your purchases are even due.

Another option, in some cases, is to indicate to your retailers that you need a down payment in order to pay for the raw materials, component parts, or inventory. If your product or service is in enough demand and you have the trust of your buyers, you may end up with advance money from them, which actually represents an investment in your company for which you didn't have to give up any portion of the company's equity.

Working with Another Company

In some cases, you may be joining with another company to enhance your ability to function in the marketplace. This is sometimes referred to as a joint venture or a strategic alliance. It may be to augment the services you provide or to enhance your selling position in the marketplace. You might even be using someone else's distribution system. In this way, you may not be paying for the additional products or services until after your sales have been expedited and you've collected the money owed. In this way, you've actually had the other company invest in your business because it saves you from investing your dollars up front.

Alternative Ways of Thinking

Keep in mind that there are more creative ways of doing most things than the conventional wisdom often reflects for those who have less imagination than you do. Money is the predicate for sustaining your business, growing your business, and reaching for that next plateau of success. There are many ways in which money can be obtained and used, some unusual. Ask your professionals what they might suggest from this standpoint relative to your particular business. You might be surprised at the answers.

Negotiating Price and Pricing Variables

IN THE PREVIOUS TWO CHAPTERS, YOU LOOKED AT some of the fundamental financial relationships created between a buyer and a seller while negotiating a business sale. Your accountant and attorney will likely handle the fine print and mathematical calculations involved in getting those relationships defined on paper. Nonetheless, you need to understand on what theories those calculations and provisions are based and how you, as buyer or seller, can make them work to your best advantage.

Toward that end, this chapter provides charts, graphs, and an amortization method and discusses pricing variables, such as size of down payment, interest rate, and length of note. While you should always consult your accountant and attorney before agreeing to any pricing option, this chapter gives you a good foundation with which to negotiate a price structure and understand the recommendations of your accountant and your attorney.

Keep in mind that a seller is dealing with two sets of figures in the negotiations. The first is a method of valuing the business based on the total purchase price derived from the operating profit concept, regardless of the amount of the down payment. The second is based very much on the amount of the down payment, because

the size of the down payment will tell buyers how much they have left in their pocket each month after making the payments on the purchase money promissory note. As you read this chapter, look for how these two sets of figures work and how they will affect the asking price of a business.

FINANCING METHODS

A buyer usually pays for a business in cash or finances it through a purchase money promissory note. Financing is often carried by the seller, but in some cases it may be carried by a third party. Whether the buyer pays cash or finances all or part of the purchase price, some price adjustments may be necessary, depending on the figures and the percentages with which the buyer and seller are working. While pluses and minuses exist in all forms of financing, the seller will minimize later complications by getting as much cash up front as possible.

An All-Cash Deal

Apart from the tax consequences, the best possible position for a seller is to receive cash for the full purchase price. The seller is relieved of any future responsibility to the business. Such an

Please note that all annual figures in this chapter may vary slightly but remain within a $5.00 difference.

occurrence is very unlikely, but if a cash deal does present itself, the seller should adjust the price to accommodate the present value of money—that is, money collected in cash now has a greater value than money paid over a 10-year period, interest notwithstanding. An all-cash deal should, therefore, offer some price advantage to the buyer in current dollars. For the seller, the obvious benefits of a cash sale also warrant that he or she consider a price break that allows a cash deal. The fact is, the more buyers are willing to put down in cash—whether in the form of a large down payment or the entire purchase price—the larger the concession they will expect in the purchase price.

The negative side of a cash sale for the seller is that if the entire purchase price of the business is received in a single tax year, the capital gains tax can be devastating. The seller will also find that the rate of interest paid by a buyer is normally higher than the interest rate the seller will get in the investment marketplace. An accountant can be very helpful in working out the differentials for the present value of the dollar, the effects of the capital gains tax, and the interest rate potential. From the buyer's perspective, the negative side of a cash sale is that the buyer who owes nothing to the seller has no leverage for dealing with potential seller misrepresentations made during negotiations.

A Seller-Carry Deal

The more common form of financing is for the buyer to make a cash down payment and for the seller to carry the balance of the purchase price at a specified interest rate and over a particular period of time. In this situation, these are the three primary variables you will encounter:

- Down payment
- Length of the note
- Interest rate

Before you examine these variables in detail, remember one last important item. Whatever money the buyer uses to purchase the business, particularly what he or she puts down in cash at the outset, is money taken from its secure investment elsewhere. The seller must be prepared to factor in the buyer's lost investment income in negotiating the sale.

NEGOTIATING THE DOWN PAYMENT

If a buyer does not make a down payment or makes a small down payment, the seller will commonly adjust the payment plan to make up for the lack of cash up front, either by increasing the interest rate on the promissory note or by decreasing the length of the note. The adjustment increases the return to the seller without imposing too onerous a burden on the buyer. However, any major adjustments can jeopardize the sale by making the business simply unaffordable for the buyer. A seller cannot raise the price if the finances of an otherwise qualified buying candidate or the business's operating profit cannot support the larger figure.

On the other hand, the buyer should not be obliged to pay more and get less. If the buyer makes a large down payment and thereby lowers the amount of the purchase money promissory note, he or she increases his or her net profit for the year by lowering the annual note payments. The buyer actually purchases a bigger annual income. This is the buyer's bonus.

The best negotiating position for the seller is not to go for a higher asking price, but to go for a larger down payment. By putting down more cash in the beginning, the buyer reduces the total loan amount that must be paid from the operating profit. The seller can show the buyer how to generate a higher annual income and the seller walks away with more cash in hand.

To demonstrate how this works, here's an example. Assume that a business with gross revenues of $300,000 per year sells for $250,000. The full purchase price is represented by a 10-year note at a 10% interest rate fully amortized—that is, the principal and interest will be paid completely at the end of the 10-year period. Assume further that the business yields a 20% operating profit, or $60,000. The full loan amount of the purchase money promissory note (PMPN) is $250,000; if the seller carries it for 10 years at 10%, the payments are $3,303 per month, or $39,645 per year. The buyer receives a net profit, after meeting the promissory note payments from the operating profit, of $20,355 per year.

In this scenario, the seller may reasonably ask for a 20% down payment, $50,000. If the seller carries the balance of the purchase price, the total loan amount is only $200,000, and the annual payments drop to

$31,716. With the larger down payment, it is easier for the buyer to make payments on the PMPN out of the operating profit. The buyer would then, after the payments on a 10-year note at 10%, enjoy a profit of $28,284. Again, a larger down payment, in addition to any possible concession in the purchase price, gives the buyer a larger annual income from the business.

In negotiating the size of the down payment, the seller should recognize that the buyer is using his or her own money, $50,000 in this example, for the down payment and is losing money every year in passive income. If the buyer's investment income was earning 8%, the buyer loses $4,000 on the cash down payment, $50,000 times 8%. The seller could reasonably adjust the purchase price by this $4,000 to the buyer's benefit.

As you can see in Table 3.1, a $60,000 operating profit could also support an asking price of $300,000, 100% of gross revenues. The payments, with the same 10% interest rate, are $47,574 per year, which still leaves $12,426 in the buyer's pocket after payments on the PMPN.

However, $12,426 may not leave the buyer enough room to handle a bad season, an unexpected employee problem, or the loss of a big customer. The seller can counter the buyer's complaints that the operating profit after note payments is too small by illustrating what a larger annual net profit the buyer will have in the future if he or she makes a larger down payment now. The seller does not have to lower the price—the size of the down payment leaves plenty of room for negotiation.

The buyer's annual net profit can rise substantially with a larger down payment. Table 3.1 shows how a 20% down payment on a $300,000 asking price will nearly double the buyer's net profit from what it would be with no down payment, from $12,426 to $21,941.

NEGOTIATING THE LENGTH OF THE NOTE

A buyer is worried about the length of the promissory note repayment period because it affects the amount of his or her monthly payment on the note. A shorter payment schedule increases the size of the monthly payment and thereby decreases the monthly income available from the operating profit.

The seller is concerned about the note's length because it affects the price he or she can justifiably ask for the business. A longer payment period lowers the size of the monthly payments and enables the seller to ask a higher price because the buyer can handle the payments more easily. The negative side of an extended payment schedule is the added risk of collecting the entire balance. Any number of elements might cause a downturn in the business; the longer the note, the greater the chances of this happening. The seller may be more interested in getting a higher price for the business than in getting his or her money more quickly on an accelerated payment schedule. On the other hand, if the seller wants to collect the balance of the purchase

---

| TABLE 3.1 | Adjustments in the Down Payment |

This table assumes gross sales of $300,000 and an operating profit of 20%, or $60,000 per year, and a 10-year note at 10% interest.

Asking Price	Down Payment	Size of PMPN	PMPN Payments per Year	Buyer's Net Profit per Year (after deducting PMPN from operating profit)
$300,000	No down payment	$300,000	$47,574	$12,426
$300,000	10% ($30,000)	$270,000	$42,816	$17,184
$300,000	20% ($60,000)	$240,000	$38,059	$21,941
$250,000	No down payment	$250,000	$39,645	$20,355
$250,000	10% ($25,000)	$225,000	$35,680	$24,320
$250,000	20% ($50,000)	$200,000	$31,716	$28,284

price more quickly, he or she must be prepared to lower the price so that the operating profit can handle the higher payments per month on the shorter note.

To demonstrate how different repayment periods affect the asking price and the buyer's net profit, look at Table 3.2, which takes the same business with annual gross revenues of $300,000 and a 20% operating profit, but with a seven-year note at 10%. With a loan amount of $250,000, the payment schedule is $49,800 per year. With a loan amount of $300,000, the payments are $59,760, just barely payable out of the $60,000 operating profit.

It is simple enough to look at the five-year amortization to see that trying to collect the money within this shorter time makes the obligation much more difficult for the buyer. With the figures used in this example, the business ceases to pay for itself, so the seller should reduce the asking price. If the seller is willing to reduce the price to accelerate the payments and realize his or her equity value more quickly, then the sale will work for both parties and it will likely take place.

NEGOTIATING THE INTEREST RATE

A promissory note commonly has an interest rate 2%–3% above the prime rate. Again, you, as a seller, do not want to jeopardize the sale by demanding an unreasonable rate. This book uses a standard interest rate of 10% for all examples. Based on prevailing rates over an extended period of time, it has proven to be a comfortable rate for both buyer and seller, based on the premise that the buyer couldn't borrow at an interest

rate that low and the seller couldn't invest at an interest rate that high. Rates other than 10% may be appropriate as the interest rate fluctuates.

Keep in mind that, regardless of the economy or the bank rates, the buyer and the seller are always in a position to discuss and negotiate the interest rate, which may ultimately be based on many personal bargaining factors. The negotiated interest rate will not affect the concepts in this book.

Usury statutes can act as a limit on the amount of interest a seller can charge, however. These statutes and limitations vary from state to state. Check in your particular jurisdiction to ensure that the rate you are using is legal.

Amortization Tables

Although amortization tables are available and you should have one, there is an easy way to have the figures handy when you need them, even without the schedule. You can use a simple method to determine the monthly and annual payments for your purchase money promissory note when using a particular interest rate and a given payout period.

The payout figures shown in Table 3.3 will give you a quick idea about how the numbers will work for your business. Amortization schedules are obtainable from any savings and loan association and most banks and credit agencies. You should prepare some of these factor schedules and become familiar with their use relative to the interest and payment-period ratio before you start discussing buying or selling.

TABLE 3.2 **Adjustments in the Length of the Note**

This table assumes an operating profit of $60,000.

Length of the Note	Asking Price	Annual Note Payment	Net Profit to Buyer
10 years at 10%	$300,000	$47,574	$12,426
	250,000	39,645	20,355
7 years at 10%	300,000	59,760	240
	250,000	49,800	10,200
5 years at 10%	300,000	76,488	<16,488>
	250,000	63,744	<3,744>

As you can see in Table 3.3, the figures of 2,124.71 for five years, 1,660.12 for seven years, and 1,321.51 for 10 years are based on a $100,000 note at a 10% interest rate. To determine the monthly or yearly obligation on a different size note, divide the loan amount by 100,000 and multiply that result by the appropriate factor, as shown in Table 3.3. That gives a monthly payment figure. Multiply it by 12 and you get the yearly promissory note payment.

PRICE STRUCTURING BEGINS WITH THE BUYER'S PERSPECTIVE

By understanding the variables and their interrelationships, a seller can then begin working backwards from operating profit to find out what yearly promissory note obligation the operating profit can support and still allow the buyer the yearly income he or she wants. The basic variables that will cause the figures to change include size of down payment, length of note, and interest rate. Once a seller knows what down payment the buyer can offer, how long the note will be, and what interest rate the seller will deal with, a workable asking price should begin to emerge. The seller will know exactly what price will work with the operating profit and the buyer's needs. If the business doesn't pay for itself and the buyer goes under, the seller hasn't made a sale.

You can determine the maximum asking price for the particular length of note you will use by applying the following formula:

> Operating profit ÷ annualized payment amount from amortization table X 100,000 = maximum asking price

On a note with a 10% interest rate, the annualized payment amount from the amortization method shown in Table 3.3 is $15,858 for a 10-year note, $19,921 for a seven-year note, and $25,497 for a five-year note. If a business is doing $200,000 gross volume and maintaining an operating profit of 20%, $40,000 per year, you can determine the maximum asking price as follows:

- On a 10-year note: operating profit of $40,000 divided by the yearly figure of $15,858 (from the amortization method in Table 3.3) equals 2.5, which is multiplied by $100,000 to get a maximum asking price of $250,000, payable from the business' operating profit, leaving no income for the buyer.

TABLE 3.3   A Simple Amortization Model

The monthly factor shown in this chart is based on a $100,000 note at 10% interest. You can use this monthly factor to determine the payments on any loan amount at 10% interest by dividing the loan amount by 100,000 and multiplying the result (shown in the fourth column) by the monthly factor.

Loan Amount	Term	Monthly Factor	Multiple (Loan ÷ 100,000)	Monthly Payments	Yearly Payments
$100,000	5 years	2,124.71	1.00	$2,124.71	$25,497
100,000	7 years	1,660.12	1.00	1,660.12	19,921
100,000	10 years	1,321.51	1.00	1,321.51	15,858
$135,000	5 years	2,124.71	1.35	2,868.36	34,420
135,000	7 years	1,660.12	1.35	2,241.16	26,894
135,000	10 years	1,321.51	1.35	1,784.04	21,408
$83,000	5 years	2,124.71	.83	1,763.51	21,162
83,000	7 years	1,660.12	.83	1,377.90	16,535
83,000	10 years	1,321.51	.83	1,096.85	13,162

- On a seven-year note: operating profit of $40,000 divided by the yearly figure of $19,921 (from Table 3.3) equals 2, which is multiplied by $100,000 to get a maximum asking price of $200,000, payable from the operating profit, leaving no income for the buyer.
- On a five-year note: operating profit of $40,000 divided by the yearly figure of $25,497 (from Table 3.3) equals 1.56, which is multiplied by $100,000 to get a maximum asking price of $156,000, payable from the operating profit, leaving no income for the buyer.

If you examine sales over recent years, you will find that the seven-year amortization gives you the most reasonable seller's asking price. The payments on a five-year amortization tend to be too difficult for the buyer. The 10-year amortization allows the breathing room needed by both buyer and seller. But, again, a larger down payment changes the working figures for both buyer and seller.

Table 3.4 (page 28) illustrates all these variables—operating profit, down payment, asking price, and length of note. If you're a seller, pay particular attention to the last column, because that is what your buyer is looking at.

Operating Profit Is the Key

Operating profit is the key to creating a selling price. As the examples above demonstrate, a higher operating profit allows a seller to ask a higher price. One of the ways a seller should prepare his or her business, therefore, is to tighten up the operating cost percentages to maximize operating profit.

As discussed in Chapter 2, you can quickly affect the operating profit on paper by reconstituting the profit and loss statement. Figure in an appropriate manager's salary and eliminate any operating costs that are more personal to the owner. Each owner will invariably have his or her own priorities in that respect.

If all your costs and payments are properly figured into your P&L, then you will likely approach a realistic asking price through some of the methods outlined above. If, for example, a seller still has two years left on an equipment contract that isn't yet included in the P&L, he or she will have to show how the buyer can meet those equipment payments and still have something left over. Then the seller can point out that, at the end of that limited payout period, the buyer can count on an additional dollar bonus as part of the profit picture. The seller may have to lower the monthly payment schedule on the purchase money promissory note for the first two years, to give the buyer a larger operating profit from which to pay for the equipment during the balance of the contract. At the end of that period, the seller can raise the monthly payments on the purchase money promissory note, because the buyer will no longer need the money to pay off the equipment.

If the seller makes the lower payment schedule on the PMPN a permanent concession on the purchase price, he or she can then point out the buyer's income will increase after paying off the equipment, because the equivalent of the equipment payments will be going from the operating profit to his or her personal income. A seller can show a buyer looking for an $80,000 per year income that he or she may have to settle for $65,000 for two years—if the payments on the equipment, for example, are about $15,000 per year. Then, after paying off the equipment, the buyer will be able to enjoy the full $80,000. Whether you are a buyer or a seller, work these differentials out with your accountant before you put them on the negotiating table.

THE PERSONAL SIDE TO NEGOTIATIONS

A seller needs to assess a buyer's goals and preferences to decide which payment plan and financing scheme the buyer will be most receptive to. A seller needs to spend time with the buyer to learn what perspective the buyer is using to look at the business. Trial lawyers often joke that if four witnesses see an accident happen from four street corners, you will get four different descriptions of the accident. It is sometimes hard to remember that there was only one accident. A seller should try to stand on the buyer's street corner to better understand what he or she is seeing.

Business-buying candidates are always looking for the largest income they can generate, which they usually equate with the largest investment they can handle. This equation, by the way, is not necessarily valid, but it seems to be the foundation for most buyers' thinking.

| TABLE 3.4 | Pricing Variables at Work |

Asking Price	Down Payment	PMPN Payment per Year	Operating Profit		Buyer's Net Profit per Year
Ten-Year Note					
$250,000	No down payment	$39,645 per year	from $60,000	=	$20,355 per year
$250,000	10% ($25,000)	$35,680 per year	from $60,000	=	$24,320 per year
$250,000	20% ($50,000)	$31,716 per year	from $60,000	=	$28,284 per year
$200,000	No down payment	$31,716 per year	from $60,000	=	$28,284 per year
$200,000	10% ($20,000)	$28,545 per year	from $60,000	=	$31,455 per year
$200,000	20% ($40,000)	$25,373 per year	from $60,000	=	$34,627 per year
$250,000	No down payment	$39,645 per year	from $30,000	=	<$9,645> per year
$250,000	10% ($25,000)	$35,681 per year	from $30,000	=	<$5,681> per year
$250,000	20% ($50,000)	$31,716 per year	from $30,000	=	<$1,716> per year
$200,000	No down payment	$31,716 per year	from $30,000	=	<$1,716> per year
$200,000	10% ($20,000)	$28,545 per year	from $30,000	=	$1,455 per year
$200,000	20% ($40,000)	$25,373 per year	from $30,000	=	$4,627 per year
Seven-Year Note					
$250,000	No down payment	$49,800 per year	from $60,000	=	$10,200 per year
$250,000	10% ($25,000)	$44,823 per year	from $60,000	=	$15,177 per year
$250,000	20% ($50,000)	$39,843 per year	from $60,000	=	$20,157 per year
$250,000	20% ($50,000)	$39,843 per year	from $30,000	=	<$9,843> per year
$200,000	20% ($40,000)	$31,874 per year	from $30,000	=	<$1,874> per year
$150,000	20% ($30,000)	$23,906 per year	from $30,000	=	$6,094 per year
Five-Year Note					
$300,000	20% ($60,000)	$61,192 per year	from $60,000	=	<$1,192> per year
$250,000	20% ($50,000)	$50,993 per year	from $60,000	=	$9,007 per year
$200,000	20% ($40,000)	$40,794 per year	from $60,000	=	$19,206 per year

A buyer who is considering a substantial cash investment is probably looking for a business growth opportunity—not merely to buy a job. The seller might, during negotiations, consider a lower down payment to ensure that the buyer has a large enough working capital reservoir to sustain the business for future survival and success.

CREATIVE FINANCING OPTIONS

Much of the premise of this book and its valuation concept is that the selling price depends, in great part, not on the real or perceived value of the business, but rather on the financial position of the potential buyer. If the purchase price and PMPN obligations do not work for the buyer, the sale will not work at all, regardless of what the seller thinks the business is worth. The business is really worth only what a buyer will or can pay.

For example, assume you are a seller and the buyer is exactly the right kind of operator, with a selling background and ready to work hard for new customers and higher sales. In fact, the buyer is exactly the kind of person you wish you had working for you before you decided to sell the business. But the buyer doesn't have enough cash to put up both the necessary working capital and a down payment. There are a number of ways to make this sale work.

Temporary Partnerships

One creative financing option is a temporary partnership. Many buyers and sellers go into temporary partnership with each other as a short-term alternative to a sale. If you are a seller, always ensure that your buyer/partner cannot build or purchase an equity position and then back out of the deal to purchase the business. Set a specific time and dollar amount for your buyer/partner to purchase your remaining interest in the business or, if your partner decides not to purchase the business, be sure you can buy back your partner's share of the business at a reasonable time and price.

No partnership situation exists in which both (or all) partners are satisfied all the time with their partners' participation. Every partnership agreement should have a buyout clause built into the contract at the beginning of the relationship. It can be based on either a specific amount of money or a formula that is easy to calculate at any time during the life of the partnership.

Using the Buyer's Assets

Another creative finance option is to examine what the buyer can put at risk. A buyer can put assets at risk in many ways, but the simplest is to execute a second trust deed, or second mortgage, on real property that has sufficient equity value. The trust deed could be for a period that expires with the last payment on the PMPN or for a period long enough for a specific amount to be paid on the note, such as equivalent to a 20% down payment, for example. Instead of a second deed of trust, a buyer could use stocks or bonds as collateral.

A buyer could even get an acceptable cosigner, but this is not so easy to do on a note that runs six figures. Finding a cosigner for a business loan is not exactly the same as having a father cosign for a Visa card for his teenager, but it could be done.

You might ask, "If the buyer has access to these assets, why not convert them to cash to meet the seller's down payment requirement?" The answer is that,

many times, for many reasons, these assets are difficult to convert to cash without a substantial penalty.

If the buyer cannot get to the assets because the timing is not right, the seller needs to consider what kind of protections can be put into the contract of sale or the promissory note. Seller protections are discussed in Chapter 14.

Allocation of Purchase Price

Much of the creativity in financing comes from the need to have a particular kind of sale fit the tax position of the buyer or seller. Depending on the state in which a business is located, you, as either a buyer or a seller, may have to pay sales tax on the sale of a business that transfers some or all of its assets.

The effects of allocation of purchase price monies to equipment and goodwill are different for the buyer and the seller. In some states, for instance, the payment of the sales tax is historically the seller's responsibility. In other states, the responsibility falls to the buyer.

If the seller is responsible for paying the sales tax, he or she will want a lower allocation to equipment, because the majority of the sales tax is predicated on hard assets. On the other hand, the buyer will want a higher allocation to equipment, so that he or she has more assets on which to take depreciation, which will cut down the taxable income from the operating profit of the ongoing business. Even with the new tax law allowing depreciation of goodwill, the time allowed to depreciate hard assets is still shorter, which will be much more advantageous to the buyer for tax purposes.

If the buyer is responsible for the sales tax, he or she will have to decide whether a substantial tax payment at the time of purchase is worth the larger depreciation factor later. If the seller is responsible for the sales tax, he or she may need to negotiate the actual allocation, because the seller wants the hard assets lower, for sales tax purposes, and the buyer wants the hard assets higher, for depreciation purposes. Sharing the sales tax burden may satisfy the needs of both buyer and seller.

Other states may not have any sales tax on a bulk sale transfer. Be sure to consult your accountant or attorney regarding the tax obligations in your state.

A Balloon Payment

The term "creative financing" has been overused in the last 10 years, particularly in the real estate market when interest rates, at one point, got too high for average homebuyers to handle the payment schedule on a 30-year fully amortized mortgage. One creative method that came into existence is a balloon payment—the balance of a loan payable at the end of a shorter term than for a fully amortized mortgage.

You could equate this to taking a 10-year fully amortized note and converting it to a five-year note, amortizing the full amount over 10 years but making the balance of the principal due at the end of the five years. Although a balloon payment scheme allows a reasonable payment schedule for the five years, the entire balance of the principal must be paid off in a lump sum or refinanced at the end of that term.

Balloon payments were quite reasonable in real estate, because many people didn't live in the same house for more than five years. They normally sold their houses, which allowed them to pay the entire note before the balloon payment came due. In addition, the housing market is relatively stable and easily financed compared with the small business market.

The balloon payment plan is much more difficult to arrange for a business purchase because banks are not as interested in lending money on business equity. If the buyer can't refinance the balloon payment, he or she is left to the mercy of the seller to refinance the balloon or take back the business on default when the buyer can't meet the balloon payment on the due date.

Both buyer and seller must beware of any creative scheme that isn't fully discussed with professional counsel: it can prove to be equally dangerous to both parties involved.

As you continue to explore more aspects of buying and selling and examine actual businesses for sale, you may want to return to this chapter. As you examine and reexamine the specifics of each potential acquisition, you will become more familiar with the figures and calculations. After a while, you will feel more comfortable with the process of negotiating price and pricing variables.

The following worksheet will also help you build a comfort zone for working with price and payment figures.

KEY POINTS TO REMEMBER

- An all-cash deal carries a heavy tax burden for the seller and affords no ongoing protection to the buyer.
- The larger the down payment, the more discount the buyer is entitled to on the purchase price.
- A longer promissory note allows a higher asking price because the monthly payments are lower.
- If the seller helps the buyer purchase the business at the right price, the seller increases the likelihood of collecting the balance of the purchase money promissory note.
- Price is based on operating profit. Anything the seller can do to cut expenses will cause dollars to drop to the bottom line and increase the asking price.

Worksheet 3.1. Price and Price Adjustments

The following questions will prepare you for negotiating price and price adjustments. You need to understand the theories and calculations behind price adjustments before you go to the negotiating table. However, as always, you should have your accountant and your attorney by your side before you agree to any price structure.

If the business is sold for cash, is the seller expected to make an adjustment in the purchase price? ❏ Yes ❏ No

Why is an all-cash deal good for the seller? _____

_____

_____

Why is an all-cash deal bad for the seller? _____

_____

_____

Why is an all-cash deal good for the buyer? _____

_____

_____

Why is an all-cash deal bad for the buyer? _____

_____

_____

Is the seller expected to make price concessions based on a larger down payment? ❏ Yes ❏ No

What is the rationale for charging a higher purchase price in return for a longer purchase money promissory note?

_____

_____

What is the rationale for lowering the selling price of a business in return for a shorter purchase money promissory note?

_____

_____

What is the key to valuing a business? _____

_____

_____

Why should the seller try to reduce costs even after putting the business up for sale? _____

_____

_____

Why should the seller be entitled to know what assets the buyer can put at risk? _____

_____

_____

What are the tax ramifications of the allocation of the purchase price? _____
_____
_____

How might a temporary partnership between buyer and seller affect the ultimate selling price of the business?
_____
_____

How can lease purchase arrangements affect the selling price of a business? _____
_____
_____

Why might a balloon note be good or bad as a finance arrangement in a business sale? _____
_____
_____

Worksheet 3.2. Price Justification

The following is a price justification for a business with a net annual operating profit of $27,420 (after reconstituting the profit and loss statement).

Aside from getting the highest price possible, this seller has two main goals: to get a high down payment and to carry the note for only five years. The seller has worked out a justification for various potential price structures.

The buyer has $100,000 in cash to invest in the business and requires an annual income of at least $30,000. Because the shop requires a working capital reservoir of $29,375, the buyer can afford a down payment of only $70,000. The manager's salary for this shop is $24,000, so the buyer needs at least $6,000 in operating profit, after meeting payments on the promissory note, to generate an aggregate income of $30,000 per year.

Scenario 1

This price structure uses the maximum asking price possible for a 10-year note at 10% interest (see the formula below on this worksheet), minus a 20% down payment.

Asking price	$173,000	Annual operating profit	$27,420
20% down payment	34,600	Reserve after paying note	5,472
Total loan amount	138,400	Manager's salary	24,000
Annual note payments	21,948	Buyer's annual income	29,472

Scenario 2

The seller is willing to reduce the asking price in return for a higher down payment. This price structure is based on a 10-year note at 10% interest.

Asking price	$169,000	Annual operating profit	$27,420
30% down payment	50,000	Reserve after paying note	8,549
Total loan amount	119,000	Manager's salary	24,000
Annual note payments	18,871	Buyer's annual income	32,549

Scenario 3

The seller is willing to reduce the asking price further in return for a higher down payment. This price structure is based on a 10-year note at 10% interest.

Asking price	$165,000	Annual operating profit	27,420
40% down payment	70,000	Reserve after paying note	12,355
Total loan amount	95,000	Manager's salary	24,000
Annual note payments	15,065	Buyer's annual income	36,355

Scenario 4

The seller is willing to reduce the asking price still further in return for a shorter repayment period. This price structure is based on a five-year note at 10% interest.

Asking price	$153,000	Annual operating profit	$27,420
45% down payment	70,000	Reserve after paying note	6,258
Total loan amount	83,000	Manager's salary	24,000
Annual note payments	21,162 (five years)	Buyer's annual income	30,258

Scenario 4 will satisfy both buyer's and seller's goals and will probably be the price structure both parties agree to. Remember: the adjustments are not strictly mathematical. Use your best judgment as you work out the figures for yourself.

Try to work out some price structures of your own. Remember: the guiding principle in price structuring is to satisfy both buyer's and seller's goals. You need to examine your own goals before you begin to justify a price structure.

Buyer's goals: _____

Seller's goals: _____

Business's operating profit: _____

Scenario 1: Length of note: _____ Interest rate: _____ Rationale for asking price: _____

Asking price	$_____	Operating profit	$_____
___% down payment	_____	Annual note payments	_____
Total loan amount	_____	Income to buyer	_____

Scenario 2: Length of note: _____ Interest rate: _____ Rationale for asking price: _____

Asking price	$_____	Operating profit	$_____
___% down payment	_____	Annual note payments	_____
Total loan amount	_____	Income to buyer	_____

Scenario 3: Length of note: _____ Interest rate: _____ Rationale for asking price: _____

Asking price	$_____	Operating profit	$_____
___% down payment	_____	Annual note payments	_____
Total loan amount	_____	Income to buyer	_____

Scenario 4: Length of note: _____ Interest rate: _____ Rationale for asking price: _____

Asking price	$_____	Operating profit	$_____
___% down payment	_____	Annual note payments	_____
Total loan amount	_____	Income to buyer	_____

MAKING THE BUSINESS DEAL

Around the world and around the town, people are making business deals. Some of them fall within the category of day-to-day arrangements: raw materials for the manufacturer, sales and distribution for the wholesaler, and products for retailers.

Synergy

Other deals fall within the category of loans, investments, acquisitions, and mergers. Sometimes, a company gets the money needed to jump-start a new program. Sometimes, an investor-participant can offer the additional talent needed to create a new impetus. Occasionally, a company will grow through acquisition. And the last is the concept of merger—sometimes a mere working relationship, known in many circles as a "strategic alliance," and other times a more formal packaging of legal entities. Many of the successes depend on the concept of synergy: two companies, each using its best strengths to combine for an effort that neither could generate as well on its own.

The Cloak Comes in Many Colors

The most interesting aspect of these concepts is the fact that there are many ways to satisfy all parties. Some professionals would lead you to believe that there are certain formats that must be followed in creating these relationships. The fact is that the methods and formats are bounded only by your own creativity.

Some companies may come to you with an idea for a new distribution arrangement. This initial suggestion could end up with your company being acquired by the other.

Here is an example. One company with a serious cash flow problem was on the verge of bankruptcy until it was pointed out that it had a portfolio of assets, particularly a strong customer base, of significant value. The conversations led to discussions of acquisition and resulted in a new venture funded by an interested third party who recognized the potential dynamics of the two businesses working in concert.

Sometimes a merger can end up with the owner of the smaller company taking a management position with the larger company and getting "a piece of the action." The acquiring company gets an employee it could not otherwise have afforded and the smaller entrepreneur ends up with an income well beyond what his or her own business could have generated in the short term. The long-term effect could very well be advantageous to everyone. Don't get locked into a format early in the discussions that precludes some creative approaches later on.

A Piece of the Action

Many entrepreneurs don't have the dollars, the people, or the energy to take the business to that next plateau. Yet they hate to sell the business, because they would be giving up the growth potential of the future that they've worked so hard to develop. Selling in an early stage shuts them out from participating in the future profits of the business. Or does it?

The answer is "Not necessarily." There are people who take products through their early research and development (R&D) phase. They may move some of these products to market, but still have others "in the drawer," ready to go, but don't have the funds to take them to market. When the business is sold, the price is usually based on the products already in the marketplace. Do the products "in the drawer" have a place in this valuation system at all? Yes, they do.

If the R&D has been finished, if the prototype has been produced, and if the product is ready for manufacture and distribution, the product has a value. Although payment for this up front might be difficult to assess because the marketplace is fickle and not always as receptive to one product as it is to another, participation in the future sales of the product ought to be a viable alternative.

The Final Equation

The actual dollars will obviously depend on the readiness of the product for sale, the costs necessary to manufacture and distribute, and the profit potential in the long term. Whether the acquiring company gains a valuable employee, a product just about ready for the distribution pipeline, or the loyalty of the customer base that may have taken years to develop, the elements of synergy during merger or acquisition must be assessed in order to build a proper business valuation.

CHAPTER 4

Your Team of Professionals

MANY BUYERS AND SELLERS THINK IT IS much easier to frame and finish the purchase of a business by leaving the professionals out of the loop at the beginning. Nothing could be further from the truth. Would you frame the basic structure of a house before consulting an architect and a general contractor? The most important time to consult professionals is before you structure the actual deal. When you develop your negotiating posture, having an accountant and attorney present can make a dramatic difference in how you arrive at the price and insert the appropriate legal provisions to protect your final agreement.

ACCOUNTANTS AND ATTORNEYS

With the complexity of tax laws and other legal concerns, the use of an accountant and an attorney is mandatory!

You must use an accountant to structure the sale to your best tax advantage. Certain basic tax considerations exist that you may already know about, many of which are included in this book. However, ensuring that each financial element works well with all the others is clearly the job of an accountant. If you fail to use an accountant early in the sale, you may suffer from costly mis-takes that are difficult, if not impossible to correct later on.

As a seller, you also need competent legal counsel to prepare all the legal protections that ensure that your sale is binding. A buyer with remorse or a good litigator can dream up many kinds of problems after a sale that you want to avoid. Even if you sell your business for cash, you certainly don't want a lawsuit down the road because of misleading or deceptive statements made in the selling documents. If your sale leads you to carry a purchase money promissory note for several years, then you certainly want the protection of knowing that your attorney has attended to all the details. The fees paid to legal counsel are the best guarantee of a good night's sleep after sale.

Sellers will sometimes argue against using an attorney by saying, "But the buyer is an old friend." It is amazing how friendships get tested when the dollar becomes part of the relationship. Be careful, not foolish. Use an attorney right from the beginning. The scenario described in Illustration 4.1 at the top of the next page reinforces the importance of having an attorney on your professional team.

As this illustration points out, the business is normally used as collateral security for the purchase money promissory note so that, if the buyer defaults on the note, the seller can take the

Illustration 4.1 Beware of Tricky Language

In the recent sale of a business, the attorney representing the buyer wanted to insert the following sentence in the purchase and sale agreement and in the promissory note: "The seller has the right to take back the business in the event that the buyer defaults in his obligations under the purchase and sale agreement or the promissory note; however, the business shall be the only collateral that the seller has a right to pursue after such a default. It is understood that no other personal assets of the buyer shall, under any circumstances, be subject to such pursuit in the event of default, a deficiency judgment, or the like."

The seller's attorney explained that including this language in the agreement could leave the seller vulnerable should the buyer damage the business in some way. The seller, realizing that her lawyer's advice was correct, told the buyer that the sale was off unless the language was taken out of the agreement and the promissory note. The buyer agreed to take it out. The sale went through and the seller was protected.

Without the advice of counsel, the seller would not have known what jeopardy was waiting around the corner. The buyer, with only the business itself at risk, would not have had a strong incentive to maintain the business at its highest efficiency.

business back. The business should, however, be used only as partial collateral, not as complete collateral. A buyer can take a large amount of money out of a business before the seller is even aware that the business is in trouble. The seller may take back the business, but only a skeleton of the once successful business may remain. If this is all the seller can go after, he or she is facing a horrible situation. Meanwhile, the buyer might have taken out of the business all of the down payment he or she made—or even more money! The buyer will walk away with a good deal of money, leaving the seller with a business that can no longer survive.

Another word of admonition, however—listen to your lawyer's and accountant's recommendations, but leave the real decision making to your own good judgment. Each part of the selling equation is based on your relationship to the business and your relationship to your own future. All of your professionals, even though they believe they are working strictly in your best interests, will often have a view quite different from yours. Be careful that their opinions are related primarily to their particular areas of expertise and not to something that is better evaluated by your own personal instinct or by conference with a family member or personal advisor.

BUSINESS BROKERS

Although the ultimate decisions will always rest squarely on your shoulders, an attorney and accountant are mandatory members of the selling or buying team. The use of a business broker, however, depends on the circumstances of the sale.

Both buyers and sellers can and do employ the services of a business broker. However, a seller is more likely to need a broker early on, to help prepare and position the business for sale. The advice here pertains primarily to sellers. (Buyers can find more information on using a business broker in Chapter 21.)

Brokers handle many different kinds of businesses. Their experience can help you, as a seller, evaluate different types of buyers. Perhaps most importantly, they examine many kinds of purchase and sale arrangements and financial packages. This kind of experience might help create a strong sale out of an otherwise weak one and can be a valuable asset.

Your broker may not have extensive experience in your particular industry or business, but it is easy enough to provide your broker with the appropriate information. A good broker will know enough to utilize the seller's experience and knowledge as selling tools. While a broker may not know the intricacies of your particular business, he or she will have more experience than you in the process of selling a business.

To equalize the brokers' advantages in the event you choose to handle the selling yourself, you need to know how they operate. One problem with hiring a broker is the 10%-12% commission normally payable at the time the business is sold. Considering that the sale may bring only a 10% down payment, the seller could be left with a cash deficit and, usually, some unpaid legal and accounting fees as well. The size of the commission is certainly worth some serious consideration. You should also consider the possibility that a buyer may make no down payment, which will leave you with an even larger cash deficit. (Although a no-down-payment deal may not be desirable, the situation does arise.)

You may face an even bigger concern, however. Ask yourself two basic questions:

- Is it possible there may be buyers interested in purchasing your business who are extremely qualified, but who do not have enough cash for a solid working capital reservoir and a substantial down payment?
- Is the broker motivated by the commission he or she will earn when the business is sold?

The answer to both these questions is clearly "Yes."

The broker's position is simple enough—if the buyer doesn't have sufficient capital for both working capital and a down payment, from which the broker will deduct his or her commission, then that buyer simply doesn't belong on your candidate list. For these reasons, using a broker may eliminate a whole category of buyer candidates. If you, as a seller, feel comfortable cutting down the size of your list of candidates and are willing to meet only those potential buyers who appear to have sufficient dollars for both working capital and a substantial down payment, then you can easily decide that you want to use a broker. However, not only is it possible to lose an otherwise qualified candidate by using such a simple dollar qualifier, it is surprising what assets and cash availability are disclosed only after the first meeting of the parties. Discarding candidates too early can be a big mistake.

By reading this book and preparing for the sale of your business, you may be able to convince a broker that you are interested in working with his or her office in exchange for a lesser commission arrangement. If you have, in fact, done much of the preparatory work yourself, such as creating a business plan presentation with the appropriate valuation formulas and the proper financial documentation, a broker might very well see the logic of your suggestion. The work done by the seller can represent many hours of tedious work that

the broker need not contemplate. And, if the broker does not see the logic of a lower commission, you may find other brokers around who are more inclined to think favorably about the arrangement. The broker who represents a business already prepared for sale may enjoy a commission more quickly, even though it may be smaller than normal.

Make no mistake, however: preparing your business for presentation requires you to do a good deal of work. You must do the following:

- Prepare your financial documentation, requiring a conference with your accountant.
- Adjust the cosmetics of the business, particularly elements that need change in anticipation of putting the business up for sale, such as repairing a shabby sign, painting the building, or replacing old and tattered point-of-purchase advertising materials. This may involve discussions with your business advisor.
- Consider legal matters affecting the business's posture for sale, such as consent to transfer the lease, which would certainly bring you to your attorney's office.
- Prepare a preliminary advertising approach, such as a letter to other franchisees if you are a franchised business. (See Chapter 14.)
- Properly evaluate the business to substantiate a fair asking price.

After you speak with your accountant and your attorney relative to the issues discussed in this book, you will be well on your way to preparing your business for sale. You may then be able to justify a lower commission rate from a broker.

The negative side to trying to hire a broker at a lower commission rate is that the broker normally splits the selling commission with the broker representing the buyer. If the buyer's broker has a choice between introducing a buyer/client to you through your broker, who will split a commission of 6% or 8%, and introducing the buyer/client to a different business proposition through a broker who will split a commission of 12%, what will the buyer's broker choose? You may lose the opportunity to present your business to that buyer because you are trying to save some dollars on the commission.

Although the commission to the buyer's broker is normally not a substantial problem, you need to consider it. Be careful that this does not work against you. If you work without a broker, but your buyer is represented by a broker, you will have to negotiate your price to accommodate the buyer's broker's fee. You will, however, be looking at a fee of 6% or less, as opposed to a fee of 11% or 12%. The key is that if you decide to work with a broker, insist on having the opportunity to meet with as many potential buyers as you want. You might want to examine all candidate applications to make your own decision about meeting them—regardless of what their financial picture might initially look like.

It cannot be stated too often that deals are made in many ways and good buyers are not easy to find. If money is your sole requirement, you may lose some very interesting candidates. If a candidate is a little short of capital, you may be able to work out a payment plan by manipulating variables like down payment or length of note. A broker may also be helpful with adjustments of this kind if he or she has previously handled a similar negotiation.

Finally, there is no magic to what a broker does. You can advertise your business and obtain mailing lists just as easily as a broker. Sometimes, of course, the daily activity of the business itself is just too demanding for you to allocate any time at all to the project of selling. The choice is yours! And it may not be an easy one to make. You must also keep in mind that if you find a buyer after your broker's agreement expires, the broker may still be entitled to his or her commission. Be sure that you understand the language in your broker agreement. (See Chapter 21.)

A Language All Their Own

Both the buyer and the seller need to understand professionals' language. Many times, people explain things that don't make sense. If they ask whether you understand, more often than you'd like to admit, you say yes when you really should say no! If the information is relatively unimportant, you avoid embarrassment and looking stupid to other people. However, selling a business is not the time to be casual about information you don't understand.

If a beloved member of your family were very ill and the doctor were explaining the alternative means of treatment, would you listen? Would you insist on understanding? Would you keep asking until you were blue in the face? If necessary, would you find someone who could interpret the doctor's language? You bet! These professionals represent you, you sought their professional advice, and you want the protection their services provide. You need to understand what they are saying.

Professionals may be very knowledgeable about their particular areas of expertise, but some of them are lousy teachers. They use the jargon of their profession every day and assume that you understand them. Sometimes, they will even ask if you do. If you don't understand, tell them—and keep telling them until you do. Nothing is so complicated that it can't be explained in simple terms if it is broken down to its basic parts. The information you are dealing with is too important to miss. It may make a big difference in your financial future.

If your professional can't explain it to you so that you understand it, get someone who can. It is absolutely essential to the relationship you need for a successful transaction.

Finally, remember that professionals, just like anyone else, may be tempted to reach beyond their area of expertise and advise you on matters that are not included in their training. This can be helpful, but it can also be harmful. When dealing with attorneys, accountants, and brokers, be careful to select only the advice that is relevant to their area of expertise and beware of their advice when it is outside their field. Some professionals have some very strange things to say about businesses they know nothing about.

Nevertheless, the experience, education, and skill that professional accountants, attorneys, and brokers offer to a buyer or seller in the early stages of a business sale are invaluable. You will always save time and money by bringing professionals into the process early and avoiding the costly mistakes you might make without their help. For more specific information regarding the role of an attorney, an accountant, or a broker in a business transfer, see Part IV.

KEY POINTS TO REMEMBER

- An attorney and accountant are necessary members of your buying or selling team. Get the team together early in the process.
- Develop a vocabulary that both you and your professionals understand.
- Make sure that, as a seller, you meet all viable buying candidates. Don't be too quick to dismiss candidates after only a cursory look.

- A seller may learn the financial qualifications of a buyer only after an initial conference. Most people do not make a full financial disclosure at a first meeting.
- Document your relationship with your broker with unambiguous language.

Worksheet 4. Assembling Your Professional Team

The following worksheet will help you choose your professional team members and ensure that they are capable of giving you the help you need to make your purchase or sale a success.

Choosing an Accountant

Have you ever dealt with this accountant before? Yes ❑ No ❑

How much work has this accountant done in the merger or acquisition field? _____

_____

What experience does this accountant have with the sale of small or medium-sized businesses? _____

_____

Get a name or names of people this accountant has represented in a similar capacity and follow up by asking those former clients if they were satisfied with this accountant's services. _____

_____

The following is a list of tasks your accountant should be willing and able to help you with. Go over it with your accountant and make sure he or she is equal to the job. You may need to supplement the list with other items, depending on the specifics of your purchase or sale. Note that some are particular to the buyer or to the seller and some are relevant to both of you.

- ❑ Ensure that the profit and loss statement, cash flow analysis, and balance sheet present a consistent and understandable financial picture of the business.
- ❑ Advise you regarding the allocation of the purchase price for the best tax advantage including the difference between an asset sale and a stock sale.
- ❑ Advise you regarding the tax ramifications of either an all-cash or a payout arrangement of the business's purchase price.
- ❑ Ensure that you meet all your tax obligations to the federal, state, and municipal authorities.
- ❑ Explain variables such as the amount of a promissory note, the length of the note, the interest rate on the note, whether the note should be interest-only or fully amortized, and how these variables affect your negotiations.
- ❑ Ensure that the payoff amounts on all leases and other obligations are correct.
- ❑ Help you examine and analyze the financial statement of the buyer.
- ❑ Help you clarify your bookkeeping so that it can be easily understood by a buyer or buyer's representative.
- ❑ Ensure that final figures for payoff to the seller are accurate.

Other tasks:

❏ _____

❏ _____

❏ _____

❏ _____

❏ _____

Choosing an Attorney

Have you ever dealt with this attorney or law firm before? Yes ❏ No ❏

How much work has this attorney done in mergers and acquisitions? _____

_____

What experience does this attorney have with the sale of small or medium-sized businesses? _____

_____

Get the names of people this attorney has represented in a similar capacity and follow up by asking those former clients if they were satisfied with this attorney's services.

_____

_____

The following is a list of tasks your attorney should be willing and able to help you with. Go over it with your attorney and make sure he or she is equal to the job. You may need to supplement the list with other items, depending on the specifics of your purchase or sale. Note that some are particular to the buyer or to the seller and some are relevant to both of you.

❏ Arrange for the lease contract on the premises to be properly assigned to the buyer.

❏ Help you structure an asking price and a negotiating posture prior to sale.

❏ Ensure that the promissory note and any security agreements are properly drafted to protect you after the sale.

❏ Ensure that all necessary certificates and affidavits are properly filed with the federal, state, and municipal authorities.

❏ Open and supervise an escrow, if necessary.

❏ File and publish under the appropriate state's bulk sale law, if applicable.

❏ Deal with problematic creditors and vendors to ensure that they do not interfere with the sale.

❏ Arrange for all equipment leases or other leases or contracts to be properly assigned to the buyer.

❏ Ensure that the language of the post-sale documentation is adequate to protect you, the seller, from having the buyer default on promissory note payments or dissipate the assets of the business before the note is paid.

❏ Ensure that your arrangement with your broker does not require you to pay unwarranted fees if a sale is not finalized.

Other tasks:

❏ _____

❏ _____

❏ _____

❏ _____

❏ _____

Choosing a Broker

What can you expect your broker to do on your behalf? _____
_____

What is a broker unlikely to do on your behalf? _____
_____

What may be most problematic in a relationship with a broker? _____
_____

What type of agreement have you worked out with your broker? What are the size of the commission, the term of the agreement, and the conditions under which you will have to pay the broker? Be sure that these aspects of your relationship are included in your agreement and defined in unambiguous terms.

_____
_____

Get a list of your broker's references and follow up with them to verify your broker's honesty, integrity, and experience.

_____
_____
_____

GETTING THE BEST FROM PROFESSIONAL ADVICE

Have you ever wondered why professionals advise their clients without ever having ventured onto the entrepreneurial plane themselves? Presumably, they have had the experience of dealing with similar situations. There are, however, subtleties that change the face of a problem and the approach necessary to the proper solution. And the problem is that you've got to be careful that the professional advisor actually knows how to properly handle your particular problem.

Fundamentals and Focus

What are the critical elements that the professional ought to bring to your problem? It is likely that his or her education has included the basics, the fundamentals that should theoretically apply to any and all problems. If your professional is a good communicator, you should be able to get a handle on these fundamentals as well. This will be your grounding in the basics on which to predicate your ultimate decision. If your pro-

fessional is unable to share this information with you so you become a member of the decision-making team, get another professional.

The other element that the professional should help you with is the concept of focus. When dealing with any problem, there are usually collateral elements that get in the way. A good professional will normally help to eliminate these collateral elements and force you to focus on that aspect of the problem that is most critical to the ultimate decision making. This focusing on the core of a problem usually saves time, money, and energy. It allows you to resolve the problem and get back to the daily details of getting the job done.

Staying Within the Field

It is unfair to criticize the average professional for wanting to take on more than is really appropriate. With the experience of dealing with many such problems, the professional is inclined to offer all aspects of that experience to his or her client. Unfortunately, portions of this advice sometimes stray far afield from the primary expertise of the professional. When this is the case, you will often be getting marketing advice from your accountant and legal advice from your marketing professional. This is the time to be careful. Although some of this advice may be helpful, since it may have been effective in other cases, your final judgment should always be to get confirmation on marketing from the marketing expert, accounting advice from the accountant, and legal advice from your lawyer. The best professionals may offer some of this collateral advice, but always with the caution that final decisions should not be made without consulting with the appropriate professional.

Monitoring the Excitement and the Passion

Lenders will often tell you that they are not interested in a product, however good it may appear to be, unless the borrower is excited and passionate about the potential of its success. The only problem with this is that excitement and passion can sometimes obscure some of the details so necessary for the success of the venture. The professional, although as excited as you are about the venture, should be able to remain objective in the face of this excitement. This is something that every professional is obliged to offer to the client.

Let the excitement prevail, but not to the extent that the essentials are disregarded.

Bringing All the Parts Together (Knitting the Fabric)

When it's all said and done, it is unlikely that any one professional's advice will be the defining factor in resolving problems or reaching that next plateau of success. More often than not, it is the combination of efforts, the teamwork of all the advisors, that will bring success. This is the reason why bigger companies have boards of directors. Each contribution becomes a part of the whole; each opinion becomes a part of the final knitting together of the fabric of success. Don't lose sight of this as you seek advice from professionals of different persuasions. The final judgment will, of necessity, fall on your shoulders ... as it should. You are the one who knows how each of the pieces is supposed to fit. You are the one who will bear the burden of failure or enjoy the fruits of success. You will not have the prerogative of blaming the professionals for advising you badly. You will need the take the best from each of them and bring all the parts together for the success of your venture.

CHAPTER 5

The Information Game

To ESTABLISH A NEGOTIATING RELATIONSHIP, both the buyer and the seller need some initial information. However, both parties are often reluctant to reveal information, particularly sensitive financial data, without proper proof that it will lead to serious and legitimate negotiations.

This early stage often sets the tone for the rest of the negotiating process. When mutual trust is established early, the process proceeds more smoothly. Many factors can prevent that trust from forming, however. This chapter discusses some of those factors, the type of information the buyer and the seller can expect early in the process, and the danger signals to look for during initial disclosures.

As a buyer, keep in mind that a good makeup job by a seller can hide many important elements you need to know about a business. The business that you are considering might not be at all that it appears to be. The seller will probably not tell you all the negatives about the business. The negatives may be inadvertently obscured or intentionally hidden.

Although intentional nondisclosure can be the predicate for good legal action, you are trying to find and procure a stable business with immediate income and growth potential, not to find a good cause for a lawsuit. Your job as a businessperson is to use your best efforts and exercise your best judgment to find and purchase that stable and income-generating business.

As a seller, keep in mind that financial stability, business experience, and ethical stature are the three key elements you want in any buyer. If you are taking cash for the business and leaving the country, you may not care about the treatment of your old customers, vendors, and neighbors. If, on the other hand, you are going to be collecting the purchase price or a portion of it over an extended time, you need to examine your buyer's financial and employment background with great care. The secret agenda of some buyers can ruin a seller who negotiates in good faith.

WHAT THE BUYER NEEDS TO KNOW
The Competition

As a buyer interested in a particular trade or industry, you must look at what the competition is offering. Who else is in the marketplace? How do the competitors present their businesses and what embellishments have they made to attract customers? In some cases, an owner is happy to discuss his or her success. In other cases, you will find it difficult to get beyond the front counter.

Some market research is easy. Look at the furniture and the fixtures. Look at the marketing materials presented to the public. Certain other items, however, may be difficult to access without the owner's permission. You may want to examine a competitor's equipment to ensure that the equipment included with the business you are buying is state-of-the-art and sufficient to put you on a level playing field with your competition. You want to look at the quality of the personnel.

If you want to make a line-by-line comparison of the business you are considering purchasing and its competition, you will need specific information from the seller. It is not unusual, however, for a seller to be somewhat reluctant to share all of this information with you, particularly financial information, solely because you indicate an interest in the business. It is not uncommon for competitors to shop their competition, to pose as buyers and examine financial information to compare just how their own businesses are doing—whether rent, cost of product, and/or labor factors are too high relative to other businesses in the industry.

You will need to convince the seller that you are a serious candidate before he or she is willing to share information about the business. If you present yourself as a serious and qualified buyer and the seller is still reluctant to share information, you may need to proceed with the purchase more cautiously.

The Customer Base

Most businesses depend on their current customer base for stability and growth. You, as a buyer, are going to be interested in the customer base for a variety of reasons.

Perhaps the most important reason is to see if the business basically depends on a small cadre of important customers who may easily change their allegiance and go to a competitor after the sale. The defection of a few big customers would make you vulnerable.

Another concern is whether you want to deal with the kind of customers on which the business depends. Fast-food operations, for example, have relatively insignificant contact with their customers and generate very little allegiance. On the other hand, many retail operations have a very close rapport with their customers, who come in for advice and counsel as well as

products or services. As a buyer, you need to recognize the difference and have the personality and inclination to involve yourself in the customer relationships necessary to maintain the business.

The danger that a competitor also wants to obtain this kind of information from a seller makes your job as a legitimate buyer more difficult. If the competitor is close enough geographically, he or she may want a peek at some of the customers or at a particular customer group to steal the business. Again, the seller will be very cautious before releasing any customer information. Disclosing your financial statement may help close the credibility gap and convince the seller that you are a legitimate buyer candidate and not someone who could put the business in jeopardy.

Curiosity Seekers

In addition to the problem of competitors, there are many buyer types who, frankly, are just curious to know what profits different businesses show based on a particular dollar investment. Some of these buyers have actually developed portfolios of business opportunities. Some of them, believe it or not, will never buy a business of any kind. They are merely amateur analysts who don't have the gumption or, in some cases, the dollars to make the investment.

Sellers don't want to expose their financials to curiosity seekers. The time devoted to each conversation with a fake buyer is a waste most sellers can't afford. You must understand the frustration of the seller in this context and be careful to create an environment of trust before you can expect to enjoy a seller's time, energy, expertise, and disclosure.

One of the other problems with amateur analysts who spend time in a seller's business is that, in many cases, the employees are unaware that the business is for sale. The more questions about the business, the more difficult it is for the seller to keep this situation under control.

On the other hand, if a seller is serious about putting the business in front of real buyers, he or she is obliged to have certain information available under certain conditions. You should understand these conditions and know what you can expect to see and when.

Look at the Business in Person

Sometimes the buyer will ask the seller over the phone to send a package of information concerning the business. Big business may have this information prepared, but small entrepreneurs rarely have time to put together packets of information. Most of their time is spent handling the business from day to day. It is more appropriate, particularly if you are calling from out of town, to come down to the site of the business and take a look. After all, if buying the business involves moving to a new area, you won't make that decision unless that area satisfies a number of personal needs and desires—yours and your family's.

If you are a serious buyer, you will also want to see the building, the traffic pattern, the surrounding area, and the general population mix. Some people don't mind working in a depressed environment; others do. Bars on the windows can often be a danger signal to a buyer by indicating the nature of the neighborhood, particularly if personnel may be working different shifts or leaving after dark. You can't see those bars over the telephone.

So which comes first, the chicken or the egg? The seller does not want to disclose a lot of information unless he or she feels the buyer is a serious prospect. The buyer does not want to make the trip unless he or she can expect the business to fulfill certain basic requirements. Many circumstances may alter the sequence, and these will vary from industry to industry. However, certain guidelines normally prevail.

The buyer is entitled, on the first round, to know the gross volume, the profit (even though profit is defined in various ways), the amount of cash required for the down payment and the working capital reservoir, and the amount of the balance of the purchase price the seller is willing to carry, if any.

Profit and loss statements, together with balance sheets and cash flow analyses, should not be necessary at this point. If you have a face-to-face conversation with the seller, you will resolve many questions. The seller should discuss what additional information he or she needs from you to allow you to continue examining the business.

Both parties can learn a lot without a single piece of paper changing hands, just by meeting and getting familiar with each other's general demeanor. When all is said and done, the dynamics of the negotiations will depend largely on the relationship and the trust that develops or fails to develop between the parties.

The Franchise and Mandatory Disclosure

If the business is a franchise, the same basics apply. The buyer should certainly visit the location and meet the owner. However, it is a good deal easier to obtain general industry information about which the buyer would normally want to inquire.

When a franchise is offered for sale anywhere in the United States, the franchisor is required to release a disclosure document to the buyer. In some states, it is called a *uniform franchise offering circular*; in others, a *Federal Trade Commission disclosure document*. This document contains information about the basic business concept, the people involved, the number and location of units, any pending litigation, and many other disclosures about the history, financial stability, management structure, and operation of the franchise (parent) company.

If you are buying a franchise, new or existing, directly from the franchisor, the required language at the top of the disclosure document indicates when you should receive it: "At the earlier of (1) the first personal meeting; or (2) ten business days before the signing of any franchise or related agreement; or (3) ten business days before any payment." (See Chapter 14 for the complete language.)

If you are buying an existing franchise from an individual franchisee, two schools of thought exist regarding the disclosure document. On the one hand, the more conservative franchisors will insist that you get the document in timely fashion. One of the document's purposes is, after all, to protect the franchisor from untrue or misleading representations made by various people about the company during the course of the initial negotiations. On the other hand, the franchisee is selling his or her own business and may sell it without using a disclosure document.

As long as the franchisor has not been suspended from franchising or has not voluntarily suspended its franchise sales activities, the disclosure document should be available to a buyer interested in an existing franchise. The seller's failure to disclose material information can lead to a lawsuit, with or without the disclosure document. More will be said in succeeding chapters regarding a seller's legal obligations to disclose. (See Chapters 14 and 17.)

The buyer's best position is to insist on the disclosure document, as long as one is available. The information the disclosure contains is invaluable. The mere existence of the information will give the potential buyer a good start on the pre-purchase research. If a disclosure document is not available, the buyer ought to question why it is not.

Too Much Information

What kind of information should the buyer be looking for? The seller will probably not give you too much information. If so, interestingly enough, that it is something to make you more careful. A seller who inundates you with information may be trying to obscure some of the more simple elements that, in a less complicated environment, would be more obvious. If you are interested in the customer base, don't be satisfied with materials on the population growth or community development. If you are asking about the terms of the lease, don't be satisfied with the building and zoning regulations or new highways and airports that are on the municipal drawing boards. In other words, be careful that the information given to you is relevant to the information you requested. If it is not, again, you should ask why not.

Before moving on, please note that this subject will come up again. Chapter 7 will lead you through the specific requests for information you need to make to a seller.

WHAT THE SELLER NEEDS TO KNOW

Remember that the sale of a business is not exactly like the sale of an automobile. When you are selling a car, you are usually uninvolved with the future of the car after the sale. With the sale of a business, on the other hand, you may carry a purchase money promissory note for a large balance of the purchase price. You will, therefore, have a very substantial interest in the future of the business and how the buyer handles it. After all, if the buyer fails, you may end up taking back the business and finding little more than a skeleton of the full-bodied business you sold.

It is in your best interest to pick a good buyer, help him or her into a success mode, and watch the business for danger signals. A buyer may feel uncomfortable with his or her seller looking on, but if the buyer still owes the seller money after the sale, he or she must understand that this is the seller's prerogative, if not the seller's obligation.

Even if there is no purchase money promissory note, your reputation in the community that you have taken years to build could be ruined in a few weeks by the wrong kind of buyer. If this holds any priority in your thinking then, again, you must be careful of the quality of your buyer.

If you were selling your car, you may not be particularly interested in the ethics or moral stature of the person buying it. When selling a business, however, you might be very concerned about these qualities in the buyer. Knowing about his or her business experience is important, if only to decide whether or not the purchase is a good idea for the buyer. After all, you know all about your business, the frustrations, the intricacies, and the demands it puts on the owner and his or her family. Your buyer will not have so clear and informed a perspective.

It is a good idea to know the size and makeup of the buyer's family and the lifestyle to which the family is accustomed. You are foolish if you don't look, with your buyer, at what family necessities and amenities the cash flow of the business can afford. Unrealistic expectations that have no chance of being fulfilled are the biggest danger to both buyer and seller.

Certainly a careful analysis of the buyer's financial history and current status is mandatory. In the event that you do not arrange an all-cash purchase, you want to know exactly what the buyer can convert to cash if the business requires more working capital than either of you anticipated. It is also important for you to take as much security as you can get for the balance owing on the purchase. You need to know what other assets the buyer is willing to put at risk. A complete financial statement will tell you just what the buyer has available. Then both parties will be equally knowledgeable about each other. (For more information on your need to have access to the buyer's financial information, see

Chapters 14 and 15 and the Sample Confidential Business Application at the beginning of Chapter 15.)

You need to know what role your buyer expects to take in the daily operation of your business. Most businesses don't do well with absentee ownership and, if the sale is not all-cash, you will have less to worry about if the buyer is involved on a day-to-day basis than you would if the buyer were merely an investor.

Find out how much down payment the buyer is willing to make, especially in terms of his or her available cash. If the buyer is willing to put a substantial amount of cash toward the purchase, that money often speaks more loudly than any words about his or her commitment to the negotiations and purchasing your business.

LEGAL ASPECTS OF THE TRANSACTION

The buyer wants to ensure that all the representations by the seller are true. The real protection the buyer has, unless he or she pays the full price in cash, is in owing the seller money. The buyer will honor this obligation so long as the business is, in fact, the business he or she expected to buy. If it isn't, the buyer is well protected by being able to withhold the payments due to the seller for the balance of the purchase price.

On the other hand, the seller wants to collect the full price for the business. More than that, the seller wants to ensure that the business will maintain its integrity until he or she has collected that full price. In order to do this, the seller must adopt a certain monitoring posture: he or she must be able to see that the bills are being paid, especially taxes of all kinds, and that salaries and costs do not exceed the appropriate ratio to sales and profit that are the very core of the business.

You can insert certain protective devices into the purchase and sale agreement to ensure that these standards are maintained. Any seller that does not use these protective devices is making a big mistake. (See Chapter 14 to learn more about how to protect your sale.)

BODY LANGUAGE

Sometimes the things we say are contradicted by the way we say them or even by the way we sit or stand while we are saying them. It is commonly assumed that people are lying, for example, when they blink a lot or when they look flushed. Sometimes, the physical aspects of conversation speak much louder than the words. Keep this in mind during the early discussions, when both parties are still getting to know one another.

Note who is at the table with the other party. Did the buyer bring a spouse or a child who expects to participate in the operation of the business? Do both parties have lawyers, accountants, or consultants? Does the buyer have a partner who will provide part or all of the financing for the purchase of the business? Each of these people represents another aspect of the buyer candidate. Some will be positives, and others will not. Your professional advisors may be able to help you interpret the role of your counterpart's family, friends, or advisors in the future of the negotiations and sale. Of course, you should always rely on your own instincts, but getting a second opinion is often a good idea.

The following chapters will return to many of the concepts discussed in Part I. However, Parts II, III, and IV will also lead you step by step through much of the work necessary to prepare yourself and your family to purchase or sell a way of life—business ownership.

KEY POINTS TO REMEMBER

- Sellers must recognize the difference between a serious buyer candidate and a casual business analyst.
- Sellers need to read and interpret the buyer's financial statement to decide whether the buyer is financially strong enough to sustain the business in all times, good and bad.
- Buyers need to examine the internal elements (such as cost of product) and the external elements (such as competition) that affect the stability and future of the business.
- Buyers must be prepared to disclose their financial position in detail if they expect the seller to carry back a purchase money promissory note.
- When looking at a franchise, buyers should be able to get all the disclosure they need on which to base a decision to buy. It is the law.

Worksheet 5. Initial Disclosures and the Dangers Involved

The success of negotiations depends in great part on the relationship established between the parties at the beginning of the process. If you establish mutual trust early on, you will find the process of buying or selling a business much easier than if you feel the party on the other side of the negotiating table is your adversary.

Use the following checklist as a guide to the preparation you need to do to begin negotiations in a positive manner and establish trust between buyer and seller.

Buyer, do you know:

Yes	No	
❏	❏	What information you need from your seller to make sure his or her business is one worth pursuing?
❏	❏	What research you need to do before you approach your seller?
❏	❏	How you will convince your seller that you are serious about pursuing sale negotiations?
❏	❏	What personal and financial information you will share with your seller at the outset?
❏	❏	Which competitors you will consult as you begin your pre-purchase research?
❏	❏	How you will approach those competitors?
❏	❏	What information competitors will be reluctant to provide for you?
❏	❏	What information you can get from manufacturers and vendors in the industry?
❏	❏	What questions you need a professional to answer—either your own professional accountant or attorney or the seller's?

Seller, do you know:

Yes	No	
❏	❏	What initial information you will share with your buying candidates?
❏	❏	How you will satisfy yourself that your buying candidate is legitimate?
❏	❏	What you will be looking for in the buyer's financial statement?
❏	❏	How you will know if something is missing or appears misleading in the buyer's information?
❏	❏	What you will do if information is missing or misleading?
❏	❏	How you will bring initial discussions to a head, to make sure you get the information you want and need?
❏	❏	If you are a franchisee, what information you will share with the buyer about the franchise company and how you will get the buyer in touch with the franchise company?
❏	❏	What questions you need a professional to answer—either your own professional accountant or attorney or the buyer's?

THE BASICS OF NEGOTIATING

Getting What You Want vs. Wanting What You Get

Sitting down at a deal-making table requires an entirely different approach than watching a movie, disciplining your child, or ordering a meal. It requires the ability to recognize the difference between negotiating and mandating, between giving orders to perform and allowing room to discuss, between satisfying all goals and adjusting some expectations.

The purpose of negotiating is to get as much as you can while the other side is getting enough to survive ... or vice versa. It is conventional wisdom that if both parties to a negotiation feel that they didn't get all they wanted, then the negotiation was a success. If one side gets it all, the other side gets nothing. This is not negotiating. And, be careful: it is not likely to be all that it appears to be.

The 10-Point Agenda

It's difficult, when approaching a business deal, to decide what would be enough to bring the negotiations to closure. Sure, you'd like it all. But, unless you have the other side over a barrel, you are not likely to find closure by insisting on winning all the marbles. A good program is to pick the 10 things you'd like to have and then list them in their order of priority—the ones you absolutely must have on the top and the ones you could do without at the bottom. Make up your mind at the beginning just which ones you can't relinquish and those that you could live without. You can use the lesser-priority items to negotiate. In other words, be prepared to adjust your expectations in the face of the other side's needs or desires.

By doing this, you will be better prepared to give up what you can do without in order to obtain the elements on which your future will depend. If approaches like this don't work, it is possible that the deal was not meant to be. To accept a deal that won't work in the long term is to make a big mistake in business. Sometimes, a deal that won't work for the other party can be a disaster for you as well.

By approaching the table in this way, you won't appear to be intractable. The other side will recognize this willingness to adjust and will, hopefully, adopt a similar negotiating posture.

The "Going for the Jugular" Syndrome

In some cases, if one party appears willing to look for a middle-of-the-road solution, that will not necessarily engender an equally friendly approach. The other side may see this "willingness" as "weakness" and immediately go for the jugular. If this is true of a party with whom you are negotiating, you must consider yourself fortunate to find this out early in the negotiations.

Anyone who will take advantage of this concessionary attitude early in the game will surely do so at every opportunity later on. If this is the tiger on the other side of the negotiating table, you ought to leave the jungle. Whatever you may win will likely carry at least an equal burden.

The Ultimate Game Plan

Using the 10-point program or anything similar to it is basically creating a business plan before you sit down at the table. You will create the reality of the business as it must exist in order to be successful. By preparing such a pro forma, what the business should look like, you will be able to judge which elements are necessary for the success of the venture and which might be good but are not mandatory for proper operation. This is how you can and should decide on your 10-point program.

If, as a buyer, there is insufficient substance to what you're buying to maintain continuity, to get to the next plateau, or to afford you the necessary dollars to make the acquisition worthwhile, don't do it. If, as a seller, you are leaving so much on the table as to be completely uncomfortable about the sale, don't do it.

Holding a Tiger by the Tail

Finally, if you should become dynamically successful in your negotiations, it is always a good caution to keep something in mind: if a deal appears too good to be true, it probably is.

PART II

The Buyer's Perspective

Committing to a Market Niche

YOU CAN INVEST IN A BUSINESS IN A VARIETY of ways. You can invest time, money, energy, and emotion. Picking a business is not like picking a horse at the track. In a horse race, win or lose, the race is over and you can forget the project until your next visit to the track. Similarly, deciding on a business venture is not like buying stock. The management of that public company is out of your control; if you don't like it, you can usually sell the stock quickly and allow the aggravation to quickly fade. Betting at the track or buying stock is a calculated risk of a relatively minor nature. It is unlikely you would put your net worth at risk in either case.

An investment in a business, on the other hand, is a commitment involving the better part of your financial empire. The investment might not require all your cash up front, but it usually requires a commitment of your entire financial portfolio behind it. You cannot make this business decision casually.

You can research either a horse or a stock at great length and, in both cases, you can get quite emotional about the results of your investment. Yet both are passive investments and neither really puts the whole framework of your life's energies to the test. Investing in a business certainly can and usually does. It really converts the financial investment into an emotional commitment.

CONSIDER A HOME-BASED BUSINESS

"Sure, I'd like to operate my own business, but I can't leave my invalid mother at home alone." This is one clear scenario for operating a business from your own home. It is not the perfect situation, which will be examined, but, since life is certainly not perfect, you will also see why it is the beginning, in many cases, of business ventures that might otherwise not have happened.

But do not be misled. Starting a business from your home is not always a product of necessity. It is often the most logical method of starting the operation at the lowest cost until the profit of the business can afford to pay for its own facility. In many cases, the move to another facility may never happen. If location is not a major factor for the success of the business you are considering, you may want to start out at home. Instead of taking on the expense and headaches of an additional site, you could buy a business without its real property or lease.

A Changing World

Years ago, few businesses operated from home. Times have changed. Years ago, businesses that didn't have an in-town address lacked a certain legitimacy. Today, the FedEx, Airborne Express, and United Parcel trucks stop in the best residential neighborhoods—and they are not all delivering packages from a home shopping television network. More and more business packages and letters are coming out of residential areas.

Many changes have led to this dramatic adjustment in the complexion of the business community. There is, of course, the fact that people are living longer than in the past. As a result, there is a substantial and growing society of elders, many of whom need attention during the day. Many others, on the other hand, are still capable of operating a business, but no longer able or willing to maintain a commute to the office. Many more single parents need to generate an income while caring for the needs of youngsters. And there are many two-parent families in which both parents want and/or need to have careers.

Along with these phenomena, also consider computer technology, which allows computer stations to be in contact with words, graphics, and sounds on an immediate basis. With the e-mail, on-line facilities in every field, and the plethora of information sources, the entire society could conceivably operate without anyone leaving home. When you combine this with cell phones and fax machines, the circuits are complete.

The latest business change to contribute to the home-based enterprise is the concept of downsizing. Companies are realizing that part-time capability without the complications of health insurance, traffic delays, time off for holidays, sick days, coffee breaks, interpersonal conflicts, and the like can improve the corporate bottom line dramatically. Many companies are taking advantage of this concept, allowing in some cases, insisting in other cases, that a certain percentage of their employees be employed from home. The computer allows this to take place with ease. No judgments need to be made about this phenomenon. It is merely a concept to be recognized as a new generation of at-home workers in the business world. Even the city fathers are in favor of more of the same. After all, working from home reduces traffic, consumption of fossil fuels, and smog.

But this is not the heart of home-based entrepreneurship. This is the world of business necessity and dividends to shareholders.

From the Boardroom to the Bedroom

The entrepreneur at home is a different story. It is really a bigger story, because it is not born of corporate America; it is born of the stuff of dreams. But be careful—home-based businesses are not all a bed of roses.

It is certainly true that you can save money on eating lunch. You can save money on office rent. You can take certain deductions on your annual taxes. These deductions include the following:

- Office supplies and equipment
- Employee wages—full or part time, including your spouse and your children, if properly documented
- Business phones and fax costs
- Magazines and other subscriptions
- Business travel
- Entertainment—but only a portion and, again, only when carefully documented
- A vehicle used for business—consistent with the percentages allowed by the IRS
- Advertising done to grow the business

But, be careful to examine this with your professional. Some compensating negative aspects must be considered before you casually address this problem, particularly if you decide to write off a portion of your home as the facility from which you operate your business.

Finally, you must be absolutely aware of one significant element—discipline!

Discipline works in a variety of ways. The workaholic must be careful to take time out for lunch. The person who is less than serious must be careful not to take too much time out for lunch. The serious entrepreneur must set a time to start and a time to finish. Those who start late and those who stop too early are equally as guilty.

There is a way of doing business. It is very much the same as the writer who says that the typewriter keys will move when they are ready. It never happens. One author claims that, aside all other things, you must sit in the chair. Nothing happens near the typewriter unless and until you are sitting in the chair. Nothing will happen with your home-based business unless and until you create a business atmosphere within which you can function as a serious businessperson with the same goals as those who jump into their offices on Wall Street each morning.

There is no lack of dignity in operating a business from your home—if you operate it in a businesslike fashion. Yes, there will be times when the children may demand more of your time than you would prefer. There will certainly be times when your elderly parents will require a little more attention than your business day allows. You must make judgments. Adjustments will be necessary. But you are the decision maker. And the goal of a successful business will be the same whether you are answering the telephone in the bedroom or in the boardroom.

Home-Based Office Needs

The first order of business involves a legal question. Does your business violate the zoning restrictions of your residential neighborhood? The more practical question might be: Does your business create a visibility that would be offensive to your neighbors?

The visibility question revolves around these four factors:

- The number of employees you have coming to work daily and where they park;
- The number and frequency of customers coming to the door for a product or a service;
- The number of deliveries coming to and leaving from the premises via UPS, FedEx, Airborne, Postal Service, or other delivery service; and
- The amount of mail delivered to the premises.

There are ways to avoid some of these problems, including using a post office box, a warehouse, and a computer link to your employees. However, the necessary or appropriate approach to the problem of visibility would best be discussed with your legal advisor.

In this same context of running a business from your home, you should be careful to note just what kind of insurance protection is afforded your business under your homeowner's policy. In most cases, protection for liability, fire, and your business equipment will require at least a business rider, if not a separate policy. See your insurance professional for the best approach.

Starting with the basics, it is clear that you will need, at least, the following items. These, of course, are in addition to the myriad of minor items, such as paper clips, a letter opener, stamps, tape, a stapler and a staple remover, pens, pencils, highlighters, and a checkbook.

Computer. A computer will give you the quick and easy means to type letters, revise draft documents, keep files, and maintain a reservoir of information from which you can easily retrieve items when they are needed. Along with the computer comes a printer and whatever software is appropriate to get you started operating your business properly. There are programs for keeping books and records, accounting and invoicing, preparing for tax time, pricing guides, and client records. Be sure that you are comfortable with handling any or all of these in-house. Be careful not to have so much sophisticated software that you end up in a nightmare with a dramatic learning curve.

The other options include an Internet connection, whether simply a modem or broadband, that will allow you to use e-mail, access the Internet, and play games. Be sure that you have an appropriate need for these options, so you don't lose time with things that get in the way of properly operating your business.

Caution—it is imperative, when using a computer, to have a backup system to protect against the loss of information in the event of a system breakdown. Some of the newest and more expensive software has built-in backup systems. If you have not yet reached this level of sophistication, be sure that you use a backup system appropriate to your needs. Using a backup disk is the beginning of the protection. If you're going to be using the computer to build a substantial reservoir of information on which your business and its survival or continuity depends, it may be time to invest in a dedicated backup system—and use it!

Fax machine. A fax machine is capable of transmitting and receiving documents almost instantaneously. This machine can also be used as a copier if your copying needs are minimal; otherwise, you may also need a copy machine. Keep in mind that the computer, with an Internet connection, can also be used as a fax machine. This enables you to send or receive information without converting it to a paper copy. Discuss this with your professional advisor.

Answering machine. A telephone answering machine or equivalent service, backed up by your local telephone company, if possible, is essential. The last thing you want to happen in practically any business is to miss a telephone call. Some businesspeople feel that a "live voice" answering service is better than a machine, but the contrary argument is just as persuasive. One device that seems to offend many callers who just want to leave a message is the answering system that lists options—if callers have the patience to stay on the line long enough to listen to the litany.

Additional phone lines. Carefully examine your need for two or more separate telephone lines to ensure availability when your business gets busy. Most telephone services have a "call interrupt" feature, which allows you some flexibility but, if you have a busy fax, you might want to enhance these options. Cost is normally not prohibitive. If you connect to the Internet through a phone line, you may want to install a dedicated line.

Magazine subscriptions. Subscribe to some magazines that are appropriate to your particular trade or industry, as well as magazines for small businesses. Check your local bookstore to get a good idea what you'll need. The ideas you find in those magazines will serve you well. In addition to the normal creative elements you may find in many generic business magazines, you will find many ideas for setting up your office in magazines about home-based businesses and home offices. Remember: if you get only one idea from a magazine, it probably was a worthwhile investment. Reading this type of material will also give you many ideas about the most critical aspect of practically every business, marketing.

Miscellaneous. In addition to obvious items like a desk and a wastebasket, you will also need sundry small items, such as a calendar, a clock, a notebook, a calculator, a filing cabinet, a book case for library usage, and a telephone book with all your business numbers—clients, vendors, prospects, associates, and professionals. Everything that happens, or should happen, while you are in your office should be recorded in your notebook. All checks received and written should be recorded when written or received. Copies of checks should be made before they're deposited.

The last item that needs to be mentioned, again and again, is that, for any business, at home or otherwise, you should have a business plan. This will tell anyone, and remind you, what purposes the business is supposed to serve and what the dollar allocations are for launching the business and for continuing it and succeeding. Your business plan should also discuss the competition, the asset structure of the business, the need for additional capital, and the purpose for those expenditures. It should have a beginning, a middle, and an end. It should be a map that can be followed from the beginning, with signposts along the way to indicate alternative directions as the economy, the competition, and the future of the industry dictate.

HOW TO FIND THE RIGHT BUSINESS INVESTMENT

You will find it very difficult and statistically unlikely that you will survive, let alone succeed, in any business venture if you don't invest all your efforts. Some people say success relies on good fortune. But as Mark Twain wrote, "The harder I work, the luckier I get." There is no magic to success, but there is an attitude about those who succeed.

The Right Attitude to Succeed

If you are going to buy a business, be prepared to invest everything, not only your money. You must invest time and energy and make the emotional commitment to succeed. If you are not sure about whether or not you will, don't do it. A positive frame of mind creates the motivation, generates the energy, and keeps the wheels moving, not only in the face of adverse circumstances, but on the smooth roads as well. A positive attitude of commitment makes success happen.

Thus, in examining the marketplace and choosing your business or market niche, you must consider the long haul and examine your personal and emotional commitment to the business you choose. If you don't consider yourself mechanically inclined, don't buy a business that is equipment-oriented or that constantly requires equipment repair or maintenance. If you are not financially oriented, don't get involved with a business that requires a high degree of financial sophistication, like a tax advisor. If you don't enjoy dealing with people, don't get involved in a business that depends on the customer relationship for its success, like a restaurant. If you are not quality-conscious, don't buy a business that depends on high-quality standards of performance, like a quick printing facility. And, for heaven's sake, if you don't like selling, don't buy a business that depends on outside sales.

Emotional Containment

The other side of emotional involvement is emotional containment. Of course, your judgment will be based, in part, on your gut reaction to the business itself. This is natural. Some people, for example, might have a real problem cleaning clogged drains or getting rid of pests and rodents. Others might be very excited about dealing with domestic animals or taking trips to exotic places around the world. It is fine to become emotionally involved in a concept, but don't let your emotions make a business judgment on which the welfare of your family and your future might depend. In other words, be careful that your positive emotions don't dictate decisions in the face of a negative business analysis.

Can You Make the Sale?

Finally, make sure the requirements of the day-to-day activities of the business match the capabilities of your own background—not the background you'd like to have, but the background you feel comfortable about really having at your fingertips. You will then be ready to examine some more serious questions, such as the industry, location, competition, and growth potential.

Deciding whether you will be successful at selling requires more research than it might at first appear. Many people consider themselves good cooks, yet they should not be in the restaurant business. The key to any business is making the sale—marketing and selling your product or service to potential customers, whoever or wherever they are. You have got to find them, sell to them, and satisfy them. You have to maintain appropriate prices, quality, inventory, equipment, and staff to make the sale. In fact, your goal is to develop the business such that you hire other people to do the day-to-day activities while you oversee the growth and future of your business.

If you like to cook, but don't like to shop for groceries or supervise a staff of waiters and dishwashers, the restaurant business is not for you. If you are not willing to keep abreast of restaurant marketing techniques—ambiance and decor, discounts and specials—then, again, you should consider another industry.

How do you feel about customer contact? Some businesses require customer contact, but no selling. Some even allow you to avoid extensive conversations with customers and outside sales altogether. However, these businesses may require heavy inventory supervision and bookkeeping, much of which is now done on computer. Computer literacy may then be important for you.

As you research the market for the industry you are interested in, look at the kinds of skills and interests other owners and proprietors possess. Illustration 6.1 shows how important the ability to deal with people and sell can be to your success.

Illustration 6.1 A Franchisor's Assessment

John Scott, former CEO of Fastframe USA, interviewed many people who wanted to buy a Fastframe franchise. He didn't look so much for people who were technically oriented or who had experience working with glass and wood and nails. Fastframe proprietors work with the public every day. He explained his approach: "I don't subscribe to the theory that salespeople are made, not born. You can teach someone how to use a bag of tools, but you can't teach them how to relate to people. And, at the end of the day, it is the relationship with the customer that is more important than anything else."

During the initial interview process, Scott would look for the ability of the prospective buyer to deal with people. "If I find someone who is clearly a fish out of water when it comes to dealing with the public, I would rather tear up the contract than take a chance. If the venture fails, not only is the owner not successful, but our franchise family will feel the pain of that failure for a long time."

Specific Research Strategies

You can follow certain basic strategies when you conduct a pre-purchase research project. Here are some that will get you started.

Develop your questions. The information you get depends on the questions you ask. The more general the question, the more general the answer. So the more specific you make the question, the more likely you will get a specific answer. You need specific answers to make an informed decision, so take the time to develop your questions properly.

Ask a competitor or franchisee. Any pre-purchase research project begins with asking a current competitor (who doesn't have to be in the immediate neighborhood) or a franchisee (if the business is a franchise) what the business is really all about.

Consult your professional. Analyze the business with your business consultant, attorney, or accountant. Let the professional give you an uninvolved, objective view of what he or she sees in relation to his or her varied experience in the business world. Your consultant, attorney, or accountant can also contribute relevant personal information regarding the particular trade or industry.

Read trade magazines. Most industries have trade associations that produce magazines to update their members on the latest technology, trends, and innovations in the industry. These trade magazines can be a valuable resource for you.

Ask a competitor or franchisee again. The person who is already in the business can give you much more specific information. He or she can speak about customer problems, profit, cost factors—the real essence of the business.

Speak to executives. Contact the executives of the franchisor or the vendors from whom the seller buys his or her goods or services. The franchisor will always try to maintain your interest in the franchise relationship by giving you the best possible picture of the industry and of the business you intend to buy. On the other hand, the vendors will give you a broader picture of the good and the bad of the industry and their reaction to the individual businesses they service. These two views

may diverge or they may support each other. In either case, it is a good way to look at more than one side of the industry.

Look at the answers. Examine the list of questions you asked and the answers you received during this process. As you become more knowledgeable in the particular trade or industry, you will find that you will be better able to construct a good question. Revise your list of questions.

Ask a competitor or franchisee again. By now you will be able to have a more in-depth discussion with a competitor or franchisee because your research has taught you so much about the business. You will likely have thought of more sophisticated questions and need to turn to the competitor or franchisee again for answers. Establishing this relationship with other owners of the type of business you hope to buy is a valuable process for your business future.

You will find as you proceed with your research that most businesses are not necessarily what they appear to be. Don't let a broker or seller convince you of some fact that you have not researched yourself. Examine and read the selling materials carefully. If you are buying a franchise, look over the disclosure document carefully and trace the company, its concept, and its competitive position in the marketplace. If you are buying an existing business, review its financial history via the profit and loss statements and the balance sheets. Do a historical analysis of the business, examine the business community on which its success depends, and get a feeling for the business impact on its current customer base. See the following worksheet for some more research strategies and sources.

Money—the Common Denominator

Finally, you need to consider your funding resources and the potential of the business to service debt and provide you with an income. You may have to pay back the money you have borrowed or replace the interest income you lost when you converted or sold your other investments to buy the business. You may simply need to make enough money to keep the business going and feed your family at the same time.

Every business must account for its sales, costs, and

income to the IRS, state taxing authorities if applicable, and any other bureaucratic agencies. You must consider your overhead, equipment, and personnel on whose productivity the success of the business depends. In addition, you must consider your customers (current and prospective), who they are, where they are, and how to market to them.

Don't ignore these issues until after you have bought the business. Begin your research early. As mentioned earlier, picking a business is not like picking a horse at the track. You can't walk away from a loss as easily.

Chapter 7 will lead you through some important specifics you should request from your seller. The research strategies presented in this chapter, combined with the appropriate information supplied by your seller, should get you well on your way to making an informed investment.

KEY POINTS TO REMEMBER

- Before you buy a business, make sure you have the right attitude and commitment to make the investment a success.
- The business you buy will require certain skills and abilities. Look objectively at the talents and experience you bring to the business before you commit any money to it.
- Doing research and asking questions may be embarrassing, time-consuming, and tedious, but they are absolutely necessary to ensure that you make the right decision.
- Your funding resources must be equal to the business' financial demands. No amount of skill or commitment will make a business a success without the necessary working capital.
- The ability to sell is a key factor to many business enterprises. If you need that skill to succeed in the business, be sure you have it before you sign the papers.

Worksheet 6.1. Making the Commitment to Succeed

While choosing the right business and negotiating a fair price are essential to your success as an entrepreneur, the attitude and commitment you bring to the venture will also influence your future success. The following checklist will help you identify your strengths and weaknesses as an entrepreneur.

Personal Commitment

Yes	No	
❏	❏	Do you think you have given the purchase and ownership of a business adequate forethought?
❏	❏	Have you considered the short- and long-term implications of purchasing a business?
❏	❏	Have you considered the effect owning your own business will have on your family?
❏	❏	Do you feel that you have a strong enough background either to understand the problems you may face as a business owner or to recognize when you need experienced professionals to help you?
❏	❏	Do you know what business skills are necessary to properly and successfully operate the business?
❏	❏	Are you aware that owning a business, no matter what anyone says, requires much more than an eight-hour day?
❏	❏	Are you prepared to invest the kind of energy and time the business requires for as long as it may take to make the business successful?

Financial Commitment

Yes	No	
❏	❏	Do you have enough money to maintain the business if it brings in less cash than you anticipate?
❏	❏	Do you have a reservoir of dollars you can draw on if sales lag for an extended period?
❏	❏	Will the money you use to help the business survive be taken away from the needs of your personal living expenses?
❏	❏	Have you analyzed just how much money you will need to properly support your family during the early and possibly nonprofit period of the business?

Dealing with Competition

Yes No
- ❏ ❏ Have you ever been in a competitive situation before, even in the corporate world?
- ❏ ❏ Are you able to cope with the disappointment of losing to a competitor?
- ❏ ❏ Do you believe competition can be healthy for a business?

Your Business Style

Yes No
- ❏ ❏ Do you consider yourself a conservative businessperson, as opposed to a risk-taker?
- ❏ ❏ If you are a risk-taker, do you have the necessary finances to support taking business risks?
- ❏ ❏ Do you feel confident that you can delegate responsibility to someone you trust to perform tasks you do not have the time or ability to do?

Home-Based Business

Yes No
- ❏ ❏ Will the anticipated business interfere with basic family activity?
- ❏ ❏ Have you discussed and analyzed this "interference" with other members of the family?
- ❏ ❏ Will the basic family activity interfere with the time and energy needs of the anticipated business?
- ❏ ❏ Do you have the discipline to separate your business activity from your family activity?
- ❏ ❏ Is there a sufficient time frame that can be devoted entirely to the business activity?
- ❏ ❏ Do you have the discipline to create timelines and priorities without having them created for you by others?

Worksheet 6.2. Research Strategies

Below are some research sources and sets of questions that will get you started with the essential primary research you should do before you make any personal or financial commitment to a business.

The Selling Portfolio

The portfolio you receive from your seller will include the profit and loss statement, balance sheets, cash flow analyses, and other financial information for the business, about which much is said in other chapters. You will also find nonfinancial data that is relevant to your understanding of the business and its industry.

Which of the following traits and talents does the business require of the owner for its proper and successful operation?

- ❏ Outside selling
- ❏ Constant training of transient personnel
- ❏ Technical know-how or hands-on technical ability
- ❏ Extensive travel

Other:

_____

_____

_____

Which of the following is the business vulnerable to?

- ❏ Climate
- ❏ Location
- ❏ Key personnel
- ❏ Substantial working capital

Other:

_____

_____

_____

How will you handle any of the above requirements? Be specific. _____

_____

_____

_____

Community Services

These include chambers of commerce, merchants associations, banks, universities, newspaper libraries, real estate agents, and even the Yellow Pages. Below are some questions you should know about the local business community.

Is the community becoming more industrialized or residential? Which would benefit your particular business?

_____

_____

Does the city or state have any plans for the immediate area or an adjacent community? Are there plans to build a road, a stadium, a convention center, or a giant mall complex? Will any of these plans be helpful or harmful to the future of your business? _____

_____

_____

SELLING YOURSELF BEFORE YOUR PRODUCT

Whether you are talking to staff, trying to make a sale, or sharing your expertise with a large audience, your preparation will be the same.

Checking Your Tools

Every presentation has a goal. In some cases, it may be to motivate your staff. In some cases, selling a product or service, the goal is obvious—close the sale. In other cases, your presentation may be to impart knowledge to your audience.

You may need audiovisual aids, computer equipment, spreadsheets, flowcharts, or merely a simple blackboard work area. You may want to prepare a handout or other materials that your audience can take away as a reminder of your presentation. But, always remember the most important tool of all—yourself, your dress, your demeanor. Making a presentation to vacationers in Hawaii while wearing a tuxedo is as silly (and likely to disturb your audience) as wearing a Hawaiian shirt and shorts at a graduation ceremony.

The Language Barrier

Addressing a jury is different from addressing a kindergarten class. Yet, interestingly enough, they have much in common. You must find and use language that communicates your information without demeaning the members of your audience by speaking down to them.

When making a sale, you should try to use language that everyone understands. Avoid using buzzwords or insider language that will often intimidate your listener. This kind of embarrassment does not engender a working relationship. It will often turn people off and create a snore factor. Once your listeners shut off, it's very difficult to get them back on track with you.

The Snore Factor

If your staff isn't listening, you will have failed to motivate them to achieve the goals you set. You will have wasted their time as well as yours. More importantly, you will have wasted valuable time that ought to have been devoted to the growth and success of the business. And there is a greater negative to consider as well. If you've lost their attention, you might have also lost credibility. Restoring credibility to establish a new focus the next time might be a great deal more difficult.

If your potential buyer has lost interest or lapsed into a snore mode, you have probably lost the sale. Certainly, a bad beginning to what you hoped might be a long relationship. Remember the old truism, "You don't get a second chance to make a first impression."

If members of your audience are responding with blank stares or, worse, closed eyelids, you have obviously created a giant snore factor. Audiences are funny. They have usually attended your presentation in lieu of alternative activities available to them. They will give you one chance. If you blow it, they will not be interested in choosing your alternative activity again. They have come to you for motivation or knowledge or the ability to better cope with the exigencies of life or business. You'd better give them something good or your presentation may be your last.

Getting Ready

Whatever your expertise or your experience, certain elements of presentation are mandatory. You must speak clearly, at a pace that people can follow and understand. You must be sincere about your perspective and sure about the legitimacy of your material. Unless using volume to accentuate a point, speak neither too softly nor too loudly.

Use graphics, audiovisuals, and handouts. Be careful that they don't interfere with your presentation by taking your audience on a different trip. If a handout might distract them, mention it but don't hand it out until after your presentation.

Don't use language that you wouldn't want your children to hear. Don't be cryptic in your approach, thinking that people will catch on and figure it out themselves. If you have an opportunity, let them participate with you, being careful not to intimidate by putting any individual to the test of responding to a question. Also be careful not to give up control of the presentation by allowing a member of the audience to take charge.

This certainly doesn't cover all the bases, but you should be aware of the need to prepare each and every time. Is it embarrassing to test yourself in front of a mirror? As long as no one is looking, why not?!

And always remember: preparing and giving a successful presentation will invariably make you more competent and professional for your next session.

The Asset Variables

A N EXISTING BUSINESS OFFERS MANY TYPES of assets, and each asset's value will eventually be figured into the selling price in one way or another. To determine the value of the asset variables, you will have to do some research on your own, consult professionals (appraisers, accountants, or attorneys), and request specific information from your seller. This chapter will help you isolate many of the variables, lead you in the right direction to determine their value, and give you some specific questions you can ask your seller to get all the answers you need.

Much of this book deals with what businesses have in common, such as operating profit, debt, and even the commitment of the owner to make the business a success. However, the differences among businesses, particularly as they relate to the value of the assets for sale, are equally important to the buy-sell process.

Service, soft goods, food, manufacturing, wholesaling, and retail businesses make up only a small portion of the business complex in a marketplace. To understand exactly what your business represents, you need to look at its components. This chapter will help you identify the more subtle elements to examine as you research your business purchase.

As you read through the following sections, consider how the various assets apply to your business and how you will research their value and ultimate effect on the business's selling price.

JUST WHAT IS FOR SALE?

Not all businesses have the same assets for sale. For instance, mail order businesses don't need to worry as much about location as retail outlets. A legal practice may not have as large an investment in equipment as a medical practice. Consider what the seller has included in the business package and how valuable each element is to operating the business.

Equipment

Every modern business relies on equipment. Sometimes people improve an initial concept without making the original equipment obsolete. In that case, buying a business with old equipment is perfectly appropriate. In other cases, old equipment can seriously affect your competitive edge. You must assess the value of the equipment for every potential business purchase.

The cost of the equipment or of equipment replacement is, in some cases, a significant dollar factor. In some businesses, on the other hand, the equipment is hardly a factor at all. Careful analysis by experts in the industry will help you make this assessment.

Be careful to check on equipment innovations on the horizon in the specific industry. What might be appropriate today could easily be obsolete tomorrow—and tomorrow might come more quickly than you anticipate. Equipment innovations could include new ways to heat with less energy, to move heavy or bulky items with smaller and/or more powerful motors, to eliminate waste more expeditiously, to freeze more quickly, or to use machinery of all kinds with fewer replacement parts required over the life of the equipment. The scope of equipment activity is endless. Be sure to make an appropriate assessment for the business in question.

Check with the appropriate state authorities involved in maintaining ownership records and ensure that there is not a lien or encumbrance on the equipment. This can sometimes happen when the equipment is originally sold or leased to protect the seller until the entire purchase price is paid or, at a later time, when a lender or a creditor wants to have some security in an item of value to protect a loan or an extension of credit. These security situations are normally found under the personal property laws of the state in which they are located or under the Uniform Commercial Code, which covers most states.

Inventory

From manufacturing businesses to retail outlets, inventory is always a factor. Inventory can be significant because the seller has allowed levels to get too high or too low. Sometimes, the inventory is totally obsolete and not worth the space it occupies; sometimes, it is so valuable that it needs to be safeguarded. Perishable foodstuffs have a limited shelf life and need to be disposed of rapidly. Certain chemicals need supervision or they may deteriorate. Certain items of inventory become obsolete because customer tastes change. Others retain their value and even outlive the business. Indeed, some items may have such utility that they can effectively be used by many people and industries.

As the buyer, you make this initial assessment. Then, based on market, wholesale, replacement, and depreciated value, you decide on the dollar amount you place on the product and the amount you are willing to pay for it as part of the purchase price. In some cases, inventory represents a modest percentage of the entire business package; in other cases, the inventory may represent the entire business package.

Make sure that you physically see, handle, count, and otherwise examine the inventory for yourself. Make sure the seller actually owns the inventory and has paid for it and that it has not been pledged or otherwise used for security. In such a case, you may not be able to obtain actual title to the property without having to face interference from some party who claims an interest for one reason or another.

Real Estate

If a seller owns the real estate on which the business is located, it may not necessarily be part of the package for sale. Many owners have confidence in the business they are selling, which means the business is a good tenant. They will want to lease the location to you, rather than selling it, because they know they can collect the rent consistently. They will be able to pay the property's mortgage and, if the area is growing, the property will be worth more with time.

You can operate the equipment, count the inventory, and stand on the real estate, but assessing the value of the lease is a little different. Consider if the business depends on the location, if the rent figures significantly in the overall business picture, or if the growth of the business may require additional space in the future. The lease and its terms are essential to the welfare, maintenance, and continuity of most businesses.

You need to understand all the terms and conditions of the lease. Some are more complicated than others and some are so obscure that only a carefully trained eye will catch the nuance. Have your professional take a close look at the lease. Here are some things to which you want to pay particular attention.

- How long is the lease?
- Is there an option to renew?
- Is the option defined in terms of the rent and other obligations?
- Is the lease a percentage lease, entitling the lessor to a percentage of your profit if your gross sales exceed a certain amount?

- Are you obliged to pay a portion of the property taxes or common area maintenance?

Then you may also need to consider some of the more subtle problems not actually in the lease itself.

- Are there any adjoining areas that you might be able to acquire should you need additional space?
- Is the lessor renting to any other businesses that could compete with or jeopardize the business you are acquiring? Does your lease protect you against such competition?

If you are not used to examining leases with a fine-tooth comb, speak to your professional advisors before you make any commitment to the business itself.

On the other hand, if you buy the property as part of the transaction and later need to move the business, the real estate could become a problem. The property may have an independent value, but if its value is overly dependent on the business that needs to be moved, you may be making a big mistake by purchasing it along with the business.

An analysis of the business is quite different from an analysis of the real estate. You must do a separate analysis to be sure of the value. Needless to say, be sure that the property is free and clear of all liens and encumbrances in the event you purchase it. Note also the possibility of an environmental infraction due to previous use of the property for which you may ultimately be responsible either for cleanup or for damages.

Building

In some cases, the real estate is not part of the sale of the business, but the building is. Paying for a building when you don't control the property on which it is located is almost always undesirable.

On the other hand, the rent for the bare property will probably be much less than it would be if the lessor owned the building as well. It is simple enough to create an equation to suggest the value of the building based on the differential of the rent, with or without a building. Then, of course, you have the question of the age, utility, and condition of the building itself.

- Does it have sufficient size for expansion?
- Is the land lease long enough to ensure that you will not have to move the building?

- Does the area lend itself to a different use of the building in the event you decide to move the business?
- Do you have the right to sublet the building in the event you choose to make such a move?

Here again, apart from doing an analysis of the business, you certainly need to have the building appraised and carefully examined. A serious roof repair, for example, could do a lot to wipe out the profit of the business. A defect in the building could lead to an expensive insurance policy or an accident and a lawsuit. If the building is for sale with the business, you are really buying two properties and you need to examine both carefully.

Highly Qualified Employees

When you buy an existing business, the employee question may be one of the trickiest issues of all. A good employee certainly appears to be a real benefit to a business. Is it possible for this same employee to be a detriment as well? Yes.

First of all, what happens when a good general manager in a particularly intricate manufacturing business, on whose capabilities the business has been dependent, moves to another state? How do you replace such a valuable person? How much would it cost for such a replacement? Is any such replacement available? How long would it take to find such a person? Companies have pension and profit-sharing plans that make it worthwhile for long-term employees to stay with the company. If they leave before a vesting, they normally cannot enjoy their full benefit package. Make sure you examine just what kind of insurance or program the previous owner has implemented to protect the business from losing its most important employees.

Many highly qualified employees are also on the front line of the business. They are in the sales department or in constant touch with the customers at the counter or on the telephone. These people actually control your customer base. In many instances, customers will buy the product exclusively because they trust the person selling it. Most markets are so competitive now that you rarely find a product that doesn't have a comparable replacement or competitor. All too often, the customer buys the salesperson, not the product.

If any employees control your customer base in this sense and decide to change jobs or work for the competition, the move could devastate your business. No legal language can guarantee total protection from the defection of a key employee in this type of situation. Make sure the business you are buying is not vulnerable to this kind of predicament. When the seller is putting a value on his or her personnel, be careful that you don't discuss this value without also considering the possibilities of losing those employees.

Customer Base

You cannot overemphasize the value of customers. Many businesses follow the philosophy that it is easier to increase your business by appealing to current customers than it is to find new customers. Your current customers already know the value of your product, how to get to your location, where to park, your basic price structure, and many subtle and personal things that affect buying behaviors.

Many businesses train their counter people to call the customers by their names. Some businesses have their counter people wear nametags to allow the customers to learn the names of the people with whom they are doing business. This personal touch can cause customers to stay with you despite discounts and other incentives offered by your competitors. As one entrepreneur said, "We have the same goods as everyone else. That's true. But the customers keep coming back because our people treat them with dignity. It really does make a difference." The relationship between personnel and customers is often the core of the business, regardless of the product or service. Customer loyalty can be a significant asset. If you are good to your customers, a time will come when they can be good to you.

Customer Contracts

Some businesses are so dependent on certain large customers that they actually have written contracts with them. One reason is that if a business has to build up a strong inventory, purchase new equipment, or hire additional personnel to accommodate the needs of a particular customer, the business owner must have some security that he or she will be able to move that inventory off the shelf and not have to let personnel go.

If a seller has a special relationship with a substantial customer because of family or personal ties, the customer may no longer be loyal to the business under new ownership. A big portion of the profit could easily be tied up in such a relationship. As you examine any business, define the large clients and satisfy yourself that they will continue to be a part of the business you are buying.

If you buy a business that depends, even in part, on such customer contracts or, for that matter, manufacturing contracts (for example, to take all the goods that a particular manufacturer can produce or to produce all the goods that a particular customer can handle), you must be careful to examine the written contracts. More importantly, examine the actual relationship between the parties and make sure it has been and will continue to be successful for both parties.

Location

Some people say that the three most important elements to consider when buying a business are location, location, and location. You may find it difficult to sell thermal underwear in Hawaii or bathing suits in Alaska. It is important that the business you buy be located in the middle of its largest potential customer base.

Your location may need to offer some or all of the following:

- Good signage opportunity so that traffic can recognize your location from both or all directions.
- Good parking if your customers depend on it for shopping convenience.
- A window to display impulse items if you have any.
- The ability to maximize space efficiency if your business is not based on customer convenience.

Logo and Trade Name

Some businesses have the advantage of longevity in the marketplace, which goes a long way to establish name recognition. Some businesses are geared to high-visibility advertising, which not only generates sales but creates corporate name recognition in a relatively short time. These businesses can be selling anything from fast food to underwear. Sometimes, name recognition can be a strong wedge for your salespeople in the marketplace, just as Microsoft is in the computer field. A logo can also be a big drawing card for consumers, like the famous golden arches of McDonald's.

If you are buying a business that has a recognizable logo or an established trade name as part of its business package, you must be prepared to pay for this market advantage. You may feel that the price is exorbitant because of this single business element and that you can sell an equivalent product or service without the use of the logo or recognizable mark. In some cases, you may be correct. The savings on the purchase may give you the additional capital necessary to fight the advantage enjoyed by your competitors with powerful logos or trade names.

In other cases, fighting the established and accepted product or service may be like tilting at windmills. Make this assessment early on. A marketing survey could help you determine the importance of the logo or trade name. In some case, it is virtually impossible to beat out a product that has years of activity in the marketplace and millions of dollars spent in advertising. The value of a logo deserves careful and objective analysis. If franchise logos dominate the marketplace, your best option may be to buy a franchise instead of an independent business.

Reputation

Following closely behind the logo and trade name question is their logical successor, reputation. Although the logo and trade name are the face of the building, the reputation of a business is represented by the activity that goes on inside and the people who work with the customer.

Part of the franchise concept, for example, is that a customer can expect to find the same product, service, and even the same cosmetic environment whether he or she is in Maine, Oregon, Florida, or California. The franchise's reputation for cleanliness, professionalism, quality of product, and consistency brings customers back to the business wherever it is located. The same can also be true of an independent. Customers expect a certain level of service and quality every time they turn to the business because of its reputation.

If you are considering buying a franchise, you may be asked to pay a higher price than you might for a comparable, nonfranchise operation because the franchise offers a nationally recognized reputation for quality. However, because of the quantity discount available to franchise companies, you may save enough on the equipment package to make up for any initial premium you will be asked to pay for the franchise reputation.

The question of paying a continuing royalty on sales to the franchise company after the purchase is quite another question. See Chapter 9 for cost comparisons between franchises and independents.

A Secret Formula

Each business, to one degree or another, is unique. Some are different because of their unusual inventory, some because of their location, and still others because they have a product based on a secret formula. Many formulas exist in the food business, which range anywhere from pancake batter to the flavoring in carbonated sodas. Other less obvious formulas consist of chemicals and other additives to increase product longevity, strength, smell, looks, and palatability.

If the business you are buying uses a secret formula of some kind, be careful that the essence of the product is properly protected under the appropriate laws. Determine the longevity of that protection, whether the formula is necessary to deal with your competitors, and whether the price you are paying is commensurate with the advantages you expect to enjoy.

Computer Hardware

Some years ago, businesses started taking advantage of computer technology to eliminate many of the manual bookkeeping aspects of the business. If you had taken a tour of one of these buildings back then, you might have been shown a room that had wall-to-wall computers, a separate air conditioning system, and a special generator that would go on automatically in case of a power failure, and even then you wouldn't be allowed to see the room because of equipment sensitivity and confidentiality.

Computers now exist that are the size of a notebook with as much power and memory as the whole complex of computers in that room. You can protect your material by access codes and move the equipment from one room to another as easily as a cup of coffee. You can send and receive information to and from computers all over the world and even send and receive pictures at the flick of a button.

The problem is that you must understand not only the nature of the equipment that you are buying, but also the part it plays in the business. In most cases, the computer is your friend and ally. Be careful, however, of those situations in which the computer is so important that anything less than perfect could jeopardize the business.

Computer Software

While the computer hardware is often fundamental to a business, the software represents the thinking technology and therefore must be equally appropriate to the task. It is your obligation to either understand the program or have someone by your side who understands it and whether or not it serves the purpose for which it was intended.

Just as the software needs to be designed or adapted to solve the problem, you need to understand it so that you are not held hostage by a system that only a few select people can handle.

Computer Capability

Finally, you need to examine whether the computer technology is really a benefit to the business. Some businesses have maintained their focus better without computer technology. Some businesses are not involved with extensive inventory problems or sophisticated price calculations. They require so little accounting work that it is more cost-effective to do the work manually. These situations, however, are somewhat uncommon.

The delicate balance is often difficult to maintain. Some people are convinced they should get a very sophisticated and expensive computer to accommodate the potential growth of the business. They argue that it is less expensive to buy all the equipment now than to add pieces and parts later on. Some businesses have been known to spend so much money on computer equipment that they use up the working capital needed to capture their customer base in the marketplace. Look at both the positive and the negative sides of the computer system you are purchasing with the business and value it appropriately.

Latest Technology

Whatever business you are considering, you will invariably find working aids of one sort or another. Ask yourself whether you need to pay for state-of-the-art equipment or whether you can get along with something more basic and less expensive.

Some of the latest technology may save some time but might be much more difficult to learn or teach. It may be much less expensive and less time-consuming to repair an older, simpler piece of equipment than a highly technical state-of-the-art machine. And the more complex machine may not prove to be nearly as cost-effective as the old standby. Look carefully and don't be fooled by appearances. Examine what is there and qualify what would best serve your interests in the short term and the long term. You may be able to work well with the original equipment until either your profit allows an upgrade or your business demands or requires it.

Absence of Competition

Competition, or the lack of it, can be a positive or a negative. Give it careful attention. The absence of competition can be as much a sign of danger as too much competition. Perhaps competitors haven't arrived yet—or maybe they have already left. Competition can be devastating or it can be tremendously important.

You will very often find a proliferation of nightclubs or restaurants in a single area of the city. This cluster of shops and clubs allows customers to come to the general area, park their vehicles, and then make their decisions. Making this scheme work is, of course, a delicate balance. Seven restaurants in one place could be very successful. The eighth could throw off the competitive balance and drive them all into bankruptcy. You have to know your business to recognize the balance in any given case.

If you are the only coffee shop in the neighborhood, for example, you might ask if others were there before. Why are they not there now? What is happening to the area? Why is rental space so readily available and inexpensive? You may buy a business that has no visible competition because all the knowledgeable people in the industry know a certain innovation is going to obsolete all current activity. Consider the silk stocking and its nylon replacement, the cloth diaper and its disposable replacement, or the metal container and its plastic replacement.

WHAT TO REQUEST FROM YOUR SELLER

You found some research strategies in Chapter 6 and will undoubtedly have to turn to professional consultants for real estate appraisals or other more complicated valuations. However, your seller is required to give you as much relevant information as he or she is able. Below are some basic disclosures you can request from your seller early in the negotiation process.

Money in and Money Out

Always start with the simplest elements. You should be looking for two things: money in and money out. What are the sources of the income to the business? What are the costs necessary to generate that income? These basic items are found on a profit and loss statement, which, together with a balance sheet and a cash flow analysis, will give you an idea of just what the business is all about.

You need to see more than one year's P&L; after all, different years will involve different elements—different competitors, employees, market factors, and cost factors. You will certainly need at least one full year to accommodate for seasonality and vacation scheduling.

Look at other barometers of the business, including the aging of receivables, how long it takes to collect for the goods or services sold by the business. Collection times will tell you how large a working capital account you need. A working capital reservoir will support your operating costs while you wait the 30, 60, or 90 days it may take customers to pay their bills. As always, have a good accountant working along with you right from the beginning of the buying process. He or she will know what all of these things are and where to find them.

Accrual vs. Cash

Keep in mind that the profit and loss statement should be on an accrual basis, to show the dollars owed at the end of the month, whether paid or not, such as rent. A cash basis presentation, on the other hand, can be very deceptive: it will show what has been paid, not necessarily what is owed. Having both will give you a much clearer picture. If you are not familiar with reading financial documents and understanding how they work together, make sure you have your professional go over these with you.

The Balance Sheet

You will need more than one balance sheet. A balance sheet shows certain elements as of the moment when it was prepared. The only way you can make judgments about long-term debt, large equipment purchases, and other substantial dollar obligations is to compare one balance sheet with another. Here again you want to be sure you understand how the financial picture is painted. If you are not sure about any of it, don't pretend you are. If you are going to operate a business, you must understand the basics. Speak to your accountant.

Some other specific questions need to be answered:

- What are the key accounts?
- Who are the key employees?
- How are relationships with key vendors established and what terms are available with each?
- What is the history of the company?
- Does the business have any current or potential litigation?
- What explains the good months and the bad months?
- What are general problems in the industry?
- What is the competition doing?

Remember: each industry is a little bit different; the smart buyer will do a complete analysis before making a judgment.

The Lease—an Asset or a Liability?

Perhaps the biggest single key of all in the retail business is the lease. With rare exception, most retail businesses fundamentally depend on location. In the case of the business that depends on local traffic for its existence and success, location is clearly a top priority. It would be frivolous to consider buying a retail business that has only a short term left on the lease. Examine whether the lease has an option to renew; if not, you must consider the problem of moving, whether there will be comparable space at a comparable price in the same marketing area. Examine the lease to ensure that the cost of the premises falls within the appropriate ratio parameters when considering the cash flow of the business, the customer base, and the growth potential. Moving the business might mean moving away from a clientele that has taken years to build and on which the business is relying for its survival and growth.

Questions, Strategies, and Results

By now you have probably developed a good list of research questions and strategies. As you continue to explore the possibilities for buying a business, consult that list of questions and strategies, revise it, and make sure you get the specific and accurate results you need.

KEY POINTS TO REMEMBER

- A business is composed of many parts. Make sure you understand what each part represents and how it contributes to the success of the business.
- One of the most significant elements to the retail business is the premises lease. Go over it with your professional advisors so that you understand its terms completely. A surprise in your lease after a sale can be devastating.
- Your customer base is your business. Know who your customers are and how to sell to them.
- A business's financial statements provide the history of the business and insight into its current value and future growth. Go over the profit and loss statement, balance sheet, cash flow analysis, and general ledger carefully with your professional advisors.

Worksheet 7. Assessing the Asset Variables

Assets are different in every business and one asset may be more or less important depending on the business and industry. Some, for example, represent capital investment for tax purposes; others are expensed in the year of purchase. Each business has its own peculiarities. The following is designed to make you think about the particular business you are purchasing and what is included in the package.

Equipment
What equipment is included in the package you are buying?

Yes	No	
❑	❑	Have you physically seen and evaluated each piece of equipment?
❑	❑	Have you or a professional surveyed the equipment to ensure that it is functioning properly and is competent to do the job for which it was designed?
❑	❑	Is the equipment currently considered state of the art?
❑	❑	Does the seller actually own the equipment and have the right to sell it to you?

Inventory
What is the size, amount, or kind of inventory you are purchasing with the business?

Yes	No	
❑	❑	Is the inventory undamaged, saleable, not obsolete, and consistent with the number, kind, size, and color that is carried on the business's books?
❑	❑	Have you checked with vendors to make sure more can be ordered and delivered in a timely fashion?
❑	❑	Have you checked the inventory turnover to make sure you are not overstocked or understocked?

Real Estate
What real estate is included in the business package?

Yes	No	
❑	❑	Does the municipality in which the real estate is located have any plans to change the zoning area from its current purpose?
❑	❑	Is the real estate comparable with other properties in the area that are used for a similar purpose?

❏ ❏ Have you examined the possibility of moving the business, leaving the property for sale as a separate entity?

The Lease
What are the terms or conditions of the lease?

Yes No
❏ ❏ Is there adjacent space that could accommodate the growth of the business?
❏ ❏ Does the municipality in which the property is located have plans for development, eminent domain, street rerouting, or other changes that could affect your business?
❏ ❏ Have you or a professional examined the lease and its terms?
❏ ❏ Are there terms under which the lease could be extended that are manageable and not overly costly?

The Building
What are the conditions of the building and its purchase?

Yes No
❏ ❏ Have you had a professional appraiser evaluate the building?
❏ ❏ Will the building have to be renovated to continue serving the purpose for which it is being purchased?

Highly Qualified Employees
What is your assessment of the current personnel and their value to the business?

Yes No
❏ ❏ Have you been able to speak with the employees?
❏ ❏ Are replacement people available in case you would need them?
❏ ❏ Have you properly examined the problem of losing customers if you lose a key employee?
❏ ❏ Have you factored into the purchase price the cost of losing a key employee?

Customer Base and Customer Contracts
What is your customer base? Is your relationship with your customers based on customer contracts? How dependent is the business to those contracts?

Yes No
❏ ❏ Will many customers be lost during the transition period, when ownership is passed from the seller to you?
❏ ❏ Have you factored that possibility into the purchase price?
❏ ❏ Have you created any devices to protect against such a degradation of the business?
❏ ❏ Are there any large customers that you may lose after the transfer of the business?
❏ ❏ Have you personally met with any of these large customers to try to ease the transition of ownership for them?

Location
Describe the location and its importance to the future of the business.

Yes No
❏ ❏ Can the business be moved and still retain enough of its customers to survive and succeed?
❏ ❏ Have you examined the competition in the area and its effect on the success of the business?

Logo and Trade Name
Describe the importance of the logo and trade name to the business.

Yes No
❏ ❏ Are you satisfied that the logo and trade name are worth the price you are paying for them?
❏ ❏ If it is possible, have you examined the viability of the business without the logo?

Reputation

What type of reputation does the business or franchise have and how important is it to the business?

Yes No

❑   ❑   If the business is a franchise, will the services and reputation you receive in return for your royalty payments be a fair exchange?

Secret Formula

Yes No

❑   ❑   If the product you are buying is based on a secret formula, are you satisfied that it is a worthwhile product that represents value for money to you and to the customer?

Computer Equipment and Capability

Describe the computer hardware and software you are purchasing with the business and its importance to the proper functioning of the business.

Yes No

❑   ❑   Are you satisfied that the computer equipment is important to the business and that it represents the latest technology?

❑   ❑   Are you sure the computer equipment will keep up with the anticipated growth of the business?

❑   ❑   Are you familiar enough with the software programs to be sure they will be a benefit and not a detriment to the efficient operation of the business?

Competition

Who are your chief competitors in the marketplace?

Yes No

❑   ❑   Would you categorize the number of competitors as adequate and appropriate?

❑   ❑   If you answered no, have you researched why the competition is too high or too low?

WHAT MAKES A BUSINESS RUN?

Whether you're an entrepreneur with one employee or a conglomerate with hundreds, the key factor in the operation of the business is people. If they are knowledgeable and inventive, their efforts will likely affect the business in a positive fashion. However, unless employees are also motivated, these efforts may fall short of maximum effectiveness.

Will Team Building Work?

Getting to know your employees is probably the first step toward creating the appropriate motivation. What makes each person tick? What will make people feel as though they are real members of the team? Many will respond to typical team-building approaches. Putting together a bowling team or a softball team often helps to create this team feeling, with the positive aspects carrying over to the business environment. Others have quite a contrary perspective. They feel that extracurricular social activities infringe on their time, their privacy, and their prerogatives. Many employees feel that it's unfair because their lack of athletic ability might be taken into account in terms of promotion or even in their relationships with others in the company, particularly management. And assurances by management that "trying is just as important as winning" do not go far in terms of reducing the anxiety over sports failure. How do you think your people would take to such a team approach?

What About Dollars?

There is clearly a relationship between responsibility and dollars. After all, the factory supervisor earns more money than the factory worker. The CEO takes home a bigger paycheck than the vice president. In most instances, the person shouldering the greater responsibility will earn the bigger salary. But because of taxes and obligations that employees take on as their salaries grow, net pay never seems to allow any extra to put away for the rainy day or the retirement fund. Certainly, talk of greater job opportunity for more money will usually be welcome. But what else is there that relates to dollars that employees are never able to find in their pay envelopes?

The Endgame

For most people, Social Security benefits will not be enough for "the good life." Retirement plans that supplement Social Security are important. The 401(k) or equivalent is one of the salary supplements that matter most to employees. Can you afford to offer such a program for your employees? Or perhaps the question should be reversed—Can you afford not to have such a program?

Much will obviously depend on your need to retain key employees. If your business is a constant turnstile of employees with little need for real experience, you might not need such a plan. On the other hand, if your business depends on the experience or knowledge of your employees, attrition can destroy your business, so such a plan may be a necessity.

The smaller business that can't afford the more sophisticated plans should seek professional advice and develop an incentive program that will allow the employees to put some dollars away. It doesn't mean that they take a part of your business; it does mean that they get some of the business's profit for their contribution that made it happen.

Job Responsibility and Job Responsiveness

Doing the same job in the same way day after day will often tend to dull the senses of the best employee. The result might be a lack of creativity and, even worse, a loss of initiative. Responsive management will always recognize the delicate balance between additional responsibility that fulfills the employee's need to grow and the burden of additional work that becomes the proverbial "straw that breaks the camel's back." Losing employees in this way is the bane of many companies. Finding the perfect balance becomes a serious management problem.

Making Sure Promotion Is Positive

Giving an employee more responsibility than he or she can handle can be the end of a positive career path. Any such promotion should be keyed to a temporary status. This allows time for the employee and management to judge if the new responsibility can be handled. In the alternative, it allows the employee to return to his or her previous status should the new responsibility fail to establish the appropriate comfort zone between the employee and the company.

The People Decision

Management decisions relative to involving employees in the growth and future of a business must factor in various elements in order to ensure success. Managers need to take into account the employees' goals, both personal and professional. The best intentions of management can often be derailed by failing to consider the people aspect of the business in the most personal way.

CHAPTER 8

Investors and Partners

S OME BUSINESS SALES CAN OCCUR IN ONE simple transaction—the papers are signed, money changes hands, and the seller goes on to begin his or her new life. Most business sales, however, require a transition period of various lengths, ranging from something as relatively simple as repayment of a promissory note to something more complicated, such as the seller acting as a paid consultant, an investor, or a partner.

Not all investors or partners are former owners of the business, though such an arrangement is one way to creatively finance a sale, as discussed in Chapter 3. Buyers often need the participation of other people for money, guidance, or actual labor.

If you are considering taking on an investor or a partner, the guidelines in this chapter will alert you to some of the issues related to sharing control of your business. The checklist toward the end of the chapter will help you focus on the issues involved.

Keep in mind that the type of investor who buys stock in a public company is not involved in the day-to-day activity of the business. The investor in a small, privately held company normally serves on the board of directors, both to protect the investment and to help direct the

financial involvements of the company. This chapter, as with this book as a whole, is directed toward the small, often family-run companies that make up the great bulk of the small business community.

THE INVESTOR PROFILE

Investors come in all shapes and sizes, with different motivations and funding. Some are interested in getting a return on their investment because the business is a start-up and will presumably produce income after it gets on its feet. Other investors are interested in a business that is doing well and has strong potential for future growth, possibly leading to the formation of a public company. Still others may recognize the possibility of duplicating the business in other markets, potentially leading to the formation of a franchise.

At a meeting of friends to consider an investment in a radio station, one potential investor said, "It might not make any money, but it will at least give us all an excuse to get together once in a while." These people have a somewhat different motivation for investing, as do people who occasionally invest because they think they are creating a worthwhile community project. Investing for camaraderie or for a charitable purpose is not just for those with a big purse. Many people do it at one time or another. This kind of investment bears a very different return, however, a return not measured in dollars.

The investor types in this chapter are those who seek a financial return, a multiple of the money invested or an interest in the growth potential of the business. While friends or benefactors may make good investors, you should always find out at the very outset of your relationship with an investor exactly what the purpose of the investment is and what it is designed to do for the investor or the investor group. A lack of this kind of understanding can create chaos whether the business succeeds or not.

The Control Factor

Money speaks loudly at the conference table. Ask yourself whether the size of an investor's dollar interest in the business speaks so loudly as to interfere with its proper operation. Investors would like to make sure their money is serving the business purpose for which it was intended and not being rerouted or diverted to someone's pocket for personal use. One way to do that is to sit on the board of directors or attend periodic management meetings where the expenditures of money and the future of the company and its activities are decided.

Management must be in the hands of those who can make the appropriate business decisions. Investors tend to protect their dollar by acting in the short term and lose sight of the long-term picture, although the long-term result is often why they invested. The securities laws work to protect investors who are not in a position to gamble with their dollars. The laws prescribe extensive disclosure documents for anyone seeking investors in a publicly held company. This disclosure normally explains that the investment is not secure and that the probability of the business's success is highly conjectural. Investors whose loss would put their families in jeopardy are certainly not the ideal investors. They tend to second-guess every business decision, looking for any misstep by management. This kind of short-term, over-the-shoulder supervision can inhibit advantageous long-term planning. Be careful about your investors and the size of their investments relative to their net worth.

The Time Factor

Every investor expects a return of investment within a particular period. You need to clearly define the length of this period when you begin the relationship with your investor. Often, this will be implicit in the document representing the investment.

For example, one investor may receive a promissory note in return for the dollars invested; this note may call for the periodic payment of interest, with the principal to be paid at the end of a certain time. Other notes may call for the obligation to be fully amortized: the principal and interest are paid periodically until the entire investment is repaid. In still other cases, the investor may receive common stock in the corporation, which will not entitle him or her to any return on investment until the corporation declares a dividend, is sold or otherwise liquidated, or has a public offering. Often, the investor participates in the company by having some combination of the above. A portion of the investment is returned and another portion remains in the company as the investor's equity participation.

In some cases, an investor may take a different class of stock that allows him or her to participate in a periodic return, depending on the conditions of the obligation or of the company. An investment of this type also may provide the investor with some voting privileges or veto power over management with regard to certain kinds of decisions.

When posturing the company for an investment that gives the investor a periodic return and voting privileges inside the management team, whether before or after you purchase the business, make arrangements to accommodate whatever return the investor expects. If an investor holds security of one kind or another to protect the investment, this security position may jeopardize the future of the company if the company needs to borrow money.

The best approach, if you must pledge assets to an investor at all, is to have the investor agree to subordinate his or her interest in the security to a lending institution if new money for growth purposes becomes appropriate. This approach makes the investor's security interest junior to the new interest of the bank, a senior security holder. Without this subordination agreement, the company would not be able to borrow additional money because the bank will not be satisfied with a second position in the security.

Make sure that time is always on your side and that you understand the rights and obligations of the parties. As you can see, a decision to handle a short-term problem can be a serious detriment to long-term goals. Have your professionals examine any pledge of the company's assets to ensure that the loss of that asset for security purposes, however temporary, will not hinder the company's ability to borrow elsewhere.

The Dollar Involvement

Unfortunately, the dollar speaks with a loud voice. If the investment is large enough to be the basis for the company's existence, you, the management, may actually be working for the investor. If the investor controls 51% or more of the participating stock in the company, he or she may hold veto power over your long-term judgments, even though you are responsible for the managing the company's activities day to day. You need to be aware of the ground rules before your investor exercises the right to overrule your management decisions. You can protect against an investor's excessive control of management, particularly if you act early in the relationship. Set priorities, anticipate the contingencies, and agree on who is responsible for which decisions.

Value to the Company

The next important factor in determining an investor's power in the company is the value of the investment to the company. If the investment is essential to maintaining the company's activities, you may have to give up some control for the privilege of going forward. If you give up too much control, the investment will undoubtedly prove inimical to the best interests of management. Remember: the investor, no matter how excited he or she may be about the business or its potential, will not normally be the best person to make decisions about the business. The investor's judgment may be skewed to making decisions that affect the investment in the short term, which is often the worst reason to make business decisions.

For every financial investment, you want to create a quid pro quo relationship—everyone gets something for something. You may want an investor in order to acquire additional inventory, property, per-sonnel, equipment, or locations. Your desire to do something more quickly or efficiently may propel your search for investors. You may even want particular investors to participate not for their money but for their ability to enhance the reputation of the company in the community or the business marketplace. Many companies ask famous athletes to lend their names to products or advertising to enhance the company image or its visibility.

You have to pay for the privilege of growing more or doing more with your business. The question is whether the value to the business and its future is worth the shackles an investor may put on the business. Be careful when you make this decision, because it is not an easy one to retract. If the business succeeds, the investor will expect to reap the rewards. If the business becomes problematic, the investor will still want something in return for the risk he or she took. Be prepared to pay the price in either case.

THE PARTNER MYSTIQUE

Partners, just like investors, come in all shapes and sizes. You must examine not only the motivation of your potential partner, but your own motivation as well. Occasions arise when you would like to have someone by your side who has extensive experience in a particular industry. You can retain and pay a consultant, you can hire the appropriate individual, or you can create a partnership arrangement. Much will depend on the nature of the business. You may start up or purchase a business because you have good ideas and creativity. However, your lack of expertise or experience in the industry could prevent the business from realizing its full potential.

For example, if you have an idea for a magazine because you understand the needs or the desires of your potential readers, you may be extremely wise to partner yourself with someone who understands the magazine business in general. A partner who understands subscriptions, advertising, list maintenance, printing price structures, and other areas in which your knowledge is limited can be very valuable. You may need a money partner because the magazine venture will likely not break even until it publishes a number of issues and builds a reputation that earns the respect of advertisers.

If you are looking for a money partner, you should get advice from an investor, not an expert. The two are very different. An expert makes sure you attend to the details of the business. An investor makes sure you don't make business decisions that could outpace the dollars you have available for growth. Three participants in a business—an expert, an investor, and the creator or founder—may be a much better balance for the future and success of any business than the somewhat singular and prejudiced view of any one participant.

The Partner Contribution

Partners and investors are not the only way to obtain money or expertise. You can buy expertise from paid consultants or hired staff. You can borrow money. On the other hand, money that the company doesn't need to pay back leaves management with less weight on its shoulders and the expertise that you can find in the next office is much better than waiting for a consultant to schedule an appointment.

Whether you choose to take on a partner or an investor or to seek other sources of money and advice, be sure that the help you get meets the needs of the business. If you give up shares in the business for an expert's help in a minor aspect of the business, you may no longer have enough shares to entice an expert when you need additional help. If you agree to share management control for a small amount of capital from an investor or partner, you may create problems for yourself later, when you need additional capital. You may have to dilute the interests of the current investors by taking on more investors. You may decide to dilute your ownership of the business by taking on more partners. This approach is very undesirable if it causes your share participation in the company to fall below 50%, a controlling interest.

The most difficult question is what to do when you take on a partner who will contribute to both management and financial strength. You want to be sure you have the full attention of your partner and that he or she is willing to participate completely. One way to help ensure that a partner participates completely in a business is to gear the partner's ownership to the time, energy, and success the partner contributes during successive periods of business growth. Any partner who says that his or her primary goal is to build the business

should find this arrangement fair and reasonable. If, on the other hand, the partner just wants to invest and not participate, you should find out early so you don't depend on someone who isn't available.

What do you do when you have a potentially great partner who doesn't have enough money to make a significant contribution to the financial strength of the company, but you want him or her anyway? One philosophy is that it doesn't matter how much a partner can afford as long as the investment is at least 80% of whatever the partner has. In other words, the partner must contribute enough money so that he or she has something at risk it would hurt to lose! The contribution must be significant to the contributing partner.

If your partner doesn't have any dollars available for investment, you could still structure a partnership by having a portion of the partner's income allocated to a fund that would eventually purchase a designated partnership interest. In other words, you can always find creative devices appropriate for your purpose. Don't decline to proceed without first exploring all the possible alternatives.

In many cases, two people want to start a business because they have had a mutual experience. Strangely enough, these kinds of partnerships tend to lack strength because neither partner has the background to contribute what the other cannot. In your situation, be sure that each partner can make a contribution such that all contributions together cover the essentials.

The Partner's Return

One last issue you need to face is the percentage of the partnership to which each partner is entitled. The ideal situation gives each partner a percentage based on his or her contribution of time, energy, expertise, and dollars. This ideal is rarely achieved. The key is to examine the contribution of each partner and make some hard decisions early on that will prevent any partner from feeling, down the road, that he or she was taken advantage of and that there should be a redistribution of investment.

Diamonds Are Forever

It is hard to conceive of a perfect partnership, because "perfect" suggests not only equal work for equal pay, but also that the partnership's longevity is beyond question. You may experience perfection in your partnership for short periods, but partners will eventually disagree on something. Each of you brings at least a slightly different experience and perspective to everything you do. The nature of your personality will cause you either to adjust to your partner or to insist that your partner adjust to you. Lack of immediate adjustment could lead to conflict; conflict, without appropriate compromise, could lead to confrontation and dispute; and dispute, without resolution, could lead to a breakup of the partnership or even litigation. The last frontier of litigation in business is the destruction of the business itself. Diamonds may be forever, but partnerships are not, and you should not expect them to be.

The most significant lesson of all, therefore, is the need to build into your partnership agreement a method for any partner to withdraw in the event of serious and irresolvable conflict. Do this in such a way that you allow the business to continue to function. In most partnerships, you will undoubtedly have "key person insurance" (also called "key man insurance"), whose purpose is to replace an important partner in the event of his or her death. Take the same care to ensure that the business continues in the event of a disagreement. After all, whatever the differences between partners, no partner wants to see his or her investment of time, energy, creativity, or money go down the drain. It is in the best interests of all partners to ensure the integrity and continuity of the business, because if one of them leaves, the others are probably going to be looking for a return of some portion of their investment. A company without profit will have a hard time returning dollars to anyone.

FORMS OF PARTICIPATION

The joint venture concept—the joining together of different people with equal or unequal participation in a business's operation—has many alternative forms.

Sole proprietorship—The simplest is the sole proprietorship in which only one person is owner and any collateral participation is by way of dollar investment, commission on sales, or bonus based on extraordinary contribution to the success of the business activity.

General partnership—In a general partnership, two or more people participate equally or in designated percentages. The problem with the general partnership is its inequality, regardless of distribution of profit. The joint and several liability of the general partnership makes any individual partner 100% responsible for any partnership obligation, whether that partner was solely or only partially responsible for the creation of the debt. This type of liability is a big danger, particularly to the partner who has the deepest pocket—the most money. The wealthiest partner is usually the person who is sued. The court can find against this deep pocket for all the damages even though the party is only partly responsible. The party who pays is entitled to sue the others for their share of the obligation, but the process is tedious and expensive and the others may not have the money to pay back their partner.

Limited partnership—The limited partnership affords most of the partners very much the same kind of protection as they would have as shareholders in a corporation. The limited partnership usually has a general partner who is completely responsible for all the activities and, in turn, for all the obligations of the partnership. The limited partners are liable for the full amount of their investment, but not for any obligation incurred during or as a result of the business activity. However, this limited liability applies only if the limited partners do not actively participate in the daily operation of the business.

Corporation—One way to protect yourself from personal liability is the corporation, which operates the business as a separate entity and is responsible for all business debts, but only to the extent of the financial capability of the corporation. The officers and directors of the corporation have no personal liability except if any of them signs personally or guarantees an obligation of the corporation or if they engage in fraud, misrepresentation, or other criminal activity. Otherwise, they are insulated against having their personal finances at risk. The shareholders are, of course, liable for the full amount of their investment. If the corporation files a bankruptcy, for example, the shareholders are not entitled to any of their investment until all the creditors are satisfied.

Limited liability company—All 50 states and the District of Columbia have adopted legislation that offers business owners a new form of doing business, the limited liability company (LLC). An LLC closely resembles and is taxed as a partnership and it offers the benefit of limited liability like corporations. Because of the newness of LLCs and the potential tax advantages and disadvantages of this entity, ask your accountant or attorney how to investigate its potential for your business.

Many variations exist within each of the above categories: you should examine them carefully before making any decision on the format you will use. Base your final judgment on both the short-term and long-term goals of the business. You will have to make part of your analysis according to the number of people involved and the extent of their financial participation, in addition to their actual involvement in the day-to-day activities of the business. Go over the alternatives carefully with your professionals.

KEY POINTS TO REMEMBER

- If you accept investments in your business, find out how much control over the business you may have to relinquish.
- Know the goals of your investor(s) or partner(s) and whether they are consistent with your goals.
- The long-term value of an investment must be consistent with the needs of the business and its ability to function in the future.
- If you take on a partner, make sure your partner's goals are clearly defined and that you both agree on a plan to dissolve the partnership if it becomes necessary.
- A business can take many legal forms. Examine them with your professional advisors and choose the best form for your short-term and long-term goals.

Worksheet 8. The Essential Checklist for Sharing Control of Your Business

The following checklist will prompt you to think about the many facets to sharing control of your business with a partner or investor. As always, consult an attorney and accountant before you finalize any investor or partnership deal.

Yes	No	
❏	❏	Are you aware that, by accepting investment capital, you are giving up a degree of control over your business?
❏	❏	Is it worthwhile for you to give up some control of your business to recognize the growth potential of the company sooner?
❏	❏	Do you know the goals of your investor(s) or partner(s)?
❏	❏	Are those goals consistent with your goals?
❏	❏	Will your business venture satisfy the goals of your investor(s) or partner(s)?
❏	❏	Do you think that short-term thinking by the investors to protect their investment might subvert the long-term goals that you have set for your company?
❏	❏	Have you considered a realistic timetable with your investor(s) or partner(s) and when the business will be able to pay back the investment, give a return on the investment, or buy out the partner, if that is your intent?
❏	❏	Have you and your investor(s) or partner(s) discussed the form of participation you will use—the legal entity, such as corporation or limited or general partnership—and its legal and financial ramifications?
❏	❏	Do you understand joint and several liability?
❏	❏	Is the expertise of your potential partner(s) worth the percentage of the business you are giving up?
❏	❏	Could an employee or paid consultant fill your need for expertise as well or better?
❏	❏	Will you be able to share all of the responsibilities with your potential partner(s), if that is what you both or all desire, including the creativity, the judgments, and the profit?
❏	❏	Because partnerships do not last forever, have you and your potential partner(s) worked out a buyout arrangement with which you are both or all comfortable, should you choose to dissolve the partnership?

WHAT IS THE MONEY FOR ANYWAY?

The concept of the initial public offering (IPO) has allowed many companies to accomplish a variety of successful business expansions. In fact, the process of raising money appears to have become a primary goal of the entire business community. It is interesting, however, that the investment programs have led to a great misconception on the part of many entrepreneurs.

The Money Isn't for You

The question of start-up capital is certainly the first order of business. Without the initial capitalization, the concept or the prototype will never get off the ground. Selling the concept and the growth potential to an investor or an investor group is the first order of business. For those companies already in the marketplace, additional capital invested in the business will often allow the company to get to the next plateau of success. The money may be used for additional locations, additional inventory, raw materials, a bigger selling organization, advertising dollars, and the like. The one thing that the average investor finds difficult to accept is the reimbursement to the entrepreneur of the money or the time that he or she has invested to get to the point of asking for the investment dollar. There are businesspeople who feel that they are entitled to be paid back for bringing the company to a stage where additional dollars are appropriate. Most investors don't concern themselves with the historical investment; they are interested in where their current investment will take the company in terms of future growth. After all, that is where their return will be coming from.

The Investor Profile

Not only are the investors totally averse to reimbursing the entrepreneur for getting the company to its present circumstance, but they are especially interested in the plans for the future that will represent a multiple return on their investment dollar. And they want the plan to be specific. If the intention is to franchise the operation, it would be a good idea to present a comparative analysis of the industry, making it very clear just what position the company will have … and how. You'd better have someone with franchise experience on the management team or the investors will consider the plan some-thing less than professional. If you're going to invest in a greater manufacturing capability, the investors will likely want to know whether the consumer market will survive long enough for the product to return revenue commensurate with the cost of construction, raw material, and the additional personnel. If you're going to accelerate your marketing effort, the investors will want to know if the marketplace can provide the additional customers that you hope to generate.

In other words, the investors are not interested in a gamble; they are even averse to those things that can be considered a calculated risk. They want a plan that has a substantial chance for success, a plan that considers as many of the contingencies as possible.

The Investment with a Purpose

It is clear that the investment dollar is looking for action. It does not want to rest; it wants to work. It wants to accomplish a purpose, it wants to succeed, and it wants to do so within certain time parameters.

The Loan vs. the Investment

When you are approaching a lending institution, it is more likely that you have a temporary problem to solve rather than a long-term plan to accomplish. Here again, the lending institution is going to want to know the reasons for the problem and, particularly, how the additional dollars will help and the method by which you expect to repay the loan with the appropriate interest. In other words, they will want to know, "What is the money for, anyway?" If you give them a well-ordered explanation and a plan that has a time frame for payment, they will usually consider your application positively. If you fail to explain adequately or your plan for repayment lacks credibility, it is likely that your request will fail.

Money is available for repair and restructure as well as for growth, so long as you prepare your plan properly. The best way to approach either a loan or an investment is to put yourself in the shoes of the lender or the investor. Ask yourself what you would want to know if someone came to you with the same request. You will probably come up with the best questions. Now, the rest of the job is to come up with the best answers.

CHAPTER 9

The Franchise Decision

I F YOU ARE NEW TO ENTREPRENEURSHIP, A FRAN-chise can offer you the comfort zone you may not experience with a nonfranchise business. The franchise company may serve as a kind of silent partner to whom you can turn for advice and assistance. Franchise companies can offer training, expert help, advertising assistance, market analysis, equipment research and development, and trade name and logo recognition.

However, none of these services are free. You will have to commit yourself to paying an initial fee to the franchise company and ongoing royalties for many years. Furthermore, you need to know how helpful and reliable the franchise company will be during your long-term relationship. The decision to buy a franchise cannot be taken lightly.

Whether you decide to purchase an existing franchise operation or start up a new business under the auspices of a franchise, think carefully before you make your decision. Compile a list of questions to examine and make sure the questions are specific. Ask for advice from professionals, franchise owners, and nonfranchise business owners.

The task is not simple. You will need to look at several issues, among them:

- The strength of the franchise company,
- The dominance of the franchise logo,
- The effectiveness of the franchise advertising in your marketplace,
- The talent that you as a businessperson bring to the business,
- The talents you lack and in which you need support,
- The kind of business, and
- The competitive element involved.

Some of the guesswork is eliminated if you buy an existing franchise. Any existing operation will have a track record you can examine, including the relationship between the franchisee and the franchisor.

This chapter will lead you through some of the factors involved in the franchise decision. It will show how franchising has changed since its dramatic growth in the 1960s and how its evolution may affect your decision to buy into a franchise company. You will learn about some of the legislation that regulates franchising and how it affects buyers and sellers. Finally, you will find a checklist in the worksheet in this chapter that will help you ask the right questions and structure your ultimate decision.

FRANCHISING—PAST AND PRESENT

When franchising started to hit its stride, around 1968, businesspeople perceived that the franchise company knew its industry well. Franchisees bought into the franchise concept knowing they would be totally dependent on the parent company for survival, growth, and success.

In those days, before computers, microchips, and satellites, the franchise concept was a good one and it worked. A person with few skills in a particular trade could be trained in a matter of weeks to operate a business. The training used proven methods to create confident and competent business owners. A franchise company was normally started by a man or woman who had taken a business concept and made it a success. This successful businessperson understood and could empathize with the day-to-day problems the franchisee faced. A certain respect and synergy existed between the franchisor and the franchisee.

The Change in Profit Distribution

As time went on, many franchisees became extremely successful and knew more about the business, certainly in their own geographic areas, than the young and inexperienced men and women whom the franchisor hired to visit and supervise franchisees.

Despite having mastered the basics of the business, the franchisee still needed someone to help deal with new and more sophisticated questions—how to expand in the marketplace and maximize growth and profit potential. Unfortunately, many franchise companies believed the franchise concept was designed to deal with the lowest common denominator, people who knew nothing about the business. Some franchise companies did not invest in support services for their more successful franchisees, because they thought the franchisees could buy the help they needed with the profits from their success. The franchisees, on the other hand, felt that, because they paid a higher royalty on their large gross revenues, they deserved more than the basics in return.

Franchising as Big Business

Matters between franchisor and franchisee really began to deteriorate when franchising became a business of its own. Rather than a distribution method that employed the energy and investment of small business owners to mutual advantage, franchising became a numbers game. Some franchise companies were more interested in how many locations they could open than how much support they could offer their current owners.

The appearance of the public company in the franchise industry, new management, and the leveraged buyout changed the face of franchising. A new generation of executives entered the game. Instead of two people working together toward a mutual goal, it was an individual franchisee who had to turn to a corporate bureaucracy for assistance and advice. The original relationship of mutual trust and support disintegrated.

Even the basic concept was lost in the confusion. One chief executive officer of a franchise giant remarked, "If the franchisee won't cooperate, I'll fire him." This executive certainly had no understanding of the synergistic relationship between the franchisor and the franchisee. Further, this person didn't even understand the basic premise that the franchisee is an entrepreneur. The franchisee can't be fired!

Some franchise companies gave up doing market research on sites because they were more interested in getting the place open. They did not update their training programs or maintain research on new equipment. They focused more on national advertising, which in some industries was not as effective as local advertising for individual franchisees.

Legislation to Protect the Franchisee

You need to be assured that any franchise company you join has worked through the corporate greed to which some fell victim in the 1980s. The economic and political trend today is toward small business, and specific legislation has been enacted to protect the individual franchise owner. The requirement for complete franchise disclosure before offering a franchise for sale essentially keeps the franchise company from making promises that it can't or won't keep. Today, this legislation is effective in all 50 states. As a franchisee, you can now depend on receiving full disclosure about the business you are buying and the company from which you are making the purchase.

While franchising has undergone many changes in the last decade, franchising as a whole has been a successful part of the American marketplace and one of the cornerstones of small business. One bad franchise company does not necessarily represent the whole industry. Franchising will continue to play a significant role in America's economy for many years.

THE VARIABLES INVOLVED IN YOUR DECISION

While disclosure documents are very helpful to a potential franchise buyer, you will also need to do some primary research of your own, research into what a franchise company will provide for you in return for your royalty payments.

Anyone who has ever operated a business will recognize that the daily activities of the business become so consuming that there is very little time to do research on new equipment in your industry, evaluate the directions your competitors are taking, follow up with your customers to increase their orders, develop a current marketing program, analyze your labor force to maintain a fair compensation package, or think about new directions your business can take.

The strength of the franchise comes from its ability to maintain its support services—services that the individual businessperson has neither the time nor, in many cases, the inclination or expertise to get involved with. A national franchise can also give quantity discounts on supplies, offer training seminars, and, of course, provide national name recognition. The availability or unavailability of these services can represent a significant factor in the success or failure of a business.

You can expect help from the franchise company with some of the various issues involved in buying a business. As you have read in previous chapters, you need to know about the necessary working capital reservoir, the competition, and the value of the business location to assess the potential for success. A franchise company can help you research these issues, but, as with any business investment, your success or failure depends ultimately on your own efforts.

Working Capital

Lack of adequate working capital, particularly in a new business, is a key reason for serious problems and even failure. In some cases, a franchise company will paint a success scenario that gives the franchise buyer a less than realistic appraisal of the working capital requirements. A responsible franchise company will be too concerned with the long-term relationship to let this happen. However, many franchise buyers, to qualify for the franchise purchase, may exaggerate their own financial resources. Don't be tempted to engage in such deception.

Competition

"Competition" is a word that can generate fear among more naive business owners. The more sophisticated businessperson accepts competition as a positive element that exposes a product or service to a wider consumer audience. In most instances, the success of a franchise in battling the competition depends primarily on the initiative of the franchise owner. However, the purpose of buying a franchise is to benefit from the franchisor's experience in the marketplace. The franchisor should have developed marketing concepts that are proven to be effective in generating a competitive advantage. The franchise company should certainly make these techniques available to the franchisee.

Location

How many times have you heard that, in most businesses, the three most important elements are location, location, and location? Although you certainly don't have to subscribe to this somewhat simplistic philosophy all the time, you cannot deny its validity in certain instances, particularly in businesses where substantial customer traffic is an absolute necessity. When a given area has many vacant sites available, the goal of site locating is simply to find the best for the business. Unfortunately, when there are not many vacant locations available, the goal is to find the best location available. You cannot expect magic from a franchise company when you look for a location for your business. Usually, all the franchisor can do is lend its experience and expertise to find you the best location available.

Future Success

The purpose of affiliating with a franchise company, whether you open a new franchise or buy an existing one, is to have an experienced partner on whom you can rely for business advice. However, the responsibility for succeeding with the business does not rest on the franchisor, but rather squarely with the franchisee.

On the other hand, the franchise relationship is based on the entrepreneurial initiative of the franchisee and the extensive industry experience of the franchisor. Successful franchisors pay heed to this relationship and offer help in every way. If the business is in trouble, the franchisee must work to fix the problem. However, the franchisor should at least participate in an analysis of the problem in order for the franchisee to work in the most appropriate direction and with the best tools to correct the problems.

Nonetheless, the law does not allow a franchisor to tell a franchisee how good a living he or she can make. The success of a small business enterprise is very much in the hands of the franchisees—their initiative, creativity, personality, work ethic, and energy.

A FRANCHISOR'S MARKETING AND ADVERTISING CAPABILITIES

One of the most important factors to a successful business is finding and selling to customers. In the early days, active selling by the franchisee was not the most significant factor in the stability and growth of the business. Most competitors were independents that didn't have the franchise companies' national buying power, the name recognition, or the allocation of dollars for local advertising. Now, most competitors are other franchises that all have similar benefits. It is now extremely important, not only for success but simply for survival, for owners to be sales-oriented, particularly in those fields where outside selling is possible. Franchise companies used to say that you didn't have to be sales-oriented to succeed. Some franchise companies are still saying this. In great part, it is no longer true. You need to assess how your franchise company will help you sell. Look especially at its training program.

The Franchisor Does Your Market Research for You

One of the services many franchise companies provide is market research. To assess your franchisor's marketing capabilities, you need to examine and evaluate:

- Your market environment,
- Your customer base,
- Your marketing priorities, and
- Your maximum marketing impact and the approach best suited to achieve it.

These concepts may seem a little complex, but they are the focus of most franchise marketing departments. Having someone develop and constantly reevaluate these concepts when you don't have the time, experience, or inclination to do it yourself has a dollar value.

Consider, for example, a retail ice cream company that failed to recognize the following facts:

- The competition was getting stronger in the marketplace.
- Yogurt was detracting from the ice cream market.
- Low-calorie substitutes were appealing to diet-conscious consumers.
- Exotic flavors were becoming popular.
- Supermarket freezers were becoming subtle, but serious competitors to on-the-street-consumption customers.

A shop owner who is involved with the daily problems of refrigeration breakdown, tardy or absent employees, delivery times, shop hygiene, and customer complaints might find it difficult to address the long-term, but ever-important demands of market research. Having a parent company there to help has a dollar value.

The ice cream shop's franchisor monitors changes in the marketplace, plans ahead with new test flavors in a few stores, and recommends changes in decor to attract new customers or draw old customers back out of their homes and into the shop. Obviously, this kind of analysis could go on and on without even addressing each industry's particular dynamics.

Is Purchasing a Franchise an Advertising Investment?

The advertising services provided by the franchise company are also at the core of many franchise relationships. Many business people consider advertising an expense of doing business rather than an investment in the future. Survival, let alone success, requires good advertising. You must tell people that you have a product or service for sale.

You could save money by not advertising if you weren't obligated to do so by a franchise contract. You shouldn't buy a franchise just for the discipline of making certain advertising commitments. Advertising is mandatory whether you are a franchise owner or an independent. Your only consideration ought to be whether the franchise company can do a more effective job locally than you can. Who will impact your customer base more? The effectiveness of a national advertising campaign depends on the type of business and the size and financial strength of the franchise company.

Some franchise companies actually develop focus group studies that tell them what the customers' interests and tastes are in a given geographical marketplace. They then develop materials that are structured to make their national or local advertising most effective. The independent just doesn't have the resources or the dollars to develop this kind of program.

In advertising, frequency is often the key to success. An isolated 10-second spot on national television may not be as effective as 10 30-second spots on a local radio station, but the cost may be exactly the same. The quantity purchasing power of the big-dollar franchise to buy multiples of advertising space in all media makes it very difficult for the independent to appear as often or take as much space in any medium with his or her spending limits.

In many industries, the franchise system ensures noncompetitive situations within its own franchise family by designating exclusive geographical areas. Keep in mind, however, that this offers only the protection of preventing another member of that particular franchise from opening a location within that territory. It does not prevent any businesses from advertising anywhere they choose!

MAKING THE DECISION

You now know some of the many variables that will go into your decision whether or not to buy a franchise. One method you can use to structure your ultimate decision is a line-by-line analysis of what a franchise company offers and how much it would cost to obtain those services elsewhere. You also need to consider whether buying an existing franchise is a better option for you than opening a new franchise or buying a nonfranchise business. The remainder of this chapter will prepare you to make those decisions and the worksheet that follows will give you some specific questions you should answer before you decide.

A Line-by-Line Analysis

As you research the prospect of buying a franchise, try to objectively weigh the pros and cons of joining a franchise family. You will need to look at several aspects of the franchise relationship, find out what services the franchisor provides, and assess the value of those services to you.

- Examine the royalty and advertising commitments of the franchise contract and relate these costs to the actual cost savings and other dollar advantages offered by the franchise.
- Compute the amount of equipment replacement for obsolescence during the average year and equipment purchases needed to remain competitive in the industry. Compare the savings offered by the franchisor's national discount price with the cost of the same or similar equipment without the franchise price break.
- Consider the research and development capability of the franchise and give it a fair and thoroughly negotiated value. Many franchise companies ease the burden of equipment research by testing, analyzing, and reporting on new equipment innovations to its franchisees.
- Assess the value of equipment service contracts you receive through the franchise. An independent who may never buy another piece of equipment from a vendor again is not going to get the same kind of service as a franchisee whose parent company acquires thousands of dollars worth of equipment from that same vendor every year.

- Calculate the value of financial coordinators and analysts whose services the franchise company offers its franchisees to go over their financial paperwork and cost-profit percentages. Independents who hire outsiders to do this face high costs for the service.

- Factor in the value of periodic seminars, an annual convention, or the periodic visits of company personnel that the franchisor may offer to help franchisees with marketing, equipment, vendors, maintenance questions, advertising, and industry updates.

- You may want to develop a cost-per-item accounting of the franchise company's services and compare it with the royalty and advertising commitment mandated by the franchise contract. The worksheet at the end of this chapter can help you get started.

How New and Existing Franchises Compare

If you buy an existing franchise, you will have the benefit of knowing the specific history of your franchisee-seller's relationship with the franchise company. A good, solid working relationship may be one of the most valuable assets an existing franchise has to offer.

You will, of course, want to consider several other issues.

- Working capital is still a primary concern, but you will have an existing cash flow from the business, so the working capital requirement will be more clearly defined and therefore much less disquieting.

- The competition is no longer an unknown, because the questions about where competitors are, what they do, and how they affect the future of the business are a basic part of analyzing the purchase.

- The question of location is eliminated, because the track record of the existing business eliminates any conjecture about the validity of the existing site.

- The question of the franchisor's cooperative attitude is answered by the actual experience of the seller. You can, of course, find out about the franchisor's attitude by questioning franchisees, whether you decide to purchase a new or an existing franchise.

- The question of the profit potential of the business is no longer a mystery. It is merely a question of carefully examining the books and records of the business in the light of its actual performance. In other words, much of the guesswork is taken out of the picture!

Does this mean you should definitely buy an existing franchise rather than a new one? Not necessarily.

In a new franchise, you have the opportunity to find the following:

- A dynamic location in a growing area, as opposed to a current location that might be in a stagnant or declining market area;

- An expandable business facility, as opposed to one whose growth potential is restricted by other buildings or zoning regulations;

- A wide-open market potential in a growing community, as opposed to a restricted business environment where all the competitors have to fight for part of a static or shrinking customer base;

- A fresh start with an opportunity to use your own personality as the basis for the relationship with your customers, as opposed to taking on a customer base that might not be consistent with your own business attitudes; and

- Many other advantages, depending on the particular industry involved.

Is it possible to find a definitive answer? Yes, though it requires a good deal of research and self-analysis.

Consider Your Needs

The franchising community today is running across different kinds of new buyers. Fewer new franchisees are gamblers and more are prudent businesspeople than was the case 10 years ago. Most are less interested in big profits than in a consistent and lasting growth pattern.

Changes in the U.S. economy during the past decade have fueled this shift. Insecurity over jobs and pensions has focused the small business buyer's attention on a secure position with retirement potential. In addition, the average franchise candidate is probably 10 years older than his or her predecessor of 10 years ago.

You should now be getting closer to deciding between a new or existing franchise. If you are a gambler hoping to make a good deal of money from buying a new franchise, you still have an opportunity as franchising moves from its adolescence to maturity. You must only keep in mind that the stakes are a little higher and the road a little more dangerous.

If you are more conservative, landing in the franchise field with a golden parachute and wanting to ensure that your retirement is relatively safe, then purchasing an existing franchise business is wiser. It gives you the benefit of the proven track record and the opportunity to improve it. Buying a franchise that has already gone through the "whether or nots"—whether or not the location is good, whether or not the competition is manageable—will prove more prudent in the short term.

The only question left is, if you buy an existing franchise, how much should you pay for it? Remember the two basic priorities. An existing business ought to provide a living wage and be able to service the purchase price of the business out of operating profit. Any payment schedule to handle the balance of the purchase price after the down payment by the buyer should not come from the buyer's pocket. It should come from the business.

Follow this philosophy and you won't have to worry much about location, competition, or break-even. You can concentrate on other things like maintaining state-of-the-art marketing techniques and cutting costs—looking toward building the business for the future and your family.

You will need to assess your own personal strengths and weaknesses as a businessperson to make the decision. Some people are very adept at taking advantage of the services offered by a franchisor and some are not. Some people have family members involved in their business organization who have good business sense. Others are not so fortunate: they have only competent but not so dedicated employees and are therefore more vulnerable to fluctuations in the marketplace, particularly with respect to personnel problems. Consider your own situation thoroughly before making the franchise decision. A worksheet follows at the end of this chapter to help lead you through the process.

Some Legal Fine Print

If you are still wondering whether to buy an existing franchise or a nonfranchise business, consider one last item. If you decide on a franchise, the franchisor needs to consent to the transfer, making the transaction a three-party contract. You are taking the seller's place in the all-important franchisor-franchisee relationship. It is the seller's obligation to explain to you thoroughly and positively what this relationship represents. The seller will tell you about royalty payments, the right of the franchisor to challenge the accuracy of these royalty payments, and the many services and advantages offered by the franchisor.

You should recognize certain basic issues involved in this process:

- The franchisor doesn't want to be in a less secure position after the sale than before the sale. When the original franchisee applied to the franchise company to buy a franchise, he or she filled out a financial application detailing his or her assets. The franchise company sold the franchise based, at least in part, on this financial strength.

- The franchisor doesn't want to give up good financial security; it wants to replace it with security of equal or greater value. The franchisor will look at your application to see if your assets and monies represent the same relative financial strength that it is giving up by releasing the seller from any further obligations under the franchise contract. The purpose of this asset strength is to ensure that the financial obligations to the franchisor are paid whether the business can afford to pay them or not. However, you should note that the continuing obligation of the seller after a sale is not the same in different jurisdictions. Ask your professional about this.

- Of course, the franchisor primarily wants to know that the cash flow of the business can support a successful transfer and that the buyer can meet the obligations. The franchisor will certainly be concerned, for example, with your ability to meet the payment schedule of the purchase money promissory note to the seller and any notes the franchisee might still owe to the franchise company. If you are unable to meet the payments on these various obligations, it is unlikely the franchisor will be able to collect the periodic royalty payments in timely fashion. The franchisor is then facing potential costly litigation to collect on its debts. The franchisor may then try to go after the other assets listed on your application.

■ The franchisor wants to ensure that its reputation in the business community will not be depreciated in any way with regard, for example, to trademarks or logos.

■ The franchisor wants an acceptable buyer under the terms of the franchise contract from the beginning. For example, the buyer normally cannot already have an ownership interest in a competing business.

■ The franchisor wants all the details in all parts of the selling agreement pertaining to the franchise company properly and clearly stated. This will afford the franchisor protection in the event of litigation between the buyer and the seller at a later time.

Even though the franchisee is selling his or her own business, it is always appropriate for the seller to comply with the disclosure law in the particular jurisdiction. If a disclosure document is available from the franchise company, you should receive one. If you are buying a new franchise, the franchise company is mandated to give you a disclosure document. See the Sample Introduction to a California Offering Circular in Chapter 14.

Franchisor's Right to Refuse or Reject a Buyer

Another legal issue to consider with regard to buying an existing franchise is the right of the franchisor to purchase the franchise for sale. Most franchise contracts contain a clause that gives the franchisor a right of first refusal. The company has the right to buy the business on the same terms and conditions as the actual offer of the prospective buyer. It cannot change the terms if it exercises this option.

If it waives this option or fails to exercise this prerogative within the option period, it is still possible that the franchisor could actually refuse to consent to the sale. Although this could be a dangerous position for a franchisor to take—it could lead to a lawsuit by the seller—it has a right to do so if it feels that the business will not be able to support the purchase price or will not be operated properly. Any legitimate reason that may put the franchisor at substantially more risk than currently exists is cause for the franchisor to exercise the right to reject the prospective buyer.

KEY POINTS TO REMEMBER

■ Positive and negative aspects exist in a franchise relationship; you must look at the franchise alternative with an eye to both.

■ Your first priority in examining a franchise opportunity is to ask for the franchise disclosure document. It contains a good deal of the information you need to know about the company.

■ Have your attorney and accountant explain all the elements that constitute your relationship with the franchise company. You need to know your obligations and your prerogatives.

■ Determine all the positive services or programs the franchisor offers, whether you need them, and if you can acquire them from another source and at what price.

■ If you feel the franchise offers you the comfort zone you need as a new entrepreneur, don't be afraid to make the commitment.

■ Once you commit to joining a franchise family, take advantage of all the benefits and services available to you.

Worksheet 9. Making the Franchise Decision

Below is a list of questions you should have answers to about any franchise company that you consider joining.

Other questions will arise depending on the kind of franchise you are interested in. Make sure you follow each line of questions until you are satisfied with the answers.

Franchise Fees
What does a new franchise cost if purchased from the franchisor? _____

_____

_____

You need to know what you will receive for your franchise fee. Whether you are buying a new or an existing franchise, list the services you will receive for the franchise fee. Be specific. _____

_____

_____

What royalties (periodic fees) are payable to the franchisor and what kinds of services can the franchisee expect in return? Are these services mandated by the franchise agreement or are they offered at the discretion of the franchisor?

_____

_____

_____

Are there any ongoing fees for services in addition to the royalty obligations? If so, what are they and what do you get in return for those additional fees? _____

_____

_____

Are there any license fees in addition to the initial fees? How necessary are these to the operation of the business? How necessary are these to the profit of the business? _____

_____

_____

What advertising commitment does the franchise agreement obligate you to make? What advertising is the franchisor committing to provide? _____

_____

_____

Does the franchisor have the right to increase your advertising commitment? _____

_____

_____

If you want to sell your franchise in the future, what transfer fees will you owe the company? What rights does the franchisor have to approve or refuse your buyer? _____

_____

_____

Check which of the following the franchise company offers and which you need. Are you willing to pay the franchise fee for the services you do not need? How much do the services cost without the franchise? Compare the services you get for the franchise fee with what those services would cost without the franchise and decide whether the franchise option would be cost-effective for you. Remember: some services the franchise offers will be hard to value in dollars, but they can be very valuable to you and must be part of the equation.

Offered Need   **Cost Without the Franchise**

❏   ❏   Research and development   _____

❏   ❏   Accounting software programs   _____

❏   ❏   Advertising and marketing plans   _____

❏   ❏   Personal visits by experienced personnel _____

❏   ❏   Flexible pricing guides   _____

❏   ❏   Standardization of signage and cosmetics _____

❏   ❏   Quantity purchase discounts   _____

❏   ❏   Equipment maintenance help   _____

❏   ❏   Initial training   _____

                Other:

❏   ❏   _____   _____

❏   ❏   _____   _____

❏   ❏   _____   _____

❏   ❏   _____   _____

Total Franchise Fee _____ **Total Cost Without the Franchise** _____

The Strength of the Franchise Company

Many of these questions may be difficult to answer on your own. They will, however, be good questions to go over with your attorney before you commit to joining a franchise.

How long has the franchise been operating? _____

How long has the company on which the franchise is predicated been operating? _____

Are the original owners still part of the franchise company? Yes ❏ No ❏

Does the franchisor's financial statement show strength or weakness? Describe. _____

_____

_____

How many franchises are in existence? _____

Where are they located? _____

_____

Make arrangements to talk to the existing franchisees and find out about their success and their relationship with the franchisor. _____

_____

What kind of competitors are in the field and will it be possible to compete with them based on advertising dollars, name recognition, etc.? What effect will this competitive factor have on the survival and success of this venture?

_____

_____

What kind of lawsuits are pending against the company? What are they based on? _____

_____

How many franchises has the franchise company terminated? What were the reasons?

What Else You Need to Know

Yes	No	
❑	❑	Will the dollars or assets you have available be sufficient for you to buy the configuration or size of franchise you want?
❑	❑	Is there a real estate requirement that may take you far beyond your financial capabilities because of the money required to rent the premises?
❑	❑	Are there any items, consumables or otherwise, that the franchisee is obligated to purchase either from the franchisor or from an affiliate of the franchisor?
❑	❑	Is there a requirement for the franchisee to have a working capital reservoir? How much is required or recommended? _____
❑	❑	Is the franchise territory protected by geographical boundaries? Under what conditions, if any, is this protection subject to forfeit? _____
❑	❑	Are there any restrictions on the goods or services that the franchisee can offer? Under what circumstances does the franchisee have the right to expand? _____
		_____
		How long is the franchise agreement? _____
❑	❑	Does the franchisee have the right to renew?
❑	❑	Is there a cost on this renewal?
		What is the renewal cost? _____

SETTING THE RECORD STRAIGHT: THE FRANCHISE AND THE INDEPENDENT

There is a lot of talk on the street about doing business with independents instead of the big franchise operations. This dichotomy needs a little more definition than just an accusation or two.

Where Did the Money Come From?

Whether you start a business as an independent or as a franchise, you will need to have dollars for all the usual start-up costs. These will invariably include such standard items as rent, deposits for electricity, telephone, etc., raw material or inventory depending on the nature of the business, signage to create and extend your visibility, advertising, salaries, and the all-important money to live on until the business has passed its break-even point and can afford to pay you, the owner, a salary. And it doesn't make any difference whether you are starting an independent business or buying a franchise. One significant difference is that, as a franchisee, you would be obligated to pay an additional amount to the franchise company for the training, the general business concepts, and the privilege of using the franchise name. You might ask yourself if you would be willing to pay for that privilege or if it makes more sense to be an independent.

Paying for the Privilege

Although there are franchise names and logos that are probably worth the price, it is clear that the franchise owner must generate a lot of business in order to amortize the cost of using them. A lesser-known or less visible name might generate less sales activity, but at least the profits go to the bottom line for the owner and not to the franchisor. In other words, there is a price for everything: only a comparative analysis will show whether the payment for the privilege is worth it.

The Advertising Differential

Whatever the business, advertising is always going to be a necessary investment in your business. The franchise company spends its advertising dollar on a national level and collects these dollars from each of its franchise operations.

One interesting aspect to consider is that advertising nationally is not nearly as effective for most small businesses as advertising locally. By paying an advertising dollar to the franchise company for a national campaign, the franchise operator might actually be using his or her advertising dollar least cost-effectively. The independent will likely be able to exercise more discretion and probably use his or her advertising dollar more cost-effectively.

The Training vs. the Experience

The franchise experience usually includes a training period for which the franchise owner will be paying as part of the initial franchise package cost. The independent already has the experience in that trade or industry and doesn't need the benefit of the training.

In fact, it is usually a very short time before the franchise owner recognizes that he or she knows a good deal more about the local customer base than the national franchise, which is always taking a more generic view of the business. Who, then, in the long term is better off?

Selling the Business

One of the most interesting questions that come up long after the start-up is whether the business is worth more as a franchise or as an independent. The fact is that the same people who were originally inclined to buy a franchise instead of setting up their own shop will be the same group of prospective buyers who will look more closely at the franchise. The reason is simple. Some people have sufficient confidence in their knowledge of the business and in their own abilities to take the start-up from scratch and some people lack an appropriate understanding of the business or confidence in their ability to operate a business without supervision. This doesn't mean that one group of individuals is better suited to business than the other. It is just that the decision requires self-analysis. People in either group could be eminently successful in the long run.

The Bottom-Line Analysis

Whether you buy a franchise or an independent business, you're operating the business yourself. Your investment, your budgets, your expertise, your initiative, and your creativity are all involved. There is no greater power being exercised in the community that gives franchisees an advantage over their independent neighbors. Anyone who thinks so should shed the veil of paranoia and get back to business. The question of 'the big guys' is yet another issue, but clearly it has nothing to do with the difference between a franchise business and an independent.

CHAPTER 10

Finding the Help You Need

MANY PEOPLE HAVE A SIMILAR DREAM—to build a successful business with an income for your family and a retirement potential for your future. The problem is that each of those people carries a different set of tools with which to do the job. Some entrepreneurs have a substantial education in accounting or engineering; others have substantial capital or access to financial support. Nevertheless, if you buy an independent business instead of a franchise, you will need help with areas of the business in which you lack expertise. Chapter 8 discussed how investors and partners can support you and Chapter 9 described some of the support services franchises offer. But what if neither of these options is for you?

In this chapter, you will learn how to find, employ, and pay for the services of experts without having to buy a franchise or take on a partner. The concept of starting and building a business has been fine-tuned by franchise companies for the past 30 years. However, you can enjoy the benefits of their experience even if you do not choose to invest in a franchise.

You will always come across people who prefer to pay the ongoing franchise royalty fees for the satisfaction of having someone to turn to in the event of a problem. These people feel much more comfortable as part of a franchise family. Others are willing to pay for the experience necessary to start the project, but have the confidence to handle the day-to-day problems by themselves. These people hire an expert to aim the business at the appropriate target and then they depend on their own talents and tenacity to achieve and maintain success. The choice is yours.

Starting, building, and maintaining a successful business involves constant activity. If you have never embarked on such an adventure, keep in mind that it is attention to detail, constant supervision, and flexible creativity that make the difference between success and failure. Your attention will, of course, be diverted by family and other activities, but it is a rare moment when the business does not occupy a part of your thinking. Having other members of the team available on whose judgment you can depend for backup is important, sometimes essential. If you can find those players early in the game, you will be many steps ahead in your search for success.

THE FRANCHISE OPTION
Saving Time and Money

If you have heard about the franchise concept and like the idea that a company has already tested the consumer market for its particular product or service, understand that if you join a franchise you will pay for that experience. This kind of experience can have a very definite value. As you continue to examine the franchise concept, you may be convinced that it is worth the money to use the company's experience to find a good location, negotiate a fair lease, buy initial equipment, acquire inventory, hire and train personnel, learn the best computer technology, and understand the best media for advertising. Then you find out about the continuing royalties.

Paying the Royalty

You may be perfectly willing to pay for the expertise and knowledge of the franchise company to get started. However, owning a franchise means paying the franchise company a royalty on your gross sales every month for the life of the franchise. The continuing royalties essentially turn the franchise company into a lifelong partner, which may not be your intention.

Some franchise salespeople explain that you should think of the royalty as merely a way of paying the franchise company back for the initial training and all the extraordinary things that it does for you during the early days of the relationship. This is a pretty good argument—until you start to add up the dollars. If you are going to pay 5% of your gross sales every month for 10 years and your gross sales average about $50,000 per month, the continuing royalties will cost you $300,000 by the end of that period. That is a lot of money to pay for the expertise that the company gave you during the early days of your relationship.

Earning the Royalty

Franchise salespeople would make a more convincing argument by telling you that the franchise company continually earns the royalties you pay over the course of the franchise relationship. The company is constantly researching the best products and services for your customers, the best way to advertise the concept to new customers, and the continual upgrades of all equipment, inventory, and state-of-the-art concepts to keep you ahead of, or at least even with, the best of your competitors.

However, after a while, you will know as much about your customer base as any franchise executive. Furthermore, the trade organizations in nearly every industry can help you to keep up with the same things as the franchise, without the fee—changing customer demands, equipment innovations, advertising philosophies, and marketing techniques.

If you need additional help from attorneys, accountants, or advertising agencies, the $300,000 that you would be paying in royalties over the 10-year period could buy a good deal of independent and professional assistance. Weigh these trade-offs carefully. Maybe you will prefer the franchise support system and maybe you will want to try to save money by hiring independent consultants.

Some franchise systems actively generate the customer activity on which your business depends. For example, some use toll-free numbers in the Yellow Pages under their logo to entice potential customers to purchase from the franchise rather than an independent business. These extraordinary types of services are yet another reason you may want to consider joining a franchise.

The one substantial element that has no equal is the trade name or logo that some franchises have promoted over many years. A familiar sign or trademark can cause an immediate and positive reaction in customers all over the country. You may want to join a franchise if a recognizable logo or trade name will give you a significant edge in the market.

THE DILEMMA

The decision between getting the services a franchise offers for a relatively fixed fee and going it alone can be difficult for the average entrepreneur. You would like to have the experience of the franchise at the beginning, but don't want to continue to pay for it during your entire business life. You would like to think that you can do it alone, but you recognize the number of failures of those who also thought they could—and then couldn't.

A good franchisor will explain to you that buying a franchise is not a guarantee of success, but rather a good insurance policy against failure. The help you get at the beginning of any venture will invariably save you time, money, and aggravation down the road. But is there any way to have the best of both worlds?

Franchise companies are particularly interested in you, as an entrepreneur, because you bring to the table all the things they need for success. You bring energy, creativity, a various valuable experiences, and money to get started. Perhaps more than anything else, you bring the fear of failure and the hunger for success. The assets and characteristics you bring to the business relationship could prove successful for both you and the franchise company. However, you have other options that offer you the benefits of insider experience in your industry.

INSIDER EXPERIENCE

A franchisor may have experience at opening your kind of business. But are there any other people with similar experience? Yes.

Some people have worked for franchise companies and left for one reason or another. Some have worked with vendors or equipment manufacturers who deal with franchise companies and independents. They gain an understanding of how each business works. Some of the former employees of franchises and vendors decide to open up shops of their own. Some are successful and some are not. The reason for their success or failure usually goes back to the tools they brought to the business. Remember: knowing how to cook does not necessarily qualify you to build a successful restaurant or a successful restaurant franchise.

If you speak with former employees of equipment manufacturers, they will be quick to tell you what they know, but it is what they do not know that is worrisome. If you speak with former employees of franchise companies, it is likely that they will know the details of running the business but will not have experienced the frustrations when things don't go according to plan. Without knowing about the frustrations, you really get only a part of the picture. No one can know everything about the business. You need to consult several sources to find the most reliable information.

How Do You Find the Right Expert?

As you examine the spectrum of business activity in the marketplace, you will start to narrow down the kind of activity that is most appealing to you. You will ask many people questions about the marketplace until you eventually learn who is most successful in your industry. As you develop relationships with those people, you can begin to build a reservoir of names, hold conferences, and narrow your list to those who are most excited about working with you. The ideal situation is to find an individual with talents and experience that complement your own. If both of you are deficient in the same areas, you may enjoy working together, but you may not achieve the success you wish for the company.

Make sure the expert you find is the expert you need. Find out about his or her expertise and decide whether it represents what you need to fill the gaps in your knowledge and experience to build a successful business.

What Do the Experts Cost?

People who tell you what to do are the least expensive. Those who show you what to do are more expensive. Those who do the job with you are the most expensive; however, they are also the most cost-effective.

You will save money on the seminars and workshops—the people who tell you what to do—by going to the library or the local bookstore and browsing in the business section. The people who show you what to do are sometimes more helpful, but they may be unable to relay some subtle details, such as the difference between a good location and a bad one. If you are going to rely on the expertise of someone else, be prepared to pay for it. Remember: you will certainly be paying less than the royalties to the franchise over a 10-year period.

The most qualified experts help others find their niche and put together a business program, and they expect to be paid for their expertise. You may be quoted a package price, but this is normally an approximation of the time it will take to do the job, properly calculated at an hourly fee. Sit down with your prospective expert and discuss in detail exactly what each of you is expected to do and the time each item will take.

Most experts want to be paid for their time and expertise but are not interested in becoming your partners. If they wanted to build a business of their own, they could presumably do it without your help. Don't be discouraged or offended if experts reject your partnership offer. It is, of course, helpful to find someone willing to participate as a partner for a portion of his or her fee. A partnership brings the upfront costs of the venture to a more manageable level. On the other hand, be careful of the expert who wants to control, as well as participate.

Whatever the arrangement, make sure you can buy out your expert partner after the business gets going. Set the buyout amount at roughly the level of the deferred fees. You should, of course, determine a certain percentage increase for the time your partner has waited for his or her money. And you should certainly arrange a compensation package for the time your partner spent orchestrating the business with you after it opened, unless your partner has already been compensated for this participation. Sometimes, it is a good idea to make the expert your partner, even if only for a short time. It is not a guarantee of success, but it is a solid hedge against failure.

Has the Concept Been Successful?

One of the questions you might be curious about is whether the expert is the right person. An expert who depends on reputation for the continuity of his or her consulting business will probably not allow you to fail after taking a fee because it would put that very reputation at risk. However, you need to decide if the expert's experience is limited to a singular portion of the industry or wide enough in scope to cover all bases. Your best option is to hire someone who currently is or has recently been the owner of a business similar to the one you intend to operate.

The Expert Looking for a Job

In today's marketplace, many people with extensive experience in a particular industry are, for one reason or another, out of work. By advertising in the right media and using your own good sense about people, you might very easily find the right candidate who can be your employee and get your business started successfully. If this person turns out to be extraordinary, he or she could eventually become your partner. Be sure to read Chapter 8, which sets out the guidelines for sharing control of your business.

KEY POINTS TO REMEMBER

- Be prepared to pay for the training and education necessary to properly understand and operate your business, whether you pay a franchise company or an independent advisor.
- You can resolve the question of paying a franchise royalty by comparing the services and benefits you receive from the franchise with the cost of those same services if you remain independent.
- If you decide to use independent experts, make sure they are, indeed, experts in their fields and the experts you need.
- When you use an independent consultant, make sure the money you pay is consistent with the your needs and the quality of the advice.
- Don't discount the possibility of finding the help you need by hiring an expert as your employee; many experts are looking for employment.

Worksheet 10. How to Find the Expert Help You Need

Chapter 6 led you through some of the important research you need to conduct before you buy a business. Look over the results of your research again, because the sources and people you consulted during your research will also be the sources and people you can turn to for expert advice if you go it alone–if you choose to operate an independent business without the help of a franchise company, partner, or investor.

The following questions will help you assemble a list of experts and consultants who can provide help or advice for your business. It will also help you realize how often those times of need may arise.

Your Abilities

Describe your education and experience in the kind of business you are purchasing. _____
_____
_____

Describe the areas of your education and experience in which you feel the most confident relative to the business you are purchasing. _____
_____
_____

Your Needs

Check the following areas in which you feel you may need help:

❏ Accounting   ❏ Personnel management   ❏ Purchasing
❏ Law   ❏ Market research   Other:
❏ Advertising   ❏ Pricing   _____
❏ Selling   ❏ Research and development _____
❏ Dealing with people ❏ Inventory management   _____

Describe any of the above areas in which your need for help is great enough to warrant hiring employees to provide continual support. _____
_____
_____

Describe any of the above areas in which you do not need to hire an employee, but you are willing to seek out and pay for experts or consultants.
_____
_____
_____
_____

Your Sources of Help

Refer again to the purchase research you conducted with the help of Worksheet 6.2.

List any people or sources who may be helpful in the above areas.
_____
_____
_____

Look at the areas in which you acknowledge you need expert help. List them here and describe the sources of help to whom you will turn to satisfy your needs.

- _____ : _____
  _____
- _____ : _____
  _____
- _____ : _____
  _____
- _____ : _____
  _____

GETTING THE ADVICE THAT COUNTS

Be careful about seeking and using generic advice when you need help with your business.

What Worked for Someone Else Might Not Be Your Answer

Conventional wisdom and standard answers will rarely solve your business problems, since the symptoms of a problem can often be the result of any of a myriad of underlying causes. The only way to know the causes is through analyzing the problem. You can't do it by guessing or by using one of the canned approaches. Every business is different in some ways. Trying to use a method of solving a problem that some other company used may be disastrous if your business is different enough to warrant an entirely different approach.

Digging for the Problem

The surface of a problem is often just that—merely the surface. To find out the source of a problem could be considerably more difficult than just noticing that there is one. In order to dig deeper to get to the source, you need a helpmate who can recognize the differences. Sometimes, this is someone in the company. Sometimes, it is someone who understands the nature of the industry you're in. And, under many circumstances, it is someone who has had the experience of dealing with problems of various sorts, someone who can see 'the forest for the trees' and not get bogged down with the day-to-day operational details.

Dollars and Cents

Even the financial aspects of a company are often addressed by standard approaches. Sometimes, it's a good idea to have 'new eyes' review the situation. Often, even the best in-house financial minds tend to see what they expect and to expect no more than they see. A fresh look might inquire about items on your profit and loss statement that no one has chosen to question in a long time. Don't ever be embarrassed at having to answer the questions—"What's that?" and "What's this?" It will certainly force you to examine things that you haven't looked at in a long time. Remember: time and circumstance in business should be a constant change. You've got to understand that looking from the outside can often reveal better insights than looking at the same things in the same way over and over again. Don't be afraid to take a critical, objective look at your business periodically.

The Simplest Things of All

In examining 'the big picture,' be careful not to exclude the simplest things of all. Are your counter people or your salespeople making the most of their opportunities when dealing with customers? You might have had a spectacular training program, but has it gotten stale? Does it need another look? And what about your design or manufacturing process? Has it reached the point where doing it the same way is wasting time … and costing money? It may be time to have an expert take that objective look to see if you're functioning in the most cost-effective way.

Don't be afraid to find something that can be corrected. Better to find it now than to examine it later, as one of the reasons why the business didn't do so well this year—or, worse yet, as one of the reasons why you are considering filing for bankruptcy, when a little warning could have saved the company.

The Ultimate Advice

There are, of course, different levels of sophisticated advice. It may be borrowing money in order to avoid an expected shortfall in sales. It may be investing to allow the company to expand by acquisition as the smartest way to accelerate your growth in the marketplace. These are the kinds of things that the average entrepreneur dreams of during the night but can't find the time to address during the day. Getting a third party to examine these dream-list items can often be the best advice you ever received. And remember: you don't have to follow someone else's suggestions—but it's a good idea to know what they are so you can make the choice.

CHAPTER 11

Don't Let Your First Mistake Be Your Last

BUYERS FACE MANY DECISIONS AS THEY research and search for a suitable business. The chapters in Part II are intended to point out some of the important issues you, as a buyer, need to consider, such as choosing your market niche, valuing the various parts of a business, and possibly sharing control with investors, partners, or a franchise company. If you are like many Americans whose job security has evaporated, you may be looking at business ownership to replace the uncertainty of your employment future. You may not have the time to research a new business venture carefully.

This chapter is largely devoted to cautioning those buyers who may be excited or otherwise emotional about buying a business. Beginning such a venture without proper forethought, research, and professional counsel is dangerous. In this chapter, you will find horror stories and success stories—and more than one word of caution.

FEELING THE PRESSURE

Many people look for a business because they can't find a job. Most people don't want to talk about it and are embarrassed to disclose their plight to others. They don't want to face the real-ity of being another statistic. If you are ready to face that reality, this chapter is for you.

People may say to you, "I know how you feel," when, in fact, they don't know how you feel at all. They try to empathize with your traumatic situation and it is comforting because it is an expression of caring. When it gets down to it, however, they really don't know how you feel. Nobody does!

In today's economy, you are not alone in experiencing these types of hardships. Many people are in line at the unemployment office. Some people walk away from lengthy careers because their jobs are eliminated. Maybe the jobs went to other countries, to younger workers, or to computers. If you have faced a similar situation, you know that the most difficult part of the problem is going home to break the news to your spouse and family with the prospect of no longer being able to fulfill their dreams and expectations. It can be a devastating experience.

The experience of losing your job can be so devastating that you may want to take more control of your employment future by going into business for yourself. Many of you are reading this book for that reason. However, you need to be careful that your fears and anxieties about being unemployed do not cloud your good business sense. Take the story of John Rayburn, for example.

Illustration 11.1 Latching onto the First Good-Sounding Idea

John Rayburn was out of a job. One day he took his son out for hitting practice at a baseball center. They had a good time. Afterwards, he was convinced that this was the business opportunity of a lifetime.

He immediately got in touch with the owner and asked him if he would be interested in opening a baseball center in another state, 3,000 miles away. The owner would participate with John in some way in the new venture. The owner was delighted to be of service. He understood just how to open a center and was anxious to participate.

John asked to see the owner's books and records to get an idea of the profit potential. The owner said he would be happy to share this information with him—for a fee of $2,000. "After all," he said, "I wouldn't want to share this information with just anyone who was merely curious." John called his attorney for advice and his attorney advised him not to look at the books and records for $2,000. It would not take John very far toward understanding the business and, if he paid $2,000 for every peek at financial records, he would be broke before he found the business that suited him best.

After John had done some initial research on his own and considered more seriously the prospect of purchasing a business, he contacted a franchise company selling a similar business. They had a good deal of financial and other important information in their disclosure document. He then discussed the matter with vendors who served baseball centers. They shared some cost and profit factors and solicited John to become a customer of theirs when he opened his business.

John asked the baseball center owner if he would be interested in helping John set up the business in the distant state, for a fee. The owner was very interested and told John that he would do it for $10,000, as soon as John found the appropriate location and signed a lease. $10,000 might be a perfectly appropriate figure for the consulting effort on which the owner was about to embark; however, one of the keys to most businesses of this type is location. For John, a newcomer to the business, to pick the location without the more experienced owner's help was foolhardy. John needed more expert advice than he could get from the baseball center owner.

Fortunately, John asked some competitors for advice and found out how important location is to a baseball center. He did not pay the owner the consultation fee, but rather sought an independent consultant for help in choosing the site for his center.

A potential partner or consultant should understand the importance his or her input has at every stage of the buying process. If the potential partner or consultant doesn't understand the importance of choosing something like a good location, you definitely need to find a new consultant.

Kathy Dixon, in the illustration below, learned the value of consulting a professional when buying a business she really wanted.

Illustration 11.2 Unable to Let Go

Kathy Dixon was enjoying a cup of coffee and a cinnamon bun at a local shopping mall. In a discussion with the owner, who was retiring due to illness, Kathy indicated an interest in the business. The pursuit was on. As the conversation got more serious, Kathy was wise enough to discuss the matter with her professionals. Several facts came up during negotiations that should have been danger signals to any buyer.

- The business was a franchise and the franchise company wanted Kathy's mother's and father's signatures on the final documents to ensure payment of the franchise royalties for the next 10 years.

- The franchise company wanted a $3,000 transfer fee for changing ownership on its books and records.

- A competitor–a donut shop–was opening right across the walkway, a fact the landlord and seller neglected to mention.

- The landlord wanted a higher rent to sign a new lease.

- The income of the business had fallen in the last 12 months.

By the time these items were factored into the financial paperwork that the seller gave to Kathy, it became very clear that the business was not profitable and its future was doubtful. If it were not for her accountant, who pointed all these things out to her, she would have bought it. She was so enamored of the business concept that she was temporarily blinded to the realities of the bottom line.

Listen to Good Advice

If you are so involved with a business idea that you cannot make an objective decision, find someone who can lend some objectivity to your decision-making process or you will regret your haste and lack of caution. Getting involved in a business about which you know nothing may seem like an exciting idea, but it's likely a disaster waiting to happen—and the worst part is that you may never know why the disaster happened.

Listening to a good friend who merely wants to be encouraging can be a big mistake. It's your money at risk, not your friend's. Someone who pats you on the back and tells you what a great salesperson you are, when you are not a great salesperson, is not doing you any favors. Your insincere friend is, in fact, doing you a great disservice.

Business owners who tell you what a joy it is to relax in your own shop and wait for the customers to come through the door, but do not tell you of the terrible frustration when they don't, are also not doing you any favors. These people may have the best motives and they may, in their particular businesses, enjoy waiting

for the customers to roll through the door. But every business is different, every location is different, and every year is different. Don't be taken in by a singular description of success. You cannot afford to be wrong.

Talk with a number of people in the industry in which you are interested. Read some trade journals and find out what the success-failure ratio is and why. Find out how locating in different areas around the country can affect a business.

For example, a fast-food company had substantial success in operating in malls and on well-trafficked streets. The company decided to open up in drive-in movie theaters. It seemed like a good idea at the time, but it turned out to be a disaster. Even businesses with successful experience behind them can be wrong.

Be careful about the advice you receive and the motives behind the advice. Be especially careful about your own analysis and judgment. Your knowledge about a particular industry may be sorely deficient, but you can study the industry and become familiar enough to develop a basic understanding. Your instincts as a consumer are probably as good as anyone else's, providing you don't let yourself be swayed by an overdose of self-indulgence or self-doubt.

Take the Time to Think It Over

Time can be very persuasive. Some people will claim that if you don't take advantage of a given opportunity immediately, you will lose it forever. Sometimes it is true that if you don't catch a wave at its crest, you will miss a singular chance. However, you can make an equally convincing argument that if it is a good idea today, it will be a good idea tomorrow. And you may add that if it isn't a good idea tomorrow, then it wasn't meant to be.

Those who insist a business transaction must be done today often have suspect motives. For example, a franchise salesperson might like to make a quota by month's end and an owner may want to get out of a dying industry before losing any more money.

Good judgments are not made under time pressure. Yes, it is often a good idea to expedite your decision making and not waste time. But gathering the information to make a carefully calculated judgment is much more important than making the decision today just because someone says you should. Let the opportunity go rather than find out after it is too late that the investment was a bad one. You can afford to let many good opportunities go by but you can't afford the bad one you chose to take.

CHECK ON YOUR AVAILABLE TOOLS

Before you jump into owning a business, capitalize on the talents, experience, and dollars you have available. You may find it very difficult to recognize the talents you have, but it is often more difficult to recognize the talents you don't have. If you have never operated your own business, don't make the assumption that managing all the daily details is easy. It is not, particularly for someone who has never done it. However, don't base your decision to buy a business on whether you can manage every aspect of it yourself. You can find people to perform the tasks you cannot, providing you recognize the need for them and have the dollars to pay for them. Keep this analysis in mind.

As you discuss with your accountant or attorney the possibility of buying a business, he or she will invariably ask you questions about your abilities and inclinations. Many businesses require a substantial selling effort to keep up with the competition. If you are not experienced in sales and, worse yet, if you don't really like this kind of customer interrelationship, don't pretend to yourself or anyone else that you can do it. Deception of others is bad; self-deception is much worse.

To find out which skills you have and which you lack, speak with those who know you best and who will give you an honest perspective. Remember: this may be the most important decision you make for many years. Don't let anything stand in the way of putting together your best information about the venture and about your talent and experience.

Educate Yourself First

Most businesses do not have anything unique about them. If you can duplicate some of the basic concepts of a business after careful examination, you may also be able to duplicate the success of that business. This learning process involves a good deal of self-education. People go through it all the time, particularly entrepre-

neurs. Many aspects of owning your own business cannot be learned in school, but only through experience and observation.

For example, many businesses are transported to other countries by foreign businesspeople. They copy what they see in the United States and duplicate equipment configurations in their own countries without the permission or involvement of the original sources, despite the attempts of international copyright laws to protect certain designs, logos, trade names, and formats. You can consider copying what you see—aside from the privileged protections just mentioned—to learn about the methodology of any given business. It is all part of the entrepreneurial exercise.

A businessperson learns every day from his or her competitors. Anyone who doesn't recognize what competitors are doing or what the innovations in a given industry represent is not doing his or her job. You have an obligation to examine every aspect of the business you intend to enter before you accept the challenge. Ask questions, take pictures, examine marketing materials, and interview personnel when possible—these tasks are all part of the process necessary for you to make an educated decision.

Giving yourself an education through firsthand research and observation has a cost—the biggest of which is the time it takes. However, you cannot decide to go into business for yourself without investing the necessary time. That's called paying for the education!

WHEN YOUR MONEY WON'T BUY THE DREAM YOU WANT

You often look at a car because the advertising suggested that it was within your price range. When you get to the dealership, the dealer tells you about all the extras that you thought were standard and the price rises well beyond your original intentions. The dealer then tells you how you can fit the payment schedule within your family budget and you end up buying the car. If you are in the market for a house and give your budget parameters to your real estate broker, you will invariably be looking at homes just beyond your original intentions. Once you have seen the upgrades, it is difficult to accept something less for your family. Besides, the broker will tell you that you can meet the payments because they will stay the same as your income rises. This might have been true years ago, but it is less so today.

You cannot allow yourself to be tempted beyond your means when you are buying a business. You cannot fit the purchase of a business within your budget. The business is your budget! You will be taking whatever reservoir of cash you have and investing in a business for the very purpose of generating a family income. You must have enough for the investment required by the seller and to establish a working capital fund to sustain the business during its formative stages. You must have enough for emergency purposes based on the nature of the business. Your emergency fund must accommodate the loss of big customers or seasonal lapses in business. You must also have enough to handle family emergencies. You are not buying a material thing; you are buying a life source. You cannot stretch it beyond the maximum capabilities of your financial portfolio.

When your money won't buy the dream you want, change the dream! Put a little reality in your life. Buy a business that fits. You can always piggyback on success. If the business works, you can expand it or buy another. You can sell it at a profit and buy something else, perhaps even the one you couldn't afford in the first place. Failure, on the other hand, doesn't afford you those prerogatives. Don't be taken in by the promise of a dream. Start with your reality and build the dream from there.

FULL DISCLOSURE FOR BOTH HUSBAND AND WIFE

Why should a business book be discussing the relationship between husband and wife? Indeed, in certain cultures, such a discussion would be offensive. In modern American society, however, where both spouses are involved in family expenditures and where, in many cases, both spouses are responsible for the generation of the family income, any discussion that excludes the subject of husband and wife would surely be lacking in reality. Whether it is the husband, wife, or significant other who decides to embark on entrepreneurship, the decision will certainly affect the entire family in both the short term and the long term.

One spouse may find it difficult to candidly discuss the personality deficiencies of the other, yet this type of candid discussion is essential to making an informed business decision. You may find it problematical to compare what the individual prefers with what the family needs. Some businesses can easily be operated by an individual. More likely, however, the business will require the attention of both husband and wife. It will require actual time involvement and constant analysis and decision making. In all cases, you can be sure, the business venture will not be completely divorced from the daily routine and involvement of the family.

Franchisors usually insist on meeting both spouses, even when the stated intention is that only one will be involved in the business. They know that the purchase of the business will invariably affect the family unit. It is normal for any seller of a business to be interested in meeting the buyer's spouse. This is particularly true if the seller is taking back a note for a portion of the purchase price.

You must set aside many of the communication problems that may exist in your marriage and create a new communication that allows the involvement, to one degree or another, of your spouse. In many cases, the necessary documents require the signature of both spouses. Certainly, the signatory will be interested in the significance of signing and the potential impact, both good and bad, of the new involvement. You might not come to a perfect agreement, but make sure that both of you at least understand the basic issues involved in buying a business.

MAKING THE HARD COMPARISONS AND THE HARDER JUDGMENTS

Buying a business at age 25 is not the same as buying one at 65. A car wash or a chimney-sweeping business requires more physical energy than a tax consultancy. One of the interesting parts of growing older is that the mind still thinks the body can handle tasks that it really can't. Make sure you understand the physical requirements and are capable of fulfilling them. Self-deception in this area can be devastating.

Before you embark on your adventure, you will have to make several decisions—whether to buy an existing business or to start a similar venture from scratch, whether to buy a franchise or a nonfranchise, and how much money you can really afford to invest while still keeping an emergency fund available. While deciding on the most appropriate business venture for yourself and your family, make a list of all the questions that need answers. Ask yourself questions about dollars you have available and talents you bring to the business. Most importantly, put on the list those things that frighten you, all the unknowns that seem to generate your biggest concerns.

KEY POINTS TO REMEMBER

- Don't let someone talk you into a business venture who has an ulterior motive—like a commission.

- Don't let your emotions lead you toward an investment that does not use your particular talents and experience. It can be fun, but it can also be dangerous.

- Examine the obvious and not-so-obvious elements of the business as you do your preliminary examination.

- Meet with your spouse and family members to ensure that everyone knows the implications of time, energy, and money required for your new business venture.

- When you can't afford to buy your dream business, change your dream!

Worksheet 11. A Pre-Purchase Self-Analysis

The following checklists will help you identify pressures and concerns that you may not recognize in yourself, but that can adversely affect your future business success.

Your Ability to Take Advice

Often, the best way to avoid mistakes is to listen to the good advice of family, friends, and professionals. If you check Yes for any of the following, you may have trouble accepting advice. Again, you may need to consider stepping back from your pursuit of a business venture and consider your qualifications as a businessperson before you put your and your family's future at risk.

Yes No

- ❑ ❑ Do you have difficulty maintaining objectivity about a business idea?
- ❑ ❑ Do you have difficulty candidly discussing your abilities and inadequacies with others?
- ❑ ❑ Do you find it difficult to take advice from professional advisors, such as lawyers or accountants?
- ❑ ❑ Do you find it difficult to find people on whose opinions you can rely?
- ❑ ❑ Do you have a hard time giving up short-term goals to achieve long-term success?
- ❑ ❑ Do you and your spouse have a difficult time communicating your fears and anxieties?

If you checked Yes to any of the above, you may find success at business ownership difficult to attain. Describe how you will deal with business problems that you cannot handle yourself. Be specific. _____

_____

_____

_____

Business Pressure

If you check Yes for any of the following, you need to consider taking a step back from the pressures and anxieties you feel about your financial and career future before you decide to buy a business. Making any investment under pressure is dangerous—buying a business under pressure can be devastating.

Yes No

- ❑ ❑ Have you lost your job and can't find another?
- ❑ ❑ Have you been forced to take a position at a lower salary?
- ❑ ❑ Are you in jeopardy of losing your job?

❏ ❏   Is your job subject to replacement by equipment or computer?

❏ ❏   Are your family needs increasing while your income remains the same?

❏ ❏   Have you been forced to liquidate hard assets to maintain your standard of living?

❏ ❏   Can you see your remaining cash and assets eroding as time goes on?

❏ ❏   Are you at an age where finding a new job is difficult because younger people are just as well schooled or just as experienced as you?

❏ ❏   Have you failed to establish any kind of retirement plan?

❏ ❏   Is your job so frustrating that it is affecting your health?

❏ ❏   Do you feel that it is almost too late to change the course of your life?

If you checked Yes to any of the above, you may feel pressured into buying a business to salvage your career or your financial future. Describe how you will prevent these pressures from causing you to overextend your financial resources or jump into an investment without having done the proper research ahead of time. Be specific.

_____

_____

_____

DO YOU REALLY WANT TO OWN A BUSINESS?

How many times have you heard a corporate employee say, "I'm tired of having to answer to my boss"? One comment that often follows is "She doesn't know what really goes on in the trenches." And the next comment is not particularly unusual: "If I owned my own business, I wouldn't have to answer to anyone!"

The Ultimate Boss

It is certainly no secret that the president of a good-sized company will usually answer to his or her board of directors. If the company has not yet reached that stature, the president will certainly be responsible to his or her investors, the people whose money has made the company possible. And if there are no directors and no investors looking over his or her shoulder, the president of the company will surely be responsive to the competitive marketplace—to the ultimate consumer, the customer. The fact of the matter is that there is no business that doesn't require responding to someone else. It is a good lesson to learn early on in business.

Advice Is Not a Mandate, but ...

Although the prerogative of an entrepreneur is to make the final decision on most matters, it is certainly good form, if not usually appropriate, to follow the advice of the people you hire. You've presumably brought them on board for the expertise they've developed, so to make contrary decisions in the face of their advice would seem foolhardy. All business decisions should be based on the best professional and experiential advice available. If you think you'd be better advised to follow your instincts rather than the experience of the marketplace, conventional wisdom would probably suggest you're not ready to become the entrepreneur. Remember: the entrepreneur is not merely a person with an idea; it's a person who can carry the idea to fruition, make it work.

At Least I'll Have a "Normal" Working Day

Unfortunately, this statement also represents a fallacy often mistaken for truth by the owner of a new business. The eight-hour day is a nonexistent concept for the entrepreneur. The five-day week is equally ill conceived. The owner usually gets to the business before anyone else and leaves last. The paperwork, for which there is no time during the busy day, is often left for the weekend when the phone stops ringing and time becomes available.

But the "Bottom-Line Profit" Is Mine

You bet! And that's why your incentive to work longer and harder than anyone else keeps you after the business day ends and after the business week is over. If the bottom line is positive, it's yours. But remember: if the bottom line is negative, this is also yours.

If all of this is true, why would you want to own your own business?!

The Equity Analysis

As you build the business, you will periodically ask, "What is this business worth?" Essentially, this means that if you wanted to or needed to sell the business, your hard work may have built something that can be conveyed to others, a business that can be converted to a passive income for you. If someone in your family has shown a proclivity for the business or an inclination to take it over, it may be transitioned to him or her. It may continue in the face of your inability to maintain the reins. In other words, it may actually have developed a life of its own without being dependent on your expertise, time, and energy. Not every business is capable of existing independently, but many are and many can be created and built to do just that.

The Ultimate Potential

The value of a business often exists outside the energy of the owner. It is often a piece to a puzzle that another company can use. As a result, it is often the subject of a merger or an acquisition by a bigger company in the same or a similar industry. Keep this in mind as you invest your energies in building your own business. It might be a very good idea for today and, sometimes, an even better idea for tomorrow.

The Seller's Perspective

CHAPTER 12

Your Retail Business and How to Package It

AS YOU PREPARE YOUR BUSINESS FOR SALE, you need to look at the component parts of a small business, as your buyer will, and learn to stress what is most appealing to a potential buyer. To accomplish these two tasks, you need to know your business and know your buyer.

Part II discussed a buyer's motivations, financing options, and negotiating postures. This chapter teaches you to look at your business objectively and to be prepared with the right answers to buyer questions—the answers that help you procure a successful sale right up to the last payment on the note. An extensive worksheet at the end of the chapter will help you analyze your business, its competition, location, and growth potential, and prepare you to answer buyer questions.

The most successful sellers exercise every effort to make their business show a strong operating profit, right up to the last minute. Remember: the size of your asking price will depend in large part on the profit your business shows. Anything you can do to maximize your business' profit, within legitimate parameters, is a must.

Packaging your business to make the most effective presentation requires you to compare your business with other businesses and franchises. You need to look at your customers, com-

petition, location, lease, and growth potential. Finally, you need to know how your business looks on paper and at the negotiating table.

THE FRANCHISE COMPARISON
Speak Well of Your Franchise

If your business is a franchise, talk about the positive aspects of the franchise relationship. Describe the various services the franchisor provides, such as the following:

- Initial training;
- Ongoing support—equipment maintenance, financial help, marketing techniques;
- Local or national advertising;
- Research and development;
- National pricing for equipment and products; or
- Competitive guidelines, including pricing guides and product recommendations.

Although there are some rare exceptions to the general rule, most franchise contracts allow you to sell your business, but only if it is sold as a franchise. Because you cannot convert your franchise to an independent business, your buyer will have to take over your relationship with the franchisor; therefore, you want to speak well of your franchisor and extol the virtues of the franchise relationship, even if your particular franchise falls somewhat short of the ideal parent company. Most unhappy situations are due to the personalities involved and not to the concept of the franchise system itself. Whether this is true in your case or not, market reality dictates that you sell the franchise system along with the franchise. Legal realities, however, also dictate that you not misrepresent the facts. For example, if the franchise company is bankrupt or no longer serving the franchisees, you need to disclose that information.

Offset the Franchise Advantages

If your business is not a franchise, then offset some of the franchise advantages. Tell potential buyers about alternative ways to obtain the same benefits as a franchisee without the franchise. If the franchisor knows how to market and advertise, then why can't you? Franchises do not possess any magic formulas for successful advertising. Your buyer can access plenty of independent services, such as maintenance, financial, and marketing services. They provide the same security as a franchise, and because they are local, they will likely be more easily accessible and better oriented to your particular customer base.

Franchises do not have a monopoly on successful pricing guides either. You can easily compare the pricing guides prepared by the franchises because franchises often distribute their price lists to customers as advertising material. You can also determine a franchise's standard price markup by making a random price sampling of wholesale prices from vendors and retail prices from competitors. Why spend the time, money, and energy to develop the same formula that the franchise companies use? The pricing guides are normally not copyrighted, and if they are, the basic content can usually be changed sufficiently to avoid any legal problems and still maintain their utility and purpose. You will know if something is copyrighted if the copyright legend appears on the first page of the material itself. The real value is in the numbers, not the format, and computations cannot be protected.

Always suggest that your buyer consult the trade organization in your particular industry. Trade organizations are geared to help newcomers to the industry. They would like to contribute to your success, and they usually have access to all the information sources you need.

A GOOD CUSTOMER MIX

Discuss your customer base with your buyer. What kinds of customers constitute a good mix for your business? Which are more profitable, and what kind of mix do you have? You know all about your customer, but does your buyer? You do not need to go through your invoices one by one and explain the nature of every sale, but you may want to give potential buyers a general view of four or five basic customer groups.

You can, of course, isolate a myriad of customer categories, from hospitals to universities, poets and songwriters to apartment property managers, from doctors, lawyers, and real estate brokers to city employees, travelers, and retirees. See how these types of customers fit into your particular industry.

Categories may change dramatically as you move from an urban marketplace to a suburban marketplace. As a seller, you need to explain your particular customer complex to interested buyers. Tell them about your customers in the most favorable light to the future of the business. Providing a general view of your customers will help the sale whether you are dealing with a knowledgeable buyer or a novice. Your buyer needs to know how to advertise to your customers, serve them, and get them to return to buy your particular service or product.

WHAT IS YOUR COMPETITION?

Defining your competition is always an interesting process. To begin with, examine the question in its simplest form.

Question: "What is your competition like?"

Answer: "Well, there are a lot of people in my industry, but I don't really consider any of them competitors. My product (or service) is so much better (or different) that I am really in a different class than the others in the marketplace."

How many times has this been the answer from the entrepreneur? Nearly always, and it is nearly always wrong.

For example, if you are selling tacos, you are in competition, to some extent, with anyone who is selling food. You are clearly in competition with another shop that also sells tacos. Yet, some taco sellers deny even this. If you sell primarily tacos, and someone else merely has tacos as an item on their otherwise diverse menu, are you in competition? This question is difficult to answer without some further analysis.

To say two shops selling primarily tacos are in competition is basic. The better taco will put the bad taco out of business. Or will it? If it is a good taco in a dirty taco restaurant, will it? If it is a good taco in a location that is difficult to find or impossible to park near, will it? If it is a taco served by an ill-groomed or impolite counter person, will it? If the ambiance is unappealing to the customer, will it? How can such a simple marketing question turn out to be such a strangling competitive analysis? And you are not nearly through with the problem.

If you are selling primarily tacos and you are near a shop that has tacos on its menu as one item among many other food choices, you may actually have a competitive advantage rather than a problem with competition. After all, the shop that deals with a specialty item might have a market advantage in many ways. The specialty shop is not trying to be all things to all people. It is looking for a market niche. It can afford to offer a variety of tacos that meet the taste of a large number of taco connoisseurs as well as those who like to reach out for a new taco flavor. It can target its advertising and marketing dollars to a more designated consumer audience. A focused product can more easily generate cost-effective advertising.

Now, what if tacos were tennis shoes? You can see that the question is not about food at all. The question is about business! Potential buyers of your business will want to know what kind of competition you have and how they can carve a niche to become the unique product or service in the marketplace.

Location and Lease

You will need to discuss your lease with potential buyers, particularly its terms and options to renew, if any. You may encounter so many buyer questions relating to lease and location that it is possible to expose you to only a few here.

Rent

For example, your buyer will want to know the terms for any rent increase. Are rent increases for any option period subject to a formula or merely to negotiation at the time the option is exercised? What if the landlord sells the building and the business must deal with a new landlord? How relevant are prices per square foot of comparable rental space within the same market area? Are you prepared to discuss this with your buyer? You should be.

You should also be prepared to discuss whether there will be rent increases during the term and what effect, if any, an increase is likely to have on your profit picture. Is there a percentage rent of any kind involved? How does this relate to gross sales or net profit? Do you understand the Consumer Price Index (CPI), how it affects your annual rental obligation, and the concept of putting a cap (maximum) on the CPI if it is pertinent to your lease and option terms? Are you familiar with expressions such as triple net lease? If it applies to your lease, you ought to be prepared to discuss it with your buyer.

What about the buyer who says: "I have a ten-year purchase money promissory note to pay to you (the seller) for the business, but I only have a lease (including options) for six years. What happens if I lose the premises?" This is not a particularly unique scenario, and you must be prepared to handle this type of concern. The answer is that a business venture is not normally designed to terminate at the expiration date of its initial lease term. The termination of a lease is a business problem your buyer should expect to deal with at some point in the life of the business.

Protective Clauses in the Lease

Are there any protective clauses that preclude certain types of business in the lessor's business complex? The buyer is certainly entitled to know, for example, if the landlord can rent to a similar business in the same complex in which your business is located. How much harm would your quick printing business suffer if a landlord allows a nearby tenant to sell photocopies? How much harm would your hamburger business suffer if a nearby tenant is allowed to sell tacos? What kind of protection is afforded?

Are there any clauses that allow the lessor to terminate the lease due to a pending sale or other unilateral reasons? It is not unusual to see leases where the landlord has a right to cancel on six month's notice for any reason, or without any reason. The landlord's right to cancel on short notice does not give the buyer very much security and could, conceivably, end your sale negotiations. Here are some other questions you need to be prepared for:

- Is the facility expandable for increased business over the years?
- Is it possible for the business to acquire the building?
- Do you have an option to buy or a right of first refusal? Do you understand the difference between the two?

Parking

In addition to knowing your lease, you will also need to address the parking situation around your business. For instance, what kind of parking is available, and what is the demand for parking in your particular business and by your particular customer? Be prepared to explain how parking is handled in your particular case.

Negotiating your lease and location may bring up hundreds of issues. Which issues become points of contention depends on your particular lease and how it could affect your buyer over the years. You must, realistically, be prepared to discuss all these aspects with the buyer. Lease and location are key factors involved in the purchase of a retail business.

Growth Potential

You may want to research your business's growth potential to make the buyer feel more secure about your knowledge of the business marketplace, and to give the buyer a better, more knowledgeable, and more positive perspective from which to examine your business. You can obtain market information from a variety of sources: the local chamber of commerce; building and zoning departments of your city or town; national statistics put out by the U.S. government; magazines or pamphlets published by your city; and trade publications carrying all kinds of statistical evaluations of the industry, the competition, and prospects for future growth.

Create a Selling Portfolio

Finally, put the information you have researched and prepared into a selling portfolio, or business plan, to give to each buying candidate.

If you are able, you may also want to look at the sales presentations the more professional franchise sales departments create. They have some interesting approaches you can use in your selling portfolio. You never really know which little piece of the presentation will prompt the buyer or his or her spouse to make the purchase. Remember: small businesses are often family businesses, and spouses, children, or parents are likely to be involved in the negotiation for the purchase of such a venture. Be prepared to tailor your presentations and negotiations to involve such intimate members of the buyer's negotiating team.

Husband and wife represent the tightest partnership of all. As you look to your own experience, you certainly recognize that the opinion of your spouse was a significant factor in any decision-making process. Sometimes, the location or customer base may be unimportant to one spouse, but of particular significance to the other. With the participating spouse in mind, it is essential that you use every selling concept you can think of in presenting your business. Make sure, if you can, that you are speaking at some point with both husband and wife. After all, if you were selling to a partnership, you would certainly want to speak with all the partners to ensure that you did not leave important questions unanswered.

Remember: the real purpose of the exercise is to find a buyer who wants to take this business opportunity as his or her new way of life—with the best equity realization for the seller.

KEY POINTS TO REMEMBER

- If your business is a franchise, make sure the buyer understands the advantages the franchise family offers.
- If your business is not a franchise, explain to the buyer the many sources in the business commu-

nity from which the buyer may duplicate the franchise benefits and services.

■ Create a selling portfolio that extols the benefits of the business and explains to the buyer about the growth potential he or she can anticipate.

■ Your buyer will be very interested in your prem-

ises lease. Be sure you understand all its intricacies so that you can answer the buyer's questions.

■ Your buyer knows the importance of the business's customer base. Be prepared to discuss this aspect of your business in great detail if the buyer inquires about it.

Worksheet 12. How to Prepare for Buyer Questions

These are questions your buyer will be asking. This worksheet will help prepare you to answer them.

Competition

Can your customers avoid using your product or service by obtaining it from another source? Yes ❏ No ❏

What kind of competition exists in your marketplace? _____

_____

_____

Is the competition a new aspect in the marketplace or has it been there long enough for you to recognize and understand its impact on your business? _____

_____

_____

Do you consider the competition a healthy factor? (Does it broaden the product or service visibility?) Yes ❏ No ❏

Depending on your answer, how will you explain the value of your business competition to potential buyers?

_____

_____

_____

Is there room in the marketplace for additional competition and will it substantially affect your business positively or negatively? _____

_____

_____

Is there a niche that you or your buyer can create that will minimize the impact of additional or existing competition?

_____

_____

_____

Is there any equipment or inventory source that would give your business a better competitive edge? Yes ❏ No ❏

If you answered Yes, describe it as you would to your potential buyers and explain how they could acquire it.

_____

_____

If you answered No, describe how and why you know you are as competitive as possible. _____

_____

_____

Location and Lease

Explain the appropriateness of your location to the business's future growth. _____

_____

Explain the competitiveness of your lease in the following categories.

Cost: _____

_____

Length: _____

_____

Options: _____

_____

Parking: _____

_____

Space: _____

_____

Expansion: _____

_____

Growth Potential

Describe how changes in the following categories might affect your business's growth potential.

Customer needs/tastes: _____

_____

Acquisition of a competitor: _____

_____

New equipment or concepts on the horizon: _____

_____

New products or services on the horizon: _____

_____

How to Determine Your Customer Base

If you have a noncash business:
Examine your invoices to determine how much your average customer spends in total and how much per purchase.

Customer	**Total Purchases**	**Dollars Spent per Purchase**
_____	$_____	$_____

Customer	Total Purchases	Dollars Spent per Purchase
_____	$_____	$_____
_____	$_____	$_____
_____	$_____	$_____
_____	$_____	$_____

Examine your invoices to determine the quality and quantity of the items purchased.

Customer	Item Purchased	Amount Purchased
_____	_____	_____
_____	_____	_____
_____	_____	_____
_____	_____	_____
_____	_____	_____

If possible, assess how much time per dollar purchased you or your staff spend with each customer.

Customer	Time Spent with Customer	Amount Spent
_____	_____	$_____
_____	_____	$_____
_____	_____	$_____
_____	_____	$_____
_____	_____	$_____

If you have a cash business:
1. Follow your customer base by examining inventory.
2. Question your staff relative to the categories listed above.
3. Ask your customers to fill out cards or respond to questionnaires, including:
   - The products or services with which they are pleased or displeased,
   - The relationship they have with your personnel, and
   - Whether you should increase or decrease your inventory on certain items.

The Franchise Alternative

If you are not a franchisee:

What franchise-type facilities or advantages, if any, could you avail yourself of? _____
_____
_____

Do these advantages supplement your own capabilities or duplicate them? _____
_____
_____

In your industry, what buying advantages (quantity-purchase advantages), if any, exist in a franchise relationship?

_____

_____

_____

How significant are franchises as competitors in your industry? _____

_____

_____

If you are a franchisee:

What services does your franchisor provide and how valuable are they? _____

_____

_____

How much would it cost to obtain those services without the franchise? _____

_____

_____

Describe the experience of being part of a franchise family and its value to you as an entrepreneur. _____

_____

_____

_____

BUILDING YOUR BUSINESS FOR THE FUTURE

Although survival is the highest-priority plateau in business, with success trailing not so far behind, people go into business for many different reasons. Some people have always dreamed of being completely independent from the corporate environment. A business of their own is the fulfillment of that dream. Other people go into business because a job is not available in their particular field, for any of a variety of reasons, which include tightening corporate budgets, innovative equipment that eliminates the need for humans, and outsourcing of manufacturing and assembly outside the country.

Young people without adequate experience and older people without adequate education have become secondary choices in the corporate job market. Interestingly, all the reasons make little difference. The fact is that small businesses have been opportunities for those creative people, young and old, for whom corporations no longer offer sufficient opportunities. The increase of these small businesses has been nothing less than phenomenal.

Recognizing the Goals

If you're operating a business, you probably ask yourself occasionally what goals your business is designed to serve. Some people are hustling every day to survive. The family gets bigger, the monthly bills swell and surge, and the idea of the business is to maintain continuity to meet this ever-increasing responsibility. Creating a foundation of stability is the highest priority.

Others have survived this plateau and are trying to build on this foundation of stability. They are reaching for the next plateau—success.

Success Comes in Many Sizes and Shapes

There are families that consider their business a generational continuity. There are others that want to build equity so they can eventually find their way into retirement. There are still others whose intention from the outset is to build a dynasty, something bigger than themselves that will survive as their mark on the historical business landscape.

Recognizing the Goals

It is important to recognize the goal, the measure of success you seek to achieve, because each goal requires a different strategy. The short-term goal will often mandate a lower investment in inventory, equipment, and personnel. The longer-term goal will often involve a longer-term investment.

Although good business theory would suggest that investment be commensurate with growth, this equation is often very deceptive, at least in terms of timing. Business experience tells us, for example, that salespeople are often paid long in advance of actual sales generated. Also, in order to manufacture more products, it is necessary to order raw material, buy or lease new equipment, and often hire personnel. This certainly represents a substantial investment in the future.

Is there a middle road to this program of investment for growth? There is certainly a delicate balance to be examined carefully. It is a question of control. Ideally, the creative entrepreneur chooses to maintain control over every aspect of his or her business growth. Giving up the necessary or appropriate degree of control, however, often turns out to be the secret to success. Trying to maintain control over every aspect of your business can be a terrible mistake. Keeping control over the most important elements is mandatory. Releasing control over the least or less critical elements will often allow you to spend more time and more energy on those things necessary to your best performance. In other words, the concept of "outsourcing" comes in many different kinds of packages, from secretarial to administrative, from manufacturing to distributing, from advertising to sales.

Can anyone make the selection for you or decide on the timing or the priorities? Doubtful. But it can be the key to your business in both the short term and the long term. Spend some time analyzing the differentials. It's worth your best energies.

CHAPTER 13

Selling the Bottom Line

YOUR BUSINESS'S OPERATING PROFIT IS THE key to determining an asking or selling price. To present the best view of the operating profit to potential buyers, you need to reconstitute your profit and loss statement, also known as your income statement. This chapter focuses on the variables that affect your bottom line, compares different profit and loss statements, and leads you through checklists to help you with your own profit and loss statement. By the end of this chapter, you should have a good idea as to the most defensible asking price for your business (notwithstanding your buyer's situation), the areas where you may need to streamline your business or eliminate excess costs, and how to present all the figures to the buyer in the best light.

OPERATING PROFIT LEADS TO AN ASKING PRICE

Chapters 1, 2, and 3 discussed how important operating profit is to developing an asking price for your business. The business must pay for itself: the operating profit must be able to support payments on the promissory note and leave the buyer with a respectable income. When you sell your business, you are really selling the bottom line, a stable operating profit from which

the buyer can pay the business's debts, including the note to the seller.

You may adjust the price up or down depending on many factors—the length of the note, the value of the business assets, or the stability or instability of the operating profit. The buyer must be able to see consistency in the cost factors that create your operating profit. Seasonality and other business fluctuations aside, the operating profit should represent a reasonably dependable bank deposit for the buyer through the year.

In fact, the buyer will look at the dependability of the profit to assess the risk involved. As discussed in Chapter 2, if purchasing the business represents a high-risk investment—because the operating profit is not stable or dependable—the buyer will want you to lower the price.

Returning to the basic premise, if the business is operated properly and your costs are within normal parameters, you should be able to formulate a basic asking price by using a multiple of the operating profit. If the price you get is too low, examine the cost factors of the business. Keep in mind that each percentage category may vary because each accountant has his or her own method of allocating items (chart of accounts) on the profit and loss statement. It might be necessary to make adjustments in these categories. Review Chapter 3 and Worksheet 3.2.

Pie Charts and the Business of Percentages

Your first priority in determining operating profit and selling price is to examine the profit picture of businesses in your market, how the percentages are supposed to work, and how the percentages can be increased by cutting costs and instituting better marketing techniques. Do a financial analysis of your shop, if you haven't already.

To do a financial analysis, do not use the profit and loss statement used for tax purposes. You need to look at the real percentages involved, taken from a particularly conservative standpoint and without any consideration to the tax advantages you can use. You can analyze most businesses by looking at the percentages with which they operate. Consider that a 1% savings on the cost of product or labor can drop quickly to the bottom line, operating profit, right into your pocket!

"The business is going out the back door" is a phrase applicable to many businesses, particularly the restaurant business. In restaurants, it means that employees are taking food home, a loss of inventory that decreases the operating profit of the business. Obviously, a correction in this type of cost inflation will help to increase the profit margins of any business. This kind of savings in turn increases the operating profit of the business. As you have already seen, the greater the operating profit, the higher the potential asking price the business can command.

A good place to start is a simple pie chart. Although each business has its own peculiarities, you can normally represent the percentages of your business by cutting a pie into four basic parts. A pie chart can be especially interesting to those of you who are statistically oriented, but it can also help you prepare a mental skeleton of the percentage parameters within which any business should properly function.

The ideal ratios for some businesses are 25% for cost of product, 25% for cost of labor, 25% for standard monthly obligations (fixed expenses, such as rent, electricity, and insurance), and 25% for operating profit (see Figure 13.1).

For a good comparison of how the percentages can work for and against your business, look at the profit and loss statements for Bob's Printing and Spry Print Shop that are located on the following pages (Table 13.1). As with any business, you want to ensure the following:

- Products or services are priced to properly reflect costs of product and labor,
- The number and kind of products or services offered for sale are within appropriate ratios to maximize profit, and
- Wastage caused by poor management is kept to a minimum.

For Bob's Printing, the cost of sales is 26.44%, the cost of labor is 25.29%, and fixed expenses are 23.62% (total operating expenses minus the labor costs: 48.91% minus 25.29%). This leaves operating profit (income from operations) at 24.64%. These figures are not far from the 25% theoretical figures in each category on the sample pie chart. This operation is run well from the standpoint of industry standards and the operating profit is good.

Now look at Spry Print Shop. The cost of sales is 35.18%, the cost of labor 30.42%, and fixed expenses are 26.96% (total operating expenses minus labor costs: 57.38% minus 30.42%). This leaves operating profit (income from operations) at 7.44%. These figures are not at all close to the ideal. This operation is not run well and the operating profit is small.

| FIGURE 13.1 | Ideal Ratios |

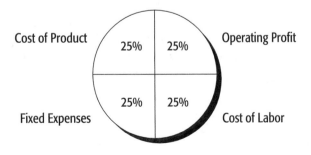

TABLE 13.1 Sample Profit and Lost Statements with Different Percentages (continued on next page)

	BOB'S PRINTING		SPRY PRINT SHOP	
	Year to Date	%	Year to Date	%
SALES				
Printing	$191,917	50.60%	$188,899	51.92%
Bindery	29,264	7.72%	21,197	5.83%
Outside Services	52,409	13.82%	64,811	17.82%
Self-Service Copiers	8,648	2.28%	27,846	7.65%
Automated Copiers	97,108	25.60%	65,201	17.92%
Merchandise	143	0.04%	(2,622)	−0.72%
Discounts	(200)	−0.05%	(1,535)	−0.42%
Total Sales	**$379,289**	**100.00%**	**$363,797**	**100.00%**
COST OF SALES				
Beginning Inventory	$3,721	0.98%	$7,186	1.98%
Purchases–Paper	26,073	6.87%	37,149	10.21%
Purchases–Supplies	2,668	0.70%	9,828	2.70%
Outside Services	27,964	7.37%	37,131	10.21%
Self-service Copiers	6,491	1.71%	23,022	6.33%
Automated Copiers	19,516	5.15%	8,376	2.30%
Allocated Sales Cost	16,556	4.37%	12,047	3.31%
Less Ending Inventory	(2,703)	−0.71%	(6,748)	−1.85%
Cost of Sales	**$100,286**	**26.44%**	**$127,991**	**35.18%**
GROSS PROFIT	**$279,003**	**73.56%**	**$235,806**	**64.82%**
OPERATING EXPENSES				
Labor Costs				
Salaries–Printing	$58,756	15.49%	$77,535	21.31%
Payroll Taxes	4,788	1.26%	7,125	1.96%
Casual Labor	1,022	0.27%	304	0.08%
Workman's Comp. Ins.	1,938	0.51%	2,538	0.70%
Group Insurance	1,839	0.48%	2,613	0.72%
Allocated Labor Costs	27,569	7.27%	20,566	5.65%
Total Labor Costs	**$95,912**	**25.29%**	**$110,681**	**30.42%**
Advertising				
Yellow Pages	$1,309	0.35%	$1,783	0.49%
1% National	3,793	1.00%	3,691	1.01%
Other	2,720	0.72%	3,714	1.02%
Total Advertising Costs	**$7,822**	**2.06%**	**$9,188**	**2.53%**

To get a truer picture of the operating profit, the principal payments on the automated copiers, which appear on the balance sheet, should be added to the monthly Cost of Sales.

These shops send a share of printing and bindery work to a central plant and are assessed a share of central plant costs, reflected in Allocated Labor and Sales Costs.

These shops contribute to a national advertising program mandated by the franchisor.

TABLE 13.1 Sample Profit and Lost Statements with Different Percentages (continued)

	BOB'S PRINTING		SPRY PRINT SHOP	
	Year to Date	**%**	**Year to Date**	**%**
Other				
Automobile Expenses	$333	0.09%	$1,206	0.33%
Cash Over/Short	97	0.03%	349	0.10%
Employee Benefits	881	0.23%	806	0.22%
Entertainment + Promo.	1,018	0.27%	1,314	0.36%
Insurance–General	923	0.24%	923	0.25%
Meetings	252	0.07%	326	0.09%
Office Supp. + Expenses	1,250	0.33%	1,803	0.50%
Operating Supplies	1,873	0.49%	2,682	0.74%
Postage	358	0.09%	756	0.21%
Allocated OH-CP	10,103	2.66%	7,362	2.02%
Parking	11	0.00%	90	0.03%
Rent	26,939	7.10%	27,953	7.68%
Repairs–Equipment	3,807	1.01%	4,120	1.13%
Repairs–Shop	458	0.12%	3,563	0.98%
Royalties	29,384	7.75%	28,567	7.85%
Taxes and Licenses	2,097	0.55%	2,447	0.67%
Telephone	1,723	0.46%	3,454	0.95%
Travel–Mtgs/Conv.	289	0.08%	1,157	0.32%
Total Other	**$81,796**	**21.57%**	**$88,878**	**24.43%**
OPERATING EXPENSES	**$185,529**	**48.91%**	**$208,747**	**57.38%**
TOTAL OPERATING PROFIT	**$93,473**	**24.64%**	**$27,059**	**7.44%**

You will notice that Bob's and Spry are both generating almost equal sales. However, Bob's cost of sales is 8.74% lower than Spry's. Bob's is spending 5.34% less for paper and supplies than Spry. Spry is spending a good deal of money on paper, which represents serious waste. Print jobs at Spry are probably being done more than once to get it right, driving up Spry's cost of product.

You will also notice that Bob's cost of labor is 5.13% lower than Spry's. Bob's personnel are functioning better than Spry's and are more productive.

As you compare each profit and loss statement, look for other discrepancies in the way the owner operates Spry Print Shop. Bob has less income from outside services, but his markup is almost 100%. (Compare costs for outside services with sales from outside services.) Spry has more income from outside services, but the markup at Spry is much less than 100%.

Notice that there are various ways to account for equipment contracts. Bob's and Spry both make payments on automated copiers. When they sell their businesses, they will have to work out with the buyer, their accountant, and the buyer's accountant how payments on the copiers will be absorbed. The size of an equipment contract and the time until it is fully repaid are differentials that can dramatically affect your price structure—differentials you need your accountant to work out. If very few payment are left on a contract, it could be paid off at closing without negatively affecting the profit on which the value is predicated.

Not all businesses will fall neatly into 25% margins. In some businesses, certain factors will be much different. For example, in a service-oriented business, the cost of labor might be 45% and the cost of product 10%. In an inventory-heavy business, the cost of product might be 60% and the cost of labor only 5%. The pie chart graphic is designed to give you a picture of the four basic elements. Let the real figures in any business flow into the chart and create a larger or smaller percentage in any one or more of the categories. Whatever the percentages, you should be able to compare any given business in that industry with the proper standards.

The Costs of Absentee Ownership

Another priority in examining your operating profit is represented by those places where profit is lost due to poor management. Whenever a potential buyer speaks of wanting to be an absentee owner, you must take the time to explain the error in that approach. In unsupervised restaurants, the steaks (and therefore the profits) go out the back door, but restaurants are not the only type of business that experiences this problem. There are many places where profits can disappear in any business. Consider the quick print shop discussed in Illustration 13.1.

Illustration 13.1 A Print Shop Example

The quick printing business is a convenient example of how quickly profits can disappear if an owner fails to manage the business carefully and effectively. As you read, try to correlate these examples with comparable ones in your business. At the counter two things can happen that directly affect your percentages:

- The counterperson isn't properly trained in sales and marketing techniques. If someone asks for stationery, it is certainly appropriate to ask if he or she needs business cards and envelopes as well.

- If your personnel do not handle the pricing of the entire job request carefully from the beginning, the profit margin will shrink. Remember: the customer normally will not tell you when you've forgotten to figure in collating or stapling.

Choice of equipment also affects the bottom line. For example, certain print jobs should be done on a copier and others on a press. The customer probably won't care which equipment you use. The manager may decide on the copier based on convenience. The owner will decide on the press based on profit—but only if he or she is present when the decision is made.

The execution of the job order also reveals potential excess cost. Sloppy camera work can force the use of duplicate plates. Sloppy press work or bindery work can lead to excess paper purchase. Bad quality can cause the customer to reject a job and the whole job may have to be done again. A supervising owner can eliminate much of this waste.

The purchase of supplies is an obvious area for cost fluctuation. Buying paper in anticipation of monthly requirements is wise because it can lead to quantity purchase discounts. Buying by the day is terribly expensive and cuts into the bottom line. You will experience further waste when your employees have to go to the paper house every day for purchases that you could have and should have anticipated.

Finally, when work is done for cash and an invoice is never written or when the press operator or the manager decides to do a favor for a friend, it also creates the potential for abuse under an absentee owner who does not anticipate such cost factors.

This example shows how easy it is to lose a percentage point on the bottom line merely by not paying attention to detail. The same types of problems apply to almost any business involved in retail or manufacturing—food, shoes, or car repair.

Whatever your success or failure with these percentages, you must be completely aware of them to have a knowledgeable conversation with a prospective buyer—especially if he or she knows anything about the business. Keep in mind that you can use this as a selling tool, whether the percentage is good or bad. If the percentage is good, you can convince the buyer that he or she is buying a well-operated business. If the percentage is bad, you can suggest where the buyer might easily improve his or her bottom-line profit with a little attention to detail. Make sure you can explain why you haven't done it yourself.

Labor Cost: A Product of Efficiency

Cost of labor also varies, depending on efficiency. In the printing business, spending 45 minutes at the counter working with one customer to find the right combination of type style, color, and quality of paper for the customer's wedding invitation is not the most effective time and cost combination. Neither is doing a printing job two or three times because the pressperson didn't pay attention to the instructions on the invoice or because the instructions on the invoice were ambiguous or misleading. People who understand the print shop business can never understand why the counterperson is often the poorest paid and least respected member of the quick print team. If your business also relies on your staff to relate well with the public, you should learn to pay for that skill. Your people behind the counter may be the only people whom your customers remember and, therefore, the people who represent your business.

An inefficient staff can lead to a cost of labor substantially higher than the norm. There is no reason why you shouldn't maintain an appropriate percentage for labor. Whatever your business, you can find out the labor cost standard.

In the quick printing business, for example, three people might operate a shop doing $15,000 per month in sales or a shop doing $25,000 per month in sales and represent an entirely different cost factor in each case. If those three people receive $5,000 per month in salaries, for example, that's 33% in labor in a shop doing $15,000 per month and 20% for labor in a shop doing $25,000 per month.

Also, keep in mind that each marketplace may have a different customer complex and that some businesses will be able to do larger volumes with fewer customers and thus fewer personnel. Another fluctuating element might be that your people have a bonus incentive for work done, invoices written, or monies deposited. Staff incentives will, of course, change the percentage to some degree, although you should always factor in good, planned incentive programs to avoid unnecessary distortions. Bonuses for exemplary work usually produce higher profits for the business— and this kind of distortion is always acceptable.

Again, keep in mind that you don't have to give a seminar about your business in all its detail each time you discuss it with a prospective buyer. But the percentages, the lease, and the customer base must always be at your fingertips to answer questions from the buyer and/or his or her professional representative, questions that they are certainly entitled to ask.

Fixed Expenses

Your standard monthly obligations, or fixed expenses, will also represent some variables, even though theoretically they should be the same each month—rent, telephone, electricity, and other utilities. On the one hand, if they stay relatively the same in actual dollars, they will change in terms of percentages of your growing gross sales. For example, a rental obligation of $5,000 per month when you are doing $10,000 per month equals 50%; that same $5,000 per month when you are doing $50,000 per month equals only 10%. Certain items, of course, will change to some degree with volume, such as telephone, electricity, and auto delivery.

On the other hand, you must also be careful to include only those items that are germane to the operation of the business from the buyer's perspective and exclude those things that are for tax purposes, such as your personal car, spouse insurance, and other personal benefits. Including these items would obviously cause your cost factors to be less realistic and throw off your profit picture. Refer to Chapter 2 and the section, "Reconstituting the P&L," to learn more about adjusting your cost percentages.

With the appropriate cautions about costs of product and costs of labor and an awareness of the obvious fluctuations in percentages depending on business volume, you can now understand the pie chart concept as a graphic picture of your business. The pie chart is a selling tool and will make it easier for the buyer to relate to costs and profit. Continue to refer to "operating profit," as opposed to "net profit," because you are not including such noncash items as depreciation and amortization and you are not concerned about the tax consequences to the buyer, since his or her financial portfolio could conceivably represent an entirely different tax obligation than yours.

KEY POINTS TO REMEMBER

- The business must pay for itself. Be prepared to show how you arrived at your bottom-line profit, and how stable and dependable that profit is, so that the buyer knows the business can pay the purchase money promissory note.
- Labor costs and labor stability are important to the buyer. Be prepared to discuss the status of your employees and any contract personnel on whom your business depends.
- When you discuss the bottom-line profit, be careful to discuss any collateral elements, such as equipment contracts that will expire shortly and leave additional money for the buyer's pocket.
- If your buyer is considering owning the business without being personally involved in the daily business activity, you need to alert him or her to the negative implications of absentee ownership.

Worksheet 13. Cost Analyses to Improve Your P&L

Marketing Analysis

Are you in close enough contact with your customers to ensure that you are carrying the proper inventory and making available the proper services for their growing and changing needs? Yes ❑ No ❑

If you checked No, how can you improve customer relations? _____

_____

_____

Labor Costs

Is your personnel properly trained and meeting performance standards? Yes ❑ No ❑

If you checked No, what changes can you make here? _____

_____

_____

How will bringing labor costs within proper levels affect the following areas of your business?

Personnel: _____

_____

Sales: _____

_____

Customer relations: _____

_____

Other: _____
_____

Product Costs
What quantity purchase or prompt payment discounts are you receiving? _____
_____
_____

How can savings be improved here? _____
_____
_____

Are you losing inventory due to poor climate controls, theft, or poor accessing procedures? Yes ❏ No ❏

If you checked Yes, what type of inventory controls do you have and how can they be improved? _____
_____
_____

Fixed Expenses
Are recurring bills (utility, telephone, delivery bills) within appropriate, cost-effective parameters? Yes ❏ No ❏

If you checked No, what improvements can you make here? _____
_____
_____

What improvements can you make in your use of space, equipment, and inventory? _____
_____
_____

Are your insurance coverage and premiums appropriate to the current aspects of the business? Yes ❏ No ❏

Sales
Is your pricing competitive and are all products and services priced consistently with industry margins and markups?
Yes ❏ No ❏

Are cash inputs consistent with changes in inventory levels? Yes ❏ No ❏

If you checked no, what is/are the source(s) of all discrepancies?
_____
_____

IF YOU'RE GOING TO SELL YOUR BUSINESS

Every business plan, regardless of the purpose for which it may have been designed, will have a section referenced "exit strategy." This section can state how a lender will be able to have a loan returned, how an equity partner will ultimately see a multiple of his or her original investment, how the business will devolve to a family member, or merely how and when the business will be sold.

The Value as a Secondary Issue

Too many entrepreneurs consider the valuation of the business, the establishment of the price for which it is to be sold, to be the highest priority. Many sellers, after the fact, recognize that this valuation is often the least of their problems. Although there are people who will tell you how complex the issue of valuation is and how expensive it can be, the reality is that the valuation concept for small businesses is relatively simple and need not be expensive at all. The real problem is how to structure the sale of the business regardless of price. As so often is the case, the devil is in the details and 'woe be unto you' if you lose sight of that very important concept.

The Buyer: An All-Important Element

Whatever the details of the sale, the most important aspect is the buyer—his or her integrity, the reasons for the purchase, and other things that many sellers consider unimportant. Since most small businesses are sold with the seller "holding paper" for the balance of the purchase price, the buyer's financial status and whatever additional security may be available should be a high priority. The buyer's background and his or her ethical reputation in the community can turn out to be a subtle reason to reconsider the buyer as a candidate. Although the buyer with the biggest purse is usually the one of greatest interest to a seller, finances are not the most important factor. After all, if you're going to be the banker and hold a promissory note for the balance of the purchase price, you should keep in mind that the buyer's purse is only an indication of his or her ability to pay; it's no guarantee that he or she is willing to adhere to the terms and conditions of the sale.

A Word About the Franchise

In the event you are a franchisee and selling your franchise, you ought to keep two things in mind. The first is that the franchise company cannot put itself in the middle of a potential sale. It would be a serious conflict of interest and conceivably cause the franchisor considerable problems after the sale. The second thing is that the franchise company is interested in perpetuating the franchise and would, logically, be more concerned about the buyer than about the seller, since the seller will be out of the picture. Be careful to understand the nature of any advice you get from the franchisor considering the long-term involvement that the company will have with the buyer.

The Flesh and the Skeleton

Many sellers feel that the security they need to support the sale and to protect the balance of the purchase price can be the business itself. This is perhaps the biggest mistake that a seller can make. In the first place, most sellers have no intention of returning to the business once the business is sold. In the second place, it doesn't take long for a bad buyer, inadvertently or intentionally, to completely destroy a business that might have taken the seller years to build. You may end up taking back the business and find that it is a mere skeleton of the business you sold, with less value and more obligations. You need additional security to protect the promissory note you hold for the balance of the purchase price.

The Last Concern ... and the Biggest

When you sell the business, be sure to remove yourself from all the ongoing obligations of the business: the lease for the premises, the leases on the equipment purchases, the bank loans for the purchase of equipment. If you leave your name on these obligations, you may be liable for them long after the buyer destroys the business and goes on his or her way.

CHAPTER 14

Finding the Right Buyer and Protecting the Sale

EVEN THOUGH YOU MUST DO MANY THINGS TO properly prepare your business for sale, you should not lose sight of a few basics. Where to look for the buyer and how to get his or her attention are two basic elements that this chapter examines. Whether you advertise by word of mouth or on television, you need to screen your candidates and narrow them down to the most serious and most qualified. To get from initial negotiations to an understanding that the sale is ready to take place requires a delicate handling, especially when you consider that you want to bind the buyer, even though the final papers may be weeks or even months away. In this chapter, you will learn how to maintain the delicate balance between protecting the stability of your business and aggressively pursuing its sale.

FINDING THE BUYER

The number of ways to put your business up for sale is almost limitless, from responding to a subtle comment at a Rotary club dinner to using the most dramatic medium of all, television. Neither of these is as crazy as it sounds.

Advertising your business on radio or television may seem quite exotic, but in the right circumstances it can be very effective. If your business is large enough to warrant such an alterna-

tive, you should consider working with a small advertising agency. You may also want to consider using a business broker, as discussed in Chapters 4 and 21.

Many sellers will find interested buyers in their social and business circles, such as someone retiring from a long-time corporate position, government, or the military. Candidates in these groups may vary in age, experience, and resources, but owning a business is a very viable and much discussed option in these circles.

Some potential buyers have not decided whether to buy a shop or open one. Many do not realize that the start-up period for a brand new store can be quite expensive and that they could exhaust their working capital base before reaching a break-even point. These more naive buyers may be persuaded to buy an existing business that is actually at break-even on the date of purchase. Bypassing the period a start-up takes to reach break-even makes buying an existing shop an interesting proposition, even when the business is not showing a substantial profit.

The Print Media

The print media is a flexible and useful tool for advertising your business. You do not need to limit your advertising to trade magazines in your particular trade. Consider the franchise magazines as well, because the franchise companies are looking for the same candidates as you are. In addition, consider local, regional, and national newspapers and mailing lists as well as the Internet.

Once you choose your medium of print advertising, you must then consider the size of the ad, placement, length and frequency, and, most importantly, content.

Advertising experts say that too much copy puts off potential readers. This is usually true; however, the ad must stop potential readers from turning the page. Once the reader passes the page without seeing your ad, it is unlikely he or she will go back for a second pass.

You have probably admired billboards yourself that are simple but effective, like "Kahlua and milk. Ahh!" or "Things go better with Coke." However, advertising a business is a little more complex. For one thing, your advertising is in the middle of other copy that is also advertising businesses for sale. How can yours be different? Keep it simple. Surround your copy with plenty of empty space. Use magic words. Best suggestion: "Widget Shop for Sale by Owner. Santa Clara County. Good Income, Low Down, Creative Financing, Full Training: (555) 815-2390."

Local newspapers can also be an effective and relatively inexpensive medium. They allow you to increase your frequency—the number of times your ad can appear. Many sellers find *The Wall Street Journal* very effective; the regional issue of the paper is normally your best source, because it will get to people who would not have to move very far.

Florida, California, and Arizona, on the other hand, tend to draw buying candidates from all over the country—particularly in the winter when people in the North are reminded how difficult it can be to survive in the snow. The ability to draw buying candidates from all over the country is particularly valuable if you are part of a franchise in which people occasionally sell their locations exclusively to move to a different climate. An open letter to other franchise owners can be very effective. See the sample letter at the end of this chapter.

Mentioning Money

Although mentioning a dollar requirement will prequalify your candidates to some degree, it can also eliminate some good candidates. To give a dollar figure that includes a working capital requirement can intimidate a potential buyer because it seems like a very high down payment. It is also difficult to explain the purpose of working capital in a short ad, since people who are not familiar with a given business will probably not understand.

For example, would the average buying candidates understand if you told them that the working capital account in a particular business is usually used to accommodate the receivable turnover period? (See Chapter 2.) Unfortunately, most buyers don't understand these terms without some further explanation. If you want to use a dollar figure as a qualifying tactic, make sure to include the working capital in the ad or reference that working capital is required. If you don't, you may have a lot of explaining to do when potential buyers respond to the ad—and then find that they need another $40,000, $50,000, or $60,000.

Keep in mind, however, that if you find a good candidate or a buyer finds this business opportunity interesting, there are a number of ways the dollar can be stretched—from a minimum down payment to a working partnership buyout arrangement. (See Chapter 3 for more on creative financing methods.) Don't be too quick to dismiss potential buyers—they are not that easy to find!

Although you can consummate a sale with a handshake at a first meeting of the parties, it is much more appropriate to consider six to 12 months to find the right buyer and finalize the sale. Remember: you're not selling a pair of shoes—you're selling a way of life.

The Disclosure, the Memorandum, and the Agreement

If you are selling a franchise, one of your first tasks is to ensure that the buyer is properly informed by presenting the franchise disclosure document. (See the language in a typical offering circular at the end of this chapter.)

After you have made full disclosure, whether you are a franchisee or not, and the parties have agreed to the basic elements of sale, your next step is to prepare a memorandum of sale. (See the sample at the end of this chapter.) The purpose of this document is to separate the buyers from the lookers. A buyer's signature on this memorandum of intent is not necessarily a consummate agreement, particularly since many buyers will not agree to the memorandum representing an actual purchase contract, but it will definitely intimidate less serious individuals and secure a down payment. In the memorandum, the parties agree that their attorneys will prepare a formal contract of purchase and sale. A personal guarantee by the buyer or lack of it is another negotiated factor that increases or decreases the buyer's ultimate responsibility and the seller's ultimate protection relative to payment of the balance of the purchase price.

The formal agreement can take a variety of forms and can be a 10- to 12-page agreement or a 20- to 30-page agreement. Its size and form depend on the personal preference of legal counsel and the kinds of protection the buyer's or seller's asset portfolio requires.

PROTECTING THE SALE

Both buyer and seller have a number of protective devices at their disposal with which to protect the sale.

Buyer Protections

The buyer's protection is the very fact of owing the seller money. A down payment entitles the buyer to begin operating the business, but if the buyer finances the purchase with a promissory note, he or she will owe the seller a substantial amount of money—money the buyer can withhold if he or she finds that the seller misrepresented anything of a material nature during the disclosure and negotiations.

A buyer may also seek a certain level of protection from the type of legal form the company adopts after the purchase. The company could become a C corporation, an S corporation, a limited partnership, a general partnership, a sole proprietorship, or a limited liability company. To a great extent, tax and liability considerations will determine the particular form. These are buyer prerogatives and the buyer should discuss them with his or her legal and accounting professionals.

Seller Protections

What do these buyer protections mean to you, the seller, and how can you protect yourself and the business you sold from post-sale trauma? The seller is entitled to a number of protective devices if the buyer takes over the business before paying the entire purchase price. You could include many kinds of protections, particularly if the buyer makes no down payment or a small down payment. These protections prevent the buyer from depleting the cash or valuable assets of the business. Some of these protections are negotiable, but some of them are absolutely necessary to protect you, the seller, from losing control of the business and its viability.

As a seller, always keep in mind that the buying corporation is only as good as its pocketbook: if the pocketbook is empty, you have no way of getting your note paid. You can, however, protect yourself in the following ways.

- Make sure you get a personal signature or guarantee on the purchase money promissory note. If the business is a franchise, the franchisor will normally require this personal signature to ensure that the post-term, noncompete covenant is respected. If it's an independent business, you want the buyer to be personally responsible for payment whether the corporation has depleted its cash or not.

- Make sure you get an acceleration-upon-default clause in the note. If the buyer falls behind on some promissory note payments, this clause will enable you to sue for the entire balance, as opposed to just the payments the buyer has missed.

- Make sure to hold the business as security for the note, so you can take back the business in the event the buyer either refuses or is unable to make payments on the note. Keep in mind, however, that it is always preferable to have security in addition to the business.

- Make sure you have the right to examine the books and records of the business if there is a default, to ensure that the buyer is not draining the business in anticipation of running off.

It is also a good idea, under any circumstances, to have the buyer obtain a life insurance policy for the amount of the purchase money promissory note, to protect yourself in case the buyer dies before fulfilling the payment obligation. In some cases, the buyer might not be critical to the proper operation and continuity of the business. In other cases, the buyer might be the key factor.

Another protection the seller may mandate is that the buyer maintain certain maximum percentages on cost of product and cost of labor, for example, to ensure that he or she doesn't drain the business and then walk away after essentially stealing back the down payment.

The financial tests listed at the end of this chapter are some of the protective devices recommended by attorneys and accountants to protect against either intentional or inadvertent dissipation of the business. They are not intended to be exhaustive but merely representative of the kinds of protections that you can use.

The suggested protection devices listed here are just some of the things that should be part of a seller protection plan. They should also allow you to better understand some legal concepts to discuss with your legal counsel.

In addition, you may wish to review Worksheet 14, which is located at the end of this chapter. It will help you review ways to protect the sale of your business.

WARNING! As always, do not use this book in the place of competent legal counsel! This book only introduces you to some general concepts involved in a business sale. Always seek professional advice concerning the issues involved in your particular transaction. (Please see Chapters 4, 19, and 20 regarding the use of legal and financial professionals.)

Disclosing the Sale to Your Employees

One other question about seller protection you ought to address is how you can protect your business from employees who may either leave or slack off while you look for an appropriate buyer. How and when should you tell your employees that you are going to sell the business? Please note the phrase, "that you are going to sell the business," not "that you have sold the business." You should address employee disclosure in the early stages of your thinking.

Sharing sales information with your employees is not just a basic courtesy, but good business sense. You may find a potential buyer among your employees. It is not unusual that an employee who seems the least likely prospect will approach a relative, friend, or customer and generate the money necessary to become a buying candidate. If that happens, of course, you would then need to share the basic dollar amounts with that individual—asking price, working capital requirement, down payment, and purchase money promissory note variables such as the number of payment years and monthly payment schedule. You would need to relate to that employee on a different level. The employee would already know the basics of the business and have some knowledge of your customers, which would give the employee quite a jump on restarting the business on his or her own behalf.

By informing employees of a potential sale, you will also be telling them that you are mindful of the effect selling the shop will have on their personal lives. They will want to know what will happen to their jobs if you sell the business. Explain that most people who buy a business are interested in the employees who contributed to its success and eager to examine the possibility of keeping as many of these people as possible.

You may need to arrange some sort of termination pay bonus for your key people, in the event the new buyer does not choose to retain their services. Keep in mind that if the business does not sell, you want to keep your employees and give them an incentive to stay as long as possible. If the business sells, you want your key employees to stay with the new owner until he or she is able to replace them. Most buyers are not able to fill key positions immediately following a takeover because they do not yet know all the nuances of the customer base, the equipment, the vendor relationships, or even the basic operation of the business.

You don't want employees to leave and take customers with them or to leave the business without adequate personnel to maintain its stability. Either of these scenarios could devastate the business and seriously jeopardize your purchase money promissory note. In all likelihood, you will have enough cash from the sale to pay the key employees something out of the purchase price that will keep them with the business for at least a minimum period. Offering your employees some kind of bonus to stay with the new owner during the transition period might be the best insurance policy you ever bought. Consider, for example, how Tony Martinez handled this situation when he was selling his business.

Illustration 14.1 Contract with a Key Employee

Tony Martinez wanted to protect the continuity of his business by ensuring that any key employees stayed with the business until the takeover was complete and the buyer could stand on his or her own. Toward that end, he made a contract with his top manager.

"As a result of your satisfactory employment and our need to assure any potential buyer that you will continue to give the business your best efforts after a sale is consummated, I have agreed to the following:

1. You will receive a bonus of $5,000 under the following conditions:

   a) You remain with the buyer, after the sale is consummated, for a period of no less than six months;

   b) In the event the buyer chooses not to retain your services for the entire six-month period, you will obtain a letter from the buyer indicating that you are not being terminated for cause; and

   c) If the buyer is unwilling to give you such a letter, then you shall keep narrative notes as to any problems you incur with the buyer during your tenure to satisfy me that your termination was not a fault of yours."

Interestingly, the contract also served to keep the manager with the business under even more trying circumstances. Tony passed away before he sold the business. His widow took over the business and, because of the letter, which she was happy to honor, the manager stayed with the business during a very difficult transition period. The letter served not only the needs of the pending sale, but also the needs of the family. It turned out to be a bonus letter in more ways than one.

In most cases, disclosing the sale to employees early on is the best course of action. The only exceptions to this rule are situations in which the details of sale are worked out quickly and quietly and the buyer intends to replace all personnel. These situations do not normally involve trade secrets or customer relationships, either of which could prove seriously problematic regardless of the buyer's ultimate intentions. Remember: if key employees have developed a personal loyalty with a few large customers, termination of those employees could cut deeply into the company's cash flow and profit. Protecting trade secrets from competitors is another reason to be cautious about the relationships with key employees. Angry ex-employees can be hard to control, even in court.

Disclosing plans to sell can be particularly tricky if you have a manager or long-term employee who has taken on some owner-type responsibilities and shows a personal concern over the success or failure of the business. In that case, your relationship with the employee will dictate how to handle such a situation.

The reason for the sale—health, insolvency, retirement—and the nature of the purchase—single purchaser, acquisition by a larger company, merger with a company of equal size—will all bear on the employee's reaction. How will the employee's reaction affect the success or failure of the sale? If you are going to take back a note from the buyer, what effect will the employee's action and reaction have on the future of the business after the sale? Look at the following examples for insights that may help in your particular situation.

Illustration 14.2 A Positive Employee Reaction

As the result of some bad expansion decisions, Lori Jamison had a serious financial problem and could not continue to operate a multi-store complex. It became clear that she had to sell one or two locations to stabilize the rest of the business.

She had a very good working relationship with all her managers and, as the result of her multi-unit activities, had left many of the daily responsibilities to the manager in charge of each location. Lori's managers took their jobs seriously and each was a stable and significant factor in the success of each location.

Although management had made some bad decisions, the industry was strong and most individual locations were doing well. Lori's professionals suggested that she afford each manager and each administrative person the courtesy of a personal meeting to make a relatively full disclosure regarding the general situation and the possibility of selling some of the locations.

Although Lori didn't know the extent of her managers' interest or the financial wherewithal of their families and friends, she indicated that she would first offer each of them the opportunity to buy the particular location that he or she was managing. After all, if the business's operating profit is big enough for the business to pay for itself, then any employee with working capital and a down payment can become a potential buyer.

Lori was delighted to find that eight managers and two administrative people were interested in the opportunity to buy. In fact, as time went on and the news spread among employees generally, additional interest came to the surface.

Two administrative people bought three locations. Lori sold the other four locations to people who responded to advertising and in every case the new owner retained the manager. The concept of disclosure was, in this case, a good idea.

▼ Illustration 14.3 Beware of Disgruntled Employees During a Sale

Linda McCain had hired an inexperienced general manager who, after two years of operation, had devastated the multi-shop operation. She terminated the general manager and proceeded to position many of the locations for sale. Because she had semi-retired during the general manager's two-year tenure, she did not have a close relationship with her remaining managers. The industry was good, but the locations individually were doing badly.

Although she offered the managers, as well as each of the administrative people, the opportunity to purchase, the situation was dramatically different from Lori Jamison's experience. Their perspectives had already been poisoned by the negative attitude of the terminated general manager. In this case, most of the managers were new; the individual shops were doing badly; there was no loyalty or even a friendly relationship developed between management and the employees; and the terminated general manager had left a negative impression on all the store managers about the business, the industry, and its future.

Two locations were consistently losing money and Linda closed them. Three managers left the organization. When Linda completed the reorganization at the end of a year and a half, the franchisor bought back three locations, a manager bought one location, Linda sold two locations to insiders, and she retained two locations herself. Linda was able to survive. However, because the terminated general manager had left the business in an unhealthy condition, Linda had her hands full with a very difficult rehabilitation process.

In both Illustrations 14.2 and 14.3, disclosing the troubles of the business and its possible sale to employees was not a dramatically negative problem. With Lori Jamison, employee reaction was very positive, and Linda McCain got help with her reorganization from a manager and two insiders who purchased locations. Although the two situations were significantly different, disclosure to employees is clearly the best approach when preparing to sell your business.

Sweat Equity Versus Absentee Ownership

If an employee, particularly a manager, buys the location he or she operates, you should keep something else in mind. Even the most dedicated employee will recognize that, as an owner, he or she would probably open the door a little earlier, work a little harder, examine the details of the day's activities a little more closely, and lock the door at the end of the day a little later. Even the most zealous manager recognizes the difference between sweat equity and absentee ownership. Allowing employees as potential buyers to examine the growth potential of the business if they owned it gives them a much different perspective than they have as employees.

A business sale in which you collect the balance of the purchase price over time requires you to have some faith in the ability of the buyer to operate the business successfully. Most buyers, however experienced they may be in the business or industry, are unknowns in many ways. Although you may be very diligent in examining the buyer and his or her history in business, you have no way to really assess his or her personality, attitude, and ability to get along with customers, employees, and vendors. It is difficult to know whether the buyer will be straightforward and honest in his or her relationships or deceptive and underhanded. The advantage to dealing with an employee/buyer is that

you probably know more about his or her personality and business sense. This comfort zone cannot be equaled with a new buyer about whom you know little. In this context, it is often a big advantage to sell to an employee, even though the dollars may be short up front and you may have to anticipate waiting longer for full payment for the business. Often, the longer wait is the smarter method of collection.

KEY POINTS TO REMEMBER

- You can advertise for a qualified buyer in many ways. Make sure the method you choose will maximize the effect of your advertising dollars.
- The disclosure, the memorandum, and the sale agreement must be properly orchestrated by your professionals to afford you the maximum protection after the sale.
- Do not use this book in place of the appropriate legal and financial professionals.
- Discuss with your professional advisors the best way to disclose the sale of your business to your employees. Remember: you may find an ideal buying candidate within your walls.
- Make sure your attorney builds the appropriate protective devices into the buy-sell agreement if the sale is not all cash.

FIGURE 14.1 Sample Sale Announcement to Fellow Franchisees

Corporation Logo
SPRY PRINT–La Mesa/El Cajon

Dear Spry Print Owner: (Letter to the existing franchisees of Spry Print franchises)

THIS is a REAL opportunity!!!!! Where have you heard that one before?

My SP locations in El Cajon and La Mesa are for sale, one or both. They are located in East County, San Diego–with the greatest climate anywhere, 70 to 80 degrees year round–in a business atmosphere of growth but with the relaxed California business pace. A perfect combination for semi-retirement.

As many of you know, my center of operations is in Northern California. I purchased these Southern California locations with my son, who has now expressed an interest in returning home to Northern California.

Attached are some financials for your perusal. The trend–positive!!!!

Price and payment schedule subject to negotiations.

Call Artie Target at (408) 111-3456 (days) or (408) 111-6543 (home, evenings) or, better yet, come down to San Diego and we'll kick the tires and kiss the bricks together.

Thanks for your consideration.

Artie Target

P.S. If you are too tied down to home, pass this on to somebody you feel may be interested in this REAL opportunity.

P.P.S. For those of you who understand SP growth potential, there is room for another SP location in the territory.

FIGURE 14.2 Sample Introduction to a California Franchise Offering Circular

---

A number of states have legislated requirements to protect their citizens from people who are selling franchises without full disclosure or, worse yet, by virtue of deceptive practices or misleading statements about the company's worth or the buyer's prospects. To protect all citizens of the United States, whether in states with such legislation or not, the Federal Trade Commission has its own requirements. If you are selling a franchise, you are mandated to observe these laws or your sale may be rescinded (called back) long after you execute the final papers. It is also possible, in some cases, that the seller could be subject to criminal penalties.

To give you an idea of the language, the following is a typical offering circular used in the state of California.

THIS OFFERING CIRCULAR IS PROVIDED FOR YOUR OWN PROTECTION AND CONTAINS A SUMMARY ONLY OF CERTAIN MATERIAL PROVISIONS OF THE FRANCHISE AGREEMENT. THIS OFFERING CIRCULAR AND ALL CONTRACTS AND AGREEMENTS SHOULD BE READ CAREFULLY IN THEIR ENTIRETY FOR AN UNDERSTANDING OF ALL RIGHTS AND OBLIGATIONS OF BOTH FRANCHISOR AND THE FRANCHISEE.

A FEDERAL TRADE COMMISSION RULE MAKES IT UNLAWFUL TO OFFER OR SELL ANY FRANCHISE WITHOUT FIRST PROVIDING THIS OFFERING CIRCULAR TO THE PROSPECTIVE FRANCHISEE AT THE EARLIER OF (1) THE FIRST PERSONAL MEETING; OR (2) TEN BUSINESS DAYS BEFORE THE SIGNING OF ANY FRANCHISE OR RELATED AGREEMENT; OR (3) TEN BUSINESS DAYS BEFORE ANY PAYMENT. THE CALIFORNIA FRANCHISE INVESTMENT

LAW REQUIRES THAT A COPY OF ALL PROPOSED AGREEMENTS RELATING TO THE SALE OF THE FRANCHISE BE DELIVERED TOGETHER WITH THE PROSPECTUS.

IF THIS OFFERING CIRCULAR IS NOT DELIVERED ON TIME, OR IF IT CONTAINS A FALSE, INCOMPLETE, INACCURATE OR MISLEADING STATEMENT, A VIOLATION OF FEDERAL AND STATE LAW MAY HAVE OCCURRED AND SHOULD BE REPORTED TO THE FEDERAL TRADE COMMISSION, WASHINGTON, D.C. 20580, AND TO THE CALIFORNIA DEPARTMENT OF CORPORATIONS AT ANY OF ITS OFFICES.

FIGURE 14.3 Sample Financial Tests

The following language in the sale agreement is recommended to a seller who takes a purchase money promissory note as part of the sale.

Buyer's operation of the business shall be subject to the following tests:

Working Capital: During each month of the calendar year 200_, the business shall maintain a ratio of current assets to current liabilities (as determined in accordance with generally accepted accounting practices, uniformly applied) of at least 1:1.

Payroll: The monthly aggregate total of all sums paid to or for the benefit of the employees of the business, including draws taken by buyer, including but not limited to salaries, payroll taxes, workers' compensation insurance payments, group insurance premiums, other benefits, and return of investments and loans, shall not exceed 30% of the monthly gross sales of the business.

Cost of Goods: The monthly cost of goods sold by the business, as determined in accordance with standards and guidelines established by the previous practice of the business and of the industry, shall not exceed 27% of the monthly gross sales of the business. This shall be in accordance with the particular chart of accounts used by the business at the time of sale.

Additionally, in the event the seller wants to keep an even tighter rein on the business, particularly when the down payment has been small (or nonexistent), a clause regarding financial reporting may also be inserted.

Financial Reports: So long as any of buyer's obligations under the Note remain unsatisfied, buyer shall permit seller (and its agents) full and complete access to the books and records of the business and shall supply seller with the following documents and information in a timely fashion:

(a) Quarterly or monthly financial statements
(b) Sales tax returns and proof of corresponding deposits
(c) Payroll tax returns and proof of corresponding deposits
(d) Royalty statements
(e) A monthly schedule of the business accounts payable showing the age of each item in months to accompany the financial statements
(f) A monthly summary of the business accounts receivable, broken down according to the age of such accounts to accompany the financial statements

FIGURE 14.4   Sample Memorandum of Sale

January 5, 2005
David Money
120 Promissory Lane
Sunnymead, California 94105

Re: Sale of Instant Printing Location referred to as (Spry Print) SP 303, located at Post and Palm in the City of Sunnymead

Dear David:

This letter will serve as a memorandum of sale with respect to the above SP location. If you sign where indicated and return it to me with the deposit noted below, this letter will then represent a purchase contract. A more formal Purchase and Sale Agreement will then be drafted consistent with the terms of this letter.

Seller is Absolute Corporation, a California Corporation, represented by Michael Dance, its President.

Buyer is a General Partnership whose partners are David and Della Money.

> You may designate the buyer to assume the debt on certain pieces of equipment. See Chapters 3 and 13.

The price is $210,000, and the business is to be sold free and clear of all encumbrances, with the exception of the Promissory Note and Security Agreement on the Kodak 200AF which is to be assumed by the partnership and payable to Kodak; the actual balance to be determined at the time of closing.

It is anticipated that the transfer of the business will take place at the close of business, Wednesday, August 31, 2005. There will be no adjustment for inventory, with the understanding that "normal" levels of inventory will be maintained until the time of sale. (Alternatively, there can be an adjustment for inventory at the close of business on 8/31/05, with the amount in excess of $_____ being a credit to the seller, the value of the inventory to be based on the Unisource price book then in use.)

> Apportioning attorneys' costs tends to ensure fairness and prevent negotiations from becoming protracted and costly.

Attorneys' costs in preparing the necessary documents will be apportioned equally between buyer and seller.

The transfer fee to SP Corporate (if any) will be allocated one-half each to the buyer and the seller.

> Making sales taxes the buyer's responsibility prevents the buyer from insisting on a large allocation to equipment for depreciation.

The down payment shall be $40,000 and shall be held in your (our) attorney's trust account (or in an escrow to be opened at Wells Fargo Bank) until the closing.

Sales tax will be the responsibility of the buyer. (Alternatively, the sales tax can be apportioned between buyer and seller.)

The balance of the purchase price shall be represented by a promissory note of $170,000, which will reflect monthly payments of $2,245.70 to fully amortize the balance over a ten-year period with the unpaid principal balance bearing interest at 10%.

> The late charge ensures that payment dates are observed, without each late payment triggering a serious rift after the sale.

The Purchase Money Promissory Note shall be secured by the business itself, the exact form of which will be discussed between buyer and seller. There shall be a $70 late charge should any payment be made more than two weeks after the due date and an acceleration clause upon a default in payment not cured within the appropriate time periods.

Permission for the sale transfer will be obtained from Spry Print Corporation (the franchisor) with the mutual cooperation of the buyer and seller. Consent to transfer the premises lease will also be obtained with the mutual cooperation of the buyer and the seller.

In the event that the location is resold, the full balance of the Promissory Note will be due and payable at that time.

Deposit to bind the sale will be $10,000.

The payables at date of closing will be the obligation of the seller. The receivables at date of closing will be either collected by the seller or collected by the buyer and remitted to the seller, with any uncollected receivables after 90 days following the closing being forwarded to the seller.

It is understood that the buyer may elect to have a representative attend the SP training course (in the event the franchisor has this policy), such training to be scheduled by SP Corporate.

As the buyer deems necessary, the present owner, Michael Dance, shall remain with the buyer for a period up to one month for a fixed salary of $2,000.

_____
David Money, Buyer

_____
Della Money

_____
Absolute Corporation,
by its President, Michael Dance

> The seller can avoid inheriting a new note holder by demanding full payment at the time the business is resold.
>
> The seller might pursue collections too aggressively without this clause.
>
> Paying the seller for his or her time causes the buyer to become independent more quickly.

Worksheet 14. Seller Protections

Finding the Buyer

Often, the first step toward protecting yourself from post-sale trauma is to find the right buyer for your business. Below are some types of buyer pre-qualifiers. Which will you use as part of your advertising for the business or as a screening process that you or your broker will use?

❏ Down payment requirement   ❏ Working capital requirement
❏ Security offered in addition to the business   ❏ Previous experience in the industry

Use the space below to write a potential print ad to offer your business in a trade magazine or newspaper. Consider also the size of the ad, its placement on the page, the frequency of its run, and the days of the week it will appear. You may want to call any magazines or newspapers you are considering to find out their policies on these issues.

As you write the ad, think about what the most important features of the business are, what prequalifiers you want to have for the buyer, whether or not you will mention money in the ad, and how many spaces per line your ad copy will occupy.

_____

_____

_____

_____

Protecting the Sale

Consider which protections discussed in Chapter 14 are most important to you. Many of the most important protections are listed below. Check which ones you want to have in your sale agreement and discuss them with your accountant and attorney.

❑ Require the buyer to purchase a life insurance policy for the amount of the purchase money promissory note.

❑ Require the buyer to maintain certain maximum cost percentages or other financial tests.

❑ Require the buyer to allow you to review the business's financial statements periodically.

❑ Require security from the buyer in addition to the business.

Some protections are not negotiable. You must be absolutely certain that some protective devices are included in your sale agreement. See the section, "Seller Protections," to review those protections, listed below.

- A personal signature or guarantee on the purchase money promissory note.
- An acceleration-upon-default clause in the note.
- The business held as security for the note.
- The right to examine the business's books and records in the case of a default.

Employee Disclosure

Sometimes, the most important thing you can do to protect your sale is to inform your employees early in the sale process that you intend to sell the business.

Who are your key employees who you think deserve to be told of your intent to sell early on and who should possibly be offered the opportunity to buy the business if they are financially able?

_____

_____

_____

If you have any employees who are so vital to your business's operation that you should make a contract or bonus offer to ensure that they will remain with the business during the new owner's transition period, list them here and describe what type of contract you will make.

_____

_____

_____

Finally, how will you describe your employees' roles in the business to the new owner? Will you encourage the new owner to keep all the employees at all costs or will you tell your buyer that the employees are not vital to the operation of the business and can be let go if the buyer finds it necessary or convenient?

_____

_____

_____

_____

CONTRACTS: AMBIGUITIES AND BAD MEMORIES

Contracts come in a variety of sizes and shapes. One such shape is a verbal contract, another is the written contract, and then there is the contract of assumptions. Whichever relationship you may be dealing with, it is a good idea to remember the basics. Although most people enter into contracts thinking that they are protecting themselves against the ultimate crisis of fraud, misrepresentation, and deception, the fact of the matter is that the basic purpose of the contract is to protect against ambiguities and bad memories.

The Verbal Contract

The verbal contract, although perfectly legal, is usually a less than adequate confirmation of a relationship. The reasons are simple.

Many verbal contracts are not only based on the words exchanged between the parties; they are also subject to the interpretation of the body language that goes along with the words. A nod, a drop of the shoulder, a raised eyebrow, or a body movement in a chair can often represent a great deal more about what the speaker is conveying than just the words themselves. In this way, an acknowledgment of a statement can be a total confirmation, a partial agreement, or a contrary position without the embarrassment of saying "No."

The worst part of the verbal contract is the question of defective memory. Although each party certainly will remember what he or she would prefer to remember, there is always the legitimate question of what really took place and whether or not any subsequent conversation changed the meaning of the original words. After all, most relationships are not encompassed in a single conversation about a singular event. The relationship is usually ongoing and changes are likely to occur during any period that could change the meaning of the original language.

The Contract of Assumptions

Very often, there will be a reason to establish a business relationship without the necessity for a written contract. The tendency will be to accept the fact that there are standards in the trade or industry that will have established precedents binding both parties. This is very much the contract of assumptions. It is also a package of vague understandings and expectations that doesn't afford much comfort when the time comes for closure. Memorializing the words in writing will usually eliminate this problem.

The Written Contract

To avoid the ambiguity of verbal contracts or the vague understandings and expectations of a contract of assumptions, it is a good idea to move the words and the expectations to paper and pen.

In this way, each party has an opportunity to react to the more obvious definitions and to question the more ambiguous terms. The reason for bringing the professional into the relationship at this point is to ensure that the language is clear and, for the most part, unambiguous. If a word or a phrase needs further definition, the lawyer will usually recognize the problem and eliminate the ambiguity before it becomes a point of contention. This does not mean that every turn of a phrase needs language to support its position. This gets silly in the extreme and often is the reason why problems come up in negotiations that tend to slow down or even destroy the negotiating process. Make sure your professional understands the difference between professionalism and perfection. There is no such thing as perfection in a contract. It is always subject to the ultimate decision by a finder of fact. The best you can hope for is to eliminate the obvious ambiguities in order to achieve closure.

Many times, the other party chooses not to sign such a memorandum, but this issue can also be resolved. Keep in mind that any court, including Judge Judy, will not give nearly as much credence to a memorandum created the day before a trial as it will to notes that are kept contemporaneously with the events as they happen. This should tell you that you should keep notes of every relationship as things happen, whether it is a situation between employer and employee or a contract between two companies.

When the Other Party Won't Sign

Keep in mind that Judge Judy will always find it difficult to determine who is telling the truth or who has the most accurate memory of the original details of a relationship. When she sees a contract signed by both parties, her ability to determine truth is enhanced.

What if she saw a memorandum and it was signed by only one of the parties? This could create a problem, particularly if the other party denies the validity or the truth of the written statements.

On the other hand, what if one party sends a memorandum to the other party and includes the following at the close of the letter or memo? "If I do not hear from you to the contrary, I will assume that the above is consistent with your understanding of our discus-sions." This language puts a burden on the party receiving the memorandum to respond to it, denying those things that are not "consistent with" his or her understanding of the discussions. By not responding in timely fashion, he or she is accepting the language. Every court will find such a memorandum determinative unless dynamic proof to the contrary is presented.

After all, what exactly is a contract? It is a relationship between two or more parties, each of whom has obligations to perform and prerogatives to enjoy. It should not be the beginning of problems; it should be the agreement that avoids them.

CHAPTER 15

The Motivations Behind the Sale

A SUCCESSFUL BUSINESS SALE REQUIRES BOTH buyer and seller to know the motivation and mind-set of the other as the negotiations proceed. The motivations of both parties have important implications long after the papers are signed. What most sellers do not realize is that the buyer's motivations often revolve around business style and concepts of entrepreneurship. How and whether your buyer delegates authority and how quickly he or she learns the business may influence whether your promissory note is paid. Is your buyer prepared for the training involved in taking over business operations? Will he or she need your help during this period?

If the buyer doesn't succeed at the business and does not meet the payments on your purchase money promissory note, your efforts to procure a successful sale have failed. Make sure that you contribute to the future success of the business by understanding the motivations behind the sale.

WHY ARE YOU SELLING?

Whether someone is interested in buying a car or a business, the potential buyer always wants to know why the seller is selling. The reason, obviously, shouldn't be that the car isn't performing well or the business is not gratifying or profitable. This will hardly motivate the buyer. Explain your reasons in such a way that the buyer can understand and feel comfortable with them. If someone is selling a car, it may be that he or she wants a better car, a faster car, or a four-door car. Why are you selling your business? Do you want to retire from business? Are you planning to move to Hawaii? Would you like to travel to Europe? Do you need to deal with health problems?

Whatever the reasons, think them through, make them solid, and make sure that your partners, professionals, and others involved in the negotiations are properly informed. You do not want to fabricate your reasons for the purpose of the sale. Misrepresenting yourself or your business could cause the buyer to rescind the sale later on. It is a good idea to discuss this with your attorney.

You must also make the selling story believable. No one, in most industries, would ever say that operating a business is easy. Business is exacting and requires constant attention to detail. If the potential for growth and profit is extraordinary, however, then the exercise is worthwhile. How you explain this paradox is important. Carefully prepare your presentation to respond to your buyer's thinking. If the business is too easy, everybody would be doing it. If the business is too tough, only the experts could handle it. Make sure the buyer understands that it is a good day's wage for a good day's labor and an equity potential in the bargain. Nobody really expects more—and nobody wants to pay for less.

Sometimes, sellers think irrationally about the value of their business. They have put much of their life, money, and energy into building and maintaining it. A seller's emotional ties to his or her business can cause a kind of paranoia during negotiations.

The value of a business is really based on the value it represents to its owner or a buyer. Value can be interpreted in many ways. A business that generates sufficient income to accommodate the needs of a family is valuable. When no one shows an interest in buying a business, it seems less valuable. When more than one person is interested in buying it, the business's value rises. You may be willing to make concessions in price and other variables when there are few interested buyers. It is quite a different story when you find that you are dealing with a qualified buying candidate. Such a motivated buyer may increase the value you perceive in your business. However, you can also blow the sale if your desire for a high selling price prevents you from properly assessing the business's value.

> ## ▼ Illustration 15.1 A Seller's Paranoia
>
> **A**l Morrow had a potential offer on his business that would have eliminated his creditor problems. Despite this good fortune, he evidenced a somewhat irrational emotional attitude.
>
> "I'll be damned if I'm going to let someone steal this business from me after all I've done to build it up from nothing. I'd rather see it go down the drain than give it away."
>
> Al was offered a fair price and probably could have consummated the deal if it were not for his attitude. Every minor point of the negotiations became a deal breaker. He became so paranoid as to believe that everyone was trying to do him in—including the buyer, the buyer's attorney, the broker, and, on occasion, even his own professional team. Everyone was suspect.

It is essential that you, as a seller, build a professional team in which you have confidence. You must give them the responsibility for helping you make decisions that will be good for you and your family in both the short and the long term. You must then accept their advice, with the understanding that it is still ultimately your decision. Remember: a fair price for both buyer and seller exists within very logical parameters. A little objectivity can go a long way in recognizing just what those parameters are.

THE BUYER'S MOTIVATIONS

In the long run, however, your reasons for selling are secondary to the buyer's motivations to buy. Your buyer's motivations may be much more subtle. You must draw them out, however, because they affect the buyer's style and approach to operating the business after you are gone, the driving forces to getting your promissory note paid.

You have every right to examine just who your potential buyers are. The Sample Confidential Business Application (Figure 15.1 on the next two pages) asks for your buyer's financial status, educational background, and business experience. However, this kind of information may not answer whether the business will fulfill his or her goals or whether he or she likes the industry, the business, the marketplace, the geography, the people, or the hours—all of which are vital to bringing about a successful sale.

You will likely encounter many types of buyers. Be prepared to deal with their different qualifications and characteristics. Here are some possibilities:

- Marketing or salespeople
- Engineers
- Shopkeepers
- Professionals
- Military people
- Blue-collar workers
- White-collar workers

Some businesses perform both manufacturing and retail sales. Manufacturing can require technical skill or experience, which can intimidate a potential buyer. You may want to reassure this type of buyer by explaining that technical people are available at a price and that the ability to sell is probably more critical to successful business.

FIGURE 15.1　Sample Confidential Business Application (continued on next page)

Confidential Information

Applicant's Full Name _____	Social Security # _____
Spouse's Full Name _____	Social Security # _____
Address _____	How long at this address? _____
City/State _____	Own ❑　Rent ❑
Business Phone _____	Home Phone _____

Personal Data

Single ❑　　　Separated ❑　　　Married ❑　　　Divorced ❑　　　Widowed ❑

Number of dependents _____　Ages of children _____ _____ _____　Monthly alimony/child _____

Record of Employment (List most recent position first. Indicate "A" for Applicant and "S" for Spouse.)

A/S	Employer	City/State	Position/Title	From	To	Income per Year

Gross Monthly Income

	Applicant	Spouse	Total
Dividends/Interest	$	$	$
Net Rental Income	$	$	$
Pension Income	$	$	$
Other Income*	$	$	$
	$	$	$
	$	$	$
	$	$	$
Total	$	$	$

Monthly Living Expenses

Rent	$
First Mortgage	$
Additional Financing	$
Other Expenses*	$
	$
	$
	$
Total	$

List Credit References (Indicate "A" for Applicant and "S" for Spouse.)

A/S	Creditor's Name/Address	Account Number	Present Balance	Date Paid

*Please itemize. If necessary, attach a separate listing.

FIGURE 15.1   Sample Confidential Business Application (continued)

Financial Data

As of _____ 20 _____

Individual Statement ❑   Joint Statement ❑   (If individual statement, a separate statement for spouse is required.)

Applicant ❑

Spouse ❑

Assets*		Liabilities and Equity*	
Checking Account		Accounts Payable	
Bank Name		Bank Loans (Unsecured)*	$
Address		Bank Name	
Account No.		Bank Address	
Balance	$		
Savings Account		Bank Loans (Secured)*	$
Bank Name		Bank Name	
Address		Bank Address	
Account No.			
Balance	$	Credit Card Balances*	$
Stocks/Bonds (Negotiable)	$		
Money Market Funds/			
Certificates of Deposit	$		
Real Estate		Taxes Due and Accrued	$
Estimated Market Value	$	Mortgages Payable	$
Type of Property:		Other Loans or Notes Payable	$
Personal Property	$		
Automobiles	$	Loans Against Life Insurance	$
How many? Year(s)		Other Debts*	$
Retirement Plans (Vested)	$		$
Other Assets*	$		$
	$	Total Liabilities (B)	$
		Equity (Net Worth) (A – B)	$
Total Assets (A)	$	Total Liabilities and Equity	$

* Please itemize. If necessary, attach a separate listing.

An ideal buying candidate is helpful, pleasant, conversational, smiling, knowledgeable, and caring. No one person has all the human elements necessary to properly operate a successful business all the time. As long as you find potential buyers who have one or some of the talents necessary to operate your business, can admit to the ones they don't have, and know how to rely on people to fill the gaps in their own experience, you have a pool of potential candidates.

Entrepreneurship and Business Style

Most buyers have read so much about owning their own business that they have what is sometimes called the entrepreneur bug. Even if they have been behind a desk in a big company for the past 20 years, they are sure that they have the qualifications to own a business. For the buyer's benefit and as a reflection on your own entrepreneurial talents, examine the differences between a do-it-yourselfer and a good supervisor. How will your buyer handle these two roles?

The goal of the do-it-yourselfer and the goal of tthe supervisor are the same—to get a job done successfully. The difference is in their methods. In many businesses, like picture framing or button making, you are a retailer and a manufacturer. You are also the advertising department, bookkeeper, inventory manager, customer service representative, procurement manager, equipment buyer, personnel manager, and salesperson. You must take control to get these jobs done.

You know the old cliché, "If I don't do it, no one will." This can be a business owner's strength; it can also be his or her greatest weakness.

> ## Illustration 15.2 A Franchisor's Evaluation
>
> Franchisors deal with the question of a potential franchisee's business style every time they sell a new franchise. John Scott, former CEO of Fastframe USA, called the type of buyers he looked for "soft entrepreneurs":
>
> It is certainly true that we are always looking for aggressive, driving, creative, self-motivated people, but you have to be careful. The man or woman who recognizes that we've spent a lot of money over a long period to "get it right," who sees the real benefits, that's the soft entrepreneur. That is the man or woman we are looking for.

Be a Leader and a Teacher

The very elements that make a good entrepreneur, doing it yourself, are the same elements that can prevent you from delegating responsibility. Sometimes, your employees know better or less expensive ways to get things done. Sometimes a previous owner or your franchise company knows the industry and the market better than you do. Take time to examine how your business can grow and leave enough room for your employees, partners, or investors to use their creativity and ingenuity. In this way, you can depend on your people to help you adapt to changing times and a changing marketplace.

Being personally involved in every aspect of your business operations at the beginning is clearly appropriate. Total understanding of each working element is necessary for your ultimate success. However, you must eventually depend on other people in order for your business to succeed. At that point, you will have two more roles to add to your repertoire: teacher and leader.

The key to converting your business style is not only delegating responsibility, but also giving the commensurate authority that goes with it. If you are going to give someone a job and then stand there while he or she does the job, then you are quite right: you might as well do it yourself. But if you have taught your people properly and shown them by your own example how you expect a job to be done and then you let them do it, you will be an effective supervisor, an important skill for any business owner. Yes, your people will make mistakes, and some may be costly, but a well-planned program of supervision will minimize the magnitude of these risks.

Give the Buyer the Benefit of Your Experience

Some businesses work well at a smaller size or with a closely knit fabric of owner participation. Other businesses function more effectively when the owner leaves the basic business operation to his or her staff. The buyer will be looking at these alternatives. It is your job to encourage this examination. While your business may have achieved its maximum productivity under your management, the business may also benefit from a change in management technique. The success of your buyer might well depend on his or her ability to recognize a better way to do something you have been doing the same way for years.

If the buyer wants to change management style, it is in your best interest to give him or her your best, objective judgment. You can operate a small business successfully in many ways. You may send some collateral functions outside, like bookkeeping to an accounting firm. Your buyer, however, may need to maintain control over such processes internally. When you start a business, you need to find the time to do almost everything yourself, yet you lack knowledge of the different job functions. As the business grows and you become more knowledgeable and efficient, you develop time savers. Share with the buyer how you underwent this process. Be careful, however, that the tale of your business education excites, rather than overwhelms, your buyer.

Learning the Business

If potential buyers are not from the industry, they will be concerned about a training or familiarization period that will enable them to successfully take over the business. You may ease their minds by telling them the philosophy of most franchise companies—they would rather sell a new franchise to someone who knows absolutely nothing about the business than to someone from inside the industry who may have bad habits that are difficult to change.

Learning the basics of properly operating a business is much more important than learning the specifics of any particular industry. Statistics show that the vast majority of franchised owners had never been involved in the particular industry before their purchase. This news should give potential buyers a much greater comfort zone if they are not especially expert in the industry they are entering.

In most franchise situations, the franchise company makes some arrangements for a training period. Some companies charge for this and some don't. In any event, you should always be willing to devote whatever time is necessary to properly orient your buyer to take over the business in the most successful way. Make sure the buyer understands that you will not leave him or her to the whim of the fates after the sale.

Remember: the buyer's success is what gets your note paid and what secures your peace of mind until he or she pays it off completely. Buyers' attitudes change dramatically when they are reminded of this during the early discussions. Also keep in mind that the time you devote to initial training or post-franchise training or even to serving in a supervisory capacity need not be without compensation. In fact, if the buyer is paying you a salary for orientation and training, he or she will be eager to release you as quickly as possible.

KEY POINTS TO REMEMBER

- You must be able to present a logical and understandable reason for wanting to sell your business.
- Be careful not to let greed or principle prevent you from getting a good, negotiated price.
- The buyer must satisfy you that his or her talents, experience, and goals are consistent with the size, profit, and growth potential of the business.
- Make sure the buyer understands the fundamental principles for operating a business successfully.
- Make sure that the buyer's personality and business style are consistent with the needs of the business's customer base.

Worksheet 15. Seller and Buyer Motivations

Below are questions that will help you analyze your motivations for selling and help you prepare for buyer questions regarding your reasons for selling.

Seller Motivations

What are your motives for selling your business? _____

_____

_____

_____

Which of your motives are most compelling or convincing? _____

_____

_____

_____

Describe your selling story, including a history of how your business attained its present success. _____

_____

_____

_____

Are there any parts of your selling story that are "material disclosures" or mandatory disclosures you need to make to the buyer? Yes ❑ No ❑

If you answered yes, make sure they are developed into your selling portfolio. Use the space below to describe them.

_____

_____

_____

What alternative selling positions might you consider to give yourself and your business the best selling posture?

_____

_____

_____

The following questions will help you analyze your buyer and his or her chances for success with the business. Your buyer's success is crucial to your ultimate success in selling your business.

Buyer Motivations

Describe the type of buyer you think you are dealing with. _____

_____

_____

_____

What particular skills or qualities does your buyer bring to the business? _____
_____
_____
_____

What skills or qualities important to your business does your buyer lack? _____
_____
_____
_____

How can the buyer supplement his or her skills or acquire the skills he or she lacks? _____
_____
_____
_____

What kind of transition period does your buyer need and how will the buyer need your services during that transition?
_____
_____
_____

WHO IS GOING TO BUY YOUR BUSINESS?

There are those naysayers who warn, "This is a bad time to try to sell your business." But is it?!

The Usual Suspects

What is most interesting is that the typical candidates are still looking. And they are not the only ones. There is the "younger group"—people who feel that their energy and innovative ideas represent the baseline for accelerated growth. There is the "older group"—people who feel that their practical experience in the industry will give them an advantage in growing a business. There are those who don't want to answer to others because they feel their business judgment is better than the judgment of those by whom they are employed. There are others who want to build something for their children. And those who have always wanted to be "the captain of their ship and the master of their destiny." But now, there are others.

The Flexible Job Market

There are many for whom there is no alternative except to be in business for themselves. They have been in industry with good jobs and good pay and good benefits ... and the job is gone. They have been "downsized." The jobs that are available neither use their experience and abilities nor generate the kind of money that has brought them to a place in the sun ... that they would not like to leave. Most of these people have saved some money over the years and they know that it will not last unless they put it to good use. These are the people in addition to "the usual suspects."

Buying a Business

Although many think about starting a business, many others recognize that buying a business eliminates a lot of the risk involved in starting from scratch. They understand that the history of an existing business can be a pretty good gauge of its future if many of the basic business elements can be maintained. A business that is capable of generating an immediate income, even though it might not anticipate an accelerated dot-com type growth, can be very appealing to someone who needs to create a comfort zone for the family and the future. The only caution is to be careful about understanding the nature of the business, its position in its industry, and its place in the competitive marketplace.

Valuing the Business for the Buyer

A good concept to keep in mind is that "a business ought to be able to buy itself." In other words, once the buyer puts a substantial down payment on the business, his or her "salary" and money to make payments on the balance of the purchase price should come from the profit of the business. With this philosophy in mind, many buyers will be willing, even eager to buy your business. This should tell you that this may very well be the best time to consider selling your business.

The Legal Paperwork ... from Both Sides

For whatever reason, both the buyer and the seller of a business always feel that they each must have the upper hand. This usually applies to all the documentation of a sale as well as the price and the terms. Those who have had enough experience will tell you that this need not be the case.

The deal must meet the rational requirements of both parties. The price must be such that "the business can buy itself." The terms must be such that the seller can enjoy the equity that he or she has earned and the buyer can enjoy the benefits of ownership and profit sufficient to feed his or her family. Finally, the paperwork must allow both sides to feel comfortable in terms of protection: the seller with some assurance of collecting the balance of the purchase price and the buyer with equal assurance that the business is what the seller represented it to be.

This, indeed, may be just as good a time to sell your business as any other, with all of the appropriate cautions still applicable.

Before the Sale

REAL ESTATE BROKERS SAY A WELL-MAINTAINED, well-manicured, and recently cleaned house sells faster and for more money than the deserted, unkempt house of a disinterested seller. The same is certainly true for a business. Take the time to invest that little extra bit of energy or creativity—or money—to make your business slightly more attractive.

This chapter focuses on how to prepare your business for sale—to cut costs and deal with outstanding debt before the sale. It also discusses how to prepare an ailing business for sale and when it may be necessary or appropriate to consider bankruptcy as an alternative.

The chapter begins with a successful and financially sound business and then examines various business problems of increasing severity—their symptoms, diagnosis, and treatment. By the end of the chapter, you will know how to deal with creditors and cut excess costs to improve your asking price. If you are concerned about needing bankruptcy protection, the chapter compares the various bankruptcy alternatives to help you decide which best fits your situation.

A SUCCESSFUL BUSINESS

Even the best-run business with an optimum operating profit has creditors. Buyers assume they will purchase the business free and clear of all encumbrances, including debt, unless it is built into the selling price. All your creditors, therefore, should be notified of a potential sale at some point.

Normally, the buyer's counsel will file a bulk sales transfer notice in the appropriate newspaper or periodical. Such an advertisement gives the buyer the protection of having notified the creditors that the business is being sold. This puts the creditors on notice to seek protection for their obligations before the sale is consummated. If they fail to seek protection on their debts after you advertise the bulk sales notice—even though they may not actually have seen the notice—they cannot then hold the buyer responsible for obligations incurred by the seller before the sale. However, taxing authorities, state, federal, and municipal, are not necessarily wiped out by such a notice and might remain a problem for the buyer after the sale.

Consult your accountant or attorney for advice regarding tax obligations and the bulk sale transfer notice. In particular, ask your attorney if your state's bulk sale law has been repealed. Numerous states have recently repealed or are in the process of repealing these laws. If your state has repealed its bulk sales law, then you, as the seller, may be asked to guarantee all unpaid obligations.

Regardless, always notify your creditors of the pending sale in a businesslike fashion to ensure a smooth transition of the business from seller to buyer. Embarrassing situations can arise if the creditors find out through third-party rumor. In cases where creditors are unsure whether you will make payment, they will probably put the claim into the escrow.

You may be wise to put your sale through an escrow, a relatively inexpensive process, which will ensure the creditors their payments in full before the business is actually turned over to the buyer and you receive the proceeds of the sale.

An escrow is a trust account held by a third party who is charged with the responsibility of holding all monies and papers until all conditions of the escrow are observed. The creditor submits his or her bill to the escrow agent and will normally take no other action, such as filing a lawsuit, that could cause the buyer to back out of the sale. As always, it is to your advantage to ensure that the buyer's relationship with all your vendors starts off positively.

If creditors are unaware of the escrow or the pending sale, they might bring a lawsuit against both buyer and seller after the fact. No matter what legal rights a creditor has, you and your buyer do not want to contend with a lawsuit after you consummate the sale.

As long as your creditors know you will bring their accounts current before the sale, they will normally not do anything to jeopardize your sale. As always, discuss this with your professional advisors when the time is right.

A GOOD BUSINESS WITH INSUFFICIENT OPERATING PROFIT

If your business is suffering from insufficient operating profit, this will affect your asking price. Reevaluate the business to find the reasons for the lack of profit. You will need to look at many potential problem areas.

- High inventory
- Unnecessary personnel
- Employee benefits
- Inadequate collection efforts
- Owner compensation too much
- Personal bills too heavy for the business to carry
- Rent increase cannot be accommodated
- Too many locations for the business to handle
- Improper margins maintained for selling purposes
- Older equipment no longer state-of-the-art
- New competitors in the marketplace
- New price structure for retail customers
- Theft by personnel of goods or money
- Maintenance costs or service contracts too costly

You can treat the problems in several ways, depending on the diagnosis. The following examples will give you a good start in finding where your problems lie. See also the worksheet at the end of this chapter.

- Do an immediate analysis of the profit and loss statement to find the specifics of the problem. Compare the statement with statements from prior years and months to find out if the problem is connected to seasonality or to a permanent change.
- Evaluate the industry to determine if the problem is widespread or if it's specific to your particular business.
- Reexamine the margins for profit potential and look for extra costs of sale that have affected the profit. Very often, businesses neglect to pass on to their customers many of the cost increases. For example, they may add pickup and delivery to their services without adding the increased costs of the service to the price they charge.
- Think about all of your employees in relation to their jobs, their incentives, and each other. Find out whether the team concept is working and what is required to make all employees more effective.
- Examine changes in customer preferences, styles, attitudes, and levels of sophistication. Sometimes, a product or service that was peripheral a decade ago becomes primary.

- Think about training or retraining employees and sales personnel. Because the marketplace evolves so rapidly today, your personnel need to keep up with sales and marketing techniques, computer innovations, and customer relations strategies.

- Consider updating your personnel manual, benefits packages, and salary scales to ensure your employees stay satisfied, challenged, and productive.

- Reevaluate your facility from the customer's perspective. Look at its size, appearance, convenience, parking, competition, and niche in the marketplace. You can too easily become complacent about your facility because you see it every day and fail to notice the cracks in the walls. New customers see these things as soon as they enter your business.

- Consider how to expand business using your existing customer base. How can you make better use of that valuable asset? How can you get existing customers to buy more product or use more services? If you have been in business long enough, you know that it is easier to build on your existing base than to find new customers.

- Look at the current advertising-marketing approach to new business. Advertising is not an expense of doing business; it is an investment. A good marketing analysis will often dictate the most cost-effective advertising approach.

- Get some research and development advice about the latest equipment technology, to maintain a competitive balance. Be careful to get an objective analysis and not just a sales pitch.

- Get a physical examination and perhaps a mental evaluation. Make sure the problems you are facing are not emotional or a phobia that might otherwise be contained. People may go through periods or phases in their lives, such as midlife crisis, which may take many forms. A physical or mental examination may reveal reasons why a business is failing.

- Consider procedures for collecting outstanding debts, including compromise and litigation. More success in collecting could be at least a partial answer to dollar problems.

- Analyze your total asset portfolio, to minimize the possibility of a business failure causing a personal disaster. An analysis of your assets will show any vulnerability of your personal and family holdings. You will sleep much better knowing that your life's savings are not at risk.

- Deal with your creditors to avoid legal action during sale negotiations. Even if your business is fairly strong, you probably have some creditors with whom your account is not current. If they find out about a sale, they may retain attorneys to protect their interests. You may want to reassure them in writing that you will take care of their accounts before closing the sale.

A GOOD BUSINESS WITH SOME STANDING DEBT

Some businesses continue successful operations despite outstanding debts on which the owners have not made payments for some time. If you have some standing debt, you may be considering selling in order to pay those creditors from the purchase price. Again, the buyer normally expects to receive the business free of such obligations.

You can handle more serious creditor problems in several ways. Your first task is always to step back from the day-to-day business details and prioritize the elements you need to resolve. The earlier you get to the problem, the easier it is to negotiate with all the people involved and the more time you have to orchestrate the alternatives. The numbers are smaller, your creditors are less frustrated, and you have more money with which to negotiate.

A BUSINESS WITH SERIOUS SOLVENCY PROBLEMS

Again, your business problems may result from a variety of causes. For example, you may have used your credit cards for business purposes or overextended your capacity to move your inventory and have a large debt to suppliers looming over the business. Either of these situations can cause creditors to start lawsuits.

If your situation has reached these proportions, your best course is to have your attorney contact the creditors directly and immediately to ensure that they don't do anything to interfere with the sale. You do not need to share these problems with your buyer because he or she is getting the business free and clear of all debt. If the problems derive from situations other than the business itself (they very often do), it is really none of the buyer's business. A lawyer normally has credibility in the business community that can eliminate these potential problems before they get out of hand.

When the escrow closes and the buyer takes over the business, these debts will be paid out of the escrow by prearrangement and will not be a part of the buyer's ongoing obligations. In fact, if one of your solvency problems is excess inventory, you may choose to sell off some of the inventory before the sale, providing the amount specified in the sale is not affected, and you can pay off the account even before the escrow closes.

BUSINESS DISASTER PENDING

If you are on the verge of business disaster, you definitely need to retain some sort of business advisor who understands your alternatives for dealing with your business problems. If you are facing some serious business problems and are not sure of your ground, get some good advice as soon as possible.

In analyzing your debt, tuck three basic words into your vocabulary: communication, consistency, and credibility.

More specifically, try to do the following:

- **Maintain communication.** However embarrassing or stressful it is to talk with someone to whom you owe money, that person is entitled to at least the courtesy of your recognition that the debt exists.
- **Create consistency.** It matters less how much you pay on an overdue debt than the fact that you pay something! Send something consistently and you show good faith and extend the patience of your creditor.
- **Don't lose credibility.** Promise to pay what you can and always fulfill your promise. "The check is in the mail" gets stale very quickly. If the check doesn't arrive as promised, you may not get a second chance—probably when you need it most.

In addition to these generic means of staving off financial disaster, your accountant and attorney will have specific steps you can take, depending on your situation.

▼ Illustration 16.1 Protect Your House and Your Business

Ted Foster bought a business for $300,000 and operated it as a sole proprietorship. He paid $50,000 down and signed a purchase money promissory note for the balance of the purchase price. The note required him to pay $3,000 per month for five years and then pay off the balloon balance of $70,000 at that time. He made payments on time until the end of the fourth year when the business got so bad that he fell behind. He still has 12 months of $3,000 payments and then the balloon payment of $70,000. The seller is threatening to take the business back if he continues to be late with his payments.

He has used all the cash he has, including the money from a second mortgage on his house. The house still has equity in it, but the bank won't lend him anymore because the salary he gets from the business is not enough for a larger monthly payment and the business cannot afford to pay him more.

Ted's biggest problem is that he has waited a long time before dealing with the situation. He has fallen behind in the promissory note payments and lost the seller's faith in his ability to recover. He now needs to step back from the day-to-day business details and prioritize the issues he needs to resolve.

First, Ted needs to deal with the balloon balance of $70,000. He paid $50,000 in cash and $3,000 per month since the purchase. He obviously has a serious investment in the business and doesn't want to lose it. Further, the business has been successful during most of this time, so the viability of the business, the industry, and Ted's ability to operate the business are not in question. The balloon balance of $70,000 due in 12 months is a serious concern if the original seller refuses to arrange for a new note and a viable payment schedule. The fact that Ted is now two months in arrears will obviously not help the situation. Rescheduling the note to pay the balloon balance on a reasonable monthly schedule is his first priority toward saving his home and business. He should contact a lawyer or an accountant immediately, preferably those who worked on the original sale.

Next, because Ted's house still has equity, he should protect it from the creditors who may bring lawsuits against him. It's probably the asset they

If, like the business owner in Illustration 16.1, you are concerned about protecting your home from creditors, you should know that you have some protection. Most states have a protective device called a homestead act. It allows you to protect a certain amount of the equity you have in the residential property in which you live. In one state, for example, you can protect only $7,500; in another, you can protect all the equity regardless of amount. Still other states have different protections for individuals and for husbands and wives. In California, for example, the protection amounts to $250,000 for a single person and $500,000 for a married couple. Check with a competent lawyer in your state to find out just how much you can protect. Once you protect your home, you can devote your attention to protecting your business.

THE BANKRUPTCY ALTERNATIVE

Many sellers think that if their business has financial problems so severe that they need to declare bankruptcy, they have lost everything. Bankruptcy does not have to mean the end for all entrepreneurs. Some types of bankruptcies allow you to sell your business in pieces to various buyers. Chapter 17 describes the circumstances under which a buyer may purchase a bankrupt business from the trustee in bankruptcy. Some sellers can continue to operate their business after the bankruptcy or resurrect parts of the business that still have value and start over.

For example, one entrepreneur in trouble found that he had no alternative but to file a Chapter 7 bankruptcy. In due course, a trustee in bankruptcy was appointed and took over all the assets to be sold for the benefit of the creditors. Even though the customer list technically belonged to the trustee, it was impossible to find a buyer who thought that it had any intrinsic value. However, the personal relationships of the business owner allowed him to start up his business immediately following the bankruptcy. All of the customers who had learned to trust him over the years didn't allow the bankruptcy to be a barrier; they started doing business with him again. It wasn't long before he opened another shop and started building the new business based on the start he got from his old customers.

No one is going to put you in jail or ask that your firstborn be sold just because you can't pay your bills. Declaring bankruptcy is embarrassing and can be a major setback to achieving your business goals, but if it is your reality, then you must reckon with it. You will do the best you can within the parameters of your financial strength, your available personnel, your innate creativity, and your human energies. But it just might not be enough. Some people want to blame market conditions, unfair competition, or the franchisor. Some blame themselves. What difference does it make? All that really matters is that you need to face the problems and deal with them.

If there is a business solution to your business problem, certainly you will take it. If you can sell the business (even without a profit) and get out of trouble, you will sell it. If this type of solution is not possible, then you must consider the alternatives. In any case, consult a good bankruptcy lawyer for all the details.

Remember these two very important things if you are contemplating protection under the bankruptcy laws.

- Certain tax obligations as well as some personal debts don't get wiped out in any event.
- If you are filing as a corporate entity, any personal guaranties or joint and several obligations leave you vulnerable to your corporate creditors. They do not get wiped out in the corporate bankruptcy proceeding. The only way to eliminate these is by filing a personal bankruptcy. If you are thinking about bankruptcy, think of all the ramifica-

tions. Speak to your attorney, particularly in the wake of any new bankruptcy legislation.

Finally, if you are contemplating the possibility of bankruptcy, be very careful about how you use the word in conversation with your creditors. Don't be arrogant. Bankruptcy is a delicate matter: even with the protection the bankruptcy acts provide, you want to handle your creditors carefully.

In your presentation to your creditors, you must be prepared to answer their questions candidly and accurately and understand exactly how the bankruptcy act works. You don't have to become a lawyer or an expert, but if you expect your creditors to pay attention to any entreaties you make regarding a bankruptcy solution, you must understand what it will do for you and for your creditors. You must be prepared intellectually and emotionally to file bankruptcy, if it becomes appropriate. If your creditors are not convinced that you are ready to take whatever steps are necessary to secure your future, they will not change their positions. If you are not willing to do whatever it takes, like actually filing the bankruptcy, the ruse may well leave you with fewer options than you had to begin with with fewer options.

A Chapter 7 Bankruptcy

The worst possible bankruptcy scenario is a Chapter 7 liquidation. Under a Chapter 7, all the money and property you own and all the obligations you owe are immediately transferred to a trustee in bankruptcy. The trustee's responsibility is to expeditiously convert your assets to cash and distribute the proceeds (after the costs and expenses of the bankruptcy) to the creditors in a pro rata manner, with some deference to the creditor status (secured or unsecured).

Once you have filed, the matter is taken out of your hands and you have no influence with respect to how creditors are paid. In fact, a bankruptcy precludes you from making any payments to old creditors, family, and friends in a preferential fashion. However, you have the prerogative of rehabilitating any debts that you choose to take on personally. You might want or need to do this if you intend to stay in business under a new name, since you may need to continue dealing with some of your creditors. Keep in mind, however, that you can file bankruptcy only every seven years. If

you take on too large a burden of debt, you may not only lose the advantage of the bankruptcy, but also create a similar disaster without having recourse to the bankruptcy court the next time around.

Certainly, many intricacies exist in the language of the act, but basically, that is all that is involved. You can protect certain things from the trustee, like a portion of the equity in your home. And certain obligations are not wiped out, such as taxes that you owe to the government. Finally, any money that you earn after filing bankruptcy is not subject to any of your old obligations, with certain exceptions, like the taxes.

You may find it difficult to see the benefit of this approach. Even though you eliminate your liabilities, you also lose all your assets. The singular exception is the equity in your home. Interestingly enough, however, losing all your assets in bankruptcy does not have to be debilitating. If you have the kind of business that depends on customer relationships, you may be able to resurrect your business contacts in a matter of minutes after filing the bankruptcy petition and none of your future earnings or assets are in jeopardy from former creditors. The trustee in bankruptcy technically owns the names of your customers, but if the relationship is personal, then no one can take that selling advantage away from you. Having the ability to resurrect your business via customer contacts is not a good reason to file the Chapter 7 petition; it is merely a way to pick up some of the pieces if filing becomes inevitable. A good lawyer or business consultant can help you orchestrate this new beginning if you find yourself trapped in this position.

If you understand how this works and can explain it to your more belligerent creditors, you may convince them that another alternative is better for them. If the trustee is obliged to sell your assets quickly, he or she will get considerably less than market value for them. A forced sale always brings bargain prices. The proceeds that creditors will be sharing may be as little as 10% of the true value of your assets. Most creditors don't even want to go through the paperwork for so little. If, on the other hand, you can convince your creditors that the business is strong and viable and that, with a little more time, they will get much more than they would in a Chapter 7 liquidation, possibly even 100% of what you owe them, they may allow you some breathing space.

A Chapter 11 Bankruptcy

Before you dive into filing a Chapter 7 petition, you must examine the Chapter 11 reorganization. After looking at Chapter 7, some people consider the Chapter 11 a much better alternative. The positive aspects of the comparison are certainly encouraging.

The Chapter 11 allows you to remain the "debtor in possession." In other words, you may continue to operate the business exactly as you did before filing the Chapter 11 petition—with one difference! After filing the petition and during the entire bankruptcy period, you, the debtor, are entitled to many kinds of relief. For example, no one can bring a lawsuit against you for any reason, all lawsuits that have been brought against you must immediately stop, and no one is entitled to harass you for any obligation incurred prior to the filing of the petition. (This relief, of course, is available to you during any bankruptcy filing.)

To take advantage of the Chapter 11 reorganization, you must qualify. This qualification entails proving to the court that the business has sufficient revenue (cash flow) to take care of all business maintenance costs and to pay at least part of the outstanding stale debt in a reasonable time. If you can't show this, both the court and creditors will see no reason for the business to continue at all. A Chapter 7 liquidation will be the more likely event.

If you can qualify, the court grants you some time (usually about 90 days) within which to formulate and present a plan to the court explaining how the business can continue to operate, pay all its current bills, and pay its old creditors. Sometimes, you can pay your creditors 100% of what you owe; other times, you can offer only a percentage of what you owe.

You may ask at this point, "If I haven't been able to pay my old debts before filing the Chapter 11 petition, what makes you think that I can pay them after filing?" Chapter 11 reorganization means just that—permission to reorganize and restructure your business in a variety of ways.

Let's take as an example a business owner with a lease for premises that are too large and too expensive and with leased equipment that the business really doesn't need. These leases are called executory contracts—contracts with certain aspects yet to be performed. Another example of an executory contract is a franchise.

In a bankruptcy, any kind of bankruptcy, you have the right to accept or reject an executory contract. If the owner was paying $5,000 per month on her old lease and now pays only $2,000 per month on a new lease, she would have $3,000 freed up with which to address her old obligations. If she was paying $5,000 per month on the two pieces of equipment that she didn't want or need, she would have $5,000 freed up with which to address her old obligations. The business could continue, she would meet her current obligations, and she would now have an additional $8,000 per month for her old obligations.

If you can free up a certain amount of money by rejecting executory contracts, you can present a plan to the bankruptcy court showing how you will pay old obligations with that money. As long as the creditors would receive more money from a Chapter 11 reorganization than they would from a Chapter 7 liquidation, the court will likely approve your plan.

The people whose executory contracts you reject (the lease for the premises and the leases on the equipment) are not left without recourse. However, their recourse is only through the bankruptcy court and the balance of their obligations is put in with all the other creditors. They may receive proportionately more than some of the other creditors, but the amount of money you pay on your plan each month will remain the same. Meanwhile, you can essentially get out of the leases and, when the plan is concluded in about five years, you will have eliminated all those obligations. The five-year period is somewhat arbitrary and will depend on the circumstances of the bankruptcy, including the nature and strength of the business and the attitude of the court and creditors. The courts are not eager to monitor these plans over an extended period. They usually allow only a reasonable payout period; nationwide, courts do not look favorably on periods longer than five years.

The bottom line is that you would be able to eliminate some debts and free up some cash monthly with which you could pay creditors on old bills. The court would reschedule your old obligations to fall within the plan presented by your counsel.

A Chapter 13 Bankruptcy

The last possibility is a Chapter 13, originally referred to as a wage earner's plan. It has been expanded to include entrepreneurs, but business owners qualify only if they operate their business as a sole proprietorship, not a corporation.

Qualification for a Chapter 13 is different from qualification for a Chapter 11. You must owe no more than $250,000 in unsecured debt and no more than $750,000 in secured debt. The reason for the larger category of secured debt is that the legislators recognized that many entrepreneurs own their own homes. These homes are secured by mortgages (trust deeds) to banks.

You must show that the business is viable and that it can support your family and pay old obligations. If you can show these things, then you may be able to take advantage of this approach. A Chapter 13 is the same as a Chapter 11 in that you continue to operate the business after filing the petition just as you did before filing. You have available the relief against lawsuits and harassment, the homestead act protection, and the prerogative to accept or reject executory contracts. Chapter 13 is different from Chapter 11 in that you pay all your *excess* cash to a trustee who deducts 10% for fees and costs and remits the balance to your creditor group. A Chapter 13 is a less expensive bankruptcy in terms of filing fees and attorney involvement. Also, the time allowed by the court to finalize your bankruptcy is somewhat less than the Chapter 11; courts are more inclined to a shorter period of time, about three years. At the end of that period, just as with the Chapter 11, you will be free from your old debts.

Bankruptcy: The Bottom Line

Bankruptcy has a negative impact on your life: you must recognize this before you decide to go forward with it. A financial housecleaning is preferable to bankruptcy, but if your creditors are not willing to give you that opportunity, you may have no alternative but to seek protection under the bankruptcy act.

A bankruptcy is embarrassing. Much of the feeling about bankruptcy depends on the national economy itself. In difficult times, all businesspeople recognize the need for a new beginning. In prosperous times, many businesspeople are much less apt to be sympathetic. Because you will consider filing a bankruptcy petition only when it is absolutely necessary, the embarrassment will normally not occupy a high priority in your thinking.

A bankruptcy affects your credit and it stays on your credit report for years. Even though you are allowed to file a bankruptcy only every seven years, many people will not be eager to extend you credit immediately after a filing. Many of your own business vendors may not be eager to extend you credit until you prove the stability of your business.

However, understanding the legal remedies can be a springboard to nonlegal settlement. For example, assume you have $500,000 in old debt. Assume further that you have assets, apart from the equity in your home, that have a market value of about $100,000. If sold by a trustee in a Chapter 7, these assets would optimistically bring $50,000. Your creditors would, therefore, get about $0.10 on the dollar. If, in a Chapter 11 or Chapter 13, you reject executory contracts to free up $80,000 a year, you could present a plan to make payments over five years which could, after deducting legal expenses, pay back approximately $375,000 of the $500,000 owed. If you settle with your creditors out of court, you could avoid the legal expenses and pay back even more to the creditors

Thus, you can make the following presentation to your creditors, plugging in the figures you calculate:

- If you file a Chapter 7, the creditors will probably get $X.
- If you file a Chapter 11 or a Chapter 13, the creditors will probably get $Y.
- If you work out an informal plan outside the bankruptcy court, the creditors will get the entire amount you owe or at least a substantial portion of it.

You can work out a nonjudicial plan with the creditors that may not take 90-120 days to be accepted by the court, will not be subject to the expenses of lawyers and accountants, and will make the full amount available for distribution to creditors.

To prove to your creditors that you are completely serious about these alternatives, you will probably have to prepare financial paperwork for them to see. It will be very similar to the information you would have to prepare for the bankruptcy court. In other words, you will be naked before your creditors just as you would be before the court; therefore, you must be prepared to file the bankruptcy petition once you allow yourself to be this vulnerable to your creditors.

Creditors are much more willing to cooperate with a debtor who has been communicative and cooperative during the normal business relationship. It is always a good idea to stay friendly with the people to whom you owe money. Don't be guilty of trying to hide from them because the confrontation is distasteful or embarrassing. It will not help your situation later, when you may need their help the most. Creditors are always willing to give up a portion of the monies owed them when they know they could lose it all and they will always accept some cash as a good-faith introduction to a repayment plan, even if they will be losing part of their debt in the long run.

KEY POINTS TO REMEMBER

- Different levels of business problems require different approaches to solve them. The least problematic may require simply good judgment. The most problematic may require a good bankruptcy lawyer.
- Make sure your business problems are serious enough to require serious measures.
- Examine your business problems carefully to see if they can be solved internally.
- Find out if your problems are specific to your business or general in the industry. They may require an entirely different solution if they are industry-wide.
- Know the differences among the types of bankruptcy protections. The outcomes for you and your family from a Chapter 7, a Chapter 11, or a Chapter 13 can be dramatically different.

Worksheet 16. How to Cut Costs and Face Serious Business Problems

Dealing with Creditors

In the space provided below, divide your creditors into the appropriate categories relating to sale disclosure. This process is important, because you may protect yourself from post-sale problems by properly disclosing the sale to your creditors at the appropriate time.

Which creditors will you notify first of an impending sale?

_____

_____

_____

What debt will the buyer take over as part of the sale? Will you adjust the purchase price to accommodate the assumption of that debt?

_____

_____

_____

Which creditors will you not notify of an impending sale? Will you be eliminating what you owe them out of the purchase price or down payment that you receive? Are you sure you will have enough cash after the sale to eliminate those debts? Will you inform the buyer of these creditors?

_____

_____

_____

Will you put your sale through an escrow? Which creditors will you eliminate by doing this?

_____

_____

_____

Are you in danger of any pending lawsuits by creditors? What will you do to protect yourself from lawsuits brought by creditors?

_____

_____

_____

Do you need to have your attorney contact any of your creditors before the sale? Will having your attorney contact them help protect you from potential lawsuits?

_____

_____

_____

Cut Costs to Boost Your Operating Profit

Throughout this book, you have learned how important your operating profit is to the process of selling your business and setting an appropriate asking price. If your business suffers from insufficient operating profit, you need to do a cost analysis of your business. Worksheet 13 has already led you through several important cost analyses. Look again at your responses to Worksheet 13 and then answer the questions below.

Step 1

Examine your profit and loss statement and your answers to Worksheet 13. What are the sources, if any, related to changes in your own business, such as inventory, employees, fixed expenses, or pricing?

_____

_____

_____

Is your cost analysis sufficient to explain your insufficient operating profit?   Yes ❑ No ❑

If you answered No, go to Step 2.

Step 2

Evaluate your industry. Contact competitors and trade organizations to see if there is an industry-wide downturn taking place.

_____

_____

_____

_____

Is this industry analysis sufficient to explain your insufficient operating profit?   Yes ❑ No ❑

If you answered No, go to Step 3.

Step 3

Examine changes in your customer base or customer preferences. Has the population of your market area changed recently, such as from families with children to retirees? Can you find any other explanations for changes in customer preferences, styles, attitudes, or levels of sophistication?

_____

_____

_____

_____

Is this analysis of your customer base sufficient to explain your insufficient operating profit?   Yes ❑ No ❑

If you answered No, go to Step 4.

Step 4

Look at the role and performance of your employees more carefully. Should your employees be more involved with customer service? Are your incentive programs adequate? Do your employees work well as a team? Do they need further training or retraining?

_____

_____

_____

_____

Is your analysis of employee roles and performance sufficient to explain your insufficient operating profit?   Yes ❑ No ❑

If you answered No, go to Step 5.

Step 5

Consider procedures for collecting outstanding debts. Also, deal with your creditors to prevent them from taking legal action. If none of these procedures have helped you, you will need to discuss alternatives with your accountant and attorney, maybe even bankruptcy. Make sure you are properly informed about all the alternatives open to you.

If you have an interested buyer, be sure you have made all necessary material disclosures relating to the poor performance of your business. If necessary, you may need to adjust the price to accommodate the buyer's needs and the business's ability to pay for itself and produce a buyer income.

The Bankruptcy Alternative

If you are considering seeking protection under one of the bankruptcy acts, you should immediately discuss the alternatives with your attorney. Make sure you are making the best possible decision. If you decide to proceed with a bankruptcy, examine which type of bankruptcy scenario is best for you. The following questions will help prepare you to meet with your attorney.

Do you understand both the positive and negative implications of a bankruptcy? Yes ❑ No ❑

What kind of tax obligations are owed by the business or by you as the owner? _____

_____

_____

What is the legal format of the business?

Sole proprietorship ❑   Limited liability company ❑

Corporation ❑   Limited partnership ❑

Partnership ❑

Are you personally liable on any of your business debts? Yes ❑ No ❑

Is your spouse signed to any documents relating to the business, such as the franchise agreement, promissory note, or lease? Yes ❑ No ❑

If your business is a corporation, have you signed any corporate credit report when applying for credit with any of your business vendors? Yes ❑ No ❑ Were there any misstatements made at the time of the application? Yes ❑ No ❑

Do you understand what 'joint and several obligation' means? Yes ❑ No ❑

Are you threatened by any lawsuits by creditors? Yes ❑ No ❑

Which of your assets may be at risk if a creditor sues you? _____

_____

_____

_____

To what executory contracts are you bound that you can reject in a bankruptcy? _____

_____

_____

_____

How much money will be available to you monthly if you reject those executory contracts? _____

_____

Before you make any decision about a bankruptcy, consult competent legal counsel.

DON'T LET MONEY GET TIGHT IN YOUR BUSINESS

Making an early assessment of a money shortfall in your business is always best. If you anticipate changes in your cash flow—that a seasonal low is coming, that you must purchase new inventory for cash in anticipation of sales, that an advertising campaign will entail expenses long before it generates sales, that hiring additional salespeople will require cash advances before they can start to bring in sales revenues—you can make decisions, borrow dollars, pledge receivables, and schedule payment to vendors in such a way that you maintain continuity of your business. Lack of planning causes such emergencies to surprise and sometimes devastate a business.

Building a Business Plan

Many business people think that a business plan is only for bigger, more sophisticated businesses, but a business plan has many uses. It is certainly true that, if you want to approach a lender or an investor, you would prepare a business plan for them to examine. It is also, true, however, that a business plan will focus your attention on the details of your business and enable you to plan for the future and avoid those unexpected potholes in the road.

Your business plan does not need to be long or intricate to include the kind of information that will allow you to plan ahead. You probably have a lot of that information at your fingertips now.

The marketing plan, for example, is a very significant part of the whole. The marketing plan you had last year will probably give you a good idea as to what your marketing plan should be for next year. After all, you don't want to duplicate the expenses for concepts that didn't work. And you certainly want to follow your successful advertising dollars with more of the same. By comparing successes and failures, costs and revenues, you can use your available dollars to your best advantage.

What about expenses? Maybe you had too much money tied up in inventory last year. Maybe you bought equipment for cash, which left you with a cash crunch, instead of paying for it over an extended period of time. Maybe you started your selling campaign too early and spent unproductive dollars on your sales program. Looking at your income statement and your balance sheet will help you avoid such unnecessary errors in judgment. Don't do these things again!

Did you put a big enough ad in the Yellow Pages? Do you need additional personnel in your manufacturing facility, in your selling organization? Would you be better off outsourcing some of your organizational efforts because it would be less costly? Should you hire more experienced personnel at your counter because your customer service has been deficient? Have you checked on your advertising to find out the cost per sale? Are your collection efforts lagging behind, causing a cash flow problem? Do you anticipate a seasonal downturn, which would require that you borrow some money?

Get Help

And, if you think that it's all too complicated and that you don't know how to develop or even read an income statement or a balance sheet, go to a professional who can explain how simple it can be. You don't need to become an accountant. All you have to do is understand enough to be able to handle your business. Don't be too embarrassed to ask. You will probably be asking the same questions as your competitors.

The financial paperwork of your company, if properly prepared and analyzed, will clarify many of the things that have happened in the company that might not have been obvious during the course of a busy season or a busy year.

It is interesting, if not amazing, how many aspects of your business become obvious and manageable by checking the marketing and financial sections of your business plan. It is amazing that the basics of a business plan for management purposes can be simple. In fact, they should be kept simple. After all, managers need to understand the comparative elements involved and they usually don't have the time or the inclination to get involved in an academic exercise. You should be able to read your business plan as you would read the scores on the sports page. By examining last weekend's records, you can find out who will be in the playoffs. In your business, you will be able to see which of the players in your field—your business and your competitors—will be the success stories.

CHAPTER 17

Negotiating the Sale of a Troubled Business

PART III HAS DISCUSSED HOW TO PREPARE A business for sale, what information your buyer will be looking for, and how to determine an asking price and defend it during your sales presentation. However, rarely does a sales negotiation go smoothly. Many issues will arise for which you will feel unprepared.

This chapter will give you some more specifics about what to expect during the negotiations, what some of your legal responsibilities are during the negotiations, and how to negotiate the problem areas of your business without losing the sale. It will also explain how to posture the sale of a business that is in serious financial difficulty or has no profit at all.

WHAT A NEW OWNER OFFERS A TROUBLED BUSINESS

Many businesses are offered for sale that show stability, vitality, and exciting prospects for the future. More often than not, however, the business is for sale because it's something less than successful. The problems may vary from lack of working capital to inexperienced personnel to obsolete equipment. Chapter 16 helped you to pinpoint potential problems, analyze them, and

decide which alternative solution may prove most effective. Depending on the severity of your business problems, you may want to have a professional advisor analyze your situation.

Selling a business is often one of the more practical solutions to a business problem. Many people don't seem able to understand why a business that is not performing adequately for the current owner would necessarily perform any better for another owner. This question has many answers, the simplest of which is that a business needs financial blood flowing through its veins and creative energy to constantly uplift and upgrade its levels of expectation. Someone who has owned a business for a long time may have lost much of this needed energy. A business owner can get tired of trying to match the competition with new and exciting advertising campaigns. An owner may not have the capital necessary for a new storefront, new equipment, or a whole new concept of inventory.

A new owner brings many things to the table—money, energy, initiative, creativity, and more. The current owner who is considering selling his or her business should not take it personally. It may simply be your time to sell or even retire. Your business needs a new leader, a new manager, a new player.

If you are a seller in this situation, turn to Chapter 16 and read or reread the steps that will help put the best face on your ailing business. Because the basis for this book's valuation method is operating profit, you will have a hard time applying that method to a business with little or no operating profit.

For example, the profit and loss statement shown in Figure 17.1 (next page) shows a shop with an annual gross revenue of approximately $220,000. Unfortunately, it has product costs of almost 34% and labor costs of 41%. Fixed expenses take an additional 22%. As a result, the operating profit shrinks to 3%—$7,173 per year! Based on a 10-year note at 10% (which gives the seller the maximum asking price), the owner of this shop would be hard pressed to substantiate a price of $45,000.

Cost of Labor

41%

34%

22%

Fixed Expenses

3%

Operating Profit

Cost of Product

If you are selling a business in similar straits, you have some work to do. Again, Chapters 13 and 16 have discussed how quickly a percentage point can drop to the bottom line, elevating your potential asking price. Examine your P&L closely and determine where you can make the most effective changes.

However, as you begin this process, you may also want to think about how you will explain in a sales presentation your business problems, the changes you have made, and the further changes a new owner can make. The danger in this kind of explanation is that the buyer will probably ask, "Why haven't you made all these changes yourself before putting the business up for sale?" But the answer, of course, lies in the very reasons for the sale—not enough money, not enough energy, not enough personnel.

YOUR LEGAL OBLIGATION TO DISCLOSE
Mandatory Material Disclosures

The first thing you need to consider in selling any business, particularly a business with serious financial problems, is what kind of disclosures you will make.

If the matter under consideration is a material fact—a fact that is significant to the business—then disclosure is mandatory. Telling someone an untruth about a material fact is a disclosure problem—it is very simply a lie. Hiding a material fact is also a disclosure problem.

If the matter is a nonmaterial fact, you may need to decide if it is important enough to discuss at all. If some tiles in a bathroom are coming loose, it's probably not material. On the other hand, if you know that it's because the plumbing is bad, that would be a material fact requiring disclosure.

If you decide the issue regarding your business is significant, the next decision is how to make the disclosure. If you make the disclosure correctly, it can be used as a focal point for further discussion. If you reveal the information badly, you could end the negotiations.

In all cases, ask yourself the question, "If I don't tell the buyer about this, could the backlash cause the sale to fall through or cause the buyer to withhold payments or start a lawsuit after the business is sold?" The answer to this question will lead you pretty quickly to the material disclosures.

Mutual Trust Ensures Payment

If the buyer is going to pay you the purchase price of the business over a period of time, you also want to ask yourself another question. "If I don't tell the buyer about this problem, will he or she wonder what other things I've failed to disclose?" If you fail to create a relationship of trust with the buyer, you will always wonder how secure the payments are on your purchase money promissory note.

For example, perhaps you purchased equipment on time at a bad price or on a bad payment schedule. If the equipment is not state-of-the-art or not appropriate to the purpose for which it was designed, your disclosure might cause the buyer to break off negotiations or, at the very least, insist on a serious change in the price of the business. Failing to make this kind of disclosure before the sale could lead to a lawsuit later. On the

FIGURE 17.1   Sample Income Statement for a Shop Operated with Poor Percentages

SALES	Year to Date	%	
Printing	$102,090	46.24%	
Bindery	13,056	5.91%	
Copier	7,389	3.35%	
Other	38,547	17.46%	
Kodak	59,709	27.04%	
Total Sales	**$220,791**	**100%**	
COST OF SALES			
Paper	$14,544	6.59%	
Subcontracts	30,564	13.85%	
Supplies	7,746	3.51%	
Equipment Rental	3,156	1.43%	
Kodak Paper & Maintenance	18,528	8.38%	
Total Cost of Sales	**$74,538**	**33.76%**	Product costs take 34% of total sales.
GROSS PROFIT	**$146,253**	**66.24%**	
OPERATING EXPENSES			
Salaries	$79,335	35.93%	
Payroll Taxes	7,386	3.35%	Labor costs take 41% of total sales.
Employee Benefits	3,000	1.36%	
Office Supplies	426	0.19%	
Postage/Freight	1,386	0.63%	
Advertising/Promotion	4,107	1.86%	
Auto Expense	4,470	2.02%	Fixed expenses take 22% of total sales.
Rent	16,326	7.39%	
Telephone/Utilities	2,604	1.18%	
Outside Services	1,164	0.53%	
Insurance	1,038	0.47%	
Property Taxes	1,014	0.46%	
Royalties	16,824	7.62%	
Total Operating Expenses	**$139,080**	**62.99%**	
TOTAL OPERATING PROFIT	**$7,173**	**3.25%**	Only 3% remains as operating profit.

other hand, if the equipment is serviceable and state-of-the-art, a bad price or a bad payment schedule will likely lead to a minor dollar adjustment in the figures at the negotiating table.

Another disclosure you may have to consider making is any large delinquencies that cause payments to exceed income. However, while this may be material with regard to your operating profit, it should not affect the buyer. If these delinquencies are paid out of

the purchase price, they will not affect the buyer after the sale in any way. This is not a disclosure problem because it is not material to the buyer.

However, an excessive equipment rental or a rent increase on the premises could be disastrous: it definitely constitutes a material fact. You must disclose such things to the buyer because they could go to the very essence of the business, its ability to survive and meet its obligations.

In some cases, the law says, "Buyer beware"—buyers need to find out certain matters for themselves or be responsible if they don't. It is always the buyer's obligation to diligently examine the business and make his or her own judgment as to the viability of the business in all respects. The buyer should consult with his or her professional advisors early in the buying process for this reason.

On the other hand, there has been much legislation—franchise legislation, for example—that requires the seller to completely disclose all material facts before selling a franchise to an individual. A seller's failure to disclose can allow the buyer to later rescind or call back the contract.

When specific legislation is not involved, common law dictates that the average buyer should be protected at least from fraud and misrepresentation. What happens in situations that are just short of fraud and misrepresentation is anybody's guess. It will depend in each case on the particular facts, the sophistication of the buyer, the intent of the seller, and the attitude of the court in any given instance.

AT THE NEGOTIATING TABLE

Successful negotiation requires timing, posturing, and expectation adjustment. When you negotiate the sale of a troubled business, the timing of certain disclosures and your overall negotiating posture take on even greater importance.

Posturing

At your first meeting with a buyer, you need to decide, for posturing purposes, whether you want to have your partner, spouse, attorney, or accountant present. You may find the first meeting easier if you meet with the buyer alone. Meeting alone allows you to do the following:

- Ask questions and offer responses that might not be appropriate if someone else were with you—perhaps items of a more personal nature.
- Assess what approach might work best with the other party. This might be much more difficult if others are at the same meeting and the other party is on guard.

- Tell the other party, "I can't really make any decisions without consulting my spouse, partner, lawyer, accountant, or banker." This is a good way out of many embarrassing situations.

On the other hand, a spouse or partner will be able to complement the perspective you bring to the table. He or she can share the responsibility of asking the right questions and will surely be able to give you a slightly different reading of the person or people on the other side of the table.

A professional at the table with you has obvious advantages. A professional advisor will likely have negotiated business deals before and can help you elicit the basic information you need to make your decision. Your professional can recognize certain peculiarities or anomalies to the buyer's presentation that a less experienced listener might miss. The question of which posture to adopt will depend on the kind of negotiating in which you expect to engage, the strength or weakness of your presentation, the length of time you expect to devote to the project, and the gravity of the timing involved.

Using a glass-top table analogy is a good way to illustrate how negotiations between a legitimate buyer and a seller should proceed. Everything from both sides ought to be on top of the table; if something is under the table, all parties should be able to see it anyway. In other words, no one should have a secret agenda.

Timing

Neither a buyer nor a seller wants to disclose information without knowing what kind of response he or she may get.

You would be unwise to tell a prospective buyer, for example, that you have already bought another house in another community. This timing secret would give the buyer some additional bargaining power.

On the other hand, the buyer doesn't want to disclose how much money he or she has available for the purchase until a price is discussed. If you have not yet discussed price, you may end up basing price exclusively on the buyer's financial position rather than on the value of the business. Pricing the business exclusively on the buyer's ability to pay is in his or her favor if the business would otherwise be priced out of his or her range. However, it is a serious disadvantage to the buyer if his or her finances can support a price well above the value and the price is therefore inflated.

A buyer is wise to begin negotiations by explaining how much money he or she needs from the business to take care of his or her family. You must then consider the buyer's income needs along with the business's value if you want to sell to that buyer candidate. On the other hand, you could start the discussion with the kind of dollars you need from the business for your plans for retirement, travel, or the anticipated purchase of a business in the future. Both you and the buyer are forced to examine each other's needs as the negotiations continue and you get to know each other, your professionals, and your families.

If an all-cash deal is possible, this kind of approach has less appeal. After all, when you are buying a used car from a stranger, it is unlikely you will have any concern with what he or she intends to do with the money or the long-term benefit it may have for his or her family.

You need to assess each negotiation as it proceeds to decide what kind of personal involvement may or may not be effective. Your professional, who has experience with negotiations, can help you adopt the most appropriate negotiating posture.

Have Your Professionals Present

Always be wary of a buyer or a seller who is not represented by an attorney. Having an attorney on your side of the negotiating table may add the necessary degree of authority and strength to your negotiating posture. While you may sometimes want to begin negotiations without your professionals, most of the time your professional advisors are the most important part of your negotiating team.

Discussing the possible purchase or sale of a business with the appropriate professional will allow you to determine your posture, your timing, and ultimately the success of your negotiations. Professional advisors will help you make an effective sales presentation, interpret the offer you are given, and determine the questions to ask to make a knowledgeable decision. Working out a deal without an attorney can be a very risky endeavor. Take, for example, the story in Illustration 17.1.

Illustration 17.1 Larceny in His Heart

In the recent sale of a hardware store, the buyer and the seller chose not to work with attorneys. Later, the buyer, Jake Thompson, felt the seller had misled him during sale negotiations. He began to threaten the seller during the repayment period and wrote him the following letter.

"I can't believe how you led me down the garden path and right into the cemetery. I am shocked at the debts people are trying to collect from me. You told me you would take care of all the debts from the down payment I made. Why did you lie to me? You told me your manager would be delighted to stay with me until I could learn the business for myself. He tells me that he has a job in Michigan and that you knew this all the time. If you think I'm going to pay you any more money, think again. I'm going to use the money I owe you to sue you, and I'm not going to stop until everyone knows just what kind of person you are."

Both Jake and the seller thought that because the business was relatively small, they didn't need to spend the money on lawyers. It just shows how badly these situations can become when both parties are left to their own devices. In this case, the seller had a little larceny in his heart and Jake didn't know how to protect his investment.

BANKRUPTCY AS A SELLING POSTURE

One of the last items you should reflect on is the possibility of using the Bankruptcy Act to posture the business for sale. If you are getting ready to sell a business that has serious financial problems and your creditors will not work with you out of court, declaring bankruptcy may be your best alternative. If the business, apart from the current financial problems, is good, you can find buyers who would be happy to buy it from a trustee in bankruptcy as part of a Chapter 7 liquidation. The trustee, whose charge is to convert the assets to cash as quickly as possible, would obviously be delighted to have a buyer waiting in the wings. And you, as the debtor in bankruptcy, may be retained as a consultant to the buyer.

Remember: any money you earn after filing the Chapter 7 bankruptcy petition is not subject to the debts involved in the bankruptcy. Chapter 11 and Chapter 13 provide similar protection. You can sell the business under the auspices of the bankruptcy court and the buyer takes over the business without the old obligations. Once again, a consulting contract is not out of the question. A consulting contract is one way a seller can enjoy a piece of the business's future after a bankruptcy. The normal bankruptcy scenario would merely close the door on any dollar benefit to the bankrupt after the filing.

Selling Your Customer Volume

When selling a business that shows little or no operating profit, you can still promote a positive aspect of your business to potential buyers. As long as your business has customers coming through the door, it has a value. To take a business from scratch usually takes time and working capital. The cost of this time can be very high, depending on the style in which the buyer is used to living. You can, therefore, argue that selling an existing business showing no profit means selling customer volume. The value of your customers should be the basis of your thinking and negotiating. If the business is showing no profit, the buyer is still purchasing customer volume, which has a monetary value.

In the face of great frustrations, closing the door and walking away may seem like the easiest path to take,

but leaving a valuable asset on the table is not fair to your family or to the investment of time and money that you have made, however unsuccessful the venture may have been. Don't lose sight of the fact that you are involved in an important decision for yourself and your family. This kind of decision deserves your best judgment and the most professional advice you can bring to your side of the negotiating table.

KEY POINTS TO REMEMBER

- Sometimes the difference between a successful and an unsuccessful business is the energy and optimism the owner brings to the front door every day.
- If you sell a debt-ridden business, you will pay old debts from the purchase price and present the business to the new owner free of its most onerous financial obligations. The new owner will have a head start toward success.
- Make all disclosures to your buyer that are material to the stability and success of the business. Anything less than full material disclosure can lead to a lawsuit after the sale and the buyer may be unable or unwilling to pay your promissory note.
- Professional business consultants and advisors have experience with all levels of business problems. Take advantage of their experience.
- You can posture a troubled business for sale in many ways, including putting it into bankruptcy. A trustee in bankruptcy is always eager to sell a business expeditiously.

Worksheet 17. Exposing the Minuses Without Losing the Sale

Material Disclosures

By now you should have a good idea what problems your business has. If you do not, reread Chapters 13 and 16 and answer the questions to the accompanying worksheets for those chapters.

List any deficiencies to which you can specifically attribute a loss of revenue.

_____

_____

_____

If you have sought the objective view of others to whom the deficiencies might appear more readily, add those deficiencies to your list.

_____

_____

_____

If you have ever used the services of professionals to analyze your business and those professionals found some deficiencies, add those to the list.

_____

_____

_____

For which problems have you been unable to find a source?

_____

_____

_____

Are you selling your business because you are unable to solve some of its problems? Yes ❑ No ❑

If you answered Yes, reread Chapter 16 and the steps you can take to cut costs and improve your operating profit. If you are still convinced you need to sell your business, read on.

Which of the above deficiencies are material, or significant, to the successful operation of the business?

_____

_____

_____

Consider how you will reveal these material facts to your potential buyer. Who will be present when you disclose this information? All partners and spouses involved in the business sale? All professionals involved on both sides? Only you and the buyer? Will you present the information in writing, to protect yourself from later accusations by the buyer? How early in the negotiating process will you present this information to the buyer?

_____

_____

_____

What advice can you give the new owner to cope with the business's problems? Are there strategies or plans you had made to resolve these problems but were unable to implement? Why were you unable to fix the problems yourself? Does the buyer bring something special or particularly important to the business that will help solve those problems—such as money, expertise, creative energy, or an enlarged customer base?

_____

_____

_____

If your business has no operating profit or is losing money and you have no prospect of resolving the problems, are there still parts of the business that have value? How valuable is your customer volume? Could you promote the equipment, location, inventory, or valuable employees as assets that have a value for the buyer? What do you think they are worth to a buyer? Discuss this with your professional advisors.

_____

_____

_____

TRUSTING YOUR PROFESSIONAL'S ETHICS

You go to your professional for business advice for two reasons. You not only want the best financial and marketing directions for your business in the short term, but you also want to ensure that your reputation in the business community will be maintained in the long term.

A Short-Term Advantage

It is easy enough to create business methods that will enable your business to succeed at the expense of your competitors, sometimes even at the expense of your own employees. You've seen this happen and probably wondered what was in the minds of the people behind those methods and whatever possessed management to agree with the concepts. Shortsightedness and greed usually precede the decision to succeed at the expense of others. Such methods may put a profit on your profit and loss statement for a given period, but the real question is will they allow you to achieve your long-term goals within your business community?

In Times of Crisis

There will be times of shortages for one reason or another. Under normal business circumstances, there might be a shortage of paper. With international situa-tions, there might be shortages of gasoline. And, in times of domestic disaster, there might be shortages of food, water, and the like. This is the time when we dis-cover those with charity in their hearts ... and those with larceny and greed in their hearts. When someone takes advantage of those who need the help the most, it is a time to remember. The pendulum has its own compensating factor and eventually swings the other way. When owners take advantage of employees in order to line their own pockets, it is a moment that needs to be recorded in memory. And it will be record-ed. And the pendulum will eventually swing the other way. Woe to those who choose the path of greed. Their day will come!

The General Rule

"Do unto others as you would have others do unto you" is certainly a simple path to follow. Its simplicity does not invalidate its wisdom. When you are choosing professionals, listen carefully to the stories they tell in terms of what they've done for other clients in the past. Get a sense of whether that kind of advice is what you want to represent you in the marketplace.

It's one thing to be competitive. It's quite another to develop a reputation that shows you going for the jugular every time. Try to find a professional who shares the same goals as you.

Many professionals are more interested in winning for their client in the short term to show how effective they can be on his or her behalf. They are not in the competitive marketplace. Many of them don't understand the synergy that needs to exist among competitors. They don't get it! They don't deal with customers and employees day to day. They don't understand that the success of a company is not due to the genius or creativity of one person, but instead a result of the continuity created by loyalty, participation, and contributions of all personnel.

All the Parts Make the Whole

You know that one of the ways you get and retain customers is that you offer quality of services or goods, timely delivery when appropriate, fair pricing in good times and bad, and a guarantee of your goods or services. This is no secret. It is the very core of a business's success.

There is another part that isn't always noticed. But it is always there. It is the method by which you do business. It's not using bait-and-switch tactics. It's not hiding behind the small print that your professional suggests you use to limit your liability to the consumer. And it's not taking an attitude of hit-and-run in terms of making a sale. The real key is that you are always ready to stand tall as a member of the community, not just as a business. It is this part of your business that makes up the whole approach to success and continuity. Don't let anyone take that away from you. It's the real staying power of success in business.

CHAPTER 18

How to Value and Sell a Professional Practice

WHILE THIS CHAPTER SPECIFICALLY DIS-cusses the sale of a professional practice, any seller can benefit from reading how to develop a price structure for a business that has some unique concerns—like a professional practice. The pricing chart used in this chapter to develop the price of a law practice as an example will give you some idea what effect a down payment and a transition period have as discount factors on an ultimate selling price. The more difficult problem of a practice dependent in great part on referrals from other professionals is examined in the story of the orthodontist, detailed later in this chapter (Illustration 18.2). The formula designed to handle this problem can obviously be used in relation to other businesses, such as a hair salon or a neurosurgical or periodontal practice, where the referral aspect is a primary source of business.

The answer must involve the resolution of two basic issues:

- Degradation of the practice because of the difficulty in transmitting the loyalty factor
- A transition period designed to minimize the negative impact of the transfer

Certainly, the loss of clients cannot be prevented. Some clients will already have a second choice lined up, whether it is a relative, friend, or merely another professional who has been patiently waiting for the day when a change would be appropriate. It is clear from experience that the longer the transition period—the period of time that the seller stays with the practice during or after the sale—the more successful the sale is likely to be.

One suggestion that has proven fruitful, although somewhat deceptive to the clients, is the development of a partnership arrangement where both buyer and seller acknowledge at the outset that the arrangement will be consummated at a certain time, a target date, and based on a particular dollar amount, a valuation given to the practice. The parties either agree to the dollar value at the beginning of the partnership or predicate it on a formula that might relate to that portion of the practice surviving the transition period. In some cases, the parties use a more complex combination of these aspects.

Most business buyers look for a business that suits their temperament, their experience, and their innate abilities. Professionals make the decision to buy a business by virtue of their education. With a law degree, one does not practice medicine; with a medical degree, one does not become a certified public accountant. In turn, the seller of a professional practice has a limited pool of buyers from which to draw. A lawyer cannot sell to a medical doctor. An accountant cannot sell to a juris doctor.

Preference and capability still play a part in a professional's decision to buy a practice. An accountant who handles primarily tax work for small businesses is not going to be interested in buying an accounting practice that deals primarily with securities work. A research scientist will not, in all probability, be interested in buying the practice of a plastic surgeon. It is equally unlikely that a trial lawyer would be interested in taking over a law practice that prepares wills and files probates.

Geography also influences the pool of buyers. Since all practices are essentially local, the buyer must consider the climate and community in which a practice is located. Even when state boards, licenses, and other requirements preclude the movement of professionals from state to state, climate will still be a consideration (with the exception of the smaller states like Rhode Island). A big city locale versus a small suburban community is also a significant consideration. To some, the ethnicity of a particular area may be important.

SPECIAL CONCERNS FOR TRANSFER OF OWNERSHIP

The kind of relationship that is established between a psychiatrist and his or her patient is not one that can easily be transferred. Similarly, when a client has disclosed all his or her personal information to an accountant or lawyer, the client may not want to make the same revelations to a stranger.

If you are selling a professional practice, you need to be prepared, to a greater extent than in the average business transfer, to introduce the buyer to your clients or patients. You need to overcome the unfamiliarity of the new owner and infuse an element of confidence into the new relationship. You cannot rush this process.

The client or patient also has the prerogative to take his or her business to another professional. Clients often take their business elsewhere when their long-time professional sells or retires. On the other hand, in the professional world, patients or clients also have some fear about looking for a new doctor, lawyer, or accountant. As a result, most people are willing to try the new professional if the buyer receives a satisfactory

endorsement from the original owner on whose advice, presumably, the client or patient has learned to depend.

Still, it is in the nature of this professional relationship that clients make many personal disclosures that have nothing at all to do with the business under consideration. Patients, for example, will often speak of their personal or business problems with their doctor, their medical problems with their accountant, and their tax problems with their lawyer. A connection develops that is very difficult to transfer to a stranger.

The best you can hope to do is present the buyer to your clients or patients as the consummate professional who has the appropriate education and experience. The process of introducing the buyer should, indeed, be a marketing program of the highest standards. As with any type of business sale, this advertising-marketing strategy is as important to the seller as it is to the buyer.

The continuity of the client base is not as dependable as it might be in a more conventional type of small business. The ability of the buyer of a professional practice to maintain the client base of the business depends in great part on the seller's willingness to devote the time and energy necessary for proper introductions.

The Partnership Period

Most conventional business sales contain an arrangement for the seller to stay with the business for some period after the buyer takes over. This transition period is sometimes referred to as the *partnership period*. During this somewhat delicate transition period, your buyer learns the idiosyncrasies of customers and employees with your help. You may want to do the following:

- Train the buyer on equipment or computer programs.
- Introduce the buyer to certain customers or accounts of particular size or merit.
- Create a continuity or comfort zone for employees.

The seller may stay on for days or months. In some cases, the seller includes this accommodation in the purchase price. In others, the seller receives compensation during this period.

In the sale of a conventional business, the partnership arrangement is a financing option. The sale of a professional practice is somewhat different. Buyers are frequently taken on as partners with the opportunity to buy out the seller after a certain length of time. The buyout could be based either on a predetermined price or on a formula to which both parties agree in the original contract of partnership.

A transition partnership has an obvious advantage to the buyer. It allows the buyer to become familiar with clients or patients under the seller's actual sponsorship. The buyer can build a rapport with each client or patient.

Some might say that a partnership period is deceptive to the clients or patients, because the seller is not going to be a partner for an extended period: the partnership is intended exclusively to consummate the sale. Whether this is a deception depends in great part on exactly how it is handled. The best approach is for you, the seller, to disclose your imminent departure to your patients or clients during the transition period.

Degradation of the Practice

No matter how successful the marketing strategy, your practice will likely experience a loss of clients or patients, a degradation of the practice, during the change in ownership. Many clients and patients will, at the very least, give the new professional a try. If the buyer proves himself or herself at that first meeting, the clients or patients are more likely to remain.

Some clients, however, will leave immediately—some because the changeover gives them an excuse to make a move they were considering, some because there are other professionals in the community with whom they are more familiar. In any case, the practice that the buyer takes over will normally not be as hardy as the one you sell. The likelihood of some kind of degradation of the practice creates a problem determining the purchase price. It is difficult, if not impossible, to assess this degradation before it actually happens.

You may be able to partially assess, during the price negotiations, which clients will stay with the new owner. In some cases, an accountant can retain clients because taxes are due shortly and because the seller has already done much of the work. A lawyer may be in the middle of a trial or final preparation of a business

reconstruction. A doctor may have followed a medical problem for a long time to maintain a delicate balance of medication and treatment, not all of which the new professional can absorb merely by going over the former practitioner's notes.

Structuring the Price

At this point, instead of reading how to prepare a price structure for a professional practice, study and compare the letter relative to the law practice on the next page and the letter on page 180 dealing with an orthodontist's practice to get two entirely different views on the attitudes of two professionals selling for different reasons. The remainder of this section discusses in detail the letters regarding the law practice.

You may notice that the concept and details of a purchase money promissory note are absent from the Sample Client Letter Establishing an Asking Price. The seller had already considered a promissory note and a partnership arrangement and had decided against both options.

Harry Aldrich was not interested in a long transition period or a partnership arrangement because he intended to embark on an entirely new career as soon as possible. He was aware that a shorter transition period meant a lower price for the practice. He was also not interested in a payout situation—he wanted an all-cash deal so that he could invest in his next business enterprise—but he recognized that he may have to compromise on this point in exchange for some negotiated payment plan. As you read the letter, you will find many of the elements discussed in this book. Note in particular the possible reduction in selling price in exchange for a larger down payment.

Harry responded to this letter with a pretty good recognition of reality. He had been given a variety of figures for the value of his business from various sources. This was the first time he had been given a rationale for any asking price.

His only comment was whether he could ask for more at the outset, even though he recognized the ultimate validity of the valuation concept. The answer is really twofold.

Once you establish an asking price, it is difficult to raise it during the course of negotiations. You should,

FIGURE 18.1   Sample Client Letter Establishing an Asking Price

January 15, 2003

Harrison Aldrich, Esq.
1200 Manomet Avenue, Suite B
Elmar, CA 92764
PRIVATE AND CONFIDENTIAL

Dear Harry:

Our current order of business is to set a value on your professional practice to posture the business for sale. As I indicated to you at our first meeting, we are going to participate in this project as a team. In order for us to do this, there are certain basics on which we need to agree. One of these is the concept of valuation.

Owner Compensation and Reconstituting the Profit and Loss Statement
One of the prerogatives of entrepreneurship is to use the business's profit as owner income. It is very difficult to put a value on a business because this arbitrary salary (owner's compensation) does not allow us to formalize the labor base of the business. The first thing we have to do is decide how much we would have to pay someone who has the necessary qualifications to replace the owner. In our case, because it is a professional position, it is difficult to make a clear assessment. However, considering the nature of the practice, the costs and expenses of living in the general area of Elmar, California, and the number of professionals available in the marketplace, I am prepared to use the figure of $35,000 as an annual income. This size salary is appropriate for someone who would be operating the business.

Another issue that we must address with some care is the profit and loss statement. We all understand that a P&L prepared for Uncle Sam is not necessarily the P&L we want to prepare for the buying candidate. After all, the IRS allows you to take certain business deductions that are personal and that the buyer may or may not include as expenses. In your particular case, you maintain a small plane that you consider essential to your practice but that another owner might not. In order to have a P&L that properly reflects the costs and expenses of the business, leading us to a realistic profit picture, we must reconstitute the P&L to eliminate those things of a more personal nature, leaving what is necessary and appropriate to the proper operation of the business. In this way, we find that your business with gross revenues of $150,000 and net revenues of $45,000 can legitimately show a net profit of $65,000 without a change in the gross business.

How to Find the Proper Value
Because the professional practice may degrade somewhat with a change in ownership, it is reasonable for the buyer to want a return of his or her investment in one to three years as opposed to five to 10 years. The conventional business can support a return of investment over a longer period because the continuity of the business and its customers is more secure.

If we then consider the actual figures of the business, plug in a manager's salary, and reconstitute the P&L, we find a profit of $30,000 per year. If we agree that, due to the degradation problem, the business should provide a return on investment in one to three years, we should be looking at a selling price of somewhere between $30,000 and $90,000. The transition period is going to be a key factor, as it would be in any professional practice. How close we come to the higher figure depends on how substantial an argument we can make for the stability of the clientele, the continuity of the business activity, and the length of time you decide to devote to the practice during the transition after the sale. The following will give you an idea as to the differentials depending on both the transition period and the down payment.

Down Payment	Selling Price	Purchase Money Promissory Note
No down payment	$120,000	$120,000
$10,000	$100,000	$90,000
$20,000	$80,000	$60,000
$30,000	$60,000	$30,000
All cash	$40,000	0

If you include a transition period in the deal, you could increase the selling price by 10%-30%, depending on the length of the period.

Keep in mind, Harry, that there is no magic to these figures. They are figures similar to those I have used in other sales, which I found to be understandable to buyers.

One last issue—the potential buyer I mentioned to you in my earlier correspondence decided against examining your practice any further due to the climate in Elmar. We need to prepare some marketing materials that present the community and climate in the best possible light.

Cordially,

Ira N. Nottonson

therefore, ask the highest defensible price. On the other hand, you must be careful not to ask a price that suggests to the potential buyer that you have severely overestimated the value of your business. The buyer may decide that your thinking is so unrealistic that a reasonable negotiation is impossible. Remember that this is not the sale of a house, where substantial negotiating for a better price is often the standard.

Getting the Project Moving: Selling

Having established the parameters within which the price should be structured, the next order of business was to get the project moving. After some discussion, Harry agreed to prepare a list of potential buyers from the general area whose names and reputations he knew firsthand. These people then received a telephone call from Harry's representative, which allowed Harry to maintain anonymity and avoid injuring his practice during these early discussions. Harry and his attorney established the following as a working scenario.

▼ Illustration 18.1 A Cold Call Scenario

"Hello, My name is Ira Nottonson. I am a California attorney and part of my practice is dealing with the purchase and sale of businesses.

"I represent an attorney who has an estate planning practice for sale within the general geographical area of Quansot, Elmar, and Haystack. I am not at liberty to disclose the name of my principal or any details about the specific location of the practice. Since we both would like to keep any such communication private, this is a very preliminary inquiry. The only question I would like to ask is whether you would be interested in discussing this matter further with me on a completely confidential basis?"

If the recipient is interested: "I would like to discuss this further, but I would rather discuss it with you when you are home. I'm sure you can understand the delicacy of the matter; I wouldn't want to feel that anyone could intrude on our conversation in any way. I'm sure you feel the same way."

If the recipient is not interested: "Why don't I give you my telephone number in case you have any further thoughts?"

If the recipient presses for some additional information: "The practice has been in place for 17 years and has a stable client base. The excellent reputation of the practitioner will precede you; all you have to do is sit down at the desk and go to work."

If the recipient asks about price: "Price is based on a mutual understanding of value. I believe very logical parameters exist within which the price of a business makes sense to both buyer and seller. If you decide to acquire the practice, you and my client will find a logical price structure that works for both of you."

Advertising the Practice

After making contact with a half-dozen candidates and finding one who might be interested, albeit not immediately, Harry decided to go forward with the next logical step. He chose the most appropriate print medium and structured an advertisement that would generate interest without risking his anonymity. He decided to use the magazine of the California Bar Association, which would reach all the most obvious and qualified candidates. The buyer would have to be a member of the California Bar Association to buy the practice and maintain it. Harry considered the possibility of reciprocity between states that might allow an out-of-state lawyer to buy the practice, but this kind of candidate would be the exception, not the rule.

The Sample Client Letter to Begin Advertising the Practice (Figure 18.2 on page 180) discusses the advertisement and is a good example of the step-by-step process he and his attorney took to advertise and sell the practice. Harry and his advisor also advertised the practice with the placement officer at all the California

law schools. They also discussed the possibility that brokers might respond to the ad. They maintained confidentiality by referring any respondents to Harry's advisor. Because Harry was so eager to sell the practice and move on to his new venture, he and his advisor agreed that the commission to a broker would be a good investment should a broker produce a qualified candidate.

Closing the Deal

The advertisement worked: it attracted candidates. Harry interviewed them and discussed the price. Professionals representing both parties became involved. Harry sold the business. The buyer is excited at having acquired a jump-start in a new community where he and his family are happy to live. Harry is on his way to his next professional adventure.

The approach taken in this section does not guarantee a successful sale. You need to work out a marketing and advertising scheme with your professionals that will work best for you. You may not be as concerned about anonymity or as opposed to a transition period as the seller in this example. Nevertheless, you can probably find the secret to a successful sale in a line from the first letter included in this chapter. "As I indicated to you at our first meeting, we are going to participate in this project as a team." In this situation, consultant and client combined their efforts for maximum effectiveness.

VALUATION OF A SPECIALTY PRACTICE

The next and more complex aspect of a professional practice is where the seller must deliver to the buyer the referrals from other professionals as part of the business. Although many businesses, professional and otherwise, depend on the ability of the buyer to build a relationship with the customer after the seller leaves, the dynamics of the problem are always a question of degree.

Usually, a retail business will maintain the continuity of its customer base so long as the quality, timeliness, and pricing of the service or product are maintained. On the other hand, the neurosurgeon depends, for the great percentage of his or her business, on referrals from primary physicians. It would be quite unusual for a patient to ask to see a neurosurgeon without

| FIGURE 18.2 | Sample Client Letter to Begin Advertising the Practice |

March 17, 2003

Harrison Aldrich, Esq.
1200 Manomet Avenue, Suite B
Elmar, CA 92764
PRIVATE AND CONFIDENTIAL

Dear Harry:

There is always an excitement about the prospect of hitting the target with the first shot. However, even though we have a candidate who, indeed, might turn out to be a buyer, we both agree that it is time to move expeditiously to the next stage of our program.

Most magazines have a closing date for submitting advertisements that usually precedes publication by many weeks; if we don't make arrangements for inserting our ad, we may miss the deadline. If the pending candidate decides to buy, we can still consider the advertising dollars as an appropriate investment. The following includes the information necessary to generate responses from serious candidates:

ESTATE PLANNING PRACTICE	24 spaces per line
SO. CAL. DESERT COMMUNITY	25
17 YRS. EXCELLENT REPUTATION.	29
TURNKEY OPERATION:150K/YR/W/	28
GROWTH POTENTIAL. SELLER WILL	29
REMAIN FOR TRANSITION. INQUIRIES	32
HANDLED WITH DISCRETION AND	27
CONFIDENTIALITY:858-555-1212	28

The number of spaces per line will be critical, but they can be worked out only when you get the parameters of the particular print format you will use. Advertising is predicated on size and frequency. Some magazines give you the opportunity to use boxes surrounding the ad or gray or white backgrounds to make the ad stand out. You need the ad to appear over a six-month period to be sure we have properly tapped the readership. Not everyone reads the whole magazine every issue. The last item to consider is the ad itself. Most ads use abbreviations, though using an extra line or longer word can sometimes be very effective. Let me know your thinking.

Cordially,

Ira N. Nottonson

having been examined by a primary physician first. The appointment would likely be set up by the general practitioner, who would recognize the symptoms requiring the need for a more expert opinion and who would have the experience to recommend a particular surgeon. One the other hand, a plastic surgeon, because of the general acceptance and proliferation of people seeking cosmetic surgery, may get the great percentage of his or her practice from a good marketing program. The orthodontics practice in the illustration below is between these two extremes, with equal numbers of patient and physician referrals.

Illustration 18.2 The Referral Problem

When Don Grimsdale decided to help his son buy an orthodontics practice, he ran across a problem that was more than he was prepared for. It wasn't the first business deal that Don had negotiated. In fact, he had, over the years, been both a buyer and a seller at different times. So, putting himself in the seller's shoes was not difficult. The problem he faced, however, was one that had not surfaced in his other business deals.

Don's son, Alex, was finishing his orthodontics program at the university. Alex had already met Dr. Bronson, the seller. They liked each other and both felt that the sale would be mutually beneficial. When Alex returned to school, he left the negotiating to his dad. Don, fortunately, sought the advice of professionals in order to establish a value for the practice. What was the practice worth, how much should he pay as a down payment, and how should the balance be paid?

With about 50% of the business coming through referrals by patients and the other 50% coming through referrals by primary physicians, the general practitioner dentists, these are the questions to answer:

- How many of these referrals will the buyer realistically be able to enjoy once the seller leaves the practice and, perhaps, the city?
- To what extent will the loyalty of referring physicians to the seller transfer to the buyer?
- What will be the deciding factors?
- Can the seller promise to deliver these referrals and to what extent can the buyer expect the the seller to fulfill that promise?
- How can this problem be handled in terms of valuing the practice?

The problem with referrals from dentists is that they are usually based on the acknowledged experience of the orthodontist or, more often, the personal relationships between the orthodontist and the referring dentists, or both. The new graduate will have neither the reputation nor the relationships.

If the practice is valued at its full potential based on the previous activity of the seller and the referral expectations go unfulfilled, then the buyer may be buying a practice of less value than expected for the price. On the other hand, if the risk of not delivering the level of referrals expected is so great as to dramatically lower the value of the business, the seller may be selling a practice of much greater value than the price would otherwise reflect.

Another significant element that must be factored into this complicated equation is the transition period, the period after the sale during which the seller maintains a relationship with the practice to help stabilize the continuity. In most businesses, this involves introducing the customers and the vendors to the buyer to establish a comfortable relationship. In some instances, it involves establishing a working environment and a familiarity with personnel. In other cases, it involves training the buyer to handle any and all aspects of the business.

In the illustration, Dr. Bronson, as the seller, is also aware of this problem, especially since his former associate and very good friend is the source for a substantial number of referrals. Even Dr. Bronson knows that, after the sale, many of these referrals will go to other orthodontists in the community instead of to his buyer.

But the seller's problem is equally as dramatic as the buyer's, especially if the seller is going to carry back a purchase money promissory note for the balance of the purchase price after the down payment. The seller doesn't want the practice to be valued based on such a risk and then find that he or she is able to deliver more referrals than might have been anticipated.

This dilemma is a good reason to establish a method by which the buyer pays for the referrals he or she gets and the seller receives payment for the referrals he or she delivers.

The seller and the buyer can agree to certain aspects of a sale, aside from the referral problem. In this case, it was agreed that if the practice remained stable—that is, the number of patients coming to the office for their initial conference remained the same, approximately 30 per month, 15 from patient referrals and 15 from dentist referrals—then the value of the business would be $500,000. It was further agreed that the seller had no control over the patient referrals. This part of the practice would likely remain the same or, certainly, would depend on the ability of the buyer—not the seller—to maintain it. Therefore, no one disputed paying at least half the value of the business, or $250,000. This amount was scheduled for payment over a 10-year period at an interest rate of 10%. The promissory note representing this $250,000 was payable at $39,100 (mathematically $39,646) per year or $3,000 (mathematically $3,304) per month.

The question arose as to how to handle the balance of the purchase price, $250,000. If the pattern of 15 referrals per month from dentists represented $3,000 per month in payments—assuming the second $250,000 was scheduled for payment in the same manner as the first $250,000 of the purchase price—then how much would the buyer owe for a single month when only 10 dentist referrals came into the office for their initial conference? They decided that the buyer would pay 10/15 of $3,000 or $2,000 for that month.

Referrals and the All-Cash Deal

The problem becomes somewhat different if the buyer borrows the money from a third party to buy the business, allowing the seller to receive all cash. This makes any payout extending over a period of time and subject to a formula impractical. In such a case, a good approach would be similar to almost any business sale where there are liable to be payments for which the buyer is responsible but that are attributable to the seller.

To handle this situation, an escrow is set up, so a third party is holding the money. The money is in escrow until a certain time period has elapsed, during which the buyer is able to find out if there are any such liabilities for which he or she may be responsible that the seller incurred before selling the business and did not disclose or for which payment arrangements had not been made, either inadvertently or intentionally.

In the sale of the orthodontist's practice, for example, it may be appropriate, if the seller is receiving all cash for the practice, to set up such an escrow for a period of six months. The escrow agreement can reflect that a portion of the money will be released to the seller, depending on the percentage of referrals that occur during the escrow period. There are many variations on this theme and the parties can presumably agree to some sort of an arrangement that will be fair. After all, if the referrals promised are not delivered, the buyer has no recourse against a seller who has received 100% of the purchase price in cash. And the bank will not be interested in the equity or lack of equity involved.

The next section looks at specifics for valuating professional practices and handling the referral problem.

Patient/Physician Referral Valuation Model

The best way to grasp the valuation process of a professional practice is to start looking at actual numbers. Take a look at the Patient/Physician Referral Valuation Model in Figure 18.3. This model, which is from the sale of an actual professional practice, shows how the numbers look for different scenarios of referrals delivered. The model is divided into three sections. The first section lists the assumptions. A change in any of these assumptions will, of course, change the entire spectrum of results on the chart.

Here are the assumptions you will need to make for your own model:

- The monthly new patient exams. This will be the method of determining just how many of the anticipated referrals are actually delivered.
- The value of the business. This figure represents the full value without considering the risk factor.
- The patient referral percentage. The critical factor is the remaining percentage from 100%, which represents the physician referrals.
- The interest on the note.
- The number of years over which the note will be payable.

The second section of the model contains the scenarios for differing rates of physician referrals delivered. This shows the dollars to which the seller is entitled, based on the number of referrals delivered out of the number that the buyer is entitled to expect; that is, the number that is expected based on the history of the practice.

The total of new patient exams annually is approximately 30 per month, 360 per year. The number attributable to physician referrals is 180 per year, 15 per month, 45 per quarter. If the seller delivers 100% of the historically expected referrals (HERs), then the seller will be entitled to 100% of the dollars that are represented by the physician referral half of the business's value. If the seller delivers 75% of these HERs, then the seller, for that period, will be entitled to only 75% of the total revenues attributable to the physician referral half for that quarter.

Next in the model, you will find some alternative scenarios, in particular, Scenarios #5 and #6 in the sec-

FIGURE 18.3	Sample Patient/Physician Referral Valuation Form

Assumptions

Current business generates 30 new patient exams (NPE) per month.
Total business value is based on 30 NPE per month.
Portion of price based on patient referrals is a percentage of the total business value.
Down payment represents portion of the business supported by patient referrals.

Business value: $500,000
Patient referral: 50%
Interest on note: 10%
Years on note: 10

First Section

Scenario		Qtr 1	Qtr 2	Qtr 3	Qtr 4	Qtr 5	Qtr 6	Qtr 7	Qtr 8	Remaining Payments	Grand Total	Second Section
1. Physician Referrals	(100%) 180/yr	45	45	45	45	45	45	45	45			
	Payment	$9,959	$9,959	$9,959	$9,959	$9,959	$9,959	$9,959	$9,959	$318,690	$398,362	
2. Physician Referrals	(75%) 135/yr	34	34	34	34	34	34	34	34			
	Payment	$7,469	$7,469	$7,469	$7,469	$7,469	$7,469	$7,469	$7,469	$238,017	$298,772	
3. Physician Referrals	(50%) 90/yr	23	23	23	23	23	23	23	23			
	Payment	$4,980	$4,980	$4,980	$4,980	$4,980	$4,980	$4,980	$4,980	$159,345	$199,181	
4. Physician Referrals	Declining 5%	45	43	41	39	37	35	33	31			
	Payment	$9,959	$9,461	$8,988	$8,539	$8,112	$7,706	$7,321	$6,955	$288,410	$295,450	
5. Physician Referrals	Cliff/12% Ramp	45	20	20	22	25	28	31	35			
	Payment	$9,959	$4,426	$4,426	$4,957	$5,552	$6,219	$6,965	$7,801	$236,246	$286,551	
6. Physician Referrals	Bathtub (15%)	45	38	33	28	32	37	42	48			
	Payment	$9,959	$8,465	$7,195	$6,116	$7,034	$8,089	$9,302	$10,697	$319,983	$386,840	
Patient Referral Note	$250,000	$9,959	$9,959	$9,959	$9,959	$9,959	$9,959	$9,959	$9,959	$318,690	$398,362	
Payment Summary												Third Section
Scenario 1	Total Paid	$19,918	$19,918	$19,918	$19,918	$19,918	$19,918	$19,918	$19,918	$637,380	$796,725	
Scenario 2	Total Paid	$17,428	$17,428	$17,428	$17,428	$17,428	$17,428	$17,428	$17,428	$557,707	$697,134	
Scenario 3	Total Paid	$14,939	$14,939	$14,939	$14,939	$14,939	$14,939	$14,939	$14,939	$478,035	$597,543	
Scenario 4	Total Paid	$19,918	$19,420	$18,947	$18,498	$18,071	$17,665	$17,280	$16,914	$547,100	$693,812	
Scenario 5	Total Paid	$19,918	$14,385	$14,385	$14,916	$15,511	$16,178	$16,924	$17,760	$554,935	$684,913	
Scenario 6	Total Paid	$19,918	$18,424	$17,154	$16,075	$16,993	$18,048	$19,261	$20,656	$638,673	$785,202	

ond section, that show both initial degradation as well as subsequent growth during the transition period leading to a variety of results representing many potential variations. Grand Total column is the amount of the payments for the entire period based on the particular numbered scenario. Keep in mind that you are looking at only one-half the total number of referrals in this model, since the other half is represented by patient referrals and is not dependent on the activity of the seller during transition.

The third section of the model shows the total payments for referrals from both patients and physicians for each of the scenarios. The Remaining Payments column represents the amount for the balance of the quarters remaining in the 10-year note, based on an average of the last two quarters on the chart. This figure can be calculated in any number of ways. This model demonstrates only one way—a method that allows for a final computation at some appropriate point after the initial period during which the referrals are most vulnerable. The degradation will, presumably, have reached a maximum level at that point, after which it is up to the buyer to maintain the balance. However, keep in mind that the growth periods in Scenarios #5 and #6 represent a more positive result. The seller then gets a definitive price based on his or her good-faith transition effort.

The Grand Total numbers in the bottom section represent the entire amount that would have been paid, based on the physician referral dollars to be received and the full complement of patient referral dollars to be received.

Your accounting professional can help you create your own models. An accountant can also show you different views of these figures, presented as a revenue model, for example, showing the actual revenue stream that the buyer would receive based on patient and actual physician referrals for each of the scenarios.

The Referral Problem—The Real Secret Formula

In many professional practices, particularly those where the practitioner is a specialist, he or she receives referrals from the general practitioners in the community. Good examples in dentistry would be periodontists and orthodontists. As previously stated, in orthodontics, the percentage of referrals in relation to the entire practice on a nationwide basis is about 50%. In periodontics, the percentage can be as high as 80% or more. It is clearly a problem that cannot be left out of any valuation concept.

If you follow the philosophy that the price must be adjusted in relationship to the risk of not maintaining continuity, then the value of these businesses would suffer dramatically. The transition period becomes even more critical than it normally appears, since it will be the obligation of the seller to deliver these referrals in order for the buyer to enjoy the full revenue stream of the business. But how can this problem be accommodated in real-dollar terms?

In other words, the seller will agree to stay with the business long enough after the sale to maintain the continuity of the referrals and the buyer will pay a price based on this promise. What if the seller fails, either intentionally or otherwise, to deliver the referrals as promised? This means that the buyer is paying for a revenue stream that he or she will never enjoy.

The alternative to this is to predicate the value of the business on the risk of non-delivery, in which case the seller is likely to receive less than the value that is ultimately delivered. Another alternative eliminates the loss to either buyer or seller. It is a formula by which the buyer pays for the referrals actually delivered. This plan creates an incentive for the seller to remain for a long enough transition period to ensure the continuity of the referral base. However, if the seller fails to deliver as promised, then the buyer is obligated to pay for only that percentage of referrals he or she is actually able to enjoy.

KEY POINTS TO REMEMBER

- The highest priority in maintaining the integrity of a professional practice after its sale is to transfer client loyalty.
- A partnership period allows clients to meet the new owner while still having the comfort of the former owner's presence.
- Potential degradation of the practice is the most serious issue in structuring the selling price of a professional practice.
- A seller is entitled to be paid for the business being sold, but the buyer should be obligated to pay only for the business that can be delivered.

Worksheet 18. The Secrets to Selling a Professional Practice

Price

You will price your professional practice very much as you would price any other kind of business, based on operating profit, return of investment, buyer income, asset variables—and, of course, the three main pricing variables: interest rate, length of note, and size of down payment. However, you will likely have to spend more time with the new owner during the transition period, and the length of this transition or partnership period will be a significant cause for price adjustment.

How long are you willing to stay with the business after the buyer takes over? _____

How much is that time worth to you in salary? _____

How much is that time worth to you to ensure that the buyer has a successful takeover and makes regular payments on a purchase money promissory note? _____

With these last two dollar figures in mind, how much price adjustment do you think is necessary for the length of time you anticipate staying with the business? _____

Partnership

If the sale of your business, professional practice or not, involves a partnership period, you should have three main considerations: the type of legal format the partnership will use, how the work and responsibility of the partners will be divided, and what the buyout clause will entail.

Use the space provided to note how you and your buyer will work out the details of a partnership arrangement. Then, as always, discuss those details with your professional accountant and attorney.

_____
_____
_____
_____

Client Concerns

A professional develops a different kind of relationship with his or her customers than the traditional business owner. Clients or patients often have a very personal relationship with their professional, which cannot be easily transferred to a new owner. How you handle your clients' concerns about the sale of your practice will affect how successful your buyer is with the business and with paying your promissory note.

Which clients or patients do you think will be reluctant to stay with the practice after the new owner takes over?

_____
_____
_____
_____

What do you think your clients' biggest fears will be about a change in ownership?

_____
_____
_____
_____

What efforts can you make to help those clients stay with the new owner? Be specific.

_____

_____

_____

_____

Degradation of the Practice
Because many of your clients will be reluctant to accept a new owner, your practice may experience a degradation of its client base after you sell. This degradation will affect the new owner's operating profit and his or her ability to make payments on a promissory note.

What efforts will you make to minimize a degradation of the practice?

_____

_____

_____

Speak to your clients about the sale before you determine your selling terms. If you anticipate that the degradation of the client base will be severe, what price adjustments will you make? Will you lower the price to get all cash from your buyer up front? Will you lower the monthly payments on the note immediately after the new owner takes over and then gradually raise them over time as the practice becomes more stable? Discuss these options with your professional advisors.

_____

_____

_____

_____

_____

THE ALTERNATIVE OF PARTNERING UP

Partnering up can be a good idea for an entrepreneur who is looking for a viable alternative to selling his or her business. It can also be a good idea for a buyer who doesn't want or isn't prepared to take on the total responsibility of operating a business.

The Rationale for Selling

The average entrepreneur will eventually and periodically face the question of selling the business, for one reason or another. Some of the reasons are sickness in the family, inability to sustain the company without hiring extra personnel, frustration with lack of adequate growth, and sometimes simply exhaustion from having sole responsibility for continuity and growth. Aside from those who are selling because the business cannot sustain itself, the above reasons are only the tip of the iceberg. And, in most of those cases, the simple answer appears to be to sell the business.

Reality Check for Sellers

One of the reasons that selling may not be a good answer is that the income usually generated from the sale of a business, even under the best of circumstances, will normally be significantly less than the income generated by the owner as an active participant. Many owners just don't examine this simple equation in the early stages of their thinking. In some cases, owners don't consider it at all before they sell. At that point, it may be too late to analyze the problem. It then becomes necessary to augment the family income by taking on another job responsibility, often less appealing than owning a business and being your own boss. For those who are interested, the other side of this coin is that you no longer have the worries of meeting payroll, maintaining cash flow, and all the other obligations of managing a small business.

And, for some people, this is better than the larger income. Food for thought.

Reality Check for Buyers

There are also many buyers who recognize their dearth of knowledge in a particular field or the fact that they have never been responsible for the totality of operating a business. They would like to contribute their expertise—technical, sales, or financial—but they want the comfort of knowing that there will be someone to help with the things they don't know.

The Synergy of Partnering Up

Think about the negatives of both buyer and seller and you will begin to recognize that an interesting alternative to selling and buying might be for the potential seller and the potential buyer to partner up.

Many authors have reflected on the philosophy that "diamonds are forever and partnerships are not." This should not be a reason to be frightened at the prospect of partnering; it is, however, a good reason to exercise the appropriate cautions.

You should always do a diligent search to find out as much as you can about your prospective partner. You should always have a document between you that explains how you can separate, should it become necessary, without destroying the business. And you must always create a trial period during which you can determine if the synergy is the right one for both of you. Personality problems may not become visible until partners face some awkward decisions on which they might not agree. Developing a method for resolving these problems may be the key to moving forward through such situations. In some cases, you will find that each of you should be in charge of particular areas of the company business due to the background and talents particular to each of you.

The Payoff Is on Results

If partnering up means that you have to give up a little income for the peace of mind you dream about, if partnering up means that you can work a shorter day or a shorter week and start to enjoy the quality of life you want so much, if partnering up means that you will be shouldering only part of the responsibility of operating the business, then you may be on the right track. And, in some cases, it is an opportunity to grow the business that, by yourself, might be much more problematic. Remember that the basic equation of synergy is that two people, working together, will invariably generate more than the two people could generate working separately.

PART IV

Legal and Financial Considerations

The Accountant's Job

THREE OF THE FOUR FOLLOWING CHAPTERS are addressed directly to accountants, lawyers, and brokers who may not have extensive experience with buying or selling a business. The fourth chapter relates the lender's expectations and perspective to the borrower. Part IV is designed to give buyers and sellers some insight into what to expect from their professionals on whose shoulders much of their success rests.

You should expect your professional advisors to help you with certain aspects of the transaction. In each case, the help should be within their scope and capabilities. These chapters will help you distinguish the boundaries of expertise and professional responsibility within which your accountant, lawyer, and broker should operate. In addition, Chapter 22 and Chapter 25 provide you insight into the demands of your lender so you can get the loan you need.

Part IV discusses difficult-to-quantify issues, such as the client-advisor relationship and what types of personal traits in the advisor will make that relationship a success. Your professionals need to stand behind you as a team throughout the process of buying or selling. These chapters, therefore, will also devote some time to how accountants, lawyers, and brokers can work together for the most successful business transfer for their clients.

The professionals to whom these remarks are directed should note that the information contained here is not designed to be a treatise. It is rather information taken from experience in the field. Hopefully, it will remind professionals of the tools that are so important and effective to the proper representation of the client.

Chapter 19 is devoted to the accountant who may not have handled many business sales. The chapter will help lead him or her through some of the elements that are of particular concern to both buyer and seller. Obviously, an accountant cannot anticipate all the business situations in which his or her advice could be helpful. Hopefully, this will be a good beginning.

As an accountant involved in a business purchase or sale, you must think ahead, place yourself in the path of business judgment, and, presumably , be there when the time comes to make the big decision. You are the only professional who is involved with the client periodically, if only to file his or her income taxes. Your advice or recommendation could make the difference between the success or failure of the sale. Educate your client to seek advice before the fact and avoid the pitfalls of judgments based on inadequate knowledge or bad advice from well-meaning but inexperienced advisors.

REPRESENTING THE SELLER
Creating the Client Relationship

Some businesspeople say that accountants should keep the figures in their proper columns and avoid being creative. Sometimes, putting the numbers in a particular column or creating a particular chart of accounts that helps a business owner with day-to-day operating activity requires creative thinking. Some accountants prefer not to participate in the business itself, but rather limit all activity to their area of expertise. Others want to be involved with the business and management decision making.

A good accountant can do a lot to help the business owner achieve his or her goals. The business owner must decide, however, to what extent he or she wants an accountant to contribute to the future of the business. The relationship, trust, and confidence that exist between a business owner and his or her accountant take time to establish.

You want to begin by making sure your client understands the need to have a good bookkeeping system, to prepare a consistent and accurate periodic profit and loss statement, and to compare balance sheets on a periodic basis—in other words, the essential elements of good financial housekeeping.

Working out the Purchase Price for the Seller

No one knows better than an accountant the need for defensible numbers. When all the philosophical aspects of the business are laid out, all the sales puffing has faded away, and all the emotional involvements have been exhausted, the buyer and his or her professionals will look at the numbers. If the numbers don't stand up, the sale will inevitably fall down.

If you have prepared a reconstituted financial statement for the sale, then you are selling a strong business that is defensible during sale negotiations. By removing from the profit and loss statement (P&L) all advantages personal to the seller, the P&L will show only those items that are basic to proper business operations. The numbers must be precise to prove that the business depends on those figures and nothing more. After all, in the final analysis, you will be explaining these numbers to the buyer's accountant. Never antici-

pate that your counterpart is less sophisticated than you are. If the buyer's accountant gets the idea that you are trying to hide something, he or she will notify the buyer that there is a problem and that every issue must be examined with care and caution. You do not want the negotiations to turn on you because the buyer gets suspicious of your numbers.

The Tax Ramifications of the Sale

You need to look at the tax aspects of the sale long before your client commits to the sale. The tax issues can often, as you know, represent the difference between a good sale and a bad sale.

The seller must understand, for example, that an all-cash sale may not help achieve his or her long-term goals. The taxes are immediate in the year of the sale and seriously deplete the potential investment dollars the seller expects to have available after the sale. Carrying back a promissory note is a constant problem, because scheduled payments to the seller will depend on the stability and success of the business. On the other hand, the interest rate reflected in the note is normally higher than an equal dollar investment would bring in the financial marketplace. The seller must carefully weigh these equations. As the seller's accountant, your job is to point out the various alternatives and refer the more complex options to a professional investment counselor.

You need to show your client the many more sophisticated levels of tax implications stemming from taking depreciation, possible recapture problems, different methods of inventory accounting, and depreciating long-term equipment purchases. Don't scare your client with a bombardment of the myriad details involved in complex tax ramifications. On the other hand, don't try to retain your client's confidence by being disingenuous about how difficult the preparation process is. Neither approach will secure your reputation as a professional. Your job is to analyze the particular problem your client faces and explain the alternatives available and what each alternative represents in terms of dollars. Then, help your client make a knowledgeable decision based on the short-term and long-term effects on his or her financial portfolio.

Presenting a Clean Set of Books

A real problem arises when the client has not maintained adequate financial records. Often, you are not the accountant of record, yet your task is to prepare financial documentation for presentation to the buyer candidate. The financial records may have been kept professionally; then the job is easy. However, they may also have been kept incorrectly, even inadvertently sabotaged, and then your job is enormous. Your experience should enable you to make an early assessment of the problem. Part of your job will be to explain the time required to properly prepare for the presentation and give the client some reasonable idea as to the anticipated costs and the reasons for them.

The Buyer's Financial Statement

Your client will want you to assess the qualifications of potential buyers. If the sale is going to be in cash, financial qualifications are less important. If, on the other hand, the seller is going to carry any part of the purchase price with a purchase money promissory note, then the question of financial stability is very important. The seller might ask for a form containing information similar to what a bank would require during the application for a mortgage loan. See the Sample Confidential Business Application in Chapter 15. The form asks about assets, liabilities, length of job and residence, and family size and obligations. Most buyer candidates are reluctant to submit these details; most sellers are not interested in serious discussions without them. At some time during initial discussions, the seller is entitled to see this information and the buyer must recognize the need to disclose it.

Although the confidential business application forms are not really difficult to read, they often require an analysis and an explanation for anyone who is unfamiliar with this presentation of financial information. As the seller's accountant, you have an obligation to ensure that the seller understands the meaning of the elements involved and that nothing appears misleading or inconsistent. The seller then has an opportunity to make a more educated judgment about the buyer.

The financial statement is sometimes done with great care and in great detail and other times quite casually and with minimum definition. In the latter case, you

should request additional information from the buyer. In either case, verify the more important disclosures. During initial disclosures, you may also want to run credit checks on any potential buyers. If your client wants additional security on a promissory note, you will need to find out the amount the buyer has still outstanding on mortgages and second trust deeds. Any available equity can serve as a support system for the seller.

REPRESENTING THE BUYER

The buyer's accountant has several jobs to perform. You need to present the buyer's financial data in a light that makes your client look financially able to operate the business successfully. However, if the buyer's resources are not sufficient to meet the capital requirements of a particular business, you also have to advise your client against the purchase. You must analyze the business and interpret the information the seller provides, the profit and loss statement, balance sheets, and cash flow analyses. You need to work with the other professionals involved on both sides of the table to work out a payment plan that provides your client with an adequate annual income.

Preparing the Buyer's Financial Statement

Your first step is to go over your client's financial resources in detail and prepare a financial statement to present to the seller. Any buyer who thinks he or she can buy a business exclusively on good looks ought to be given a very large dose of reality. P.T. Barnum may have been correct when he said there is a sucker born every minute; however, there are not that many suckers around these days. If a seller is going to take a down payment and carry back the remainder of the selling price, the seller wants a buyer with sufficient capital resources to weather occasional storms and make note payments on time.

You will have to discuss the financial statement with your buyer in some detail. It cannot be deceptive, misleading, or simplistic. It must contain a real picture of the entire asset portfolio of your client. If there are things your client would prefer not to disclose, you need to give your professional advice about the ramifications of any failure to disclose.

Explaining the Purchase Price to the Buyer

A buyer is basically interested in two things.

- The ability of the business to generate an immediate income.
- A cash flow sufficient to pay the balance of the purchase price after making the down payment or, if the sale is in cash, a reasonable return on investment.

The income must be consistent with your buyer's needs and the purchase price must be able to come out of the cash flow of the business in a reasonable time period, about five to 10 years maximum. The actual dollar amount is negotiable, but you should never lose sight of the buyer's goals. Don't argue over price just for the sake of winning.

The appropriateness of the price must be based on your client's resources and needs and on the business's operating profit, not on any emotional involvement. Always keep in mind, however, that two businesses similar in all other respects can bring much different prices if they have been operated differently. The owner of one may have reconstituted the profit and loss statement to present a much more accurate picture of the business than the owner of the other. Don't let your buyer be deceived by the numbers alone until you have evaluated their accuracy and validity. You know how deceiving they can be.

The Profit and Loss Statement

A seller needs to present the buyer with a map showing how the business developed from its inception or at least over the past few years. The buyer will want to examine this history in light of the particular industry. The buyer will be able to analyze comparative months, seasonality problems, differentials due to competitors opening or closing, utility of new equipment, and the ability of the business to service debt. Without this financial tracking, the buyer would have no idea as to the validity of the business. This financial history is one of the best looks into the future.

A road map can have too much detail, including every little town and village along the highway, or it can have too little. The same is true for the profit and loss statement (P&L). As the buyer's accountant, you must know enough about the business your client is pur-

chasing to decide what level of definition its P&L should have. If the seller presents a reconstituted P&L during the sale negotiations, your client may ask you, "How can you have a reconstituted profit and loss statement for the buyer when it's different from the one prepared for the IRS?" As Chapter 2 points out, the P&L leaves room for some flexible recordkeeping with regard to expenses personal to the owner.

The P&L's flexibility may also allow a creative accountant for the seller to represent different aspects of business operations. A good accountant will design a P&L to serve whatever purpose he or she chooses, consistent with industry and professional standards and the needs of the client.

As the buyer's representative, you must be careful to recognize the difference between those expenses personal to the owner and those basic to the operation of the business. For example, the choice of a particular car may be personal to the owner, but the use of some vehicle, with its associated costs and expenses, may be mandatory for the business's pickup and delivery service.

The Balance Sheet

A balance sheet is a business standing still and a P&L is a business in motion: your client may need for you to explain this difference. The buyer must know how to read and interpret each financial record, as each has a particular statement to make. If it sounds like your job as an accountant involves teaching your client, you are right. With today's tax implications—particularly the personal liability of the individual, regardless of corporate protection—the buyer must understand at least the basics of the financial map. Without such an understanding, your client may end up as one of P.T. Barnum's suckers. These buyers do not make good clients.

Impress upon your client that a single balance sheet does not provide enough information for judging the progress of a business. The change of numbers shows the progress or lack of it during the long-term activities of the business. By going over the basics of the balance sheet, you will enable your client to quickly monitor some of the long-term business decisions that are so often lost in the details of day-to-day business activity. For example, the P&L will show the monthly interest being paid on a long-term obligation, but not what the total obligation is over the years of the particular lease, note, or purchase contract. This information is found only by examining two or more balance sheets.

The General Ledger

The balance sheet and the P&L represent the financial map of the business. You must make it clear to the client that these two reports cannot be prepared without a general ledger. The general ledger is the engineer's tool to initiate and design that road map. This ultimate reservoir of information allows the accountant to find all the detail necessary to prepare a clear financial picture of the business. As the buyer's accountant, you should prepare a chart of accounts that will allow you to designate and access each element of the business and put it in its proper category to analyze the business. Your client must keep the chart of accounts clearly and accurately.

The Need for Detail

Every business functions within certain parameters to be most effective. Some must maintain a particular ratio between labor and revenue to realize a profit. Others require a particular ratio between cost of product and revenues. Still others require a particular inventory level. The ratios you analyze depend on the type of business your client is purchasing. Many of the appropriate ratios can be found in the financial road map, providing it has sufficient detail. Without a detailed financial history, your client cannot properly analyze the business.

For example, if you are looking at a service business that has experienced an increase in labor costs without a commensurate increase in the price for services, you should recognize this as a danger sign to the profit of the business. An increase in cost of product without an increase in retail pricing structure is another signpost of danger.

Taxes

A buyer faces even more precarious tax obligations than a seller. Your client must realize the personal liability of federal, state, and municipal tax obligations, such as sales taxes, payroll taxes, excise taxes, personal property taxes, and real property taxes. You must ensure that, whatever the posture of the business, the buyer never, never, never falls behind on any of these obligations.

Costs and Fees

Closing costs, whether in the sale of a house or a business, are invariably a surprise to the parties involved. By the time the buyer gets through the escrow costs, rent, deposits for gas and electricity and telephone, accountant's and attorney's fees, and other incidentals that arise, the buyer has depleted the cash reservoir he or she thought might be available for working capital after the sale.

Make sure your client doesn't have to face this surprise at the last minute. In the end, your client will be grateful that you discussed costs and fees early in the process.

Employee Requirements

Learning the employees' salary and bonus structure is only the beginning of your client's investigation into the business's employee requirements. For example, some sales may come from outside commission salespeople, who are not only a labor factor but a control factor as well. They may have more control over some big customers than the buyer would prefer. Bring this issue to your client's attention as a concern you should both examine.

Each business has its employee benefits, from a health program to vacation plans and accrued vacations for older employees. The buyer may even be obliged to honor some strange bonuses that the seller initiated at some point for some reason. You have an obligation as a financial investigator to find as many of these problem areas as possible. Unfortunately, being an accountant involves not only examining what you see, but also searching and finding the things that are not so obvious.

Although it is not your job as the buyer's accountant to restructure the business, your advice in this context can be tremendously helpful. Your experience will have put you in touch with various outside services and state-of-the-art equipment for maintaining good financial bookkeeping. Examine with the buyer which of these might eliminate excess personnel expenses. You may help the buyer make the difference between a brilliant first year and a mediocre one.

After all, many sellers are interested in selling their businesses because the financial maintenance, among other things, has just become too onerous in terms of costs and/or time. If you can bring these alternatives to the attention of your client, you may help him or her recoup your entire fee for the year. This grateful buyer could become a long-term client.

The buyer can create a positive atmosphere in the business and solidify the relationship between the business and its employees in many ways. If the business is big enough and profitable enough, then creating plans to ensure employee longevity is appropriate, in some cases even necessary, to the continued success of the business. In other cases, this may be an opportunity for the owners of the business to begin developing a retirement plan and conditions may be just right to take advantage of some of the tax benefits available. A business owner could make big mistakes without good advice from a competent accountant, a pension administrator, or other investment advisor.

The S Corporation

Most businesspeople, without much legal or accounting background, think that the corporate entity is the answer to all personal liability situations involved in the business community. They are not aware that taxes are normally excluded from this protective device and that most people in the business community require personal signatures or guarantees to corporate contracts of any substance. You must ensure that your client understands the rationale behind both of these exceptions.

In the event, however, that the corporate entity can still serve a good purpose, you must explain to your client that a C corporation could represent a double tax on the business profits before they make their way into his or her pocket. The corporation pays a tax on the profit of the business and the shareholder pays a tax on the dividend if the profit is distributed.

When you explain that in the S corporation the tax is on the profit of the business only—it is taxed only once—you will have a very grateful client. Be careful to

point out, however, that profits are assessed to each partner and a tax is payable on those profits whether the partner actually receives the money or not. Carefully discuss the alternatives with all the appropriate professionals to avoid this situation. One approach might be better than another based on the kind of business, the kinds of investments that have been made, or the financial position of the investors.

Borrowing Money for the Business

You also need to explain to your client the potential dangers of borrowing money on behalf of the corporation. If your client submits a credit application on behalf of the corporation to a company from which your client's business expects to obtain products or services, your client is not completely protected by his or her corporate position. If the application is faulty— if it contains information that is incomplete or untrue—the officers and directors of the corporation may be personally liable. Unfortunately, many clients fill out these applications, thinking nothing of it. By the time their accountant gets to the problem, it is too late.

Your job is not so much to find money for the business as it is to know when it is a good or bad idea to borrow it. Your client faces many options for obtaining money and needs your advice as to which is the best. A buyer has the following options:

- Discount retail prices to generate additional cash flow.
- Discount receivables to a bank or other institution.
- Get a long-term commitment by applying for a loan secured by hard assets or accounts receivable.
- Sell stock or other participations in the business.

In fact, you can find a myriad of ways to service a money problem without necessarily borrowing. Make sure your client understands the alternatives.

Investing Retained Earnings

Finally, you may be called on to help your client decide what to do with excess profits. Your client should obey three important rules of investing: the investment must have security, return, and flexibility. If an investment meets the first two criteria but not the third, business immediacies may require taking back the investment early. The penalties may eliminate whatever profit your client anticipated. In the worst-case scenario, the officers and directors who made the decision might be liable to the shareholders for bad judgment.

You want to have an eye on all your client's needs as you assist with purchase negotiations. You must look at the business in relationship to all the other financial aspects of your client's personal and business life. If you don't, you could misdiagnose the problems and give bad advice.

If you can develop a relationship of mutual trust with your client, you will probably save your client money in the long term. You will be able to catch mistakes before they happen. Most clients are beginning to realize that asking the professional for advice, before the fact, saves money most of the time.

Finally, whether you will be representing the buyer or the seller, you may want to review the Accountant's Checklist below to help you better represent your client.

KEY POINTS TO REMEMBER

- Never underrate the value of a strong relationship with your client.
- As accountant for the seller, your first priorities are to work out the selling price and its tax ramifications, prepare the financial disclosure documents, and examine the financial capabilities of the buyer.
- As accountant for the buyer, your first priorities are to prepare his or her financial statement, explain the seller's financial disclosure documents, and ensure that your client will have an adequate working capital reservoir.
- The buyer must be able to understand and discuss the financial history of the business, including the balance sheet, the profit and loss statement, the cash flow analysis, and the general ledger. If your client cannot do this, you need to educate him or her.

Worksheet 19. Accountant's Checklist

These questions are not intended to represent a complete checklist for every sale. They are intended to remind the accountant that each sale is different and that there is more to properly representing a client than merely preparing the documents.

Representing the Seller

Yes	No	
❏	❏	Do you enjoy getting involved in the negotiating process and does your client want you involved in the negotiating process?
❏	❏	If you checked No, are you satisfied that you can serve your client adequately without being involved in negotiations?
❏	❏	Have you explained the difference between a profit and loss statement prepared for the IRS and one prepared for the buyer?
❏	❏	Are you satisfied that your client understands the difference?
❏	❏	Does your client understand the financial numbers related to the sale well enough to explain them to the buyer?
❏	❏	Have you discussed the tax ramifications of the sale with your client, particularly the tax payable in the event of an all-cash sale?
❏	❏	Does your client understand the difference between an asset sale and a stock sale?
❏	❏	Do you and your client have a clear picture of what you are expected to do during the course of the selling process?
❏	❏	Does your client have an idea what your fee will be depending on what aspects of representation and documentation you are asked to participate in?

Representing the Buyer

Yes No

- ☐ ☐ Are you responsible for helping your client prepare his or her financial statement to submit to the seller?
- ☐ ☐ Does your client understand the dangers of disclosure and nondisclosure related to preparing an honest and complete financial statement?
- ☐ ☐ Does your client have a realistic view of the purchase price he or she can afford and whether or not it is appropriate to his or her investment capital and short- and long-term goals?
- ☐ ☐ Does your client understand the difference between an asset sale and a stock sale?
- ☐ ☐ Do you and your client understand what you are expected to do during the pre-sale, negotiation, and post-sale periods?
- ☐ ☐ Does your client have an idea what your fee will be depending on what aspects of representation and documentation you are asked to participate in?
- ☐ ☐ Have you explained to your client the tax and liability considerations related to the various legal entities, such as a C or S corporation?
- ☐ ☐ Does your client understand the difference between a profit and loss statement prepared for the IRS and one prepared for the purpose of selling the business?
- ☐ ☐ Does your client understand how to determine a manager's salary and relate it to his or her potential owner's compensation and overall profit picture after taking over the business?

SERVICE FEES OF PROFESSIONALS—GOOD AND BAD

What Does a Professional Cost?

It is always a little disturbing when professionals can't explain why their fees are higher than those of the average artisan.

If you ask, which you always should, lawyers will tell you that their expertise, made up of education and experience, allows them to charge more than the average electrician or plumber for each hour of work. They will also tell you that a given job, transactional or court-associated, will likely fall within a certain time frame. They will, upon further inquiry, indicate what the low-end charge might be, as well as the alternative of the high-end charge, depending on the length of time it takes to bring the matter to closure. In this way, you will at least be able to judge whether your business budget can stand the cost ... before you decide to go forward. Accountants will usually extend this same courtesy with regard to time and cost.

Brokers are in a different category. They usually charge by a percentage of the sale. The reason is different. They handle a variety of deals, of which only a few ever come to fruition. By taking a percentage of the ones that close, they can depend on the statistics to carry them through. It's a little bit like the insurance salesperson who makes 100 calls knowing that, if one of them buys, all the work has been worthwhile. This statistical value works on many levels. Even the sophisticated investor knows that, if only one of his or her investments works well, it will make up for the ones that didn't. And the ones that didn't are usually in the majority.

When the Fees Are "over the Top"

But when the time allocated and the fees involved are "over the top" without a valid reason, the consumer has reason to complain. There are those people who value businesses, for sale and other purposes, who will tell you that it will take weeks or even months to arrive at a business valuation. There are prices in the marketplace that run from $10,000 to $35,000 at the latest estimates.

The fact of the matter is that a business valuation, for purposes of satisfying most business needs, can be done in one day and should cost the price of a professional's day. It is unlikely that this day's activity will come to a price of $10,000 or more.

It is certainly true that the paperwork necessary to satisfy a court for litigation purposes or an accounting firm for estate tax purposes or a mediator for divorce purposes or the kind of substantial paperwork that is used for stock valuation and other sophisticated paper trails will require additional work. It is also true that the larger, more sophisticated companies may require additional time. In some cases, the "breakout" of an individual's interest may require some refinement. In other words, there are many variations on the job, depending on the purpose or purposes to be served by the valuation.

However, the average small businessperson is interested in the basic parameters within which a buyer and a seller might find comfort in a selling situation. Although it is true that businesses can be valued in various ways, every business is not a rocket science project. It is also true that a 35-page analysis of the industry of which your business is a part is probably overkill in most situations. Keep it simple. Pay for what you need. And be sure to get some estimates of time required before you pay a king's ransom for a pot of stone soup.

CHAPTER 20

The Lawyer's Job

A LAWYER MUST BE A GOOD LISTENER, A clear thinker, and a skillful tactician. Lawyers obviously need good communication skills, not only to argue cases, but also to explain issues to their client and to advise the client on which alternative is the shortest, least expensive, and most productive. Finally, a lawyer must be a good presenter to convince the other party—another lawyer, a judge, a jury, or a board of directors—with logic, emotion, and substance, to achieve the result desired by the client.

A lawyer cannot afford to make a mistake on a client's behalf. To a client, it could mean as little as a bump in the road or as much as life itself. To the lawyer, it could mean censure, disbarment, or, in the case of criminal involvement, incarceration. Lawyers sell a strange product, time and expertise. Neither is something you can feel, look at, drive, or put away. Both are intangible.

While selling or buying a business, your client may not be able to point to any one thing you did to help the transfer succeed for him or her. However, with a skilled lawyer, a buyer or a seller will benefit from good representation and sleep well at night.

The checklist at the end of this chapter will help you identify those areas in which your client needs the most legal help. Be sure to review Worksheet 20 with your client.

CREATING THE CLIENT RELATIONSHIP

Every lawyer knows that you don't instill confidence in a client by telling him or her what school you attended, whether you were on the law review, or how much money you made last year. On the other hand, each of these things means something a little different to each client. They become part of the picture for the client.

The substance of the relationship, however, is based on a much more personal level. The relationship is often based on things over which you exercise little control—your voice, your demeanor, your clothes, your desk, the pictures on your wall, or the location of your office.

You build the most satisfactory relationship by listening to the problem and responding to the issues objectively and dispassionately. By listening and responding appropriately, you give your client a comfort zone, confidence in a professional who appears to understand the problem and to have a clear picture of how to most expeditiously serve the client.

To ensure that you can best serve your client's needs, you need the most accurate and reliable information from him or her. If your client is concerned about disclosure, it may be because he or she doesn't know who may ultimately have access to the information disclosed. By explaining the attorney-client privilege and stressing that it can be waived only by the client, you may be able to satisfy your client's concern.

Some lawyers look at every problem from a negative perspective and think of reasons why the client won't be able to buy or sell a business on advantageous terms. Other lawyers address the sale in a positive way to maximize the benefits to the client. Your best approach is to remember that the client is looking for a lawyer who can get the job done. If you fulfill your purpose in an appropriate time frame and for a reasonable fee, you have indeed gotten the job done.

REPRESENTING THE SELLER
Defending the Selling Price

Whether the price is set by the client or by a professional appraiser whom the client has retained, it is incumbent on you, as the client's representative, to understand the price structure and be prepared to defend it. Understanding and defending does not mean you interfere with the valuation of the business; however, a price that is clearly out of line will eventually lead the buyer or his or her professional advisors to cancel the deal. You will have charged a fee with little concern about the ultimate result sought by your client, to sell the business.

Many clients fail to make appropriate adjustments in their price expectations because they're emotionally involved with the business. At that point, it is necessary for you to put logic before emotion by explaining what price your client can realistically expect. A lawyer cannot do any better under the circumstances.

Preparing the Initial Memorandum

You are well advised, as counsel for the seller, to prepare an initial memorandum to memorialize the basic elements of the sale, early on. This memorandum can reference the fact that more formal documents are being prepared, but the memorandum will also call for a down payment. When the buyer candidate puts down hard cash to bind the deal, even though he or she may be able to retrieve these dollars if the deal falls

through, it brings the parties much closer to a real discussion.

With buyer's remorse a chronic problem, you must act to tie the deal down in whatever way you can, pending the preparation of final documents. The memorandum must be simple to read and understand and contain no ambiguities. Put in as many of the basics as you can without detracting from the simplicity of the document. The purpose of the exercise is to get it signed and a down payment in the bank or into an escrow of some kind. (See the Sample Memorandum of Sale in Chapter 14.)

Preparing the Final Documents

Because documents very often survive the relationship between attorney and client, it is always a good idea to go over the final document with your client to ensure that he or she understands the language, including those elements in which legal language has no simple equivalent. Have your client take notes and add those notes to his or her copy after the sale is consummated to be sure your client can resurrect the proper interpretation of the language whenever necessary. Like everything else you do as an attorney, this kind of extra service will earn you the reputation of making your client's best interests your highest priority.

Protecting the Seller Until the Balance Is Paid

If the buyer's particular expertise is essential to the survival and success of the business, what would happen if the buyer died before the purchase money promissory note is paid off? The seller may have difficulty getting the dollars he or she anticipated from the sale. One solution is to have the buyer take out an insurance policy for the balance of the note with the seller as beneficiary.

What if the buyer fails at the business? If the original down payment was large enough and if the seller has the right to take the business back, the seller may still be able to achieve his or her goal by selling the business again, even if for less than the original purchase price. What if the buyer has not only failed at the business but also run the business into the ground? The seller will take back a mere skeleton of the business he or she sold. This is what you should seek to protect the seller against. (See Chapter 14 for more on seller protections.)

After the sale, the seller should be able to monitor the business as long as any part of the purchase price is still outstanding. Some sellers merely want assurances that the taxes are paid; other outstanding debts are usually easier to negotiate if the seller is forced to take the business back. The seller also wants to ensure that salaries and other labor costs are held to a certain percentage of income to be sure that the business is not being systematically destroyed. Some sellers even go as far as to seek assurance that the cost of product stays within certain parameters. The more sophisticated will even monitor the advertising. You need to arrange for your client to monitor the business during the repayment period.

Much depends on the type of business involved and the size of the down payment. In fact, much also depends on the amount of supervision to which the buyer is willing to submit. You, as seller's counsel, will have to make the judgment once you and the seller have developed a good working relationship.

REPRESENTING THE BUYER
Explaining the Selling Price

You will not make the ultimate decision whether your client buys a business. Your job is to examine pricing alternatives and explain the ramifications of each potential price structure. It is not your prerogative to accept or reject the price of a business; as long as the price is sensible, however, you have certain obligations to the buyer. You must examine with the buyer various issues regarding money. Does your client have the following?

- Enough income to pay the bills, including the purchase money obligation, if any?
- Enough money as working capital for the business to survive and prosper?
- Enough money to feed his or her family while paying the promissory note and building the business?

Make sure your client is aware of these issues. Then he or she should use good judgment and, hopefully, the advice of a good accountant.

Protections for the Buyer

A buyer is invariably emotionally involved in the project of buying a business. After all, not only is the buyer investing very substantial time, money, and effort, but also the future of the family and the buyer's retirement are probably at stake. It is incumbent upon you as buyer's counsel to offer whatever objective, dispassionate advice you can to temper this emotional involvement. You are not expected to know everything about every business; however, very much like a bar examination, it is not as necessary to know the specific answers to the questions as to recognize the questions themselves. The buyer must satisfy himself or herself as to the answers. These questions could include the following:

- The history of the industry
- The adequacy of the equipment included in the purchase
- Competitors and what they mean to the potential growth of the business
- The personnel as an asset or a potential problem
- The ratios of labor and cost of product to the income stream
- The seasonality of the business, if any

You should be able to recognize that answers to these questions could dramatically change the buyer's perspective. You would be doing your client a disservice if you did not enter into this area to at least some degree.

Examine the Lease

The longevity of a business in a particular location could substantially affect its success. If your client needs to move the business or face a dramatic increase in rent or rental equivalent, such as taxes or common area maintenance, it could devastate profitability. You should look at the lease and lease options carefully to avoid these potential problems.

Many options to renew leases state that rent will be discussed at the time the lessee chooses to exercise the option to renew. This is hardly an option. It is merely an opportunity to negotiate. Explain this to the buyer, along with any of the other ambiguities that so many leases contain.

Broker Agreements

Discuss also any agreements with brokers for commissions at the time of sale. These types of commissions can lead to very tricky situations; you should scrutinize any relationship that the seller had with a broker at any time. If a seller has had relationships with other brokers before the current one, an earlier contract may still create problems. If a former broker brings a lawsuit against the seller, the buyer might become embroiled in the problem, like it or not. Be careful to look out for this hidden danger for your client.

Examine Any Franchise Agreement

Some lawyers think that because they have eaten at a McDonald's they understand franchising. This kind of thinking can be a dangerous mistake. There is really no reason for it. State and federal legislation has made the lawyer's job much easier in this regard. Buying a franchise is not much different from buying any business, if you find out just what the business is all about.

Your first step is to request the franchise disclosure document from the franchise company. It will, by law, contain the nature and history of the business, the people who are responsible for the operation of the franchise company, and any obligations the buyer is about to take on. This information will lead you to any other questions about the local marketplace and competition. See also Chapter 9 of this book or *Franchise Bible* by Erwin J. Keup (Entrepreneur Press, 2004) for more information on buying or selling a franchise.

Long-Term Leases and Contracts

While you cannot save your client from every lurking disaster, long-term leases or contracts your client purchases with the business are places where potential disasters can hide. Long-term obligations, whether for equipment or for buying or selling products, can have unforeseen long-term consequences for the business.

Take a quantity discount purchase, for example. If a new component is designed that makes the product obsolete before the entire quantity is sold, your client will be buying a deteriorating inventory. If a seller wants to get out of the business because he or she has a long-term lease on equipment that is about to become obsolete, raise the issue with your client as a possible deal breaker.

Legal Business Entities

There are several forms of holding title to a business. An owner may be a sole proprietor, a general partner with one or more partners, the general partner in a limited partnership, or the president of a corporation. On a more subtle level, you can control a business in many ways without appearing to be the driving force on a day-to-day basis, such as by controlling the money or corporate stock.

As the buyer's lawyer, you need to assess just what your client is ultimately trying to accomplish and then recommend which form of ownership is most appropriate under the circumstances. Explain also that your client may have a reason to change the form of ownership as the long-term goals of the business change. For example, the company may grow to a stature that warrants a public offering. If the company goes public, a different corporate package may be necessary to facilitate large investments while allowing present management to stay in control of the day-to-day activities.

The Personal Signature

The average businessperson understands that the corporate form of ownership affords the owner a certain amount of protection. Unfortunately, many business relationships that the owner would like to protect against, like leases and long-term purchase arrangements, require either a personal signature to the contract or a personal guarantee. The corporation cannot protect against this.

Many people do not understand the ramifications of their signature on a legal document. They are even unaware that "The Corporation, by Jack Terry, President" is an entirely different signature from "Jack Terry." You need to ensure that your client clearly understands the dangerous difference between the two. The first signature will bind the corporation to a contract but will not create an obligation on Jack Terry the individual. The second signature, on the other hand, will bind Jack Terry to the obligation regardless of whom or what he may purport to represent.

Since a corporation can be costly and problematic to use as a business entity, the decision to incorporate depends on the kind of business and business obligations for which the owner expects to be responsible. Your client needs to understand the potential holes in corporate protection.

Joint and Several Liability

Some less sophisticated business people think that if they sign a document along with other people, they are responsible for only a portion of the obligation. They are devastated when they find out their signature obligates them to the entire debt. Certainly they may have the right to seek contributions from the other signatories; however, if they have the most money, their money will invariably pay the bill long before contributions come from the others. Make sure your client understands joint and several liability.

The Partnership Relationship

The best relationships will have disagreements. That's only natural and logical. The best framework for a partnership agreement is to have, from the beginning, a method by which either partner can get out or buy out the other. It is a good idea to explain to your client that one partner can legally bind the other to long-term business obligations. A decision that might appear to be brilliant at one moment may turn out to be terrible in hindsight. The partnership agreement must be drafted carefully to keep either partner from binding the partnership to a long-term obligation detrimental to the future of the business.

Collections and Contracts

Someone who has acted as a sales representative for a large company may never have dealt with the problem of collecting from the accounts he or she sold. That type of buyer merely picked up a commission check at the end of the week, verified that the commission was properly calculated, and made the deposit. Operating a business, particularly collecting for the goods sold, is a new world for many of these people.

Entering into contractual relationships with customers may also be new territory for a person who formerly just took orders. Any long-term, contractual arrangement that is important to the success or survival of the business should always be reduced to writing, partly to avoid ambiguities and partly to help secure payment. You must decide how much education your client needs about collections and contracts to survive and prosper in the business after buying it.

Employee Relations and Contracts

The employees of a business can either be incidental to the core elements or, in some cases, actually be the core elements of the business activity. Losing key employees can devastate an otherwise successful business. You need to examine any contractual relationship between management and employees. If no documented contracts exist, you still need to get into the substance of the relationship. Suggest to your client that he or she examine the employees' loyalty and what, if any, promises have been made to the employees that the new management will be obliged or expected to keep. If the business is large enough to involve a union, you may need to consult an attorney who specializes in labor law.

How to Handle a Bulk Transfer

The purchase of a business can involve the acquisition of stocks or assets. In the case of stocks, the buyer is knowingly taking on the full responsibility of the corporate business. In the case of assets, the buyer's intention is normally to take on only what he or she can see—what is disclosed.

But what about the things you or your client cannot see? The question of the buyer's responsibility to the seller's creditors can be problematic. In most jurisdictions, technically, creditors can be notified officially by publishing notice of the pending sale. They are then obliged to put their claims in the escrow and are precluded from seeking payment from the new buyer. Some jurisdictions have legislation under the title of a bulk transfer of assets; others reference the sale in different ways. It is appropriate to check your particular jurisdiction to ensure that the law has not been repealed.

Buying Assets Free and Clear

Because your client expects to purchase most of the business assets free and clear of any outstanding debt, you need to verify that no one else has an interest in the property. Check all the appropriate agencies for the filing of legal documents that indicate an interest in the property by someone other than the seller. Check any filings made under the Uniform Commercial Code to ensure that no others hold title to the property that your client is presumably buying.

By examining any outstanding contracts or debts on the business assets, you will also examine any contractual relationships between the seller and vendors and manufacturers with whom the seller does business. If you cannot find a filing on record, the chances are greater that your client is getting the assets he or she expects.

Issues Beyond Your Expertise

Many lawyers like to think of themselves as a one-stop shop, a place where clients can address all legal problems. With the constant passage of legislation in every area of the law, it is practically impossible for the average lawyer to keep up with the changes in every field. Smart lawyers maintain an up-to-date understanding of their own specialty and seek advice from others when their practice takes them into an area away from their expertise.

In dealing with a business purchase or sale, you may need help in these areas:

- Labor law—to deal with unions or other employee concerns
- Securities law—to deal with stock participations in public companies (sometimes, private companies as well)
- Litigation—to deal with lawsuits ranging from collection on delinquent accounts to contract issues, to protection of proprietary interests and intellectual property, etc.

You may be able to handle a given matter without being affiliated with another office; sometimes, a little advice in the right direction can save you time and save your client a lot of money. Your own good judgment should prevail.

In other areas of the law, the experience of dealing with the people involved is just as important as the law itself. In negotiating the specific elements of a lease, for example, your experience and negotiating skills are as valuable as your knowledge of the law. You must depend on your judgment in many of these situations. After all, the highest priority is always to serve your client most professionally and expeditiously.

Be sure to review the worksheet below to help you cover these important issues with your client.

KEY POINTS TO REMEMBER

- Your first priority is to create a relationship with your client that instills confidence and to explain the attorney-client privilege.
- As attorney for the seller, make sure you and your client understand your responsibilities regarding preparing the sales presentation, negotiating the purchase price, and protecting the sale.
- As attorney for the buyer, make sure your client understands the premises lease, any franchise agreement, and any contracts with vendors, customers, manufacturers, or employees.
- As attorney for the buyer, you may need to educate your client regarding the rationale behind the purchase price, available cash flow, personal liability, and relationships with partners and investors.

Worksheet 20. Lawyer's Checklist

These questions are not intended to represent a complete checklist for every sale. They are intended to remind each professional that every sale is different and that there is more to properly representing a client than merely preparing the documents.

Representing the Seller

Yes No

❑ ❑ Do you have a strong relationship with your client so that you know the information he or she gives you is reliable, honest, and complete?

❑ ❑ Does your client understand attorney-client privilege?

❑ ❑ If you do not have sufficient experience in buying and selling small businesses, do you have reliable professional advice you and your client can turn to for help?

❑ ❑ If you are not familiar with the business for sale, have you discussed the business with your client enough to understand its most important elements?

❑ ❑ Does your client understand what material disclosures are and the dangers of material nondisclosure?

❑ ❑ If your client accepts a purchase money promissory note for some or all of the purchase price, do you know which protective devices to include in the sale agreement to prevent post-sale problems?

❑ ❑ Does your client have an idea what your fee will be depending on what aspects of representation and documentation you are asked to participate in?

❑ ❑ Does your client understand the difference between the sale of assets and the sale of stock?

Representing the Buyer

Yes No

❑ ❑ Have you examined the feasibility of the purchase from the buyer's perspective?

❑ ❑ Have you examined the business's lease to ensure that your client is properly protected from future problems such as rent increases or arbitrary lease termination clauses?

❑ ❑ Have you examined all equipment and short-term leases to make sure your client is getting the title, value, and maintenance agreements he or she expects?

❑ ❑ If your client is purchasing a franchise, have you examined the uniform franchise offering circular or other disclosure documents and discussed their implications with your client?

❑ ❑ Have you discussed the different legal entities, such as a C or S corporation, sole proprietorship, general partnership, or limited partnership, so that your client understands the tax and legal implications of each?

❑ ❑ Have you cautioned your client regarding personal guarantees and using his or her personal signature, the ramifications of joint and several liability, and the proper manner in which to sign a corporate document?

❑ ❑ Have you examined with your client the relationships between the business and its vendors and manufacturers to ensure that these relationships do not contain any surprises?

❑ ❑ Does your client have an idea what your fee will be depending on what aspects of representation and documentation you are asked to participate in?

❑ ❑ Does your client understand the difference between an asset sale and a stock sale?

BEING YOUR OWN LAWYER

There are many sources from which you can access legal forms that you can fill out yourself instead of seeking professional advice. There are books that proclaim that you can draft your own legal documents. There are Web sites that will allow you to access whatever form you might consider appropriate to your current needs. There is even a franchise that services those who want to prepare their own legal documents. All are careful to point out that they merely provide an alternative for those people who already know what they want. But do these people already know what they want? Do they really understand the rule against perpetuities? Do they know the implications of using the words "per stirpes" in a will? Can they recognize the difference between an option to buy and a right of first refusal in a lease? What are the dangers that lurk in this land of do-it-yourself legal advice?

Referring the "Real" Problems

Even the do-it-yourself legal services franchise is quick to say that it refers all legal questions or complicated litigation to attorneys. The problem is that some legal language is obviously complicated, requiring legal advice, while other language, which appears to be self-explanatory, harbors legal questions that are not so obvious but the implications of which could be disastrous. If the layperson does not recognize these questions, what is the position of the client who uses the form without being aware of the consequences? The client is not even in a position to sue for reparation since, in practically all these instances, the form or the advice is usually followed by the legal caution, "None of the above is designed to take the place of professional advice and the author takes no responsibility for language or lack of language that is ultimately determined to be inadequate or inappropriate."

The Starting Point

It is certainly true that, in the context of everyday business, the individual usually knows what his or her prerogatives and obligations are in a business relationship. This often is referred to as "the deal points." If the parties spell these out and agree to them, the creation of a legal document should do little more than put the deal points into language that is clear and unambiguous, so that nothing could be interpreted in more than the one correct way. Even the most practiced professional can be guilty of failing to perfect such a document. However, the chances are that the relationship will be better delineated in the hands of a professional than in the hands of the layperson.

Many businesspeople now are drafting the deal points themselves and then seeking professional advice to ensure that the language is clear and unambiguous. This is certainly a better approach than to merely fill in the blanks in a form.

What's It Going to Cost?

It is true that professionals cannot often give you an exact cost with respect to legal actions, primarily because they cannot gauge how much time is going to be required to finalize a matter. On the other hand, they can probably give you a pretty good range of costs relative to preparing documents. On this basis, you can find out early what the cost of preparation will be and compare this with the time you would need to devote in order to do the job yourself. The biggest part of that equation is the calculated risk you will take by not having the professional examine the language to ensure that it is unequivocal, an insurance against problems in the future.

The Team Effort

Most attorneys today want to meet with the client and, by conferencing about the facts, are in a position to expedite the paperwork cost-effectively and professionally. As with so many things, if the context of the agreement is small or the time frame of the relationship is narrow, it is not likely that the paperwork will exceed a minor cost. On the other hand, if the matter is complicated or the time frame of the relationship is extensive, the paperwork might be substantial. On this basis, the cost will be higher. Keep in mind that if the relationship is such that it requires a lot of definition, the cost for preparation might be much less expensive than losing in litigation because of inadequate or improper preparation. Remember: don't be penny-wise and pound-foolish when the dollar implications of the relationship are formidable.

CHAPTER 21

The Broker's Job

N O ONE CAN BE AN EXPERT IN ALL BUSI-nesses. Nonetheless, the broker's obligation is to understand the nature of the business that he or she is negotiating on behalf of a client. After all, if a broker is only going to obtain signatures on the listing agreement, what real value does he or she have to any buyer or seller? A broker must never forget that his or her client is dealing with tremendous emotional pressure.

Every business has its nuances. No one would expect a broker to be as practiced at the business that he or she represents as the seller. It is, however, incumbent on the broker to have a fair understanding of the basic elements. You should discuss the business with your seller/client or buyer/client carefully. You need to appreciate just what the seller is putting on the market and the kind of involvement for which the buyer anticipates paying. You should read whichever section of this chapter is appropriate—"Representing the Seller" or "Representing the Buyer"—or both sections and then, to review your responsibilities to your clients, refer to Worksheet 21 at the end of the chapter.

REPRESENTING THE SELLER
Creating the Client-Broker Relationship

The client-broker relationship is referred to differently in different jurisdictions. The most restrictive is the exclusive authorization to sell. Under this kind of agreement, the broker is entitled to collect a commission on the business sale whether he or she brings the particular buyer to the table or not. As long as a sale is consummated with a buyer who was introduced to the business during the term of the agreement, whether by the broker or not, the broker is deemed to have earned the commission.

This may seem unfair. Clients should recognize, however, that in some cases a broker spends an inordinate amount of time and even a substantial sum of money to advertise the business—time and money for which the broker cannot be compensated unless and until there is a sale.

This type of agreement can also call for an earned commission if the sale takes place after the agreement has expired, as long as the broker prepares a list of buyer candidates and gives it to the client within a certain time frame. Indeed, if the seller withdraws the business from the market or interferes with a sale that might otherwise have taken place during the term of the broker agreement, the broker might still be entitled to the commission. You can, of course, develop other less stringent broker arrangements.

The commission is another element you and your client need to consider. Most brokers earn a 10% commission when a business is sold, but the percentage could be less or more. A broker may even work without a commission. Some brokers charge for their time, with a bonus tied in if the business is sold.

The type of agreement and the amount of the commission are, in a sense, secondary considerations. The key issues are disclosure and mutual trust. The client must feel that the broker is experienced, competent, and trustworthy. The broker must feel that the client is realistic, honest, and trustworthy. Full disclosure will always eliminate the ambiguous and uncertain elements between you and your client.

Preparing the Asking Price

If an asking price is substantially below the market value of the business, the business may sell quickly, but the seller may lose a good portion of his or her earned equity. If the business is priced too high, it may remain unsold, much to the chagrin of both the seller and the broker. As a result, your obligation as a broker is to find a selling price that maximizes the equity position of the seller while ensuring that you are positioned in the marketplace to attract the largest number of qualified buyers.

To find the asking price, always examine the marketplace from the perspective of the potential buyer. After all, the deal must serve the buyer's goals or there's no sale. You know from experience that there is no magic to price. The buyer is looking for two things: an immediate income consistent with his or her needs and a cash flow that can essentially pay the purchase price of the business. The real question is what income is consistent with the buyer's needs. If the necessary income is too much for the business to handle without restructuring the price far below the seller's expectations, then the buyer is the wrong candidate.

On the other hand, the seller must be given the appropriate dose of reality based on the number of other businesses available in the same profit range. It is the seller's prerogative to set the bottom selling price—and it is the broker's job to analyze, advise, and counsel the seller.

Remember always, as the broker, that price is based on much more than just the dollar amount put forward at the beginning of the negotiating session. Price can be adjusted by many items with which the seller is normally not very conversant. Here are some of these variables:

- All-cash vs. a carryback
- The amount of the down payment
- The interest on the note
- The time the seller is willing to carry the note
- The possibility of a consulting contract for the seller as part of the purchase price

Any one of these could turn out to be the key to the sale, the point that allows the buyer and the seller to succeed in their negotiations. Explain these pricing variables to your client at the beginning of your involvement. By discussing price structuring with your client, you will show that you have a handle on the nuances of selling and that you are the best-qualified person in the field to handle the sale for the seller.

Preparing the Business for Sale

The key to an attractive business is good housekeeping—cosmetic, hygienic, and financial. You can play an important part here.

Walking through your own home, you don't often see the crack in the wall, the bookcase that looks disheveled, or the kitchen tiles that need to be replaced. Walking through someone else's house, you will likely notice many of these things. Business owners frequently do not see the cobwebs in the corners, the torn carpet, or the plastic panel coming off the counter. It is your job to point these things out. In some cases, a small cosmetic change can make a difference in the price; in other cases, it can determine whether or not you make the sale. Don't ever hesitate about bringing these things to your client's attention.

A new bookkeeping system can help put a better face on the business and get it ready for sale. The bookkeeping system should be easy to access, read, and understand. If the buyer can understand it, you will spend less time with the buyer's accountant. In addition, the books must tell the financial story of the business. Remember: whatever it is that you are representing for sale, the information must be honest, accurate, and easy to access. Anything less will suggest that someone is trying to hide something from the buyer, which will make a sale more difficult, if not impossible.

Whatever the reality of the business, it has a value. The business might not be valued as high as the seller would like, but it has a value. A good broker is interested in maximizing that value without distorting the facts or the reality of the business. Your reputation for honesty, candor, and conciseness is, indeed, your stock in trade. If it becomes tainted, you may become less effective in the business community. You will be of little value to your prospective clients.

If the business has a substantial price, you may even want to structure a business plan. A business plan can take many shapes, from a few pages to something as complex as a franchise disclosure document. Because writing a business plan is time-consuming and expensive, discuss it with your client.

Preparing the Seller's Negotiating Position

For every negotiating session, there are three basic categories of consideration:

- Things your client must have
- Things your client would like to have
- Things your client is willing to concede

Before every session, you should confer with your client to ensure that you both understand which items fall into those three categories.

Other essential elements to consider may be collateral to the asking price.

- How long is the seller willing to remain with the business after the sale for training, supervisory, or introduction purposes? This is often called the *transition period*.
- Should the receivables be part of the sale or not? If so, should they be calculated at 100% of value or something less?
- Is the real property, if there is any involved, included or not? If so, what should its value be? This gives the seller greater flexibility in negotiating the total price structure.

The broker must constantly stress that negotiating is searching, not demanding. Buying and selling are based on compromise, not mandate.

Discussing the Buyer's Financial Statement

Unless a business owner looks at financial statements regularly, discrepancies will probably not be obvious. You must examine the statement with your client for three purposes.

- To find out if there seems to be anything missing or misleading about the statement.
- To make a preliminary judgment as to whether the statement qualifies the buyer financially.
- To determine whether there are any assets that can serve as additional security in the event the sale is not all-cash.

If any information is missing, you may want to order a credit report, check on some of the bank accounts listed to confirm balances, and even make calls to business and personal references. After all, the broker's job, among others, is to ensure that the seller has enough credible information on which to make a satisfactory sale.

Marketing the Business

Marketing the business can involve various things, from preparing a business plan to examining the basic categories of potential buying candidates. You, as the broker, will normally go to your largest source of candidates. Yet, this is not necessarily the best approach and, in some cases, this source can be exactly the wrong reservoir from which to draw.

If, for example, you are dealing with a business that may be vulnerable to employees or creditors if its pending sale becomes known, you are then bound to maintain confidentiality. The need to maintain confidentiality might severely limit your ability to expose the business to a broad spectrum of buyer candidates. A broker's mistake in such a situation can prove devastating to the client. It can even lead to litigation, which is the last thing a broker wants to consider in the course of his or her business activities.

In the case of a professional practice—law, accounting, or medicine—disclosure to the wrong people can cause the professional you represent to lose confidence in you, which could cause you to lose clients. In the case of a manufacturing business, inappropriate disclosure can mean the loss of customers significant enough to destroy the future of the business.

You must carry this responsibility with great care and exercise discretion. Discuss confidentiality with your client and put the details of the disclosure problem in writing. You will then have the necessary guidelines to reduce the possibility that you'll err inadvertently.

On the other hand, you may find in some situations that the best and most logical candidate is either a customer or a competitor. In either of these cases, your job is different. With a customer, you are dealing with someone who at least knows the nature of the product or service being offered. You must then find out what qualifications this customer has as a potential buyer. With a competitor, you don't have to sell the concept of the business. You merely have to convince him or her that acquiring the business will not negatively affect his or her total business operation, but rather increase revenues and profits.

A customer or competitor will have a head start understanding the particular business and the industry itself. A stranger to the industry requires a different approach and a more detailed education about the business and the industry.

Advertising the Business

Each broker has his or her personal preferences for advertising media. Much, of course, depends on the business and its industry. For every industry, you will invariably find a trade magazine. Advertising in this medium will get to the people who already understand much about the business you represent. On the other hand, advertising in a newspaper where people are looking for jobs might be a very good way to reach people who recognize that owning a business eliminates the need to ever look for a job again.

Because size and frequency are the keys to advertising, particularly in the print media, you must decide just how much of an investment is appropriate. After all, if you spend enough money, you may find a buyer and make the sale—but you may also use up all of the commission you made on the sale. And, what if, after

such an extensive expenditure, you don't find a buyer? It is easy enough for the seller to say, "But that's your job!" You are not acting as a charitable institution. If you and the seller agree that an extensive advertising campaign is what the seller wants, it is completely appropriate for you to also discuss the seller's investment in that campaign. If the seller is obliged to put his or her money into advertising the business, it may make his or her input into the decisions more reasonable.

Working with the Accountant and the Lawyer

As you handle more business deals for both buyers and sellers, you will become so familiar with some of the paperwork and protective devices that they will become almost second nature. However, the experienced broker must distinguish between the elements within his or her domain and those in the domain of other professionals, particularly the accountant and lawyer. Giving accounting or legal advice to your client may cause those professionals to become less cooperative and put your own professional practice in serious jeopardy should your advice be off target. You should understand the roles of other professionals so that you can explain and interpret their advice to your client and occasionally offer interesting sidebars to the other advisors on your client's team.

Make sure your client has a good lawyer and a good accountant. Each of these professionals has a specific role to play in preparation for the sale and the period following the sale. The protective devices and tax implications of a sale that is not all-cash are important to the seller. Leaving your client unprotected after a sale is a big mistake. It is sometimes difficult to know exactly when the representation ends. Working with good professionals eliminates this danger and brings high endorsements from a satisfied client

REPRESENTING THE BUYER
Understanding the Business

In some cases, you may deal with a buyer who is a competitor in the field. The buyer understands the nature of the industry and all the positive reasons for the potential acquisition. Your job then is to ensure confidentiality, confirm the revenues the seller is presenting, and make sure there are no substantial negatives for the buyer.

If a potential buyer is familiar with the business as a customer, you may need to point out the negatives. A customer or other type of buyer who is not familiar with the day-to-day frustrations of operating a business may be too excited or emotional about the purchase to see potential dangers. If you think your commentary on the negative aspects of the business might prevent the sale from happening, you are right. But what is your role as the buyer's representative? Is it to ensure that he or she buys something—or that he or she buys something that is likely to survive and succeed?

Your job is not to decide whether or not to buy, but to ensure that the buyer makes a knowledgeable decision based on all available information. Some information may be difficult to find and some may not be positive; however, you should certainly give the search for it your best effort. The business may not be the best for a particular buyer because of his or her personality, inclinations, aversions, or lack of basic knowledge. You can point these things out to your client; the ultimate decision is not in your hands. In all these cases, you should monitor in writing the progress of a sale. In part, this will show where you are at every substantial stage of the buying process. It will also ensure that the buyer cannot later accuse you of bad advice you never gave.

Rationalizing the Purchase Price

Although purchase price is based on various factors, the acquisition must serve two basic purposes for the average buyer: it must generate the income the buyer requires and provide sufficient cash flow to service the purchase money promissory note or pay back the dollars borrowed for the purchase. Other, secondary reasons for buying may be as diverse as building equity for retirement or fulfilling the requirements for an alien to obtain a green card for permanent resident status.

A business that provides owner income and that services debt is the only kind of business a broker is normally dispatched to find. Buyers often view owner's compensation in a sole proprietorship as all the money available to the buyer after the sale. You must point out to your client that the cash flow to service the purchase money promissory note must also come from this

source. If the seller handles more administrative activity than the buyer can handle until the buyer learns the business, the buyer may need additional personnel or contracted help, all of which must come from that same income source. The buyer may not be able to fulfill salary expectations as early as he or she would like.

The Buyer's Financial Statement

The seller will be interested in the financial and, to some extent, the personal background of the buyer. If the sale is not all cash, the information is essential to ensure continuity of the business. If the sale is all cash, the seller may still want to ensure that his or her vendors, customers, employees, and associates are going to be getting a fair deal from a competent businessperson. The seller may request the buyer's financial information before serious negotiations get under way, when neither the seller nor the buyer is sure what purchase arrangement they will structure. The seller asks for this information, in part, to ensure that the buyer is a serious candidate. Only serious candidates normally disclose this type of personal information.

On the other hand, although the information submitted must be complete, truthful, and not misleading, the buyer need not disclose many things that are mandatory in a bankruptcy petition or a mortgage loan application. The degree of disclosure depends on the buyer; as the buyer's broker you can help protect some more personal elements.

For example, potential inheritances, interests in capital assets (real estate) with others, and minority interests in unlisted stocks are not necessary disclosures to consummate the sale and could unnecessarily put these assets at risk. Keep in mind that the buyer must exercise a certain caution at this point. Although your advice is appropriate, you are wise to have an accountant examine these disclosures to be sure your client is adequately protected.

How to Package a Loan

Putting together a package for a loan involves three basic elements:

- A picture of the business, including its history, current financial status, current management, and competitive position in the marketplace

- The growth potential of the business, including whether its equipment is state-of-the-art and whether its management is up to the task of maintaining success in a competitive marketplace
- The reason for the loan, including a defense of the purchase price, how the investment capital will be used apart from the purchase, and the business's stability for loan repayment and future growth

All these elements can be stated in different terms and with somewhat different priorities, but the lender needs to know where the money is going and when it is going to be returned. Then ask how stable the business is and how secure the investment.

Where to take the loan is the broker's biggest problem. You probably have personal contacts in the banking and investment community. Keeping these sources viable is one of the keys to making investment capital available as and when your client meets the necessary criteria and the business opportunity is a good one.

Working with the Accountant and the Lawyer

Some brokers feel that their job is to orchestrate the basic elements of a purchase and then suggest to the client that he or she bring an attorney and an accountant to the table. Many clients agree with this procedure, because they think bringing other professionals into the game later means lower fees. The smart broker knows that neither of these propositions is true.

Because your most significant contribution to the buy-sell process is to bring a willing buyer together with a willing seller, it is your obligation to harness the strongest team to do the job. That means working with a good accountant and a good attorney. Bring them in before mistakes happen in the preliminary negotiations. Once statements are made to the seller, it is difficult to go back and change them. Once the buyer has agreed to certain conditions of sale, even though they may not yet be in writing, it is difficult to retrench without causing a serious rift in the buyer-seller relationship. The cost of correcting an error can be significantly greater than the cost of using an accountant and an attorney from the beginning. By getting the right advice from the professionals before mistakes happen, negotiations will be smoother and the purchase more fulfilling for the buyer.

Your Role in Pre-Purchase Research

The question of the extent of the broker's obligation to the buyer is always open. If your client purchases a house with a big hill behind it, you might suggest a geological survey be performed. If your client buys rural land with the intention of building a house, you might suggest a percolation test before signing the papers. These suggestions ensure that the purchase serves the basic purpose for which it is made. To what extent does this obligation apply to the purchase of a business?

The broker's obligation to recommend market surveys or other analyses does not extend beyond your knowledge or experience. The representation does not oblige you to become an expert in the field or industry of which the business is a part. You can become very involved in pre-purchase research and analysis. Your level of involvement depends on the size of the business, the purchase price, and the relationship you have with the buyer, both personally and professionally.

If you want to really get involved in finding out about the nature of the business and its prospects, you take on a serious task. Just like the preparation of a business plan on a seller's behalf, an analysis can take many shapes. It can be as simple as a rough look at the marketplace or as complex as a presentation submitted to generate corporate investment or to take a company public. You would be involved in price comparison and analyzing the competition and the competition's quantity purchase advantages or disadvantages. You would do an analysis of population growth, traffic and shopping habits of the neighborhood, including public transportation or parking availability, the location of the business and comparative rents, potential for future growth, and availability of personnel.

Regardless of the level of market analysis you decide to undertake, as the buyer's broker you should research the competition at least superficially. For example, many fast-food merchants don't consider a neighboring merchant a competitor if it is not selling the exact same food product. A newcomer to the industry may think that 10 fast-food neighbors are a competition problem. You may want to point out the phenomenon of shopping mall food fairs. Customers go to them not really knowing what they will be in the mood to eat. All the food concessions are congregated in one place to draw lunch traffic to the area. This concept has proven quite successful. Although it is not your prerogative to intrude on the buyer's decision-making process, you do want your client to have enough information to make an educated decision.

No one can foretell the future, yet business is based on guessing the need for a product or a service. The ability to anticipate the needs of the customers is the key to success for many entrepreneurs. It is hardly your job as the buyer's broker to look into the future and advise your client whether he or she is making the right decision by acquiring the business in question. However, you know how blinded your client can be by the emotional involvement of the decision.

Whatever business is under scrutiny, have your client analyze whether it is dependent on a strong or a weak economy. Make sure your client asks the simplest of all questions, whether the population size and the traffic pattern surrounding the location will deliver a strong enough customer base. If you look at these questions with your client, your client will have the advantage of another, somewhat more objective perspective from which to consider the important decision.

KEY POINTS TO REMEMBER

- Always document your broker-client relationship in writing.
- Although you do not need to be an expert in every business, you should learn enough about the business and the industry to properly represent the buyer or the seller.
- As the seller's broker, you need to understand and help present and defend the price of the business.
- As the buyer's broker, you need to negotiate the price based on the business's assets and its position in the marketplace.
- A delicate balance exists between a price that is too low, allowing the business to sell quickly but losing some of the seller's equity, and a price that is too high, which prevents a sale from taking place.
- You must work with the accountant and lawyer as an effective professional team to maximize success for your client.

Worksheet 21. Broker's Checklist

These questions are not intended to represent a complete checklist for every sale. They are intended to remind the broker that every sale is different and that there is more to properly representing a client than merely preparing the documents.

Yes	No	
❑	❑	Are you comfortable with your knowledge of the preparation, negotiation, and documentation of a small business purchase or sale?
❑	❑	If you checked No, do you have professional advisors whom you or your client can contact for further assistance?
❑	❑	Have you explained to your client the different kind of broker-client relationships?
❑	❑	Does your client understand the different levels of responsibility you may assume based on the type of relationship you agree on?
❑	❑	Have you explained to your client the basis of your fee and what activities you perform to earn the fee?
❑	❑	Do you have a basic understanding of the business and industry you are examining on your client's behalf?
❑	❑	If you checked No, do you have professional advisors whom you or your client can contact for further assistance?
❑	❑	Have you done a valuation of the business for your client and explained the parameters within which a negotiated price is likely to take place?
❑	❑	Does your client understand the difference between an asset sale and a stock sale?

Representing the Seller

Yes No
- ❏ ❏ Have you helped your client prepare the business for sale, including the appearance, books and records, lease, and any other documentation the buyer is likely to examine?
- ❏ ❏ Have you discussed the ways to advertise the business for sale and the costs of each method?
- ❏ ❏ Have you made contact with the other professionals on the seller's team?

Representing the Buyer

Yes No
- ❏ ❏ Have you and your client gone over your client's financial statement together?
- ❏ ❏ Do you and your client agree that it is your responsibility to examine the growth potential of the business and do a market analysis?
- ❏ ❏ If you checked No, are you satisfied your client will have an adequate picture of the business's growth potential from another source?
- ❏ ❏ Have you made contact with the other professionals on the buyer's team?
- ❏ ❏ Are you satisfied that you know where your responsibilities lie compared with the responsibilities of the buyer's other professional advisors?
- ❏ ❏ Does your client understand the difference between an asset sale and a stock sale?

NEGOTIATING IS A CROOKED PATH

It is said that a straight line is the shortest distance between two points. This may be a geometric certainty, but nothing could be farther from the truth on a practical business level.

The First Bid

In buying and selling a business, the first bid is the most vulnerable. It essentially sets the stage for the entire negotiating process. It sets a high or a low that becomes difficult to adjust since it is not yet involved in contest and gives the initiating party an open book within which to start writing. It creates the framework for both parties, not just because of the things it includes but also because of the things it fails to include. It is to be created with great care since it creates many parameters within which the subsequent negotiating will take place. It is essentially the skeleton of the deal.

The Second Bid

Although not quite as critical as the first bid, the second bid represents the fleshing out of the skeleton. It further defines by its inclusions and exclusions the edges of the envelope beyond which neither party will likely venture.

Some examples are appropriate to make the point. The first bid is usually for the seller to set the minimum price for the business. In the response (second bid) the buyer may agree to this price or negotiate for a lower price and then speak about the length of time to pay the price. The next response may be to ask for a down payment, a program of payments over time, and the interest rate. After that, come various elements, including requests for additional information about the business known as "due diligence," the transition period during which the seller will stay for introductions, training and the like after the sale, and whether the seller will be paid additionally for this accommodation and over what period of time.

The Next, and the Next, and the Next

Then, some of the legal elements come into play: the noncompete agreement to be signed by the seller at the time of sale, additional security to guarantee the balance of payments, etc. As you can see, there is practically no end to the myriad details that will eventually enter into what both parties may have envisioned as a relatively simple business deal and that, most of the time, bring the parties to an agreement of some kind.

The Ability to Compromise

Negotiating is the process by which two parties come to a position that satisfies both in part and neither completely. It is essentially dependent on their ability to compromise. You must decide which items on your agenda are deal breakers—those things without which you can't make a deal (these should be few)—and which items are of interest but for which you don't need absolute compliance or full capitulation to make a deal. Until you identify all of these items, don't start your negotiating.

Negotiating Posture

Knowing how serious the other party is and to what extent he or she will go to make a deal is important.

Equally important is the posture you assume, which will tell the other party how serious you are. A party who feels inclined to either alternative—to make the deal or to walk away—is not as easy to work with as a party who is ill and needs to leave the business or a party who must have the business is order to get a visa.

Attitude is a big part of this game scenario, since it often tells the other side just how far you will go or not go. It will also tell how much you can push or not push. This negotiating posture is all-important. Knowing how far to push is important, because without this knowledge your pushing can blow the deal. Know your limits and you will come out with what you need to make the negotiations a success.

CHAPTER 22

The Lender's Job

WHETHER YOU WANT TO BORROW money to take your business to the next growth plateau or to survive a current crisis or to buy a business, your approach to a potential lender is going to require a similar presentation. This chapter will help you find the money for your business.

Remember that there are basically two types of lenders. One lender will loan you money and expect you to return it with interest for the period during which you are using it. The other lender, sometimes called an investor, an angel, or a venture capitalist, will advance money on the basis of participating in the business—this lender comes along for the ride. There are, of course, combinations of lending and equity participation for investors, although banks do not normally engage in combinations of lending and ownership.

You should understand that both lenders have the same goal: they want a return of their investment and a bonus within what they consider an appropriate time frame. Your job is to create a comfort zone so they can feel secure in your ability to allow them to achieve their goal. This is often called the *exit strategy*, which will be better defined in further discussion. Since the approach to getting the money is more often borrowing from the bank, this will be your basic reference.

KNOW THE BANK AND THE BANKER

Banks, just like any other businesses, are not all things to all people. Each bank and each banker will tend to have a positive attitude toward those businesses about which they are most knowledgeable. After all, the lending decision must be based, in great part, on the banker's understanding of the particular business's competitive position in the marketplace, among other things. This is good reason to examine two aspects of the lending relationship early on:

- Know which industries the bank is most likely to receive positively.
- Be prepared to present information about the industry of which your business or prospective business is a part, the size of the business in relation to its competitors, and the particular niche market your business occupies.

Also make sure that you're in the correct department at the bank. Different bankers may well cater to different industries and, certainly, different bankers will have different levels of dollar responsibility. There is no point in talking to a banker about a loan for $250,000 when his or her dollar authority maxes out at $50,000. Also keep in mind that you can do some preliminary work and often save a lot of time by knowing what the bank requires as a minimum for the ratio of assets/income to loan amount. When you ask a banker for this information, your question also tells him or her that you have enough financial knowledge to be credible.

THE BUSINESS PLAN

Bankers are not interested in participating in your business. Their product is money. Their expertise lies in the value of money—what a certain amount can generate during what period of time with what degree of security. Notice the word "security," rather than "certainty." You must understand that they are not so much interested in whether you can achieve your goals as in whether they can expect to get their money and you should expect them to be looking for additional security for their money, as we will discuss.

However often you have examined and reexamined the basic concept, the necessary elements, and the sequential aspects of business plan preparation, you must recognize which of those elements are going to be of the highest priority to the bank.

Focus on the Numbers

Bankers will go immediately to the numbers to see if a discussion is worthwhile. There are many significant elements, each of which may ultimately play a part in a bank's decision. The first order of business is to find out if the dollar request is within the bank's lending parameters. The second order of business is to examine the nature of the business's activity to get a sense of the business's ability to repay a loan. These are both aspects of the numbers.

Venture capitalists and bankers have different points of view. Venture capitalists are primarily interested in the future of the business and what kind of a dollar multiple they might anticipate. Bankers are more interested in the historical financial picture, which might give them some assurance of stability and, in turn, the ability of the company to generate a payment schedule on the loan. As a result, bankers will be looking for the income statement, the rate of growth, the balance sheet, and three to five years of historical information documenting what growth plateaus had been reached within what time frames and the money it took to achieve those goals.

Although tax returns will ultimately be required, primarily for confirmation purposes, it is not likely to be a requirement until after the application is actually in place. Similarly, a personal financial statement will also be required. This, of course, allows the bank to see just what other assets might be available as additional security for the loan. (Remember the reference earlier to additional security.)

MAKE YOUR CASE

How are you going to make your case for a loan? You should know what you are going to say. Bankers are not interested in your ability as an extemporaneous speaker. They are interested in the content of your remarks and the excitement that represents the energy, creativity, and initiative so necessary to the success of any entrepreneurial effort. In other words, bankers want to know that you're just as excited about and interested in the future of the business as you want them to be.

You should, of course, be prepared for questions. But, to begin, you should prepare what you want to convey. Practice it on others, perhaps people who might be friendlier and not involved, seeing if you can get a positive reaction to the approach you intend to take. Trial attorneys often set up mock juries to see what reaction they are likely to get to a particular kind of presentation. Why shouldn't you?

Remember that the banker who sees your application likely knows nothing about your business or even of the industry of which your business is a part. It is incumbent upon you to create a picture of both that is easy to recognize. Keep in mind that a banker could be handling from 50 to 150 business applications. He or she must have enough information about your business to be comfortable, especially if the banker is going to make a subsequent presentation to an underwriter.

For example, if your business deals in bauxite ore, make sure that your explanation includes the fact that bauxite is used in toothpaste. Without that information, the banker may never recognize the practical value of your product or service. Without that recognition, it will be impossible to make any assessment of your position in the marketplace—the real world. Don't take for granted the fact that people understand this reality without your telling them. This assumption could be your first and last mistake.

Who's Managing the Business?

However exciting an industry or a business within a given industry may be, every business success is attributable to intelligent business management. Every bank is going to look at a loan application with particular interest in the people on whom the business will depend for its continuity and success. The experience of management personnel and key operational people is going to impact the decision on any application. The banker is going to want to know the people in charge of every aspect of your business' operation.

If, for example, your business plan indicates that a substantial portion of your required capital is going to be used for marketing, you can be sure that the banker will be interested in the background and experience of your marketing executive. If a big portion of your loan is allocated to manufacturing, the banker will look to the background of your executive in charge. If your intention is to replicate your operation by franchising concept, the banker will certainly want to examine the experience and prior successes of the individual in charge of creating the franchise program. Don't lose sight of this all-important aspect of your operation.

Where Is the Money Going?

Even though a given banker might not be familiar with your business or your industry, they are all practiced in the concept of what kinds of dollars it will take to achieve certain levels of activity and, in turn, generate certain levels of sales and revenues. It is your obligation, as part of your business plan, to explain how you will use the money, what levels of activity you intend to achieve, what business plateaus you hope to attain, and the relationship between this growth and the ultimate goal—profit.

Do your best to think like a banker. If you create a scenario in which you use every dollar to achieve your basic goals, it may be too tight a fit for the average banker. Bankers need to know that there will be enough money available to handle the inevitable contingencies, those things that invariably happen regardless of the most careful planning based on the most extensive investigation and the aggregate thinking of the best minds. If you build a fair margin for error into your business plan, the banker will be more inclined to assess the investment as a minimal risk. Be careful to address this question at every stage of your thinking.

The Risk

Although there are many specific negatives that will crop up and that you will need to address, there is one that ought to be obvious but that many loan applicants fail to recognize. It was mentioned earlier that the banker wants to know that you're just as excited about and interested in the future of the business as you want them to be. The banker also wants to know that you have a risk in the future of the business just as you expect them to take by lending you money.

Many entrepreneurs see the bank loan as an opportunity to get reimbursed for the dollars that they have invested to get the business started. Any lender, whether a lending institution or an investor taking an equity position, will be quite disturbed at the thought that you will not be risking your own money as you ask them to risk their money. They want to know that their investment is going to contribute to the growth of the business and not to compensate you for your original investment of time, money, or both.

Don't Forget the Sizzle

Banks are notoriously and historically known as dry institutions, but don't let that throw you off. As noted earlier, the banker is interested in both the content of your story and the excitement in your presentation. In other words, he or she is interested in the sizzle of your story as well as the meat and potatoes of your presentation. If there is any excitement in your industry, the reputation of your management team, or the particular niche you occupy in the competitive marketplace—anything that makes your business more interesting or explosive than the business next door—make sure to present it as a significant part of your business picture. The banker will never get a feeling for this excitement if you don't tell about it!

Keep in mind that very often the banker will need to sell the loan to an underwriter. The banker will need all the tools to build a credible picture. Make sure you fill his or her toolbox with anything and everything that might help. You may get another bite at this apple, but, except under certain circumstances, the first bite may be the most important.

Special Circumstances

Some experienced financial people have a slightly different approach that would be defined as "special circumstances." They suggest that you apply first at a lending institution that you feel will likely reject your loan. The purpose would be to use the application as a test, to get an impression as to which items prove effective and which items are not so well received. This will allow you to restructure your application for maximum effectiveness without prejudicing your loan with an institution that is likely to approve it.

There are two schools of thought in this regard, so you should discuss this tactic with your financial advisor before making any such decision. Since the banking community in any given city might be very close-knit, with bankers sharing stories with each other, such an approach could cause a dangerous backlash. Be careful before making this decision.

Get out of the Bank

Although your first meeting is likely to be at the bank, keep in mind that bankers like to see the collateral available. Invite the banker to visit your business—and make sure to do so clearly and early. A good banker is going to have a good idea what to look for.

There is, of course, the story of the banker who was processing a loan to an oil company and specifically examined the oil reservoir owned by the borrower. It wasn't until much later that the banker made a terribly unpleasant discovery. The oil tank was three-quarters full of water and then just topped off with oil.

Most situations, of course, are not so rife with fraud. However, keep in mind that the slightest variance from total truth and candor can lead any banker to quickly deny a loan application—no matter how good it looks!

Exit Strategy

In any plan, the concept of exit strategy must always be an integral part. Whether a lender is lending money or an investor is taking an equity position, the questions of 'return of capital' and 'return on capital' are high on the list of priorities. You must build into your presentation the method by which the company expects to repay the loan or the method by which the investor can anticipate the growth of his or her investment. Also include the method by which he or she may ultimately expect to convert the equity position to cash—to cash out. The sophisticated investor usually recognizes that there are basically three ways for this conversion to take place:

- The company may grow so dramatically as to be in a position to pay a dividend to its shareholders. Most small companies will prefer, however, to use these extra dollars to either invest in new equipment or personnel or retire any existing debt that the company may be carrying.
- The company may present such a positive picture of growth as to attract a bigger company that might be interested in acquiring it.
- Management may recognize the potential of taking the company into the public marketplace, which could make every investor's share worth a multiple of the original investment.

There are, of course, other ways to convert, some of which are less optimistic than others. In the event of a bankruptcy, for example, the investor may get part of the original investment returned but only after all creditors are paid. The likelihood of a return of any kind to the investor is quite conjectural, as you might well imagine.

Remember that the bank will not be actively participating in your business and your profit, although it may build in a power to veto larger expenditures that it might not consider totally prudent. Be careful that you don't end up with a partner in decision making as part of your loan package. The bank's inclination to protect its investment in the short term might turn out to be inimical to the long-term goals of the company.

Keep in mind that, however excited you may get the banker about the potential of your business, you must nonetheless convince him or her that you can repay the loan over a specific period of time within the structure of the business as you've presented it.

THE ESSENTIALS OF YOUR APPLICATION

In considering your loan application, the bank is looking at many factors. Make sure that you have addressed all of them. These are the primary factors:

- Profitability of the business

- Liquidity of the business
- Solvency of the business

The answers to these questions drive the bank's analysis of your application and its decision on your application:

- What is the ability of the company to repay the debt?
- How much equity do you have in the business?
- How do the industry, the competition, the economy, and the interest rates look for the foreseeable future?
- What is your personal credit history?
- What is really available in terms of your personal guarantee, the availability of any second trust deeds, liens on equipment, or liens on receivables?
- What kind of profits, depending on the success or lack of success of the business plan, will be available to repay the loan?
- How fast are sales growing? Is profit commensurate with sales growth? If not, why not? And how long will this period last?
- What can be turned into cash, if necessary?

Last, but not least, keep in mind that, although banks will not take an actual equity position in a company, they may be able to advise you as to alternative sources of investment capital—depending on the size and scope of the risk involved.

Follow Up

Finally, don't forget that simple, basic courtesies still matter. Don't expect the bank to do the job without your help. Your loan application should be a joint effort. Send a thank-you note whenever you consider it appropriate because someone has helped you in the process. You never know the extent to which such a courtesy may find its way to the right desk.

Stay on top of the process. There is certainly a difference between bothering someone and following up. Make sure you understand the difference. Being a pain in the neck will not help your cause, but being an interested applicant can make a big difference.

THE BIG DECISION
Rejection

You understand by now that there are many reasons for which a bank might reject your application for a loan. You also understand that rejection by one bank does not necessarily portend rejection by others. Banks have different philosophies, different levels of participation, and different criteria depending on industry, size of loan, purpose of loan, and competitive position in the marketplace.

So, if you get rejected, don't fold up your tent! Go to the banker, in the correct frame of mind, and ask for his or her reasons for rejecting your application. You might, under the right circumstances, even ask him or her for advice as to which institution might be a good bet for you to try next. You might find that an adjustment in your business plan or your application might make a big difference in your next attempt. And from this follow-up interview you might find out that by making some changes in your method of operation, you might be a much more suitable candidate for a loan six to eight months down the road ... at the same bank!

Acceptance

If the bank accepts your application, you might think that it's the end of the process. Actually, it might still be quite near the beginning. The bank may have approved your loan based on the general health and stability of the business but, at this stage, you might not yet have addressed some of the more mundane aspects of the loan. Consider the following issues.

- What is the method of funding? Is it a line of credit to be used as activity demands, is it based on periodic approval by the bank based on certain criteria, or is it a complete funding at one time?
- What is the interest rate? Is it different from what you've anticipated, because of a change in the federal rate since the time of your original inquiry or application? Does the risk that the bank is taking demand a higher interest rate?
- Is the repayment schedule more difficult than you anticipated in your repayment plan? Was the subject of your collateral security specifically addressed?

- Was your all-important and ever-present personal guarantee factored into your thinking, except under the most extraordinary circumstances?

After all, if you're not willing to take the risk, why should they? You should keep in mind that both collateral security and a personal signature can be reduced as you pay off your loan. Although it's unlikely, the bank may release any security that is in excess of the current balance.

THE BANKRUPTCY LOAN

At this point we should consider another type of loan application, by a company that has declared a Chapter 11 bankruptcy.

It is fairly obvious that, given the choice, the average banker would prefer to exclude from his or her portfolio any business that has declared bankruptcy. However, for those who understand the implications of a Chapter 11 bankruptcy, the reconstruction of a business, investment in such a project can often represent a lesser risk than normal and an opportunity to recapture the loan with greater security in hand and over a shorter period of time. It also means that there will be considerably greater supervision over business operations. In some cases, an earlier loan by the bank may be

at risk; an additional loan could help restructure the business and, conceivably, rehabilitate the original lending position. An accomplished Chapter 11 might be well received by a knowledgeable banker.

You should not expect, however, to get any advice from the bank with regard to such position. There are potential liability problems with respect to any such advice and this is not within the purview of normal banking activity.

KEY POINTS TO REMEMBER

- Make sure your business plan shows your knowledge of the marketplace, your financial goals, and your competitive position.
- What the lender knows about your business will likely be limited to the information you present.
- Although lenders will assess risk primarily on your financial history, their examination of your management team will always be a high priority.
- Every investor will be particularly interested in how you handle your exit strategy—how the lender gets paid.
- A rejection can, in many ways, be converted into a learning process for the next presentation.

Worksheet 22. Know the Lender's Job

These questions are designed to better prepare you for meeting with the lender and financing your business. The better you understand the lender, the better your chances of providing all the information he or she needs.

Do you understand the role of the lender and his or her primary goal?   Yes ❑ No ❑

How will you handle this? _____

_____

_____

What is the difference in the motivation between the lender and the investor? _____

_____

_____

_____

How do you propose to handle each of them? _____
_____
_____

What is the purpose of a business plan? _____
_____
_____

Indicate four or five elements that every business plan should contain.
_____
_____
_____
_____

Is the lender more interested in a strong product with a weak management team or a strong management team with a weak product? _____
_____

How will you handle this as a small businessperson with a small business management team? _____
_____

Which is the easier problem to fix for the investor—management or product? _____
_____
_____
_____

Why is it not the same for the lender? _____
_____
_____

Is it better to underestimate revenues and surprise your lender with unexpected growth or to overestimate revenues, to get the loan, and then explain why the reality was short of the expectations? _____
_____
_____
_____

What are the dangers of each approach? _____
_____
_____

Do you know what kinds of loans your bank historically makes? Yes ❑ No ❑

Do you think this information is important? Why? _____

_____

_____

Do you know what kinds of loans your investor makes? Yes ❑ No ❑

Do you know what that investor expects in terms of return on investment over what period of time? Yes ❑ No ❑

Do you think this information is important to know before you apply? Yes ❑ No ❑

How should you handle a bank's rejection? _____

_____

_____

Should you follow up with your bank representative? Yes ❑ No ❑

What are the advantages to following up with your bank's representatives? _____

_____

_____

_____

Do you think the bank will be interested in the purpose to be served by the loan? Yes ❑ No ❑

Will the bank be interested in how long you expect to take to achieve those goals? Yes ❑ No ❑

Do you think the bank will be interested in a contingency plan, in the event you fail to perform within the anticipated time frame? Yes ❑ No ❑

How will you handle this? _____

_____

_____

_____

Do you understand all the elements involved in a loan, besides the bank merely saying yes? Yes ❑ No ❑

Name four of these elements. _____

_____

_____

Is one of them the rate of interest on the bank? Yes ❑ No ❑

Are you willing to personally guarantee a bank business loan? Yes ❑ No ❑

Are you willing to personally guarantee a business investment? Yes ❑ No ❑

What is the difference? _____

_____

Why would this interest the bank? _____

_____

_____

Do you expect to get your original investment back from the bank loan? Yes ❑ No ❑

What do you think the bank's position would be on this question? _____

_____

_____

What does the lender expect to see in terms of an exit strategy? _____

_____

_____

Do you know how much this is likely to cost? Yes ❑ No ❑

BORROWING WHEN YOU CAN'T GO TO THE BANK

Conventional wisdom will tell you that if you can't borrow from your bank when your business needs some help, your options for borrowing are over. As the famous song goes, "It ain't necessarily so."

The Strange Game of Rejection

Usually, when one lender finds your application lacking, another will likely have the same response. Strangely enough, quite the opposite is true in some cases. There are organizations that will lend money to "existing small businesses that cannot qualify for conventional bank financing." These organizations are funded primarily by lending institutions that cannot lend money to those businesses that do not fall within the basic requirements of the banking community.

What Is Their Real Game?

Although most of these organizations are nonprofit, they serve a number of purposes. The basic concept is that a business, if given a chance, may be able to rise to the level of conventional bank lending. At this point, the banking community will have contributed to the

local business marketplace and, in some cases, created a business relationship with a successful business that might never have achieved that level of success.

The "real game" is probably most visible in the fact that the loan does not have a prepayment penalty. In other words, these organizations want the borrowing business to be able to repay the loan as soon as it can, because that probably means that it has achieved a level of success that will enable it to apply for money with a conventional lending institution.

The Two Basic Plans

There are loans for businesses that have been in existence for at least one year. The business must submit evidence that it cannot obtain conventional bank financing. The loan level is usually up to $150,000.

There are loans for start-up businesses that have been operating for less than one year. These loans are usually smaller, up to $25,000. The institution may have a geographic limitation, in that you must be operating your business within its service area. In addition, with respect to a start-up business, the loan will normally be no greater than one half of the total project cost. This ensures that the entrepreneur has his or her own assets at risk as well.

The Basic Requirements

This is not a handout. There are formal requirements and the criteria for the loan are every bit as detailed as those used by other lending institutions. Your application must be accompanied by a serious, well-developed business plan with cash flow projections, an understanding of your position in the competitive marketplace, a marketing concept that makes sense, and the other basic elements that suggest strong management competence. A good personal credit history is required as well as personal and business balance sheets.

Keep in mind that these alternative lenders are also interested in borrower risk. Any lender will always want as much comfort in terms of security as the borrower has to offer. There is a basic tenet to lending that the borrower should have most of his or her available collateral at risk. After all, if the need for a loan isn't important enough for the borrower to be risking assets, why should it reach that level of risk for the lender? Although the loans usually allow up to five years for repayment, most of these lenders would like to see a business plan that suggests the business will reach a break-even point within a year. For additional information on this kind of lending, speak with your local banker.

PART V

Contract Elements

CHAPTER 23

The Noncompete Nondisclosure Issue

THERE ARE TWO ASPECTS OF THE NONCOMpete question that the owner of a business or the buyer of a business must understand. The first is the problem when an employee leaves his or her employer in order to join a competitor in the same marketplace. The second is the problem when a business owner sells the business and then starts a competing business.

This chapter addresses the issues and dynamics of both noncompete and nondisclosure issues. They need to be examined in detail, because both have become the core elements of substantial litigation and deserve additional attention.

WHEN A BUSINESS IS TRANSFERRED

Someone who buys a business should certainly be entitled to the comfort of knowing that the person selling it is not going to set up a competing business across the street immediately after the sale. This would lead to the seller contacting old customers and moving them into the new business and away from the business recently sold. It could jeopardize and maybe even destroy the business acquired by the buyer. This is why the buyer may require as part of the terms of the sale that the seller sign an agreement not to compete—a very usual request.

In general, a noncompete clause must be "reasonable." This means that it must be justified by some reasonable circumstances and involve reasonable consideration: the sale of a business would qualify on both counts. It must also be reasonable in geographic scope and in duration. Determining what is reasonable in terms of scope and time can be problematic. In fact, the only question a court usually has with noncompete clauses is whether the terms are reasonable in relation to the geography and the length of time during which the seller is precluded from competing.

WHEN AN EMPLOYEE LEAVES

The situation in which an employee leaves to go to work for a competitor is, perhaps, the more prevalent noncompete problem. It may come as a surprise that, in many states, a noncompete agreement between employees and an employer is not enforceable. The reason for this is that the broad interpretation of such an agreement would suggest that it is in restraint of trade. Technically, yes, it is a restraint of trade. After all, a noncompete agreement is designed to legally keep an individual from engaging in a lawful occupation in the venue of his or her choice. The key to a noncompete agreement that courts would enforce is in the language that would make a specific case an exception to the general rule.

The critical element is that, in the sale of a business, the departure of an employee can be detrimental to the buyer, the seller, or both, because both buyer and seller are likely to be vulnerable.

Most small businesses are not sold for cash, but rather with a down payment, leaving the balance of the purchase price to be paid over a period of time. If a key employee unexpectedly leaves the business shortly after the sale, the buyer may believe that the seller misrepresented the business, even though the seller may have known nothing of the employee's intention to leave. The buyer may feel justified in not making payments on the balance of the purchase price.

The departure of the employee, then, could jeopardize the seller's ability to collect the balance of the purchase price. The question, unfortunately, may have to be resolved in court.

Is there a way to protect against this possibility? To the extent that contract language can prevent an employee from leaving, the answer is no! To the extent that contract language can protect the balance of the seller's purchase price, the answer is yes! The key is in the drafting of the purchase and sale agreement. The buyer must acknowledge that the employee structure of the company will be a responsibility of the buyer and not the seller. The seller may be protected if both parties reach this agreement with a complete and mature understanding of its implications.

Trade Secrets and Nondisclosure

An agreement to keep former employees from making disclosures about trade secrets to a competitor or any third party is usually enforceable. The relationship to the information, however, must be carefully defined. The information must be specific to the extent that it is either a development or an accumulation of data that has taken a substantial investment to acquire or that others could acquire only through a substantial investment.

The information must also be considered valuable not only when it is protected from disclosure to outside sources but also when it is protected within close confines, even within the company itself. If the company does not consider it important enough to protect it, why should the court?

Ultimately, this is the question: does such disclosure give an unfair commercial advantage to a competitor who has not invested in its development?

Special Access

The relationship of the employee to the company can have significant bearing on the enforceability of noncompete or nondisclosure language in a contract. An employee who is at the management level and who has management discretion or prerogatives is likely to be held to a higher standard than those who are not at that level. The special nature of management or executive personnel suggests that they have special access to the private, proprietary, and protectable information so necessary for the maintenance, continuity, and success of the business.

However, keep in mind that the nondisclosure or noncompete language is contractual. It is not inherent in the employer-employee relationship.

Follow these guidelines:

- Noncompete and nondisclosure language must be carefully designed and delineated.
- Noncompete and nondisclosure language must have consideration, as in any other contract. That is, the employee must accept the language as part of his or her employment arrangement; it cannot merely be tacked on at some point after the fact.
- Although clearly a question of fact, the relationship must be one of trust and confidence that prevails on the management level.

WHAT WILL THE COURTS SAY?

The language used in drafting noncompete and nondisclosure agreements is obviously important. No matter how artfully you draft the document, however, keep in mind that if the employer chooses to enforce the contract or the employee chooses not to abide by it, the court must accept the language. It is important that the document carefully define the essential elements: the relationship, the information to be protected, the length of time involved, and the area within which the person is not to compete.

Here is an interesting point. Some courts will examine the language to see if it is reasonable and then decide, on that basis, to enforce it or not. In other words, some courts will take the language as they find it. It is both reasonable and appropriate or it is not. If not, it is simply not enforceable. Other courts take the position that the parties intended for the protection to exist even though the agreement was actually drafted by one attorney or another. These courts tend to rewrite the language in order to make it acceptable and enforceable. In other words, if the language prohibits competition within the Commonwealth of Massachusetts and the court deems the geographic scope to be too extensive, the court may rewrite the language to include only the cities east of Worcester.

Remember that litigation is expensive, in terms of money, time, energy, and sometimes image and morale. An employer must make a careful judgment, before the fact, as to whether the cost of legally enforcing the noncompete or nondisclosure agreement is worth the protection it is intended to provide.

Temporary Restraining Order

When an employer seeks to enforce a nondisclosure agreement, the first order of legal business is for his or her lawyer to seek a temporary restraining order to prevent any dissemination of the protected information until the entire problem can be examined and resolved by the court. Otherwise, if it took weeks or months for the case to come to court and for the judge to rule, the judgment would obviously be after the fact. Such a protracted decision would not afford any comfort to the employer's company. In order to prevent unauthorized disclosures, the lawyer will ask the court to make a preliminary judgment even before both sides are heard and all the facts are determined. This must be done in order to maintain the current status and prevent any such disclosure before the court has an opportunity to fully examine the facts.

This may seem like a prudent solution, but there's a problem—cost. The lawyer must examine the entire case in order to make this plea to the court for a temporary injunction. This means that the cost of the temporary restraining order could conceivably be the most substantial part of the legal costs of the entire action. It shouldn't come as a surprise to the commercially sophisticated employer that this figure could be from $5,000 to

$50,000. This should certainly suggest that an employer give a lot of thought to the question of enforcement before deciding to go forward with a legal action.

The Intimidation Factor

From the employee's perspective, a nondisclosure agreement certainly deserves an equal amount of attention. Before choosing to violate the language of the contract, the employee must consider the following questions:

- Is the employer likely to go to court to enforce it?
- Is the court likely to find in favor of the employer?
- Do I have the money necessary to mount a defense?
- Is the gamble of risking this contest worth the dollars involved in the activity in question?

As you can see, even if the contract language is never enforced in court, it certainly serves as an intimidation factor that would cause the employee to think before he or she disregards that language.

Also, consider that a company that is contemplating hiring the former employee—even if part of the reason is to access privileged information—must understand that it could then easily become part of any legal action brought by the former employer. In other words, the new company might be brought into the action as a party defendant on the allegation of having been involved in a conspiracy to obtain the privileged information. The former employer could also take legal action against the hiring company for interfering with a contractual relationship or interfering with an advantageous business relationship. Either of these actions could result in substantial damages against the hiring company. As you can see, there are good reasons why each of the parties involved should give serious thought to the consequences before entering this very conjectural arena.

The Exit Interview

This is one of the reasons why an employer should always conduct an exit interview when an employee is leaving because of termination or expiration of a contract relationship. It lays the groundwork for a clear understanding of what is expected of the parties after the relationship ends. It is an opportunity to review any such language that might have been inserted in a contract at the outset of the relationship.

The Danger with Salespeople

One of the biggest problems in the highly competitive marketplace is the aggressive nature of outside selling. Although some businesses have always depended on outside sales in the form of distributors or an internal sales department, there are many businesses that used to rely on advertising in various media. Today, the one-on-one relationship appears to be the most successful method of product presentation. In this context, many businesses are not satisfied with the somewhat passive aspect of the media. They are interested in a much more aggressive sales posture.

When you hire a salesperson, you are putting him or her in direct contact with your customers. In many cases, the customers don't care or don't know that you are the owner of the business. They are concerned only with the person on whom they depend for the timely delivery, quality, and fair pricing of the service or product they are buying. With this in mind, it is clear that the business relationship with your client or customer is not really with the company at all; it is with the sales representative of your company. If the salesperson decides to move to a competitor, your customers may very well end up at the competitor's counter as well. It is a clear and present danger.

Not Everything Is Protectable

Many things, even those that appear relatively mundane, can be protected if the company affords the information sufficient dignity to warrant its protection as valuable and secret. These items can include customer lists, business plans, financial information, research data, and methods of instruction.

However, you can't keep an ex-employee from using his or her knowledge of the trade and his or her general skills as a salesperson, an engineer, a paralegal, and so on. Generally, those things that are public knowledge or that can be learned by participating in a particular industry would be difficult to protect unless the company can show that its methodology is different enough to warrant a special or peculiar presentation. The question of proof becomes the key—and don't forget the costs involved in proving it.

So What Is the Answer?

The answer doesn't lie so much in the language of the contract. It is easy enough to recognize that even the most carefully drawn language in a contract is not only subject to the ultimate discretion of a court but also dramatically expensive. The real answer lies outside the contract relationship of the parties.

One of the reasons for companies to create profit-sharing and pension plans, such as the 401(k), is that the investment by both employer and employee gives the employee a reason to remain with the company. Years ago, the loyalty factor was the primary adhesive element. Today, with corporations showing as much downsizing as loyalty, the vested dollar becomes the higher priority.

Even without the substantial investment in the more sophisticated plans, the small businessperson can create this vested-dollar incentive. When you hire a salesperson or a key employee without whom the business would not be as strong or whose absence could even mean the loss of substantial clientele, you can set up a plan.

In many sales situations, a contractual arrangement is made that provides for a salesperson who leaves the business to continue to receive a percentage of the normal commission for any accounts that he or she sold while with the employer. This percentage usually declines over time until the dollar amount reaches zero. At the same time, the new salesperson receives the other part of the commission, a percentage that rises as the percentage paid to the former salesperson declines.

For example, when a salesperson leaves, he or she might get 80% of personal sales for the first year, 60% in the second, 40% in the third, and so on down to zero, while the new salesperson might get 20% in the first year, 40% in the second, 60% in the third, and so on up to 100%. This arrangement can be orchestrated in various ways. It is usually predicated on the salesperson leaving under pleasant circumstances and there are usually no payments at all if the salesperson leaves to work for a competitor.

In addition to this, part of the salary or compensation arrangement for a new employee could be for a certain percentage or dollar amount to be deposited in an escrow account, a holding account, which would continue to build up during the employee's tenure. When the employee decides to leave the business, this escrow account is subject to distribution—but only under certain terms and conditions. Sometimes the money held in escrow is distributed over a period of five years. This arrangement creates an incentive for the employee to think carefully before leaving to work for a competitor.

One Last Caution

Be sure that you examine these alternatives with your professional in order to be sure that you are not violating any laws mandating parity among employees for anything that falls within the area of profit-sharing and pension plans.

KEY POINTS TO REMEMBER

- In the purchase of any business, seller's agreement to a noncompete clause is mandatory.
- Trade secrets and other proprietary information subject to nondisclosure must be afforded the appropriate dignity to ensure its protection.
- Noncompete language must be reasonable in terms of both time and geography in order to be likely enforceable.
- The more practical approach of the dollar incentive is becoming more prevalent in the business marketplace than the threat of legal enforceability.
- Whatever the problem of disclosure, never lose sight of the legal costs involved in enforcement.

Worksheet 23. Avoiding Noncompete and Nondisclosure Problems

The best way to avoid noncompete and nondisclosure wranglings is to arm your business with a plan. This worksheet will help you prevent conflicts and/or brace for noncompete and nondisclosure problems. Use this worksheet to get to know your business environment and plan accordingly.

If You're a Seller

In situations where certain employees are critical to the continuity of the business in the short term, a smart seller uses an incentive plan. One such plan is to offer a bonus to an employee who agrees to stay and give his or her best efforts during some period of time subsequent to the sale. This will ensure a more comfortable transition for the buyer and, in turn, give the seller a more secure feeling about the success of the business after the sale and about receiving payments on the balance of the purchase price according to schedule.

Can you think of other ways to provide such protection? For variations on this kind of insurance program, before and after a sale of the business, see your professional. _____

_____

_____

If You're a Buyer

To one extent or another, business owners have a relationship with their customers. Relinquishing this relationship is one of the elements of the sale. Make sure that the seller gives up the right to this business relationship as part of the purchase. Otherwise, you will be buying much less than you anticipated.

What kind of protective device will you expect the seller to sign? What period of time and what geographic area do you consider reasonable? _____

_____

Assess the Environment

What kind of information do you need to protect—and from whom?

From your customers? _____

From your vendors? _____

From your competitors? _____

From your employees? _____

What information can you protect?

Secret formulas? _____

Customer lists? _____

Methods of operation? _____

Financial information? _____

What kind of 'dignity' is necessary in order to afford your information the protection to which you think it's entitled?

_____

_____

_____

How do you achieve that 'dignity'? _____

_____

_____

_____

From what category of employee can you expect confidentiality—hourly, management, technical, sales, etc.?

_____

_____

Is access to proprietary information an important element? _____

_____

_____

How much protection do you expect to get from a confidentiality agreement? _____

_____

_____

_____

Is it necessary that you have a confidentiality agreement at the beginning of the employment relationship? Why or why not?

_____

_____

_____

How will you handle this? _____

_____

_____

_____

Should this be a factor when considering the enforceability? Yes ❑ No ❑

Do you think it's a good idea to have them even though enforceability is conjectural in your legal jurisdiction? Yes ❑ No ❑

What kind of information is difficult to protect? _____

_____

_____

In your business, can you develop an incentive program to help protect against information disclosure? Yes ❑ No ❑

What kinds of programs are usually most effective? _____

_____

_____

What is the greatest danger in hiring a professional outside salesperson to contact your customers? _____

_____

_____

_____

CAN YOU REALLY PROTECT AGAINST DISCLOSURE?

The problem of employee retention has become more visible in today's intellectual melting pot. Years ago, a good idea was usually the beginning of a long journey. It involved accessing raw material, developing a cost-effective manufacturing process, understanding the market to choose the best advertising approach, and hiring the most appropriate people. Now, with business moving faster and the Internet opening up markets, a good idea might be minutes away from execution and profit. One of the problems with this accelerated production schedule is that the idea, taken by a competitor, could find its way to market before the first company can even set up a second management conference to assess its potential. And what happens when one of the management team decides to move across the street to a competitor ... with that idea?

Can You Keep an Employee from "Crossing the Street"?

Many employees will leave their company because of personal conflict with peers or supervisors. Some will leave because they have been offered a better opportunity for advancement or for a substantial increase in pay. What if the offer for opportunity or pay is predicated not on the quality of the individual but rather on the quality of his or her information? Should it make a difference? If so, what kind of a difference should it make?

You might have all your employees sign an agreement not to disclose confidential information if they leave the company for any reason. But what, exactly, is "confidential information"?

There is a controversial legal theory known as "inevitable disclosure" that suggests that a person who moves from one business environment to another that is similar will disclose, even if unintentionally, whatever is in his or her intellectual toolbox. In other words, ethics notwithstanding, the mere use of one's experience in the field and general knowledge would constitute a disclosure. If this is true and the courts accept this concept, you'd only have to show as evidence of disclosure that the employee "crossed the street." You wouldn't even have to prove intent. This theory of "inevitable disclosure" runs counter, of course, to the traditional belief that a company shouldn't be able to prevent an ex-employee from making a living. After all, if someone who has been an engineer for 20 years leaves a company, it wouldn't be fair to expect that person to get a job in a fast-food outlet.

Industrial Espionage and the Subtler Problem

But what happens when a competitor is so determined to find out about the trade secrets of a company or desperately needs the customer list of a successful competitor that it entices an employee to either disclose the information or cross the street for a new job? The first of these is in the category of industrial espionage and is easier to recognize and deal with. The second of these is more difficult to define.

The Question of Enforcement

Whether or not you can protect against any such disclosure depends very much on the law of the particular jurisdiction in which you live, the discretion of the court on the question of intent, and your ability to show the significant value of the information and the nature of your damages. All of the above factors represent a long, tedious road at best. And—make no mistake about it—this road also represents a very expensive ride! It is not a trip to take lightly.

The Real Answers

There are really two ways to protect against such a problem. The first is to give the information you want to protect the proper dignity. It should be made available only to key employees on a "need to know" basis. Certainly, each part of a project can be isolated from other parts, which means that the employees working on either part will not necessarily be aware of the other. Yet, it is also true that certain employees, of necessity, will need to know all the information in order to put the parts together for the finished product. Whenever the information becomes significantly valuable, it should be protected as best it can. This is not always easy and is usually not foolproof.

The better answer is to provide incentives for the employees by creating the most advantageous retention plan the company can handle. Being "penny-wise and pound-foolish" is clearly contrary to the best interests of management in the long term. You've got to make the employees feel that the company is theirs, that giving information to the competition is not in their best interests.

But don't forget the key! Words, phrases, and promises are easy to make, easy to break, and, more often than not, will fall on deaf ears. If your intention is to protect and benefit your company and you recognize the dynamic vulnerability of disclosure, put the game plan together *now!* Tomorrow's lawsuit could have been avoided by action taken yesterday. Do it now!

CHAPTER 24

The End of the Franchise Contract

W HAT HAPPENS WHEN THE DANCE IS over? When you own your business, it can go on forever. When you own a franchise business, the relationship eventually comes to an end. Then what do you do?

It is certainly true that buying a business of any kind is quite traumatic, since the decision will obviously be far-reaching in terms of both time and money. To do a reasonably good job in the due diligence phase of examining the business and the industry takes a lot of work. Making judgments about working capital, personnel, training, equipment, and the myriad other things that constitute the basic structure of the business is mind-boggling. And it all must be done.

Then, in the case of a franchise, the buyer must examine the relationship under which he or she will be operating the business: this is a critically important element to consider. To say the least, all the factors involved in making the decision whether to go into business as an independent or as a franchise affiliate can be overwhelming. Is this any time to consider what the alternatives will be when the franchise contract ultimately comes to an end? Unfortunately, the answer is "Yes."

ALL FRANCHISE CONTRACTS ARE NOT THE SAME

Although time and legislation have created a basic format that most franchise companies follow, franchise contracts are not all alike. The amount of the royalty payable, most often calculated on the gross sales of the business, may vary from 1% to 10% or more. Some royalties are payable weekly; some are paid monthly. There is often an advertising commitment in addition to the royalties. The percentage for advertising also varies from company to company. Some of the advertising dollars are allocated for national advertising, some are allocated for local advertising, and sometimes the franchisor has complete discretion in placing the advertising dollars.

Although you will certainly want to examine many of the above aspects of the franchise contract in comparison with others in the same industry, most franchise companies have adjusted their royalty and advertising concepts to conform to industry standards. They usually correlate in some way with the amount of the profit that the franchise is expected to generate. After all, it would be silly for the franchisor to expect to collect revenues that would leave the franchisee without any income. It is unlikely that you will find a dramatic difference between one franchise company and another in the same industry. On the other hand, you should always make this initial comparison to be sure that you are not looking at an exception.

Long-Term Plans

All the elements of the franchise relationship relative to dollars and cents should certainly be factored into your business plan. The question that is difficult to consider in the early stages of your entrepreneurial adventure is what is the purpose of your long-term plans? If you are in your early 20s, your judgment about the future may be considerably different from what it might be if you were in your 50s. Some people buy a business with the intention that it will be the family business for more than just a single generation, that ownership will pass to the children. Other people buy a business with the intention of building it into a dynasty that will consume all of their intellect, energy, and emotion for a lifetime. Still others have shorter-term goals that suggest taking the business to a particular plateau and then converting their earned equity to a retirement income by selling the business. There are yet others, depending in part on the industry chosen, who recognize that they are essentially buying a job from which they can't be discharged and that they can abandon at the appropriate time should they choose to do so.

Why Did They Become Franchisees in the First Place?

This, of course, brings us to the very nature of the franchise relationship. Without belaboring the concept of the franchise, suffice to say that most entrepreneurs choose the franchise route because they lack the experience, education, or confidence to do it alone. They want to take advantage of the experience of the franchisor that, in most cases, has been considerable over an extended time. This enables the neophyte entrepreneur to enjoy many of the franchisor's benefits, including training, supervision, and quantity discounts with vendors. The neophyte also benefits from research and development that most entrepreneurs have neither the time nor the ability to do themselves. The beginner can also reap the marketing and advertising savvy, which is difficult, if not impossible, to attain on an independent's budget. He or she also has the opportunity to meet with franchisees from all over the country and compare notes with peers who may share private and proprietary aspects of their business with other franchisees with whom they are not in direct competition. Yes, these are reasons why buyers look to the franchise rather than scale the mountain by themselves.

The Norm in the Seller's Marketplace

Most entrepreneurs, whether by design or by default, seem to end up in the category of converting their earned equity into a retirement income. Still others find, after giving the business their best efforts, that the profit is not sufficient to warrant maintaining the franchise relationship: the royalties are dollars that the owner would prefer to keep.

In the first instance, it is appropriate to recognize the difference in ultimately selling your business. Do you think it will be easier to sell it as a franchise or as an independent? Do you think you will be able to get more money for it as a franchise or as an independent? These questions are especially interesting because they can vary according to a range of factors, especially geography.

The Questions of Advertising Impact and Visibility

Franchise companies, as noted earlier, collect monies from their franchisees for basically three reasons. The first is because they need the money in order to service the franchisees, to be available when a franchisee needs help or advice. The second is because they need money to sell the concept of the franchise to others who may become franchisees. The third is to advertise the products and services, to bring customers to the franchisees. This advertising generates revenues for the franchisees from whom the franchisor gets royalties and advertising dollars. This is the cycle. The bigger the franchise name and the more recognizable the franchise logo, the more likely that entrepreneurs will want to buy franchises and, presumably, the more likely that franchisees will enjoy a favorable equity position when they sell their franchise.

On the other hand, if the name and logo do not have this commercial impact and if the franchisee feels that he or she no longer needs the services provided by the franchisor, then the question of the franchise name becomes a lower priority. At the end of the contract, if the franchisee does not renew it, the lack of a franchise contract might not impair his or her ability to sell the business at all. In fact, if a buyer realizes that he or she can operate the business as an independent rather than as a franchise, he or she must also recognize that dollars not paid as royalties to the franchisor become profits for the owner.

Since most businesses are valued, at least in part, on the basis of profit, it is easy to recognize that a business might sell for a higher price as an independent rather than as a franchise. This, of course, is based on the ability of the owner to continue to function equally as well as an independent. This may or may not be problematic, depending in great part on the industry, as you will see later on in the chapter. The businessperson must also reflect on the fact that the noncompete clause of the franchise contract might prevent him or her from continuing in the same business after the franchise relationship ends.

The Length of the Contract

The same differences among franchises are true with respect to the length of the contract. Some are for as little as five years and some are for as long as 25 years. Occasionally, you will even run into a franchise contract that suggests it is in perpetuity—in other words, forever. As the old saying goes, time flies when you're having fun. Certainly that's true when you're busy and, as an entrepreneur, you will be busy. The five-year contract or even the 25-year contract comes to an end faster than you might think.

You are constantly told that in business you must always plan ahead. That wisdom applies in this case. You should examine the length of the contract, your long-term plans for yourself and your family, and the limitations on competition specified in the contract.

The Language of Limitations

The typical franchise contract has language in it to the effect that, for a certain period of time and within certain geographical boundaries, the franchisee and any representative or affiliate of the franchisee are precluded from competing with the business. The language of these limitations differs from contract to contract: any

franchise candidate is encouraged to read and understand these differences. Even if you are permitted to continue the business, you might have to give up the telephone number that is listed under the franchise logo in the Yellow Pages. After all, the logo belongs to the company, which is entitled, if not obligated, to protect it from use by a nonfranchise. In some industries, losing the telephone number in the Yellow Pages could devastate the business.

The Geography

Since most franchise contracts designate a certain geography to each franchise, the noncompete language usually uses the same geographical boundaries. The language will state that the franchisee is precluded from participating "in any competitive business located or operating within the statistical market area of the terminated franchise."

Some problems are created when the franchisor tries to prevent competition not only within the area that was allocated to the terminated franchise but also within all franchise territories anywhere. Such language is contained in a paragraph that precludes the franchisee from operating in a competitive capacity "within a fifteen (15) mile radius of the franchised location or within fifteen (15) miles of any other franchised or company-owned store." Another franchise agreement uses the same language, but specifies an area of no less than 25 miles. In the case of a national franchise, such language could preclude the ex-franchisee from working anywhere! Without knowing whether a court in your particular state would enforce this restriction, what would be your immediate reaction to this kind of limitation?

What Is "Reasonable"?

It is interesting that one franchisor tries to eliminate the question of "reasonable" by asking the franchisee to sign a contract with language that avoids the potential conflict at the very outset of the agreement: "the franchisee acknowledges that the terms and conditions of this covenant are fair and reasonable with respect to both the time and distance restrictions." Some attorneys suggest that this precludes the need for a court to decide on the reasonableness of the restrictions. Other attorneys suggest that the court will not necessarily accept this decision by the parties and will accept or reject this decision after a fair hearing on the facts. The decision will depend on the court and the disposition of the judge, factors over which you as a franchisee will have little or no influence.

Not Just the Franchisee

In order to prevent former franchisees from the clever strategy of operating under someone else's name, most of the contracts contain language that is quite inclusive. Here's an example: "franchisee and each of its principals agree not to engage within forty (40) miles of the approved location, either directly or indirectly, as an owner, officer, director, shareholder, partner, employee, consultant, or agent in any activity competitive to the business of the franchisor or which is similar to or conducts its business in a manner similar to, or be involved in any manner."

Here's another example of language that makes the restriction pretty tight: "as a disclosed or beneficial owner, investor, partner, representative or agent or in any other capacity." Some language even attempts to include those who may never have had any relationship to the original contract: "through a member of any immediate family of the franchisee or its owners or otherwise."

Whether or not any court would enforce much of this language is conjectural in the minds of most attorneys. The restrictive language stands as valid unless challenged, however. The language that the franchisor will use to temper this very restrictive language will often be such as this: "the restrictions of this Section shall not be applicable to the ownership of shares of a class of securities listed on a stock exchange or traded on the over-the-counter market that represent 5% or less of the number of shares of that class of securities issued and outstanding." It obviously doesn't leave very much room for any sort of participation short of a minor investment in a publicly traded company.

The Adjusted Compromise

Occasionally, you will find language that is somewhat surprising, in favor of the franchisee. You may surmise that it emanates from a company with a different sense of morals or ethics. It might, however, be a compromise that was made between the franchisor and the franchisee to keep peace in the franchise family. It might, in other words, be a compromise that was either designed to avoid litigation or developed during a litigation situation. Here is an example: "For one (1) year following the earlier termination (but not expiration) of this agreement, franchisee shall not directly or indirectly, own, operate, or have any interest (as an owner, employee, director, officer, salesperson, representative, or agent or in any other capacity) within the exclusive franchise area or three (3) miles of the location of the store authorized by this agreement." The exclusion of the word "expiration" gives a prerogative to the franchisee that is most unusual.

Negotiating the Contract Provision

What about requesting a change in the franchise contract language before you commit to signing it? Keep in mind that the franchise relationship depends on consistency among the franchisees. If one franchisee finds that another has a much different contract or one in which the language has been materially changed, the franchise's cohesiveness could be destroyed as the result. It is for this reason that it is not normal for you to make changes in the franchise contract. It is possible. And there are certainly areas where minor adjustments might be made. But, as a general rule, don't think that you can substantially adjust the terms and conditions of a franchise contract. The reasons are obvious. You would not want to find out after the fact that someone else has a more advantageous contract than you do, would you?

Contract Language Aside

Perhaps the biggest question to be answered in this context is whether there are reasons that will prevent an independent from competing with the franchise after the contract expires because of things that have nothing to do with the noncompete language itself. As one franchisor said, "If there isn't a secret formula or some other exclusive, proprietary item that is susceptible of absolute protection, there better be some special prerogatives that the ex-franchisee, now the independent, cannot enjoy without being a part of the franchise company."

This kind of prerogative can take many forms. In the case of one fast-food company, the franchisor actually produces the product in frozen form, eliminating the need to measure ingredients, knead dough, or design the final product. If the franchisee were to leave the fold when the contract expires, he or she would no longer have access to the product. The owner would have to create an entirely different product that would have neither the quality nor the customer appeal of the franchised product.

In another company, the franchisee is totally dependent on the use of certain vendors whose pricing structure is extremely beneficial to the franchisees because of the quantity of purchases made by the franchisor through its network. If a franchise turned independent, he or she could no longer benefit from this discount structure and the profit margin would decrease to the point that it was unlikely to be sufficient to support the business.

But I've Got the Customers!

In some cases, building the customer base is the biggest problem in a retail business. If you have a loyal customer base, it might not make a big difference that you are now selling cookies instead of cake or tea instead of coffee. In some such situations, the product or service may change enough to avoid the noncompete language but still appeal to the customer base. It might be an unusual situation, but it does happen.

Of course, this is exactly what many franchisors are trying to protect against. After all, if the product is designed to create an ambiance of relaxation within which the product is sold, is it the product or the ambiance that is the real moneymaker? And if the ambiance can be maintained with a different product, has the franchisee actually used the franchisor's advertising dollars to build a business that can now be used for an alternative product? On the other hand, many franchisors would not care if this happens, since they are more concerned about their product or service than about the customer base.

THE ULTIMATE CONTRACT COMPROMISE

Many franchisors have recognized the problem of enforcing such restrictive language and have tried to accommodate the problem in a different way. They have acknowledged that, whatever the franchisor has invested in the trade name and whatever it has done to help create a successful enterprise for the franchisee, all franchisees will not want to renew their franchise obligations at the time the contract expires. In fact, long before the contract expires, many don't feel comfortable paying the royalty. Unhappy franchisees are not good for the propagation of the system. The unhappiness, in some cases, has a way of spreading like a cancer and it certainly isn't a good idea to suggest that a new franchise candidate talk with a franchisee who may convey a message of dissatisfaction.

The answer is to give these unhappy franchisees a way out, one that may be painful to their pocketbook but that will not hurt the franchise. Money is often the answer.

In some cases, the franchisor has suggested a dollar buyout equivalent to a percentage of the last year's gross income. In other cases, the franchisor tries to create a present value based on the average royalties being paid annually, then multiplied by the number of years left on the contract.

In order to avoid this being called a "penalty," which the courts are hesitant to enforce, the language that is used to describe this buyout is "liquidated damages." This means that the amount is theoretically equivalent to the loss the company would incur when the franchisee leaves and no longer pays the royalty to which the company would otherwise be entitled. Even though the franchisee signs the contract that contains this language, most lawyers feel that the reasonableness of this dollar amount is still subject to the opinion of a court. This is especially true when the percentage or the dollar amount does not appear to related to the real dollars involved and suggests that it is, in fact, a penalty and unenforceable.

For example, "franchisee agrees ... that the damage to franchisor's business arising from a breach of the provisions of this covenant not to compete are difficult to assess and that payment to franchisor of forty-five percent (45%) of the revenues related to franchisee's breach would be reasonable and franchisee agrees to pay, and franchisor agrees to accept payment of that amount as liquidated damages for such breach." Would you consider that percentage a reasonable compromise?

Of course, if the amount designated in the contract or a negotiated amount is acceptable to a franchisee who wants out of the contract, then the concept certainly serves its purpose for both parties—they don't end up in court.

The language involved in these noncompete situations is difficult to understand and even more difficult to interpret. It is the kind of question that you must discuss with your professional. Remember: the long-term consequence of your signature on any contract is something you must consider at the beginning of any relationship.

KEY POINTS TO REMEMBER

- Check the length of the franchise commitment in order to ensure that its expiration coincides with your personal plans for the future.
- Although it may not appear to be a high priority when buying a franchise, it is important to note the conditions under which you can continue in business after your franchise expires.
- Do you think your customers will be loyal to you even if you change the name of your business or do you think the absence of the franchise logo will mean losing your customers?
- Have your professional explain the reasonableness and the potential enforceability of your franchise expiration language in your state.
- Make sure you understand the limitations of staying in business if you choose not to renew your franchise contract.

Worksheet 24. When the Franchise Contract Ends

The end of your franchise contract—whether five, 10, or 50 years—may seem like a distant destination, but it's right around the corner. Because there are so many franchise contracts up for renewal since the franchise explosion of the '70s and '80s, this is a booming area of law. This worksheet will help you plan and prepare for the inevitable end of the contract.

Before you signed your franchise contract, did you examine the alternatives available to you at the expiration of the contract period? Yes ❑ No ❑

After you signed your franchise contract, did you examine the alternatives available to you at the expiration of the contract period? Yes ❑ No ❑

Just before the expiration of your franchise contract, did you examine the alternatives available to you at the expiration of the contract period? Yes ❑ No ❑

Do you think you can survive in your business marketplace without the help of the franchise? Yes ❑ No ❑

Do you think the franchisor will allow you to survive after your franchise contract expires? Yes ❑ No ❑

What does your franchise contract say on this subject? _____

_____

_____

Do you think the language is enforceable in your jurisdiction? Yes ❑ No ❑

Would you like to have an answer to this question? Yes ❑ No ❑

Are there cost benefits that will no longer be available to you if you fail to renew your franchise contract?
Yes ❑ No ❑

Will these negatively impact your survival and success? Yes ❑ No ❑

Is the trade-off a worthwhile one?   Yes ❏ No ❏

Are those cost benefits equivalent to the royalty dollars that you will be saving?   Yes ❏ No ❏

Do you have enough time to create a marketing program to maintain the continuity of your business after leaving the franchise?   Yes ❏ No ❏

Have you thought this problem through?   Yes ❏ No ❏

Have you spoken with others who have maintained a successful business after leaving the franchise?   Yes ❏ No ❏

Do you think such a conversation would be a good idea?   Yes ❏ No ❏

When you are ready to sell your business, do you think it will be easier to sell as a franchise or as an independent?

Do you think the value will be greater or lesser in each case? _____

_____

Do you think that you are still getting value for your money as you pay your royalties to your franchisor?
Yes ❏ No ❏

Can you find equivalent services outside the franchise for less than the royalty payments?   Yes ❏ No ❏

Do you think you can survive as an independent without being affiliated with the franchise logo in the Yellow Pages?
Yes ❏ No ❏

Does your franchise contract prevent you from using the same telephone number?   Yes ❏ No ❏

If it does, have you prepared for this contingency?   Yes ❏ No ❏

Does your franchisor have the right to take over your premises lease when your franchise contract expires?
Yes ❏ No ❏

THE FRIGHTENING ASPECT OF BEING SUED

If you've been in business for any substantial period of time, it is quite likely that you've been involved in a lawsuit or the threat of a lawsuit. As with so many things, the fear is usually greater than the ultimate result.

The Initial Contact

The standard in the practice of law is that an attorney notifies the "responsible party"—you—in writing that he or she represents a person who feels that he or she has a claim against you. This is usually referred to as an "alleged" claim since it doesn't attain the dignity of an "actual" claim until it's proven. The letter is usually couched in very dramatic language, suggesting that you have either done something wrong or failed to do something that you were obliged to do. In either case, this notification is for the purpose of setting the record straight, at least according to the person who is making the claim, and making it clear that, if you do not take care of the matter immediately to the satisfaction of the claimant, the matter will be taken further ... usually meaning that the matter will go to court.

This letter should not necessarily alarm you, since it is designed to give you a chance to examine the facts and resolve the matter without it going any further. Contact your professional for advice!

The Lawsuit

If the matter is not resolved, the claimant will then initiate the lawsuit, which has some frightening side effects to be sure. In the first place, if you do not respond within the appropriate time frame, you can be "defaulted." This means that you've lost the lawsuit without even preparing and presenting your side of the story. This is not a good idea, since the amounts involved might be arbitrary and you might have been able to minimize the amounts if you had been represented. Contact your professional for advice.

The Worst Part of the Language

When you get the "pleadings"—formal declarations setting forth the claims and referencing all the issues involved in the lawsuit—you will undoubtedly be surprised. You must remember that, just as with any arbitration or negotiation, you usually can't increase the amount you want after you start. As a result, the attorney representing the claimant will accuse you of just about everything and set the potential recovery at such an amount that you might not even recognize the original problem. When you read the terrible things you are alleged to have done or those obligations that you failed to fulfill, you might even think that the claimant is talking about someone else. Don't be thrown off by this excessive language, these extraordinary allegations. It is all part of the process.

The Effect on Your Psyche

One of the most significant problems in any litigation is that it takes so much time. You will be asked to file answers to interrogatories, a series of questions intended to get to the core of the matter, and you will need to examine all the important details of the claim, the defense to the claim, and the potential counterclaim. All of a sudden, you will note that the lawsuit is taking as much of your time as your business. It actually takes on a life of its own and consumes much of your leisure as well as your sleep. You should begin to see that you ought to examine any and all alternatives before you let your business and yourself fall into the litigation abyss.

The Trial

If you think that preparing for trial has affected your time, consider the time elements involved in the actual trial. You will likely have been deposed, asked to answer a variety of questions by the claimant's attorney, prior to the actual courtroom activity. Preparing for this deposition is terribly important and requires a lot of time, since the questioning is exhaustive and can take hours. The trial itself can take many directions, since both sides are likely to bring in "experts" to testify on behalf of their positions—and there is an expert prepared to testify on any side of an issue.

The key to most trials is "the truth of the matter" and truth is usually based on credibility. Who will the court or the jury believe? Are the results of trials fair? The prevailing party will usually say that they are and the losing party will often take the opposite side of the argument. Before you let yourself fall into the category of being a participant, be careful. Consult with a professional whom you trust. It may be the best advice you will ever receive.

And if you have an argument with your franchisor, which is not unusual considering the length of most franchise contracts, consider the element of compromise before you allow yourself to fall into the abyss of litigation.

PART VI

Revisiting the Essentials

CHAPTER 25

Revisiting the Financial Issues

How much do you know about finances? How do you absorb and use financial information? We are all different in our knowledge, experience, and processing. Since understanding financial basics is a predicate for understanding the entire topic of business valuation, this chapter has been added to ensure that, whatever your background, education, or learning disposition, the information is packaged from a slightly different perspective. In this context, this chapter uses definitions as well as charts. If we are to be accused of redundancy, our defense is that we want to make sure that you understand the financial issues.

THE BALANCE SHEET

The balance sheet is a document to which many entrepreneurs fail to give the proper respect. They think it is a tool that is more important to the accountant at tax time than to the owner of the business during the course of his or her activity. Nothing could be further from the truth. This section explains the basic elements and presents some of the reasons why the balance sheet is important, whether you're buying a business, selling a business, expanding a business, or just surviving.

Structure and Components

The balance sheet consists of three components structured into two sections. The first section is Assets (what you own). The second section is made up of Liabilities (what you owe) and—depending on the legal form of the company—Owner's Equity or Stockholders' Equity (what you have invested and earned, which will always show the difference between assets and liabilities). The balance sheet represents the financial position of the company at a moment in time. To understand the financial health of the company, you must see more than one balance sheet over a period of time to understand the direction the company is taking.

The layout of the balance sheet is as follows:

Assets
Current Assets
  Cash
  Marketable Securities
  Accounts Receivable
  Inventory
     Raw materials
     Work in process
     Finished goods
  Prepaid Expenses

Long-Term Assets

  Property, Plant, and Equipment

  Furniture and Equipment

  Machines

  Building

  Land

  Accumulated Depreciation

Total Assets

Liabilities

Current Liabilities

  Accounts Payable

  Accrued Expenses

  Income Tax Payable

  Short-Term Notes Payable

Total Current Liabilities

Long-Term Liabilities

  Long-Term Notes Payable

Total Long-Term Liabilities

Total Liabilities

Stockholders' Equity

  Capital Stock/Paid in Capital (cash or other contributions to the business)

    Retained Earnings

Total Liabilities and Stockholders' Equity

What Is a Balance Sheet Statement?

A balance sheet statement is a snapshot of the financial support structure you need to be able to make sales. Now, let's look at how we define the structure of the three segments—assets, liabilities, and owner's or stockholders' equity.

1. Assets are the part of a business that helps support and pay for the work of a business or, to put it another way, the work the business needs to do to complete a sale.

Assets divide into two categories: current assets and long-term assets. Current assets include cash, accounts receivable, marketable securities, and inventory. These are defined as current because they can be easily converted into cash. Long-term assets include equipment, buildings, and land. These assets have a life of over one year and cannot be converted to cash as easily as current assets. Long-term assets continue to make it possible for a company to build widgets or provide a place for a company to do whatever work must be done to

complete a sale. Assets include prepaid expenses—expenses paid in advance, such as insurance, leases, and deposits—and accumulated depreciation—a tax deduction the government allows for the purchase of certain assets based on the life of the assets.

Cash listed on the balance sheet comes from sales made with cash or from sales made on credit. Cash also comes from investments or from lines of credit that a company maintains with banks. Cash pays for inventory and for the daily operations.

2. Liabilities are commitments (debt) that a company incurs to support business operations. Liabilities are divided, like assets, into two categories: current liabilities and long-term liabilities. Current liabilities include accounts payable, accrued expenses, income tax payables, and short-term notes payable (lines of credit). These debts are totally paid off within one year. Long-term liabilities include long-term notes payable. These are debts that are paid over time, such as an equipment loan or a loan for a building or land.

3. Owner's/Stockholders' Equity is the difference between assets and liabilities. Equity is divided into two basic categories: Capital Stock (investments in the company, cash or other) and Retained Earnings (net income earned and retained by the company). The Retained Earnings appear on a balance sheet only after the company has been in business for one year. Retained Earnings maintains the records of earnings and losses directly from the profit and loss statement (income statement).

The Balance Sheet as a Reference Point

Unlike the profit and loss statement, which shows you a picture of the business in a chronological way, month to month, the balance sheet does not represent a chronology. It's a picture of the business at a moment in time. In order to understand that kind of picture, you will need to compare two balance sheets.

For example, if December 2003 shows a loan outstanding in the amount of $120,000.00, you will need to look at a month in 2004 to see what the balance is. If the balance of the loan in December 2004 is $60,000.00, then you know that you paid $60,000.00 on the loan between December 2003 and December 2004. It is likely that you paid $5,000.00 each month during that 12-month period. You can then plug this figure into your profit and loss statement (which likely contains only the interest payments on the loan) and you have a clearer picture of the monthly obligations of the business.

	December 2003	December 2004
Liabilities	$120,000.00	$60,000.00

What can you learn about the trends in your business?

Your balance sheet will show you, at any given time, your receivables and your inventory. If your receivables were larger this year than last year and your inventory was less this year than last year, you probably made more sales this year than last. *But* what if your receivables are all past due? What if a lot of your receivables are from the previous year's sales? This might mean that many might not be collectable. This is not good news!

	December 2003	December 2004
Assets		
Receivables	$200,000.00	$300,000.00
Inventory	$50,000.00	$20,000.00

The above scenario could represent an increase in sales from one year to the next, which would be very positive, but if the $300,000.00 is broken down into $150,000.00 in current receivables and $150,000.00 in last year's receivables, still owed, this picture could represent a serious negative situation.

On the other hand, if your receivables were lower this year than last year and your inventory was more this year than last year, you might have made a mistake in the number of units you chose to produce and were unable to sell enough of them. This could be bad.

	December 2003	December 2004
Assets		
Receivables	$300,000.00	$200,000.00
Inventory	$20,000.00	$50,000.00

But when you look at your sales picture, you might notice that you've sold much more this year than last year. This might mean that you've collected more on your receivables and have an appropriate amount of inventory left at the close of the year. This could be good.

It is interesting to note that finding the incremental payments on long-term obligations requires reading two or more balance sheets. Although the interest on long-term loans and leases will be found on the P&L, the only way to obtain the principal payments on those loans is to look at two balance sheets. The amount on the current balance sheet will indicate what is still owed. The amount of the current balance sheet, deducted from the previous one, will show what's been paid during the period of time between the two balance sheets. This amount of principal payments can then be added to the P&L and then divided by months to get a more realistic picture of the incremental payments required to pay off both the interest and the principal. Failure to do this will result in an unrealistic picture of the business and its profit potential.

THE PROFIT AND LOSS STATEMENT

The profit and loss statement (P&L) (also known as the income statement) is an ongoing account of the sales and expenses related to those sales during the course of the months and years of a business.

The first section below explains in basic narrative form the line items on a typical P&L. Keep in mind that this is basic. Considering that a P&L, initially, is for the benefit of the entrepreneur, it can have as many line items in each category as the business owner chooses. The owner may want to compare products or services from one time frame to another to see which of them is the most profitable in terms of time, margins, or numbers sold. He or she may want to compare expenses, like advertising expenses, to see which appear to have been more cost-effective from one year to the next. The idea is to make the P&L readable so that it becomes a tool of the business and not an academic exercise.

As has often been said, you don't have to be an accountant or a lawyer in order to properly operate a business. If that were the case, there would be very few small businesses in the American marketplace. The nature of financial paperwork is that it can be as simple or as complex as you like. The better approach is to keep it simple, understand the basics, and then proceed to make it as complicated as you like. An entrepreneur can deduce many things from a comparative analysis of two or more P&Ls, as will be shown later in this chapter.

WHAT IS A PROFIT AND LOSS STATEMENT?

There are basically five elements involved in a profit and loss statement (P&L):

- Sales
- Cost of Sales or Cost of Product
- Gross Profit
- SG&A
- Profit

Sales. These are the revenues generated by the company. Sales are often broken down into line items so the reader can see which products or services have a larger margin of profit. If the person preparing the financial picture is doing a complete job, he or she will prepare a set of 'assumptions' that explain the purpose of each line item under Sales. This will also be important as you examine trends in the business.

Cost of Sales or Cost of Product. This represents the cost of raw materials or component parts necessary to prepare the product for sale. This category should also have a set of assumptions indicating the nature of the materials or components necessary to produce the product or service. Again, the reader will be able to compare the costs and get a better sense of the business on an ongoing basis. The figures will show which items are potentially problematic, in terms of either availability or price.

Gross Profit. This is the difference between Sales and Cost of Sales or Product. There are variations due to the different approaches that people take to keeping financial records, even in the same business. Some businesses will put sales *commissions* under Cost of Product, since they relate directly to the amount of revenues or sales produced. These same people will keep sales *salaries* under SG&A, because they represent expenses of operating the business *regardless* of the volume of sales. This is one of the reasons why it is sometimes very difficult to do a comparative analysis of two like businesses, since each may present its financial picture somewhat differently.

SG&A. This represents *all* the other costs of operating the business. The acronym stands for salaries, general, and administrative expenses. This is where the problem of most businesses starts because it includes rent, telephone, gas and electric, deliveries, cleaning, and every other aspect of keeping the business alive *regardless* of whether you sell a little or a lot or, indeed, anything! This SG&A section must be carefully examined to ensure that the business can make a profit. The line items under SG&A should be sufficiently designated to allow for a comparative analysis. If, for example, a line item says "Advertising," how will you know how much of that figure is for Yellow Pages (an expense that created sales) and how much is for mailers (an expense that didn't create sales)? If you don't find the answer to this in the assumptions, be sure to ask. Also, be sure that you see the notes on "What Is a Balance Sheet Statement?" to ensure that you include both the principal and the interest payments in the SG&A section of your P&L. Failure to do so will give you a deceptive profit picture.

Profit. This is the bottom line. It can be a positive number or a negative number, indicated by parentheses ($) or angle brackets <$>. A positive number means that the company made money after all the expenses of properly operating the business. The accountants then differentiate among different kinds of profit. For example, they will use terms like EBITDA—earnings before interest, taxes, depreciation, and amortization.

In examining the profit of a company, there are some key factors to look for. One of these is to ask if the owner's salary is included in the SG&A or if the owner takes his or her compensation out of the profit of the business. You should recognize the tremendous difference in the answer to this all-important question.

The Difference Between Accrual and Cash

The P&L is usually built on the accrual method of accounting. This ensures that it properly reflects sales (even though not yet collected) and the equivalent expenses against sales (even though not yet paid) and will show how the business is doing. The difference between building a P&L on an accrual basis and building it on a cash basis is significant. You need to understand both, as they indicate, in different ways, the financial status of the business. (See Figures 25.1 and 25.2.)

This is a business profile of a company that doesn't sell for cash. The cost of sales represents money paid for the goods when purchased, whether or not the company sold any or collected for any. The people to

FIGURE 25.1   Basic Cash Flow Projection–Accrual Basis

	Jan	Feb	Mar	Apr	May	Jun	Jul	Aug	Sep	Oct	Nov	Dec	Total
Sales Made	$5,000	$5,000	$5,000	$5,500	$6,000	$6,500	$7,000	$7,000	$8,000	$8,000	$9,000	$12,000	$84,000
Cash Collections	$-	$-	$2,500	$2,500	$5,000	$5,000	$6,000	$6,000	$7,000	$7,500	$8,000	$4,000	$53,500
Cost of Sales	$2,500	$2,500	$2,500	$2,750	$3,000	$3,250	$3,500	$3,500	$4,000	$4,000	$4,500	$6,000	$42,000
Gross Profit (accrual)	$2,500	$2,500	$2,500	$2,750	$3,000	$3,250	$3,500	$3,500	$4,000	$4,000	$4,500	$6,000	$42,000
SG&A													
Rent	$2,000	$2,000	$2,000	$2,000	$2,000	$2,000	$2,000	$2,000	$2,000	$2,000	$2,000	$2,000	$24,000
All Other Expenses	$1,000	$1,000	$1,000	$1,000	$1,000	$1,000	$1,000	$1,000	$1,000	$1,000	$1,000	$1,000	$12,000
Profit (Loss)	($500)	($500)	($500)	($250)	$-	$250	$500	$500	$1,000	$1,000	$1,500	$3,000	$6,000
Cumulative	($500)	($1,000)	($1,500)	($1,750)	($1,750)	($1,500)	($1,000)	($500)	$500	$1,500	$3,000	$6,000	$6,000

Note that on an accrual basis it doesn't make any difference whether money was received or not.

The accrual concept shows the progress of the business, not the progress of collections.

Costs are deducted from sales made rather than from monies collected.

When using an accrual basis, you ended up at the end of the year showing a $6,000 profit.

Do you think you ought to know the difference between the two: cash and accrual? When trying to find a true value for your business, you might want to understand both.

FIGURE 25.2   Basic Cash Flow Projection–Cash Basis

	Jan	Feb	Mar	Apr	May	Jun	Jul	Aug	Sep	Oct	Nov	Dec	Total
Sales Made	$5,000	$5,000	$5,000	$5,500	$6,000	$6,500	$7,000	$7,000	$8,000	$8,000	$9,000	$12,000	$84,000
Cash Collections	$-	$-	$2,500	$2,500	$5,000	$5,000	$6,000	$6,000	$7,000	$7,500	$8,000	$4,000	$53,500
Cost of Sales*	$2,500	$2,500	$2,500	$2,750	$3,000	$3,250	$3,500	$3,500	$4,000	$4,000	$4,500	$6,000	$42,000
Gross Profit (cash)	($2,500)	($2,500)	$-	($250)	$2,000	$1,750	$2,500	$2,500	$3,000	$3,500	$3,500	($2,000)	$11,500
SG&A													
Rent	$2,000	$2,000	$2,000	$2,000	$2,000	$2,000	$2,000	$2,000	$2,000	$2,000	$2,000	$2,000	$24,000
All Other Expenses	$1,000	$1,000	$1,000	$1,000	$1,000	$1,000	$1,000	$1,000	$1,000	$1,000	$1,000	$1,000	$12,000
Profit (Loss)**	($5,500)	($5,500)	($3,000)	($3,250)	($1,000)	($1,250)	($500)	($500)	$-	$500	$500	($5,000)	($24,500)
Cumulative	($5,500)	($11,000)	($14,000)	($17,250)	($18,250)	($19,500)	($20,000)	($20,500)	($20,500)	($20,000)	($19,500)	($24,500)	($24,500)

Note that the people to whom sold you goods in January and February don't even start paying for the goods until March. This is a business profile of those who don't sell for cash. Note also that, although payments are good for most of the year, December is good for sales but not for collections. As a result, you might be short of cash in December and you might make arrangements to pay your December rent in January in addition to January's rent when you have better collections.

Even though you have accrued $84,000 but only received $53,500 in CASH. Note that by paying the December rent in January of the following year, your CASH costs for the current year will be $2,000 less and your actual CASH COSTS for the following year will be $2,000 more. This will change your PROFIT picture on a cash basis in both years. It will not change your picture on an ACCRUAL basis.

*Note that this is money paid for the goods when purchased whether you sold any or collected for any.

**Remember that profit (or lack of it) is being recorded on a CASH BASIS; deducted from collections, not from sales. On a cash basis, you will be in the hole in the amount of $24,500 at year end. Do you think the business will be worthwhile?

whom the company sold goods in January and February don't even start paying for the goods until March.

Note that, although payments are good for most of the year, December is good for sales but not for collections. As a result, the company might be short of cash in December and might make arrangements to pay its December rent a month late, with its January rent, when its collections are better. By paying the December rent in January of the following year, cash costs for the current year will be $2,000 lower and cash costs for the following year will be $2,000 higher. This will change the profit picture on a cash basis, but it will not change the picture on an accrual basis.

The profit (or loss) is being recorded on a cash basis; it's deducted from collections, not from sales. Even though it accrued $84,000, the company received only $53,500 in cash. On a cash basis, the company will be in the hole $24,500 at year-end. Do you think the business will be worthwhile?

What Is Cash Flow?

In analyzing a business in terms of making a loan or an investment, a lender or a potential equity participant will want to see a cash flow analysis. This person with the money will want to know which periods will require a cash reservoir to achieve the anticipated goals or, in the case of a new business, how long it will be before the business will reach a break-even point (when the income will be equivalent to the costs necessary to produce that income) and begin to register a real, bottom-line profit.

Forecasting cash flow is especially important, aside from what your profit and loss statement may look like at the end of the year. After all, the profit and loss statement is usually developed on the basis of sales made but not necessarily collected and purchases made but not necessarily paid for—accrual accounting. On the other hand, cash flow is the actual dollars spent vs. the actual dollars collected—cash accounting.

Although cash flow is particularly important in a business involved in seasonal activity, where monthly sales rise and decline, most businesses need to address the subject for other reasons. When buying products for resale, hiring a salesperson, or creating an advertising campaign, it is essential that you anticipate the dollars needed for the expenditure long before you expect to earn the dollars based on these expenditures.

Working on the basis of day-to-day requirements can be terribly problematic without having the necessary cash available. If you need to buy inventory or parts or start making payments on equipment or additional personnel, you will be paying out in advance, sometimes significantly in advance, of bringing in the money to meet these payment obligations. If you don't have a sufficient working capital reservoir (enough money in the bank), you must have a lending source that will take you over this financial hurdle. This will invariably mean you will need a relationship with a lending institution that allows you to borrow money in some way, such as a simple loan or a line of credit.

Lenders will want to understand the reasons for this temporary financial problem and they will insist on seeing a cash flow forecast. The best forecast will obviously be based on the previous year's activities—providing, of course, that you had a previous year. If you have no such history, you need to back up your forecast with assumptions that are credible and believable based on the marketplace, with the support of purchase orders, existing inventory, and the like.

The banker or other lender will want to look at your balance sheet, particularly at your cash availability, your existing inventory, your purchase orders, your accounts receivable, your accounts payable, and your current and long-term obligations. Essentially, they will make judgments based on the ratios of your assets to your liabilities. They will often give you an advance based on your receivables, but only a percentage of this figure, depending on the age of these accounts and the reputation of the people who owe you the money. They will consider advancing dollars based on the amount of your inventory, under the assumption that this inventory will convert into sales. They will note the purchase orders for new goods or services and, depending on the credibility of those accounts, may advance money against those purchases. In other words, lenders want to assess the validity of your business practices, the financial position of the company, and the time and dollars you've already invested in your business.

What Is a Borrowing Base?

When a company applies for a loan, it may grant the lender a security interest in its receivables and/or inventory as collateral. This security interest is the borrowing base. A bank uses the borrowing base to monitor the financial health of the company to determine that it can lend money or to evaluate the financial performance of a company to which it has made a loan.

The type of loan that will require a borrowing base is a revolving line of credit (RLC). Banking institutions of all kinds will use a borrowing base when making a loan to a company, to determine how well a company is performing and achieving its goals relative to its projections. The bank and the company will agree on a borrowing base when a loan is executed. If a company is overperforming or underperforming its goals, the bank will use the borrowing base to evaluate the situation and determine how to help the company. The terms of a note may require that the company submit a borrowing base to the bank monthly, quarterly, or annually.

Key ratios that help determine the company's ability to repay its debt include the current ratio (current assets divided by current liabilities) and the total debt/equity ratio (total debt divided by total equity). For manufacturing companies, key ratios will also include accounts receivable days (average gross receivables divided by the quotient of annual net sales divided by 365), accounts payable days (average payables divided by the quotient of annual purchases divided by 365), and inventory days (average inventory divided by the quotient of cost of goods sold divided by 365).

A borrowing base certificate will look like the sample shown in Figure 25.4. The compliance ratios used in this certificate measure management's ability to manage the assets and liabilities on the balance sheet. For instance, the top ratio of debt to tangible net worth is simply debt divided by net worth. The bank is requiring that the debt/worth ratio be equal to or less than 5.0:1. This means that, in the most extreme case, for every $5 of debt, the company has $1 invested in net worth. If the company goes over that ratio, the bank can no longer lend it any money. The actual figure shows that the company has $1.91 of debt to $1 of net worth. This is evidence to the banker that the company knows how to manage its finances appropriately and that the bank can keep lending money to the company.

And What About a New Business?

When you have a totally new business and want to show your potential lender, partner, or investor how you intend to handle the money that you're seeking, you have a problem: no history. So you need to create the future of the business in financial terms. Sophisticated businesspeople, including lenders, are aware that a new business will not likely generate a profit immediately. The question is "When will that happen?" By creating a future year, based on serious and credible investigation, you should be able to show how long it will take for the business to reach its break-even point.

In the early stages of the business, you will be spending more than you're earning and go deeper into the hole each month, using the investment dollars. This will represent a cumulative loss. Lenders expect this to be the case. What lenders want is a credible picture of the time when you not only will have reached the break-even point but also have earned back the dollars spent earlier, when you will start generating a profit. This will give the lender (and you) a timeline for your success.

Although this may present a fairly simplistic view of the lender relationship, it should give you an idea of the parameters that your company should contemplate when borrowing. It is clearly essential for you to take advantage of professional advice to ensure that your presentation is prepared most appropriately.

A Real Example with Assumptions

Figure 25.5 (page 255) is the cash flow statement for a new school, with income projections for the first three years.

THE COMPARATIVE ANALYSIS

It is obvious that looking at longer periods for a comparative analysis will give you a better definition of "differences" than looking at shorter periods. The month-to-month activity change could easily be an aberration caused by any number of factors. The year-to-year comparative analysis is much more likely to give you a better sense of the differentials in real terms. In this context, see Figure 25.6 (page 256).

FIGURE 25.4 | Sample Borrowing Base Certificate

Borrowing Base/Compliance Certificate
For XYZ Trading Co.
As of March 31, 2004

Borrowing Base

1.	Total US A/R book value as of 3/31/2004	$507,442
2.	Less: A/R 91 days or more past due	$222,195
3.	Eligible accounts (line 1 – line 2)	$285,247
4.	Loan value of accounts (80% of line 3)	$228,198
5.	Total A/R book value as of 3/31/2004	$106,112
6.	Less A/R 90 days or more past due	$36,369
7.	Eligible accounts (line 5 – line 6)	$69,743
8.	Loan value of accounts (80% of line 7, $800,000 max)	$55,794
9.	Inventory as of 3/31/2004	$493,537
10.	Loan value of inventory (50% of line 9)	$246,769
11.	Sales purchase orders as of 3/31/2004	$7,263,321
12.	Loan value of sales purchase orders (60% of line 11)	$4,357,993
13.	Maximum line amount $5,000,000.00	$4,888,753
14.	Banker's acceptance owing lender	$94,869
15.	Present line of credit balance owing lender	$860,000
16.	Total due to lender	$954,869
17.	Line amount due or available unused line amount	$3,933,884

Compliance Ratios	Notes	Required	Actual
Debt to			
Tangible net worth	= or <	5.0:1	1.91:1
Tangible net worth	= or >	$1,000,000	$710,376
Consecutive days out of debt	= or >	30	30
Personal liquidity – A/R XYZ	= or >	$500,000	$500,000

The undersigned represents and warrants that the foregoing is true, complete and correct, and that the information reflected herein complies with the representations and warranties set forth in the loan agreement between the undersigned and the bank dated _____.

XYZ Trading Company, Inc.

By _____

Title _____

Compare services and products in the years referenced. Such an analysis should give the reader good reason to consider a change in the direction of the company.

Sales (revenue) shows the same decline for both Company A and Company B. However, with Company A revenue from services carries a cost of product of 10%, while revenues from products, which remains the same for all four years, carries a cost of product of 50%. What if these were reversed, as with Company B? Would you think that this trend required your serious attention? It certainly would if you were concerned

FIGURE 25.5   Pro Forma Cash Flow Statement

Assumptions	Jan	Feb	Mar	Apr	May	Jun	Jul	Aug	Sep	Oct	Nov	Dec	Yr 1 Total	Yr 2 Proj	Yr 3 Proj
				2 classes	3 classes	4 classes	4 classes	5 classes	5 classes	6 classes	6 classes	6 classes		6 cls/mo	8 cls/mo
Sales*	0	0	0	$2,304	$3,456	$4,608	$4,608	$5,760	$5,760	$6,912	$6,912	$6,912	$47,232	$82,944	$110,592
COS															
Teacher Salaries	$-	$-	$-	$480	$720	$960	$960	$1,200	$1,200	$1,440	$1,440	$1,440	$9,840	$17,280	$23,040
Class Supplies	$-	$-	$-	$30	$45	$60	$60	$75	$75	$90	$90	$90	$615	$1,080	$1,440
Total COS	$-	$-	$-	$510	$765	$1,020	$1,020	$1,275	$1,275	$1,530	$1,530	$1,530	$10,455	$18,360	$24,480
Gross Profit	$-	$-	$-	$1,794	$2,691	$3,588	$3,588	$4,485	$4,485	$5,382	$5,382	$5,382	$36,777	$64,584	$86,112
Expenses															
Phone	$75	$50	$50	$50	$50	$50	$50	$50	$50	$50	$50	$50	$600	$600	$600
Legal/Accounting	$-	$-	$-	$-	$-	$-	$-	$-	$75	$-	$-	$75	$225	$225	$225
Advertising	$500	$500	$700	$700	$700	$700	$700	$700	$600	$600	$700	$700	$7,600	$7,600	$7,600
Postage	$200	$-	$1,000	$-	$1,000	$-	$-	$-	$1,000	$-	$-	$-	$3,200	$1,000	$1,000
Mailing List															
Referral	$-	$300	$-	$-	$-	$300	$-	$-	$-	$300	$-	$-	$900	$900	$-
Printing	$-	$1,050	$-	$-	$-	$-	$-	$-	$-	$-	$-	$-	$-	$-	$-
Cleaning	$-	$-	$-	$-	$-	$-	$-	$-	$-	$-	$-	$-	$-	$600	$600
Office Staff															
Salaries	$-	$-	$-	$-	$-	$-	$-	$-	$-	$-	$-	$-	$-	$20,000	$30,000
Maintenance	$-	$-	$-	$-	$-	$-	$-	$-	$-	$-	$-	$-	$-	$-	$-
Utilities	$-	$-	$-	$75	$75	$75	$75	$75	$75	$75	$75	$75	$675	$675	$675
Insurance	$-	$-	$-	$-	$-	$-	$676	$-	$-	$-	$-	$-	$-	$-	$-
Rent	$-	$-	$-	$1,000	$1,000	$1,000	$1,000	$1,000	$1,000	$1,000	$1,000	$1,000	$9,000	$12,000	$12,000
Start-up Costs	$4,500	$-	$-	$-	$-	$-	$-	$-	$-	$-	$-	$-	$4,500	$-	$-
Banking Costs	$100	$-	$-	$25	$25	$25	$25	$25	$25	$25	$25	$25	$325	$300	$300
SG&A Expenses	$5,375	$1,900	$1,750	$1,850	$2,850	$2,150	$2,550	$1,850	$2,750	$2,050	$2,050	$2,125	$29,250	$43,900	$53,000
Net Income	($5,375)	($1,900)	($1,750)	($56)	($159)	$1,438	$1,038	$2,635	$1,735	$3,332	$3,332	$3,257	$7,527	$20,684	$33,112
Cumulative Income (Loss)	($5,375)	($7,275)	($9,025)	($9,081)	($9,240)	($7,802)	($6,764)	($4,129)	($2,394)	$938	$4,270	$7,527			

Assumptions: 8 students per class @ $144 each
Teachers = $240 per class

*****Note:** Many businesses don't account for sales until all invoices are mailed 30, 60, 90 days. This is cash collected over time. Cash collected over time is accrual accounting. When a business collects cash at the time of a sale and accounts for all sales in this manner, it is defined as cash accounting.

FIGURE 25.6 Profit and Loss Statement (Income Statement) for a Comparative Analysis

Company A

	2004	2003	2002	2001	
Sales (Revenue)					
Services	$30,000	$40,000	$50,000	$60,000	
Products	$30,000	$30,000	$30,000	$30,000	
Total	$60,000	$70,000	$80,000	$90,000	
Cost of Product					
Services	$3,000	$4,000	$5,000	$6,000	10%
Products	$15,000	$15,000	$15,000	$15,000	50%
Total	$18,000	$19,000	$20,000	$21,000	
Gross Profit	**$42,000**	**$51,000**	**$60,000**	**$69,000**	
SG&A (Salaries, General, and Administrative Expenses)					
Advertising	$1,000	$1,000	$1,000	$1,000	
Legal/Accounting	$200	$200	$200	$200	
Rent	$3,000	$3,000	$3,000	$3,000	
Utilities	$800	$800	$800	$800	
Total	$5,000	$5,000	$5,000	$5,000	
Net Income or Loss	**$37,000**	**$46,000**	**$55,000**	**$64,000**	

Company B

	2004	2003	2002	2001	
Sales (Revenue)					
Services	$60,000	$60,000	$60,000	$60,000	
Products	$0	$10,000	$20,000	$30,000	
Total	$60,000	$70,000	$80,000	$90,000	
Cost of Product					
Services	$6,000	$6,000	$6,000	$6,000	10%
Products	$0	$5,000	$10,000	$15,000	50%
Total	$6,000	$11,000	$16,000	$21,000	
Gross Profit	**$54,000**	**$59,000**	**$64,000**	**$69,000**	
SG&A (Salaries, General, and Administrative Expenses)					
Advertising	$1,000	$1,000	$1,000	$1,000	
Legal/Accounting	$200	$200	$200	$200	
Rent	$3,000	$3,000	$3,000	$3,000	
Utilities	$800	$800	$800	$800	
Total	$5,000	$5,000	$5,000	$5,000	
Net Income or Loss	**$49,000**	**$54,000**	**$59,000**	**$64,000**	

about the difference in profit! In addition, it would also tell you what direction your company is taking.

SG&A stays the same whether you are generating greater or fewer sales. If you no longer need space for product, could you save money on your SG&A? What about rent and utilities?

KEY POINTS TO REMEMBER

- A balance sheet represents a moment in time. You will always need to compare two or more balance sheets to note the movement of the business's financial position.
- A profit and loss statement (also known as an income statement) is usually prepared on an accrual basis. This shows what the business looks like, assuming that all receivables are collected and all payables are paid, even though they might not be.
- Showing a business's activity on a cash basis will be significantly different in most cases from the same financial picture portrayed on an accrual basis.
- A borrowing base includes the totality of the financial picture of a business, which allows a lender to properly assess and minimize risk.
- In the cash flow forecast of a new business, assumptions explaining the details of line items are especially important for a potential lender or equity participant.

Worksheet 25. Revisiting the Financial Issues

The following questions emphasize some of the most important points you need to consider in order to better understand the purpose of properly developing your financial paperwork.

Why do you need more than one balance sheet to understand the movement of your financial picture?

_____

_____

What are the three basic sections of a balance sheet? _____

_____

What is the difference between long-term and short-term obligations? _____

_____

Why are the principal payments on long-term notes and lease obligations not included in your profit and loss statement? _____

_____

How can you find the principal payments on a promissory note or long-term lease obligation?

_____

_____

What is your profit and loss statement designed to show you? _____

_____

What is the purpose of using assumptions as part of your profit and loss presentation? _____

_____

What is the difference between the accrual and cash methods of accounting? _____

_____

Why is cash flow so important to a new business? _____

_____

What does EBITDA mean? _____

_____

What are the basic elements involved in a borrowing base? _____

_____

What will a comparative analysis of two profit and loss statements tell you? _____

_____

Why is this important? _____

_____

GROWING AT THE RIGHT SPEED

A good track coach will tell you that it's not always best to run as fast as you can. If you're running the hurdles, you have to pace yourself to get to each hurdle in stride; if you're running a long race, you've got to conserve energy for the final lap. Good business coaching has a similar set of values.

Running Faster than Your Legs Can Move

Selling a service without the equipment necessary to produce it is courting disaster. One answer is to have someone else produce it, which reduces your margins. Another alternative is to buy or lease the equipment, which represents a cost against sales. Selling product without adequate inventory is a similar problem.

You can buy as you sell, but the price per product will be much higher than if you buy in quantity. These are the kinds of management judgments that must be made every day. The time to make this judgment is usually before you go out to make the sale. In other words, make sure that you are prepared to deliver the product or service you sell before taking on the responsibility for fulfilling the orders. And know what your margins are for survival and success. Running faster than your legs can move will, more often than not, cause you to fall.

Growing with Grace

Timing and investment are two critical elements that you need to examine constantly. You ought to make decisions about both before considering the business aspects of selling. Make sure that your figures are correct and that you have adequate capital to make the things happen that are the core elements of your business. If you don't have adequate backing, slow down. Work on a time schedule that will allow you to grow and maintain. Many businesses fail because management didn't take the time to reflect on the basics of time and investment. Growth is based on the ability to meet the essentials of sale, production, collection, and profit. Make sure that your priorities are in order before you start.

Incremental Growth vs. Accelerated Growth

Remember the old story of the tortoise and the hare. Taking on more than your business, your personnel, or your available capital can handle may give you great satisfaction in the thinking stage—but it will undoubtedly give you a big headache in the implementation stage. Good business judgment will often dictate that incremental growth can, in the long term, be a more satisfactory approach to growing your business.

There are, of course, those situations where big dollars and big potential can suggest going to the public market, creating a franchise operation, or opening simultaneous operations to impact your competitive marketplace. But the caution is that every accelerated growth situation has its negative and potentially disastrous side if all of the implications are not considered early on with great respect. Many people have succumbed to this temptation only to regret their decision because they did not properly prepare.

Watching the Slower Economy

Whatever the conventional wisdom may be about the current economy, it doesn't hurt to build a little caution into your business decisions. Making a big sale is good business only if the buyer can afford to pay for the service or the product. Collecting in timely fashion can often become the key to solid business activity. It is sometimes easier to make the sale than to collect on it. Don't get too far behind in your receivables. Sales may fulfill your corporate ego, but only real dollar profits will keep your business alive and growing.

CHAPTER 26

Revisiting the Core Elements of This Book

A S YOU SPEAK WITH PROFESSIONALS ABOUT the valuation process, you will find that they reference a variety of approaches to the concept. They will invariably discuss a comparative analysis of other businesses in the same field. For public companies, they will reference the stock prices and ratios. In fact, they will boggle your mind with figures that can be manipulated in various ways.

It is interesting that buyers' and sellers' goals, although sometimes taken into consideration, are pretty low on the totem pole. And yet, the entire buying-selling process depends on these people who are the reason for this process. You cannot lose sight of this fact.

To ensure that the basics of the people involved are never excluded from the process, this short chapter that concludes this book begins with a discussion of why people buy businesses and why people sell businesses.

FOR A SELLER: WHY DOES SOMEONE BUY A BUSINESS?

It is certainly easier to recognize the reasons why a buyer wants to acquire a business than it is to understand a seller's motives, but be careful. All is not necessarily what it appears to be.

A buyer's reasons are important because most small businesses (businesses with gross revenues of $10,000,000 per year or less) are not normally sold for cash. The buyer makes a down payment and then pays the balance over time, usually in the form of a promissory note, often carried by the seller for five to 10 years. It is important, then, to know the buyer's qualifications, including education, experience, family involvement, and financial history, including current assets and liabilities. A seller can't make a careful judgment without knowing these elements.

Here are a half-dozen potential problem areas in the sale of a business that should cause a seller to take precautions.

The buyer who can pay cash is clearly the least problematic sale from the seller's perspective. So long as the seller's presentation doesn't contain misrepresentations that could be the basis for a lawsuit, the seller will be out of the picture and have no financial interest in the success or failure of the business after the sale. The only disadvantage is that the buyer who is willing to pay all cash will likely want a substantial reduction in price … to which, by the way, he or she would be entitled.

The buyer who says that the compensation available to him or her after the sale will be adequate to support the family can be problematic.

If the seller is going to carry back a promissory note for the balance of the purchase price after a down payment, he or she better be sure that buyer is telling the truth and that exigencies won't change that truth. If the buyer needs to take more money from the business, it might be at the expense of the seller's promissory note. There are ways to protect against this contingency; be prepared to discuss it with your professional.

A buyer with substantial dollars may be acquiring the business as an investment with the idea that he or she will be an absentee owner. Even if the operation is handled by a family member, the seller needs to be careful about this. It is well known in the business community that absentee ownership, more often than not, can spell disaster. Additional protections will be needed if this appears to be the case.

If the seller will be carrying a note for the balance of the purchase price, whatever the situation, it is always appropriate to ask for financial protection in addition to the business itself as security. This can be in the form of additional equities such as stocks, bonds, second or third trust deeds (mortgages) on real property, and the like. Even if there is little equity left in the real estate after mortgages, it is a very substantial and intimidating risk to the buyer and his or her family becasue it could prevent the property from being sold.

In most businesses, a key factor to maintaining the business is to have adequate working capital for growth, for continuity, and for the unexpected. If a buyer is taking over the business with little or no additional capital available, any glitch in the normal business activity may cause the business to falter. In such a case, the buyer usually needs to ask the seller for a hiatus in note payments. As a seller, be sure that you don't get caught in this situation. You will essentially be financing a business that you no longer own just to protect the payments on your note. In addition, most of those problems get worse before they get better. Be cautious.

If a buyer wants to change the format of a business, the seller needs to be sure that it doesn't change the original concept to the extent of hurting the buyer's ability to function in the marketplace. Converting a successful women's clothing shop to a child's clothing shop might seem like a good idea. If this is the buyer's plan, he or she should have purchased one. If the buyer converts to an entirely different competitive market-place, the change may very well prove disastrous and he or she may never pay the seller's note. On the other hand, a creative buyer may want to augment the products or services offered and this may be a great idea. As a seller holding a promissory note, it is your obligation to ensure that the judgments are appropriate to survival of the business. It is an ongoing obligation until the promissory note has been completely paid.

Although it is impossible to examine all the potential problem areas in the sale of a business, the above examples should cause any seller to seek the appropriate professional advice before making the commitment.

FOR A BUYER: WHY DOES SOMEONE SELL A BUSINESS?

It is impossible to cover all the myriad reasons why the owner of a business puts it up for sale. If you're buying, you should be aware of at least the following half-dozen reasons, because they may affect you.

Age has its prerogatives as well as its failings. The physical and intellectual demands of a business can be wearing. As time passes and an owner gets closer to the golden years, it may become more difficult for him or her to operate the business. Those who can anticipate the difficulties early enough will decide to sell while the business is still healthy and needs only a strong leader to continue its success. Others have maintained their health and abilities, but decide that the time has come to stop working and start enjoying life more fully.

Illness of the owner or illness in the family that forces a move to a different climate or a simpler way of life is often a compelling reason to sell. If this is the premise for the sale, keep a sharp eye for the possibility that it might not be the whole story. Remember: even a covenant not to compete, an essential element for the buyer in just about every business sale, might not provide sufficient protection, if it applies only to the owner but not necessarily to his or her family or key employees. You should not be consistently cynical, but certainly you should exercise the appropriate cautions. In legal terms, this is called "due diligence." In lay terms, it's basic protective thinking.

Some business owners hadn't thought about selling until they were approached by a competitor or a "downsized" executive looking for a new opportunity.

These sellers are not any easier to deal with; in some cases, they may be even more difficult than most. Although they did not come to the decision to sell as much as the decision came to them, they will now be as anxious to maximize their equity as anyone who has prepared the business for market many months before presentation.

There are younger owners for whom the romance or excitement of the business has worn off. They may or may not have been really successful but have handled the business at least adequately. They are now ready for their next adventure and want to convert the equity of the business into dollars for their next business. There is nothing particularly problematic about these buyers so long as you have some comfort in knowing that they are not going to create a business like the one they're selling … across the proverbial street. Very often, these sellers will not have maximized the potential of their business because they've always had the "second dream" on their minds. This might be an interesting opportunity.

The caution in dealing with younger sellers (or any sellers, for that matter) is that they may be selling the business because they can read the writing on the wall; they may recognize the next level of sophistication in their trade or industry and innovations that might obsolete their current product or service and the cost might be prohibitive. It is something to consider when you are investigating the industry of which this business is a part.

This is a good reason to consult someone who knows more about the business than you. It is the old franchise axiom, "investigate before investing."

And then, of course, there is the owner who knows something that you don't know. Maybe it's something about his or her source for raw materials, component parts, equipment, and the like. Maybe some of his or her key employees are about to leave, possibly taking some key clients along. Maybe a giant competitor is opening shop close enough to the business to cause a problem. Maybe the city is going to restructure the street on which the business is located. It might be almost anything! If you're going to buy a business, it is your obligation to become knowledgeable in every aspect relative to its survival and potential success. Anyone who suggests that you rush to judgment before taking adequate time for this necessary examination is giving you bad advice. The dark room holds its secrets only until you turn the light on. After that, all becomes clear.

Although it is certainly true that you could hold an auction for the sale of your business, it is also true that you could merely close the door and sell off your assets. Neither of these approaches would likely result in a satisfactory conversion of your equity into cash. The idea is to find the parameters within which to arrive at a price that is logical for both buyer and seller. If you do this far enough in advance, you will have an opportunity to maximize the sales and minimize the costs of operation, leading to the highest price potential for the business.

WHY VALUE A BUSINESS?

Valuing a business is very much like writing a business plan. It is usually intended to serve a specific purpose—the business valuation in anticipation of selling, the business plan in anticipation of borrowing. But these should not be the primary goals. The real goal is to give the owner an idea of where he or she stands, what needs to be done to maximize the conversion of equity to retirement or to satisfy the requirements of a lender.

Building a valuation should not be done the day before preparing a selling presentation. It should not be done because a buyer is waiting for the answers. It should be done because you need to know the answers in advance in order to work on those things that need attention long before a presentation is anticipated.

As you look at your preliminary valuation, you should examine the last few years on the basis of a comparative analysis. And always start with the basics.

Are profits up because you've improved your margins by buying raw materials or component parts at lower prices? Or are profits up because you've increased your sales to customers? If you've improved your margins but sales are down, you will want to know why.

Are you taking less compensation from your business? Is your lesser compensation predicated on increased costs of doing business? You will want to know what these increased costs are. Are your competitors dealing with the same problem? How have they handled the problem to ensure that profits continue to maintain?

Are you spending more time at the business but not seeing any improvement in either sales or profits? You certainly want to know why this equation is not more positive. If any of these questions and answers suggest a trend in your business, you will need to know this and factor this into the risk aspect of your selling presentation. Is your business vulnerable because your customer base is small, because the loss of any customer could cause chaos? This is certainly another of the risk factors that the buyer will be looking at.

Are you aware of your competitors and what they are doing to market and advertise? You must be sure that your marketing approach and advertising dollars are being used most cost-effectively. It's very difficult to explain to potential buyers that they can improve their sales by adjusting their marketing and advertising after the sale. They will invariably want to know why you didn't do it before selling.

Is your inventory up and are your receivables down? This is a simple barometer that should take you to your sales department. Why did you order as many products or as much production in anticipation of sales that didn't materialize? Did you make a mistake or did the economy cause a few surprises? And you will need to see how many of your receivables are recent and how many have not been paid for a long time. Are you still doing business with the people who have not paid? They may be using you as their banker—which is not likely the business that you intended.

Have you analyzed each employee's job category and whether employees are performing up to expectations? Where are your key people and what is their performance rating? In the event of a sale, which of them are likely to stay under new management? Are any in a position to become competitors to your buyer?

Have you ever thought of such a situation? If you're going to carry a promissory note for the balance of the purchase price, this issue could become particularly problematic.

The problem of valuing a business is that most entrepreneurs don't attend to this very important matter until the 11th hour … just before they need to make a selling presentation. The key to selling is to understand the valuation concept long in advance of any such sale. The above references represent only some of the elements of the business that you need to consider. Waiting too long will invariably mean that you will be leaving money on the table during selling negotiations. Remember: in any negotiations, you need to be in control. In order to do that, you must be able to anticipate the questions and have credible answers. Losing this credibility means losing the negotiating battle. Don't let this happen. Get a valuation done early.

KEY POINTS TO REMEMBER

- Most businesses are not sold for cash. The buyer usually makes a down payment and then pays the balance of the purchase price over time.
- Both buyer and seller should be sure that the buyer has adequate working capital to ensure against any glitch in the economy or otherwise.
- The buyer should make sure that the seller (together with family, friends, and associates) will not become a competitor after the sale.
- The purpose of a business valuation is to help the seller increase his or her equity in the business long before a sale become necessary or appropriate.
- A business valuation should ensure that, after the sale, there is sufficient profit for the buyer to draw an income and make payments to the seller on the balance of the purchase price.

Worksheet 26. Revisiting the Core Elements of This Book

The following questions emphasize some of the most important points you need to understand about what motivates buyers and sellers as well as the basic information involved in a business valuation.

For the Seller

Do you understand why it's important for a buyer to fully understand the nature and obligations of the business you are selling? What could happen if he or she fails to understand these things?

_____

_____

Why is it important to get additional security to ensure payment of the promissory note for the balance of the purchase price? _____

_____

Why do you think that the right to take the business back in the event of default is not adequate protection?

_____

_____

Why is it a good idea to ensure that the buyer has adequate working capital? _____

_____

What is the problem with a buyer who expects to be an absentee owner? _____

_____

What kinds of protective devices should you build into the buy-sell agreement in such a case? Will that kind of protective device be helpful in a normal sale situation? _____

_____

For the Buyer

Why is it a good idea to have some of the purchase price held after the sale? _____

_____

Why is it necessary for the buyer to investigate before investing in any business? _____

_____

How important is it to get a noncompete clause in the buy-sell agreement? _____

_____

Why is it important to understand the relationship between the seller and his or her employees?

_____

_____

What alternatives are available to you if you find that the seller misrepresented material facts during the negotiations?

_____

_____

Before the sale is consummated? _____

_____

After the sale is consummated and there is a promissory note for the balance of the purchase price?

_____

_____

After the sale is consummated and there is no promissory note for the balance of the purchase price and no other monies held in escrow? _____

_____

Why Value a Business?

As a *buyer*, how can you determine the risks of the business before you buy it? _____

_____

_____

As a *seller*, how can you determine how to increase your equity before a sale? _____

_____

_____

WHAT ARE YOU LOOKING FOR?

One of the funniest statements you will ever hear is from the person who says, "I'm glad to be leaving the corporate world and going to work for myself: less pressure, more time for my family, less aggravation." If you have already embarked on "The USS Entrepreneur," you will likely be laughing. If you are thinking about it, take this caution from the old musical standard before you take leave of your senses: "It ain't necessarily so."

Quality of Life

It may be true that you can more easily pick your time to work and to play. That depends, of course, on whether you are willing to work 17 hours a day in order to play for two or three. This, by the way, ought to leave you with four hours to sleep, give or take a little. Waking up at 3:00 a.m. wondering if you're going to make payroll is something that did not happen to you as a corporate employee. It was someone else's problem. Your sense of calm and your comfort zone regarding paying your own bills were built into a certain envelope that had fairly defined edges, your paycheck. Going into business on your own means losing this comfort. If this is the quality of life you dreamed of, don't let anyone stand in your way.

The Confidence Factor

In your corporate life, you probably had a job you knew. You probably worked within a certain set of parameters and were confident in your ability to shoulder the known responsibilities. As an entrepreneur, all bets are off. You might be dealing initially with a business about which you know less than you'd like. You'll certainly be involved with a myriad of details, none of which you ever handled in your old job. There will be marketing, selling, margins, financials, production, customer satisfaction, advertising, and on and on it goes. If you can't handle it, you'll need to get someone who can. This costs money and will dilute whatever profit you depended on to take care of your family.

Charging the Customer

Whatever your product or service, you will need to charge a price that will make you competitive or your potential customer will buy from another source, either because it is less expensive or because it has more value. You will need to do an analysis of your costs: your costs for products to be sold, your costs of component parts necessary for your final product, your costs of equipment to produce the product or service you sell. If you make a mistake in answering these questions, your longevity in business may be severely curtailed. If you can build the appropriate equation, you may survive and even succeed.

Enjoying the Game

Success, of course, comes in many different packages. There are those packages that are filled with dollars and an equal amount of aggravation. Is this your dream of success? There is a package that contains less money and less aggravation as well. And then, there is the package that allows you to enjoy your family and your leisure time but may give you less income than you enjoyed in your corporate employment. Understand and accept that it is unlikely you will find a package that contains it all. Life is composed of equations … and compromises. On balance, you need to give something up order to enjoy something else. Make sure you know what will be your best plan for maximum enjoyment before you start on your new adventure. It's always best to check for water in the pool before you jump off the diving board.

Index